THE
TYRANNY
OF OIL

Also by Antonia Juhasz

The Bush Agenda: Invading the World, One Economy at a Time

To Kevin at Sarah, In peace,

THE TYRANNY OF OIL

THE WORLD'S MOST POWERFUL
INDUSTRY—AND
WHAT WE MUST DO TO STOP IT

ANTONIA JUHASZ

WM

WILLIAM MORROW

An Imprint of HarperCollinsPublishers

THE TYRANNY OF OIL. Copyright © 2008 by Antonia Juhasz. All rights reserved. Printed in the United States of America. No part of this book may
be used or reproduced in any manner whatsoever without written permission except in the case of brief quotations embodied in critical articles and
reviews. For information address HarperCollins Publishers, 10 East 53rd
Street, New York, NY 10022.

HarperCollins books may be purchased for educational, business, or sales
promotional use. For information please write: Special Markets Department,
HarperCollins Publishers, 10 East 53rd Street, New York, NY 10022.

FIRST EDITION

Designed by Renato Stanisic

Library of Congress Cataloging-in-Publication Data

Juhasz, Antonia.
    The tyranny of oil : the world's most powerful industry—and what we must
do to stop it / Antonia Juhasz.
        p. cm.
    Includes bibliographical references and index.
    ISBN 978-0-06-143450-1
    1. Petroleum industry and trade—United States 2. Petroleum industry
and trade—Political aspects—United States. I. Title.

HD9565.J84 2008
333.2'72820973—dc22   2008025912

08 09 10 11 12 WBC/RRD 10 9 8 7 6 5 4 3 2 1

To my family, for your unending support:
Joseph, Suzanne, Alex, Jenny, Christina, Linda, Paul, Branny, Emma,
Eliza, Simone, Gabriel, and Lucky

To the activists, for the hope you spread
and the change you create

*For the ignorance of the public
is the real capital of monopoly.*

—HENRY DEMAREST LLOYD,
WEALTH AGAINST COMMONWEALTH, 1894

Contents

1

Big Oil's Last Stand

Within days of the New Year, 2008 began with three landmark events. Oil reached $100 per barrel for only the second time in history as gasoline prices began an ascent toward the highest prices in a generation. And on January 3, Senator Barack Obama became the first African American to win the Iowa Caucus. Voter turnout broke records as well, with four times more registered Democrats voting than had turned out in 2000. Senator Obama was reserved yet purposeful as he delivered his historic victory speech. He chose to highlight just a handful of policy issues in the fifteen-minute address, making his focus on oil all the more significant. Obama forcefully declared that he would free the United States once and for all from "the tyranny of oil" and then pledged to be the president "who ends the war in Iraq and finally brings our troops home." An already raucous crowd met these pronouncements with thunderous applause and waves of cheers.

"The tyranny of oil" powerfully encapsulates the feelings not only of Americans, but of people the world over. Without viable and accessible alternatives, entire economies suffer when increasing proportions of national budgets must be used to purchase oil. And on an individual level, families, facing the same lack of alternatives, forgo basic necessities when gasoline prices skyrocket. Communities that live where oil is found—from Ecuador to Nigeria to Iraq—experience the tyranny of daily human rights abuses, violence, and war. The tyranny of environmental pollution, public health risks, and climate destruction is created at every stage of oil use, from exploration to production, from transport to refining, from consumption to disposal. And the political tyranny exercised by the masters of the oil industry corrupts democracy and destroys our ability to choose how much we will sacrifice in oil's name.

The masters of the oil industry, the companies known as "Big Oil," exercise their influence throughout this chain of events: through rapidly and ever-increasing oil and gasoline prices, a lack of viable alternatives, the erosion of democracy, environmental destruction, global warming, violence, and war. The American public is fed up with Big Oil. In 2006 Gallup published its annual rating of public perceptions of U.S. industry. The oil industry is always a poor performer, but this time it came in dead last—earning the lowest rating for any industry in the history of the poll.[1]

For a time, it was the rare 2008 presidential candidate who would speak out against the tyrants behind the tyranny of oil. The earliest denunciations came from Democratic senator John Edwards, who came in second and just 8 percentage points behind Obama in the 2008 Iowa Caucus. Edwards repeatedly stated the need to "take on Big Oil," and decried handing the "keys to the corridors of government over to the lobbyists for the big oil companies."[2] Statements such as these quickly earned Edwards the title of the "Populist candidate" for president, as did this one made on January 28, 2008, when Edwards announced that there are "two Americas that exist in this country: there's one for the lobbyists, for the special interests, for the powerful, for the big multinational corporations and there's another one for everybody else. Well I'm here to say that their America is over!"[3] Edwards took his script from Congressman William Jennings Bryan, who represented the Populist and Democratic Parties for president in 1896 and who declared, "On the one side are the allied hosts of monopolies, the money power, great trusts . . . who seek the enactment of laws to benefit them and impoverish the people. On the other side are the farmers, laborers, merchants, and all others who produce wealth and bear the burden of taxation."[4]

As the 2008 election progressed, both Obama and his leading Democratic challenger Senator Hillary Clinton went increasingly on the attack against Big Oil, and each was eventually called a "Populist candidate," their words sounding an alarm similar to one made over one hundred years earlier by the Populist movement against corporate trusts generally and Standard Oil in particular, the company from which many of today's oil giants descend.

John D. Rockefeller founded the Standard Oil Company in 1870. By the 1880s, Standard Oil controlled 90 percent of all refining in the United States, 80 percent of the marketing of oil products, a quarter of the country's total crude output, and, in this preautomobile era, produced more than a quarter of the world's total supply of kerosene.[5] Standard Oil was renowned for both the ruthlessness and the illegality of its business methods. Dozens of court cases were brought against the company, and Standard Oil was broken up by three separate state-level injunctions. Its response was to change states, making federal action imperative. In addition to the producers, refiners, and other sellers of oil that Standard Oil bought out, bribed, bullied, or burned down, masses of people across the country were enraged by its exercise of control over their government.

Standard Oil was not alone. It had perfected the use of the corporate trust, and hundreds of other trusts soon followed. A *trust* is a combination of corporations in which a board of trustees holds the stock of each individual company and manages the business of all. While the company operates as one giant conglomerate, the individual companies maintain the legal status— and in many cases, including Standard Oil's, the legal fiction—of independence. At the time, the word *trust* quickly became synonymous with any large corporation.

A newspaper cartoon from the era depicts the U.S. Senate. Towering above the seated senators, three times their individual size, stand grossly obese men representing the trusts. Each man is dressed in top hat and tails. Standard Oil, the most dominant, is the only company depicted by name among the "copper," "iron," "sugar," "tin," "coal," and "paper bag" trusts. Above them a sign is posted: "This is a Senate of the monopolists, by the monopolists, for the monopolists!" Off in the far left corner is a small sign that reads "People's Entrance," below which is a bolted and barred door marked "closed."

A great groundswell of citizen action emerged in response to the power of the trusts. People across the nation came together in what has since been called the Populist and Progressive movements to bring about change. Some groups sought revolution, but what the collective effort achieved were fundamental reforms, including new laws on campaign finance, workers' rights and protections, public health, and the first national antitrust laws. The intent of the antitrust laws was to break the power of the trusts over the government. In 1911 the federal government used the Sherman Antitrust Act to break up Standard Oil into thirty-four separate companies. Standard Oil would not regain its singular dominance and consolidation of the industry, or the political control it held at the height of its power in the late 1800s.

The 1911 breakup largely failed over the course of the next decade, however, due to the absence of effective government oversight. Primarily to address these failings, new antitrust laws and, most importantly, a new government agency—the Federal Trade Commission (FTC)—were later introduced to tighten the government's control over antitrust violations by U.S. corporations. The FTC remains the most important government agency in charge of regulating corporate consolidation and collusion. Still, while the nation's antitrust laws were fairly well applied to domestic oil operations, the largest oil companies functioned in the international arena as a cartel. From approximately World

War I to 1970, the three largest postbreakup companies, Standard Oil of New Jersey (Exxon), Standard Oil of New York (Mobil), and Standard Oil of California (Chevron), joined with Gulf, Texaco, BP, and Shell to form a cartel, earning them the nickname the "Seven Sisters." These seven companies owned the vast majority of the world's oil and controlled the economic fate of entire nations.

Over the decades, many strategies to rein in the power of the Seven Sisters were proposed, debated, and even attempted in the United States. These included reducing the flow of oil the companies could bring into the United States, state-owned refineries, a national oil company, and massive antitrust action against the oil companies. Some of these efforts were successful, but most were not. It was the oil-rich nations operating as their own cartel, the Organization of Petroleum Exporting Countries (OPEC), which ultimately brought down the corporate cartel. By the mid-1980s, the OPEC governments had taken back full ownership of their oil. The Seven Sisters, which in 1973 earned two-thirds of their profits abroad, turned their attention back to the U.S. market that they had largely abdicated to the smaller "independent" oil companies. Big Oil's new mantra was "Merge or die," as the companies first bought up the independents and then each other.

The Reagan administration ushered in the first frontal attack aimed at dismantling the antitrust policies of the United States. Reagan's FTC initiated a new and radically permissive attitude toward corporate mergers that was carried on through each subsequent administration. As stated quite matter-of-factly by Jonathan Baker, an antitrust attorney for the Clinton administration, the "older concerns about protecting small business and preventing concentrations of political power have been discarded."[6] Since 1991, government regulators, under the direct and heavy influence of the nation's largest oil companies and their lawyers, have allowed more than 2,600 mergers to take place in the U.S. oil industry. The mergers have resulted in the near demise of the independent oil company, refiner, and gas station in the United States.

The mergers of the megagiant oil companies have all taken place since 1999 and remain the largest mergers in corporate history. Exxon merged with Mobil, Chevron with Texaco, Conoco with Phillips, and BP with Amoco and then Arco to create the largest corporations the world has ever seen. Shell also participated in the merger wave by purchasing several "baby-Standard" oil companies.

The mergers helped Big Oil reestablish its footing as a major owner of oil. While nowhere near its Seven Sisters "glory years," Big Oil's oil reserves are impressive nonetheless. Were the five largest oil companies operating in the United States one country instead of five corporations, their combined crude oil holdings would today rank within the top ten of the world's largest oil-rich nations. ExxonMobil, Chevron, ConocoPhillips, Shell, and BP exercise their control over the price of oil today throgh these individual holdings and through participation in the crude oil futures market. The futures market has replaced OPEC as the principal determinant of the price of crude oil. It is largely unregulated and prone to excessive speculation and manipulation.

The mergers also allowed the oil companies to take control of the refining and selling of gasoline in the United States in the style of Standard Oil. They have forged a mass consolidation of these sectors, yielding rapid increases in the price of gasoline and oil company profits. "Big Oil has created a market on the brink, manipulating inventories and refinery capacity to the point that the slightest supply disruption sends prices—and company profits—skyrocketing," Connecticut's attorney general Richard Blumenthal told a congressional committee in mid-2007. "There is sufficient supply, but these newly created industry giants use their huge market power to keep a stranglehold on the spigot."[7]

Riding on high oil and gasoline prices, the oil industry is far and away the most profitable industry in the world. Six of the ten largest corporations in the world are oil companies. They are, in order, ExxonMobil, Royal Dutch Shell (Shell), BP, Chevron, ConocoPhillips, and Total.* According to *Fortune*'s 2007 Global 500 listing, the ten largest global oil companies took in over $167 billion in profits in 2006 alone†—nearly $50 billion more than the top ten companies in the second most profitable industry, commercial and savings banks.

The largest publicly traded oil companies operating in the United States and those with the greatest influence on U.S. policy-making are ExxonMobil, Shell, BP, Chevron, Conoco-Phillips, Valero (the forty-third largest global corporation), and Marathon (the ninety-second largest global corporation). Each is either a direct descendant or has purchased direct descendants of Standard Oil. They are among the most powerful corporations in the world. These companies are Big Oil.

Big Oil is experiencing a level of power that has only one historical precedent: that of the Standard Oil era. And like Standard Oil, the companies appear willing to do anything to maintain their position. With over $40 billion in pure profit in 2007, ExxonMobil is the most profitable corporation both in the world and in world history. Its profits are larger than the entire economies of ninety-three of the world's nations ranked by GDP. ExxonMobil had the most profitable year of any corporation ever in 2003 and then proceeded to surpass its own record every year for the next five years.

Wal-Mart edged out ExxonMobil as the world's largest corporation in 2007 by just barely surpassing its sales—$379 billion compared with ExxonMobil's $373 billion. Wal-Mart's $12.7 billion in profits, however, were a mere one-third of ExxonMobil's. In fact, ExxonMobil's profits were more than *twice* those of the next three U.S. companies on the Fortune 500 list *combined*: Chevron with $18.7 billion; General Motors, which *lost* $38.7

---

* The others are Wal-Mart, General Motors, Toyota Motor, and Daimler-Chrysler.

† The most recent date for which international comparative data is available.

billion; and ConocoPhillips with $11.9 billion. Similarly, in 2006 ExxonMobil's profits were nearly twice those of the next two U.S. companies combined: United Airlines with $23 billion and Citigroup with $21 billion.

As described by *Fortune* magazine in 2005, ExxonMobil was "the most powerful U.S. corporation by just about any metric. It surpassed General Electric to become the most valuable U.S. company by market capitalization ($375 billion). It pumps almost twice as much oil and gas a day as Kuwait, and its energy reserves stretch across six continents and are larger than those of any non-government company on the planet."[8]

ExxonMobil is not alone. Each major American oil company—ExxonMobil, Chevron, ConocoPhillips, Valero, and Marathon—has surpassed its own record-breaking profits in almost every year for the last five years. Combined, they earned more than $80 billion in 2007 profits, making them the sixty-seventh largest economy on the planet. There is simply no comparison with any other industry in the United States. For example, the U.S. defense industry, which has also been experiencing some of its most profitable years of late, does not come close. The top five U.S. oil companies took in almost four times more profits in 2007 than the top *sixteen* U.S. defense and aerospace companies combined: $80 billion versus approximately $21 billion. The eighteen most profitable pharmaceutical companies took in about $43 billion in profits. In 2006 Big Oil had somewhat of a financial rival in the nation's commercial banks, the top five of which had about $73 billion in profits. However, following the mortgage crisis, the twenty-five most profitable banks took in just $70 billion in 2007 profits. All other industries—including cars, computers, insurance, telecommunications, tobacco, coal, and entertainment—are not now, and for years have not been, even worth adding up; their profits are a pittance in comparison to Big Oil's.

The oil industry argues in public that while its profits look large, its profit *margin* is not. In testimony before the U.S. Congress in April 2008, for example, ExxonMobil senior vice president J. S. Simon explained, "[I]n 2007, the oil and gas industry earned, on average, about 8.3 cents per dollar of sales—near the Dow Jones Industrial Average for major industries of 7.8 cents per dollar of sales."[9] Simon measured the company's net income as a share of its total revenues. In ExxonMobil's shareholder report, however, the company uses a very different measure—the company's return on capital employed (ROCE). As ExxonMobil argues in its 2007 annual report, "The Corporation has consistently applied its ROCE definition for many years and views it as the best measure of historical capital productivity in our capital-intensive, long-term industry. . . ." Using this measure, ExxonMobil is far and away more profitable than any other comparable U.S. industry. ExxonMobil's global operations made a 31.8 percent rate of return on average capital employed, nearly 24 points higher than the average return for all nonfinancial U.S. corporations in 2007 and 18 points higher than that of the manufacturing sector in 2006 (the most recent date available).[10] As for the oil industry as a whole, *U.S. News and World Report* urges readers to look at shareholder equity available for investment. Using this measure, the oil industry, at 27 percent, was nearly 10 points higher than that of other manufacturers in 2007.[11]

Shell and BP are headquartered in The Hague and London, respectively, but each has powerful, influential, and sizable American affiliates. Each is a leading U.S. campaign spender, heavily influencing and benefiting from the American political system. Shell and BP, combined with their five American sisters, garnered an incredible and unprecedented $133 billion in pure profit in 2007—the equivalent of the combined GDPs of the forty-two poorest nations in the world, including Fiji, Kyrgyzstan, Bhutan, and Sierra Leone.

What does $133 billion in profits buy an industry?* It bought

---

* I use profit as a measure of power (versus sales, stock value, or assets, for example) because I am most interested in how the industry uses its "excess cash."

the oil industry at least eight years of a U.S. "oiligarchy": a government ruled by a small number of oil interests. The oil industry spent more money to get the George W. Bush administration into office in 2000 than it has spent on any election before or since. In return it received, for the first time in American history, a president, vice president, and secretary of state who are all former oil company officials. In fact, in 2000 both George W. Bush and Condoleezza Rice had more experience running oil companies than they did working for the government. Every agency and every level of bureaucracy was filled with former oil industry lobbyists, lawyers, staff, board members, and executives, or those on their way to work for the oil industry after a brief stint of government service. The oil industry got what it paid for: an administration that has arguably gone further than just about any other in American history to serve Big Oil's interests through deregulation, lax enforcement, new access to America's public lands and oceans, subsidies, tax breaks, and even war.

Americans tried to change course in 2006 by replacing the Republican Congress with a Democratic-controlled House and Senate. Democrats pledged in their election campaigns to take action against the oil industry, climate change, and the war in Iraq—all three of which are intimately and rightly connected in the public's mind. The Democrats failed to deliver. Far too often, Big Oil's money appeared to be the reason why. In one particularly glaring example, the Center for American Progress investigated the relationship between votes and campaign contributions in connection with HR 2776, the Renewable Energy and Energy Conservation Tax Act of 2007. The bill would have eliminated $16 billion in oil and gas industry tax breaks to fund clean energy alternatives. Between 1989 and 2006, members of Congress who voted against the bill received on average four times more money in campaign contributions from the oil and gas industry (approximately $100,000) than those who voted for the bill (approximately $26,000). The bill ultimately died.

Similarly, Oil Change International compiled voting records

for the five most important bills on the Iraq war: the initial 2003 vote authorizing the use of force in Iraq and the subsequent supplemental war funding bills in 2003, 2004, 2005, and 2006. From 1989 to 2006, members of Congress who voted for all five bills received on average eight times more money from the oil and gas industry (approximately $116,000) than those who voted against the war (approximately $14,000). And the war rages on.

Big Oil does not only wield its financial purse at election time, it impacts daily policy-making through its unprecedented spending on lobbyists. In fact, the millions of dollars it spends on elections is small potatoes compared with the tens of millions it spends lobbying the federal government. From 1998 to 2006, ExxonMobil alone spent more than $80 million lobbying the federal government, over *fourteen times* more money than it spent on political campaigns. Combined, ExxonMobil, Chevron, Shell, BP, Marathon, and ConocoPhillips spent $240 million lobbying the federal government from 1998 to 2006—more than the *entire oil and gas industry* spent on federal election campaigns from 1990 to 2006.

There is simply no comparison between the financial reach of the oil industry and that of organizations working on behalf of consumers, the environment, public health, communities living near oil production or gasoline refining facilities, and groups working in support of alternative energy, antitrust enforcement, or the protection of human rights. Through lawyers, lobbyists, elected officials, government regulators, conservative think tanks, industry front groups, and full-force media saturation, the oil industry uses its wealth to change the public debate and, more often than not, achieve its desired policy outcomes.

Yet for all its enduring power, Big Oil finds itself in a precarious position today. While it is at its financial and political pinnacle, it faces the greatest threat to its existence in its one-hundred-and-fifty-plus-year history: oil, the resource on which it depends, is growing far more difficult to come by.

In 1938 King Abdul Aziz of Saudi Arabia asked, "Do you know what they will find when they reach Mars? They will find

Americans out there in the desert hunting for oil."[12] The Americans in Saudi Arabia in 1938 worked for Chevron. While not (yet) busy on Mars, Chevron's employees and those of every major oil company are today just as committed to finding and acquiring every last drop of oil as they were seventy years ago. They are working to expand access to oil in "traditional" areas such Iran and Iraq, while seeking out new frontiers below the ocean floor, atop the Rocky Mountains, and in the depths of the tar-filled earth. In mid-2007, Chevron's Paul Siegele stood 200 feet in the air atop Chevron's Cajun Express floating oil derrick 190 miles off the coast of Florida. "A decade ago, I never even dreamed we'd get here," he said, looking out across the Gulf waters, considered one of the world's most promising new oil regions. "And a decade from now, this moonscape could be populated with rigs as far as the eye can see."[13]

A comparison of Chevron's outlook in 1938 with that in 2007 paints the stark reality facing today's oil industry. In 1938 Chevron was sitting on Saudi Arabia's Ghawar oil field, which was and remains the largest oil field in the world. It encompasses some 1.3 million acres and now contains at least 55 billion barrels of oil lying about 6,000 feet below the desert sand.[14] By the mid-1980s, Saudi Arabia had fully nationalized its oil—oil that Chevron, along with other U.S. oil companies, had previously owned and controlled. Today, Chevron's Cajun Express, at a cost of more than half a million dollars *per day,* is drilling 26,000 feet below the ocean surface in the hope of someday producing oil from the 19,200-acre Tahiti field. Chevron hopes this field may yield as much as 500 million barrels of oil, or just about enough to cover twenty-four days' worth of oil consumption in the United States.

While Mars may yet prove to have oil, for now Chevron and the rest of the oil industry are stuck with the oil on planet Earth. Unlike in 1938, today the Earth is just about tapped out of conventional oil. There are no new Ghawars—or anything even close. There are no new vast, untouched reserves sitting close to the earth's surface just waiting to be discovered. In fact, even with phenomenal advances in technology, no one has made such a discovery in more than forty-five years. This, of course, is not for lack of trying. From Canada to China, Mexico to Brazil, Nigeria to Iraq, Malaysia to Greenland, California to Florida, through ice, sand, silt, and rock, over the course of the past one hundred and fifty years and at an incalculable cost, we have scoured the globe in search of oil.

Oil is a nonrenewable natural resource: when a reservoir of oil is depleted, no new oil emerges to take its place. Since about 1960, the rate at which the world has consumed oil has outpaced the rate at which we have discovered new fields. Today we find only about one new barrel of oil for roughly every four that we consume.[15] Meanwhile, it is estimated that the world will consume 120 million barrels of oil a day by 2025, over 50 percent more than we consumed in 2001.[16] We are therefore forced to confront a bitter reality: the world is fast approaching the point at which conventional sources of oil will decline until they are forever gone.

"Conventional oil" is the kind of crude we have been living on for the last one hundred and fifty years. Simplifying quite a bit, while petroleum means "rock oil," conventional oil is found essentially in liquid form in reservoirs below the ground, and all that is needed to get it out is a traditional derrick, which drills through the earth to reach the reservoir and draws up the oil. "Unconventional oil" (often called "frontier oil" or "frontier hydrocarbons"), by contrast, is not found in reservoirs but rather in small quantities deeply embedded within other substances such as tar or rock. It must first be removed from these substances—at great environmental and financial cost—before it can emerge as a liquid.

More than 50 percent of the world's remaining conventional oil is found in just five countries: Saudi Arabia, Iran, Iraq, Kuwait, and the United Arab Emirates. In 2003 the Bush administration, composed of former and future oil company executives, led the United States into war against Iraq on the pretense that Saddam Hussein had weapons of mass destruction. The same administration is now threatening war against Iran while establishing permanent U.S. military facilities across the region, including in Kuwait and the UAE. The administration supplies arms to Saudi Arabia while negotiating for greater access to that nation's oil for U.S. oil companies.

The rest of the world's conventional oil is found in comparatively small amounts in fourteen other countries: Venezuela, Russia, Libya, Nigeria, Kazakhstan, the United States, China, Qatar, Mexico, Algeria, Brazil, Angola, Norway, and Azerbaijan.[17] If you map the massive increase in construction of U.S. military bases and installations and military deployments around the world under the Bush administration, you will see that they directly follow oil locations and oil transit routes. New U.S. military installations in Central and South America, West Africa, and elsewhere raise the threat of new military action in those regions. The costs to people who live in those countries and along those routes are mounting, from human rights abuses, environmental destruction, military occupation, and war.

Oil production in most of the world has reached or is nearing its peak. Production in most Middle Eastern countries, on the other hand, is not expected to peak until 2025. This means that an even greater percentage of the world's remaining oil will be consolidated in just a few Middle Eastern nations.

The realization that oil is being concentrated in the Middle East has led many to argue that the United States should become more "energy independent." In response to this sort of view, Sarah Emerson of Energy Security Analysis Inc. explained in 2002, "The trouble with diversifying outside the Middle East . . . is that it is not where the oil is. One of the best things for our supply security would be to liberate Iraq."[18]

Outside of the Middle East, the oil that is left is becoming more technologically difficult, expensive, and environmentally destructive to acquire. Conventional oil is found offshore below the world's ocean waters, making its production risky, environmentally harmful, and destructive to coastal communities. Among the largest unconventional sources of oil are the tar sands of Canada and the shale regions of the midwestern United States. In addition to the problems just listed, the process of removing the tar and shale from the earth, extracting the oil, converting it into liquid, and refining it into gasoline is far more energy-intensive and ozone-depleting than traditional methods of oil production and thus contributes more to climate change.

Climate change and global warming are increasingly critical issues. Including 2007, seven of the eight warmest years since records began in 1880 have occurred since 2001, and the ten warmest years have all occurred since 1997.[19] Burning fossil fuels, primarily oil, natural gas, and coal, increases atmospheric concentrations of carbon dioxide (CO_2), the principal greenhouse gas. The more greenhouse gas there is in the earth's atmosphere, the more of the sun's heat is trapped near the earth's surface; the more heat that is trapped, the higher the planet's temperature; the higher the earth's temperature, the more ice melts, oceans rise, and extreme weather results. All of which would be better described as "climate chaos" rather than mere "climate change" or "global warming." Just to *stabilize* current greenhouse gas concentrations in the atmosphere, it is estimated that the world must reduce emissions of these gases by 50 to 80 percent by 2050 or even sooner.[20]

The United States is by far the largest per capita contributor to global warming—releasing 30 percent of all energy-related CO_2 emissions in 2004 (the most recent date for which data is available)—primarily from our cars and trucks.[21] The United States is also the largest consumer of oil. With just 5 percent of the world's population, the United States uses almost 25 percent of the world's oil every year.[22] In fact, Americans consume as much oil every year as the next five countries—China, Japan, Russia, Germany, and India—*combined*.[23] On average, each American uses nearly 3 gallons of oil per day. Products made from petroleum, such as plastics, linoleum, nylon, and polyester, fill our lives, but it is the car that dominates our oil consumption.

Nearly 70 percent of all petroleum consumed in the United States is for transportation. This includes trucks, trains, and planes, but cars rein supreme. One out of every seven barrels of oil in the world is consumed on America's highways alone. In fact, the population growth of cars in the United States is greater than that of people: a new car rolls onto the street every three seconds, whereas a baby is born only every eight seconds.[24] Americans are increasingly aware that this consumption is unsustainable. Many of us would like to see fewer cars on the road, cleaner-burning renewable alternative fuels, more and better public transportation, more pedestrian-friendly downtowns, better rail systems, and electric cars. This is where we collide head-on with the economic clout of the oil industry.

Big Oil would like us to believe that it is part of the solution, that it has seen the writing on the wall and knows that the future is clean energy. The companies' advertising campaigns would have us believe that they are in fact using their vast resources to embrace a clean, green, sustainable, and renewable energy future. Do not believe the hype. Chevron spends 60 percent more money *in one day* on the Cajun Express than it spent in the *entire year* of 2006 on all its investments in clean energy alternatives, approximately $500,000 compared to $300,000. The same ratio holds true for each company, and in most cases is far worse. None of the companies invests more than 4 percent of its entire annual expenditures on clean, renewable, alternative forms of energy. If you take just one message from this book, let it be this: Big Oil is deeply committed to remaining Big Oil and is putting all its considerable resources behind this effort.

The major oil companies have merged, bought up and pushed out rivals, and otherwise expanded their size. At the same time, they have used their unprecedented bankrolls, subsidized by our tax dollars, to experiment with expensive, risky, and environmentally catastrophic methods of scraping through tar, burrowing under mountains, and diving into the deepest depths of the ocean to get every last drop of oil left on the planet. All the while, they have stood directly in the way of meaningful efforts at change.

Lee Raymond, then the CEO of ExxonMobil, warned in 2003, "As demand increases while our existing production base decreases, we come squarely to the magnitude of the task before us."[25] The "task" is determining how far we are willing to go to get what is left of the world's remaining oil and how this critical decision will be made.

Deciding as a public that we want to end the tyranny of oil is not enough. We must also end the tyranny of Big Oil. This book will explain why, and how, this must be done. Big Oil thrives on secrecy, a lack of transparency, and control over information. We can only address its power by pulling back its veil.

2

The Birth and Breakup of Standard Oil

Corporations, which should be carefully restrained creatures of the law and servants of the people, are fast becoming the peoples' masters.
—PRESIDENT GROVER CLEVELAND, 1888[1]

I have ways of making money that you know nothing of.
—JOHN D. ROCKEFELLER[2]

Nearly 75 percent of Americans believe that big business has too much influence over the federal government, according to a 2006 Gallup poll. In fact, the only industry that Americans like less than Big Oil is the U.S. government.[3] Many people also believe that the power of corporations over the U.S. government—especially that of Big Oil—is impenetrable. If history is a guide, this simply is not true. One hundred years ago, mass movements of people across the United States joined together to fundamentally rewrite the relationship between corporations, the government, and the public. It was one of the most radical and transformative periods in U.S. history and a period to which our own time bears much resemblance. Corporate executives were working hand in glove with elected officials to advance interests widely held to be contrary to the overall economic health of the people and the nation, including waging wars for corporate profit and imperial expansion. In response, people organized against unchecked and unprecedented corporate power in what is today known as the Populist or Progressive Era.

Ultimately, this era did not yield the more radical changes desired by some, but it did bring about regulation: specifically, the first federal laws in the United States to protect labor and regulate corporate activity, and the financing of political campaigns. The Sherman Antitrust Act was among these new regulatory tools to rein in the nation's "epidemic" of megacorporations.

Then, as now, oil lay at the heart of much of the struggle, while John D. Rockefeller's Standard Oil, like its largest descendant today—ExxonMobil—reigned as the most formidable corporate power. Standard Oil's rise was part of a mass consolidation of economic and political power into the hands of a few megacorporations in the decades following the Civil War. In 1865 these companies emerged from the war heavily supported by the U.S. government with tax breaks, subsidies, and protection from both foreign and domestic competition. They were also free from government regulation—including the absence of just about any worker rights and consumer protections. These policy choices were justified, their supporters contended, because the companies needed unimpeded growth to match the expansion of the American economy.

Unregulated, the corporation did what it does naturally: whatever it could to enrich the bottom line. In describing the tactics and practices used by Standard Oil, the Interstate Commerce Commission, the first regulatory commission in U.S. history, did not mince words: "unjust discrimination," "intentional disregard of rights," "unexcused," "illegal," "excessive," "extraordinary," "forbidden," "so obvious and palpable a discrimination that no discussion of it is necessary," "wholly indefensible," "patent and provoking discrimination for which no rational excuse is suggested, "obnoxious," "absurd and inexcusable," "gross disproportions and inequalities," and "the most unjust and injurious discrimination."[4]

Rockefeller built Standard Oil into the first major industrial monopoly in the United States and established the model that all others would seek to follow. Ida Tarbell writes in the introduction to her 1904 book *The History of the Standard Oil Company* that Standard Oil "was the first in the field, and it has furnished the methods, the charter, and the traditions for its followers. It is the most perfectly developed trust in existence; that is, it satisfies most nearly the trust ideal of entire control of the commodity in which it deals."[5] The New York State Senate concluded after its hallmark investigation of Standard Oil in 1888, "Its success has been the incentive to the formation of all other trusts or combinations. It is the type of a system which has spread like a disease through the commercial system of this country."[6]

Following Standard Oil's lead, the nation's largest companies merged and consolidated their own efforts by forming trusts. A "trust" is a combination of corporations where a board of trustees holds the stock of each individual company and manages the business of all. At the time, the word *trust* quickly became synonymous with any large corporation. The trusts gobbled up their smaller competitors and forced out of business those that they could not buy. The companies then used their size and economic clout to influence political decision-making on their behalf. Again Rockefeller set the standard, perfecting the art of the political contribution. As power was consolidated in the hands of a few great companies, the rights of workers, farmers, consumers, and smaller businesses shrank accordingly.

All across the country, people responded with resistance, rebellion, and a demand for fundamental change, including new legal structures to support not only their rights but also the nation's flagging democracy. Farmers, women and children factory workers, African-American railway workers, longshoremen, suffragists, Anarchists, Communists, Socialists, Wobblies, and many other groups organized for change. On May 1, 1886,

350,000 workers at over 11,500 establishments all across the United States went on strike. In the course of that year, there were more than 1,400 strikes involving some half a million workers. By 1904, there were on average more than 4,000 strikes *per year.*[7] The objectives of the strikers sound almost trite today, as they are rights that most American citizens now take largely for granted: the eight-hour workday, the forty-hour workweek, a minimum wage, worker safety, the right to form unions, compensation when injured on the job, and the right to work under legal contracts enforcing mutual commitments between employers and workers.

The 1890 Sherman Antitrust Act was designed to protect small businesses—and thereby support the overall economy; to keep business within the realm of government regulation—and thereby protect workers and consumers; and to keep businesses small enough so that economic clout did not become political clout—and thereby protect democracy. The law would ultimately be used to bring down Standard Oil, and it remains the foundation of all U.S. antitrust policy today. However, from the 1980s until today, the original intent of the law has been all but forgotten, and the mergers of megacorporations, including the descendants of Standard Oil, have been allowed to proceed virtually without restriction.

At the center of the Progressive and Populist Movements were the "muckrakers," journalists who dug up the dirt and brought sunlight to shine on the crimes committed by corporations and the politicians who supported them. While she hated the nomenclature, Ida Tarbell, author, historian, and journalist, was one of the most influential muckrakers of her day. Her blistering sixteen-part, two-year-long exposé of John D. Rockefeller and his Standard Oil Company ran in *McClure's Magazine* from 1902 to 1904. When the series was released as a book in 1904, one journal described it as "the most remarkable book of its kind ever written in this country." Daniel Yergin, in his landmark book *The Prize: The Epic*

Quest for Oil, Money and Power, describes Tarbell's book, saying "Arguably, it was the single most influential book on business ever published in the United States."[8] It was the nail in the coffin for the nation's most hated trust and its premier robber baron.

As for Rockefeller, Yergin describes him as "the single most important figure in shaping the oil industry."[9] It is a common characterization and is undoubtedly true. However, Rockefeller earned this and even greater acclaim despite the fact that neither he nor his company contributed to the discovery of oil. He did not develop the technology to drill for oil, pump it out of the earth, turn crude into kerosene for lamps or gasoline for cars, or move it through pipelines around the earth. On the contrary, Rockefeller did more than just about any other individual in history to undercut the efforts of those who made these discoveries and to push them out of the oil business altogether.

Nor did Rockefeller found the first oil company, introduce the ideas of vertical or horizontal integration to the oil industry, or invent the concept of the corporate trust.

Yet Rockefeller unquestionably deserves Yergin's title, because he mastered the fine art of mass consolidation and achieving unprecedented profit with little regard for the human, social, or broader economic costs of his actions. In Rockefeller's words, "The growth of a large business is merely a survival of the fittest."[10] For more than a century, the direct descendants of Standard Oil, including ExxonMobil, Chevron, and Conoco-Phillips, have dutifully followed Rockefeller's business model.

Yet all of Standard Oil's descendants should pay heed, for John D. Rockefeller personally sowed the seeds of his own demise: a peoples' movement committed to, and ultimately successful in, breaking up the Standard Oil Company.

THE MUCKRAKER AND THE MONOPOLIST

The [eighteen-] eighties dripped with blood. Men struggled to get at causes, to find corrections, to humanize and socialize

the country; for then as now there were those who dreamed
of a good world although at times it seemed to them to be
going mad.

—IDA M. TARBELL[11]

The way to make money is to buy when blood is running in
the streets.

—JOHN D. ROCKEFELLER[12]

"The Yankee Struck Oil"

Ida Tarbell was born in 1857 in Erie, Pennsylvania, just two years
before and thirty miles away from the nation's first big oil strike.
On August 27, 1859, the cry went out across the country, "The
Yankee struck oil!" when Colonel Edwin Drake of New Haven,
Connecticut, made history by drilling the first successful oil well
in the United States in Pithole, Pennsylvania. Tarbell's father had
provided the family with a modest but secure living from farm-
ing, selling lumber, and captaining a boat, but was preparing
to move them all to Iowa to try their hand in the great western
expansion. He quickly changed plans when he learned of Colonel Drake's find. The family moved to Pithole, where Tarbell's
father built and sold oil tanks. When Ida Tarbell was twelve, the
family moved to Titusville, Pennsylvania, then the heart of
America's oil production, where both her father and her brother
would ultimately earn their living as small independent oil producers.

Ida Tarbell's mother had been a schoolteacher before marry-
ing and filled the house with books and magazines. One of Tarbell's earliest remembered pleasures was lying on her stomach
reading through *Harper's Weekly*, the *New York Tribune*, and
even the *Police Gazette* (read without her parents' permission) in
which she read weekly updates on Titusville's renowned "seamier"
side of drunkenness, prostitution, and gambling. Another early
pleasure was science. In her 1939 autobiography, *All in a Day's*
Work, Tarbell describes the moment when the "naturally engrained

curiosity" that would serve her well throughout her career was first revealed. As a small child she decided to conduct a floatation experiment by throwing her baby brother into a brook. The baby, demonstrating that he did, in fact, float, "as his little skirts spread out and held him up," proceeded to float away. Luckily, a man working nearby heard the boy's cries, dove in, and saved him.

The more significant results of Tarbell's curiosity would emerge later. She was one of the first women in the United States to attend college, and after a short, unfulfilling two-year stint as a schoolteacher, she began her career in journalism at the *Chautauquan Magazine* in 1882. It took another twenty years for Tarbell to write about the topic that likely had the most profound impact on her life: oil.

Growing up virtually in an oil field leaves one with few illusions about the reality of oil production. Tarbell writes in the first pages of her autobiography, "No industry of man in its early days has ever been more destructive of beauty, order, [and] decency, than the production of petroleum."[13] While there was little love lost between Tarbell and oil, she felt an unshakable devotion to those who produced it, her father, brother, friends, and neighbors among them. She writes with unreserved pride about the hopes and commitment of the local producers to use their oil wealth to build up and support their communities. For a time, they were successful. Tarbell writes with equal passion, however, about the devastation brought about by Rockefeller's consolidation of the industry. "But suddenly, at the very heyday of this confidence, a big hand reached out from nobody knew where, to steal their conquest and throttle their future. The suddenness and the blackness of the assault on their business stirred to the bottom their manhood and their sense of fair play, and the whole region arose in a revolt which is scarcely paralleled in the commercial history of the United States."[14] The impact was quick and profound on the young Tarbell, who by the age of fifteen had developed a firm "hatred of privilege" and made a personal commitment to work on behalf of social and economic justice.

Tarbell spent the next twenty years exploring revolution and revolutionary figures. Her specialty was the historical biography. Her subjects were Madam Roland (Marie-Jeanne Roland de la Platière), Napoleon, and Lincoln. Her books on the latter two were both best sellers, and all three provided excellent preparation for her later study of John D. Rockefeller. Tarbell explained that the people of Pennsylvania came to view Rockefeller much in the way that "English commoners" viewed Napoleon—"as a dread power, cruel, omniscient, always ready to spring."

"Devil Bill"

While Tarbell counts among her ancestors Rebecca Nurse, who was hanged for witchcraft in Massachusetts in 1692, John Davison Rockefeller's most notorious ancestor was his father, William, better known as "Devil Bill." In *Titan: The Life of John D. Rockefeller, Sr.*, his foremost biographer, Ron Chernow, variously describes Rockefeller's father as a bigamist, accused rapist, trickster, schemer, flimflam man, and a "sworn foe of conventional morality who had opted for a vagabond existence."[15] Rockefeller's father, like Tarbell's, also made money from oil. But in Devil Bill's case, his profits were made as a snake-oil salesman, making wild claims about the oil's curative properties—some true, most not—to gullible customers. For a time, John lived with his father, his mother, his father's girlfriend, and his four siblings—the children of both women. While still married to John's mother, Devil Bill moved to Canada to live with another wife and family.

John Davison, named for his mother's father, was born on the family's small farm in New York in 1839. He spent the majority of his childhood living with just his mother, older sister, and three younger siblings. His mother, a devout Baptist, strict and violent disciplinarian, and thrifty spender, was the rock of his childhood. She relied on her eldest son to fill in for her husband's constant absences. When not attending school, Rockefeller would cut wood, milk the cow, draw well water, tend the garden, help with the family's shopping, supervise his younger siblings, manage the family budget, and concoct schemes to earn money.

As a small child he bought candy by the pound, divided it into small portions, and then sold it at a tidy profit to his siblings. At age seven he "shadowed a turkey hen as it waddled off into the woods, raided its nest, and raised the chicks for sale."[16] He earned money by helping neighboring farmers dig up potatoes, until he realized that he could make money far more easily by lending the farmers money and charging interest. He explained that during this time "the impression was gaining ground with me that it was a good thing to let the money be my slave and not make myself a slave to money."

Rockefeller did not finish high school or attend college, choosing instead to attend business school. Upon graduation at age sixteen in 1855, he took his first job as a bookkeeper. By age twenty, he and a partner had formed their own business selling produce. The outbreak of the Civil War in 1861 did nothing to slow the young man's progress. He simply paid a "substitute" to take his place in the military and proceeded to make a fortune selling supplies to the federal government.

THE RISE OF STANDARD OIL

For hundreds of years, whale oil provided high-quality illumination for candles and then lamps. But as inevitably happens with nonrenewable natural resources, the whales of the Atlantic were nearly wiped out, and the whalers were forced to sail farther and farther afield to more dangerous and expensive waters to meet the world's growing demand. The whalers made a fortune as the increasingly limited supply and growing demand enabled them to charge higher prices for their product. Consumers and naturalists, however, demanded a change. Once the technology was developed to drill for rock oil and pump it out of the ground in large quantities, petroleum quickly replaced whale oil as the world's primary source of illumination.

In 1860, just one year after Colonel Drake struck oil in Pithole, at least fifteen refineries were operating in western Pennsylvania and five more in Pittsburgh. Pipelines carried the oil from the field to trains that then carried it to refineries. The railroad came to Cleveland in 1863, putting the city in a position to compete in the oil-refining business. That same year, Rockefeller, now age twenty-four, and his partner used their war bounty to purchase the largest of Cleveland's thirty refineries. Two years later, Rockefeller bought out his partner and built a second refinery.[17]

Rockefeller quickly moved to put as much of the oil business under his direct ownership and control as possible. He bought the trees used to build oil barrels, the tank cars and boats to carry it, and the warehouses in which it was stored. He stayed away, at least initially, from the oil wells themselves, finding production too risky and coarse for his tastes.

A problem that would plague Rockefeller's corporate descendants more than a century later, in the 1980s, became increasingly evident to him by the late 1860s: oversupply. There were too many producers pumping too much oil, too many refineries turning out too many finished products, and prices for his products were too low. His solution—to take control over the refining sector in order to reduce the quantity of oil that would be turned into finished products and eliminate the competition—would be dutifully followed by his corporate descendants. Rockefeller decided to build his own giant refining and marketing business to function as the sole buyer and seller of refined products. This would allow him to control supply and price.

First he needed capital. In 1870 he brought in four partners, formed the Standard Oil Company in Ohio, and quickly set out to buy up the competition. Rockefeller sought to maintain as much secrecy and distance between himself, Standard Oil, and the public maneuverings of the company as possible. He appeared little in public and said even less. His agents spoke in code and tried to appear to work on behalf of independent companies rather than Standard Oil. As one commentator, J. C. Welch, wrote in 1883, "If there was ever anything in this country that was bolted and barred, hedged round, covered over, shielded before and behind, in itself and all its approaches, with secrecy, that thing is the Standard Oil Company."[18]

Standard Oil's tactics were infamous for both their ruthlessness and their success. If a refiner would not join or sell, Standard Oil would cut its own prices, even operate at a loss if necessary, to force the competitor out of business. Once the competition was beaten, Standard Oil's prices would rise again. If the refiner remained recalcitrant, Standard Oil was known to orchestrate "barrel famines"—buying up every available oil barrel so there were none left for other producers to use. Standard Oil would cajole, threaten, bully, lie, cheat, steal—even, on occasion, make expert use of a well-placed fire—to achieve its ends. As one refiner, Robert Hanna, explained, the threat from Standard Oil was more than clear: "If you refuse to sell, it will end in your being crushed."[19]

In addition to owning the refineries, Rockefeller sought to control supply by taking hold of the transportation sector. Rockefeller could not buy up the corporate giants that ran the railroad industry as he had bought out the small oil refiners, but he could and did enlist them as willing coconspirators. In 1871 Rockefeller invited a few select refiners to join with Standard Oil under a front organization, the South Improvement Company, to carry out a massive rebate scheme. The South Improvement Company guaranteed the railroads a bulk supply of oil to ship on their rails; in return, the railroads doubled their rates on the oil it shipped for all of the South Improvement Company's competitors. Those refiners and producers who could not afford the new rates were effectively put out of business.

During one of the many legal investigations into the rebate

scheme, the vice president of the Erie Railway Company was asked, "The effect of this contract would have been a complete monopoly in the oil-carrying trade?"

"Yes, sir," he replied, "a complete monopoly."[20]

A congressional committee declared of Standard Oil, "Your success meant the destruction of every refiner who refused for any reason to join your company, or whom you did not care to have in, and it put the producers entirely in your power. It would make a monopoly such as no set of men are fit to handle."[21]

The Great Oil War

Suddenly, overnight, the price of transporting oil on the railroads doubled. For the small independent operators in Pennsylvania, the price increase was enough to ruin anyone in the industry who did not, in the phrase of the time, "go over to the Standard." In response, three thousand people met in the Titusville opera house in February 1872 to fight back in the manner of the day: they organized a union. The Petroleum Producers' Union pledged that no oil would go to anyone known to be in the South Improvement Company. They vowed to bring down the "Great Anaconda" of Standard Oil. Ida Tarbell recalled when her father joined the union and the struggle: "the night when my father came home with a grim look on his face and told how he with scores of other producers had signed a pledge not to sell to the Cleveland ogre that alone had profited from the [railroad rebate] scheme."[22]

There were nightly organizing meetings, regular protests, and marches. Trains of oil cars loaded for members of the South Improvement Company were raided, the oil poured out on the ground, and their buyers evicted from the exchanges where oil was sold. Tarbell expressed the opinion of most people in the oil region when she wrote, "I looked with more contempt on the man who had gone over to the Standard than on the one who had been in jail. I felt pity for the latter man, but none for the deserters from the ranks of the fighting independents."[23]

The Petroleum Producers' Union successfully cut off the flow of oil from Pennsylvania, leaving Rockefeller's refineries nearly idle. The union took its demand for the end of the rebate scheme and the end of the South Improvement Company to the Pennsylvania state legislature, the U.S. Congress, and to President Ulysses S. Grant. Grant shared their concerns, telling the union representatives, "Gentlemen, I have noticed the progress of monopolies, and have long been convinced that the national government would have to interfere and protect the people against them."[24] The Pennsylvania state legislature found the South Improvement Company to be the "most gigantic and daring conspiracy" the United States had ever seen. In April 1872, just months after the oil war had begun, the legislature repealed the South Improvement Company's corporate charter, and the oil regions proclaimed victory, heralding the slaying of the Standard Oil Company "monster."

The oil war was a pivotal moment in the lives of both Tarbell and Rockefeller. For Tarbell, the war instilled a powerful belief in the strength of people's movements, as well as a deep personal commitment never to find herself in the economic power of any man. She writes that at age fourteen, she got down on her knees and prayed to God to be spared from marriage.

The most lasting effect of the Pennsylvania oil war on Rockefeller was arguably his personal exposure. Rockefeller had largely succeeded in avoiding public scrutiny until the oil war drew the public's attention. His ability to keep his identity secret was part of his power; according to Tarbell, his secrecy had fostered among the people of the oil regions the unsettling sense that an omnipotent and omniscient specter ruled over their fate. That is why, when his identity was finally known and the depths of his schemes revealed, Rockefeller was so personally reviled. The oil regions had succeeded not only in uncovering Rockefeller's plot but also—at least for a time—in blocking it. From this point on, the American public viewed Standard Oil as a company that the public should and—perhaps more importantly—could control.

Never one to take a defeat lying down, however, Rockefeller used the collapse of the South Improvement Company to buy up his former coconspirators in what would go down in history as the "Cleveland Massacre." By the spring of 1872, Rockefeller owned twenty-two of Cleveland's twenty-six refineries. Public scrutiny and the law aside, neither Rockefeller nor the railroads ultimately changed their practices, and Standard Oil continued to grow, until, by 1879, Rockefeller controlled a full 90 percent of all refining in the United States.[25]

The people of the oil regions tried everything they could to maintain their independence from Standard Oil. They even invented, designed, and built the first oil pipeline capable of carrying oil from Pennsylvania to the coast, allowing them to bypass the railways altogether. But their victory was short-lived. Standard Oil took over this pipeline and every other pipeline and gathering system carrying oil in and out of the oil regions. In this way, Rockefeller was able to reduce oil output to the exact amount that would ensure his desired price for his refined products. If that meant that half, two-thirds, or more of the oil producers were left to sit idle, without work or income, so be it. Rockefeller had no qualms about the practice, as he shared none of Tarbell's faith in the oilmen: "Whatever their backgrounds, [the producers] were highly individualistic and unlikely to take a long view and think of the common good, even if a workable plan had presented itself."[26]

The people of the oil regions were not easily beaten. They continued to demand reform. In 1879 they were once again victorious when the Grand Jury of Pennsylvania handed down an eight-count indictment against Rockefeller, his brother and business partner William, and seven other Standard Oil men, charging them with "a conspiracy for the purpose of securing a monopoly, forming a combination to oppress and injure those engaged in producing petroleum, to extort from railroad companies unreasonable rebates and commissions, and by fraudulent means and devices to control the market prices of crude and refined petroleum and acquire unlawful gains thereby."[27] Rockefeller avoided the ruling by exacting a promise from the governor of New York not to approve any extradition order from Pennsylvania.

THE STANDARD OIL TRUST

Three years later, in 1882, the state of Ohio rescinded Standard Oil's corporate charter and dissolved the company, declaring Standard Oil "adjudged to have forfeited and surrendered its corporate rights, privileges, powers and franchises, and that it be ousted and excluded therefrom, and that it be dissolved."[28] Regardless of how many courts found Standard Oil's practices illegal, however, time and again Rockefeller determined that he did not need new business practices but rather a new corporate model and better political allies. He refused to accept defeat in himself or others (a trait that may well have contributed to the "nervous collapse due to overwork" suffered by his son, John D. Rockefeller Jr., at the tender age of thirteen).[29]

After the state of Ohio dissolved the Standard Oil Company, Rockefeller formed the Standard Oil Trust of Ohio in 1882. Rockefeller was the head of the board of trustees, which was charged with the general supervision of the fourteen wholly owned and twenty-six partly owned companies of the trust. For Rockefeller it was one in a series of corporate devices he used to establish the appearance of competition when in fact no competition existed. Instead of one giant monopoly, he wanted the world to see several distinct companies; instead of one corporate chieftain, he wanted the world to see dozens of separate executives.

Rockefeller remained in charge, and the separate corporations continued to work as one company, but the trust provided a convenient charade of separation. The trust could argue that it did not operate as a monopoly, because it was not one company and its component parts had no legal relationship. In the words of one Standard Oil executive testifying before the New York state legislature, it was simply a "pleasant coincidence" that the businesses happened to work together "in harmony."[30] Of course, as the courts would later rule, Rockefeller's trust was a ruse. Nevertheless, the business world was sold on Rockefeller's model, and a flood of new corporate trusts soon formed across the nation.

Between 1898 and 1904, the number of companies forming into trusts in the United States nearly quadrupled, increasing from 82 to 319, while swallowing up approximately 5,300 previously independent businesses.[31] The trusts, whether they were in timber, steel, coal, paper, wheat, or the rails, consolidated their purchasing and selling power and controlled prices after the model of Standard Oil. They progressively shut out small and independent businesspeople all along the chain of production as they increased their power vis-à-vis their workers, consumers, the economy, and the nation. The trusts were also deeply interconnected, as the nation had not yet passed the prohibition on interlocking directorates. In addition to his control over the Standard Oil Trust, Rockefeller personally sat on the boards of thirty-nine other corporations.

First published in 1942, Allan Nevins and Henry Steel Commager's classic American history textbook, *A Pocket History of the United States*, provides a clear description of the problems associated with the trusts, which could equally well apply to the impact of today's megacorporations: "Local industry dried up, factories went out of business or were absorbed . . . and neighbors who worked not for themselves but for distant corporations were exposed to the vicissitudes of policy over which they had no control. . . . It created a system of absentee ownership more far-reaching than anything known heretofore to American history. . . . It centered in the hands of a few men power over the fortunes of millions of people greater than that wielded by many monarchs. . . . It created new aggregations of capital powerful enough to influence policies of state and even the national legislators, foreign as well as domestic."[32]

Not only were there more trusts, but they were yielding the first large class of truly wealthy individuals in U.S. history. There were two hundred times more millionaires in the United States in the 1890s than there had been in the 1840s, the number increasing from fewer than twenty to more than four thousand. There were also an additional 120 Americans with over $10 million each.[33] One analysis in 1890 found that more than half the country's wealth was held by just 1 percent of U.S. families, compared with about 29 percent in 1860.[34] While inequality was certainly not new to America, by the 1870s the United States experienced its first broadly universal encounter with vast income inequality stretching across the nation, massive and heretofore unprecedented wealth accumulation by a small industrial class, and the emergence of a plutocracy: a government for the wealthy.

Government for Sale

The power exerted over government officials by these wealthy individuals and corporations was nothing short of scandalous at the time and would be shocking to us today if it were not so familiar. "From New Hampshire to California, from New Mexico to Montana, legislators were up for auction," declares the *Pocket History.* "Everywhere the great corporations had their lobbyists who engaged in shameless bribery or, where that failed, in blackmail." A grand jury investigating conditions in Missouri at the turn of the nineteenth century concluded that for twelve years corruption had been accepted in state legislation "without interference or hindrance."[35]

A legal textbook from the time, *Leading Cases Simplified,* warned students, "Do not pay much heed to the decisions of the Supreme Court of Pennsylvania—at least, during the past ten or fifteen years. The Pennsylvania Railroad appears to run that tribunal with the same success that it does its own trains."[36] The Petroleum Producers' Union offered this description of the Pennsylvania legislature in 1878: "Our present lawmakers, as a body, are ignorant, corrupt and unprincipled; . . . the majority of them are, directly or indirectly, under the control of the very monopolies against whose acts we have been seeking relief. . . ." As for the Ohio legislature, one newspaper wrote, "The whole Democratic Legislature was made rotten by the money that was used to buy and sell the members like so many sheep."[37]

Rockefeller's approach to electoral politics was much the same as his business model: complete consolidation. "It was a matter of constant comment in Ohio, New York and Pennsylvania that the Standard was active in all elections," states Tarbell. "Rarely did an able young lawyer get into office who was not retained by the Standard."[38] Standard Oil had allied legislators in the federal government and every key state within which it operated. Among other efforts, they helped to prevent the passage of bills that would have made the use of pipelines and rails free and held off for years the passage of federal antitrust and interstate commerce bills.

"From his headquarters at 26 Broadway in New York, Rockefeller controlled a corporation unique in the world's history," noted Anthony Sampson in his groundbreaking 1975 book, *The Seven Sisters*. "It was almost untouchable by the state governments which seemed small beside it, or the federal government in Washington, whose regulatory powers were minimal. By bribes and bargains it established 'friends' in each legislature and teams of lawyers were ready to defend its positions. Its income was greater than that of most states."[39]

H. H. Rogers, one of the most senior and powerful directors of Standard Oil, told Tarbell in response to her question about its manipulation of legislation, "Oh, of course, we look after it! They come in here and ask us to contribute to their campaign funds. And we do it,—that is, as individuals. . . . We put our hands in our pockets and give them some good sums for campaign purposes and then when a bill comes up that is against our interest we go to the manager and say: 'There's such and such a bill up. We don't like it and we want you to take care of our interests.' That's the way everybody does it."[40]

Standard Oil trustee John D. Archbold wrote to Senator Joseph

Foraker of Ohio in 1900 about a bill opposed by Standard Oil: "It is so outrageous as to be ridiculous, but needs to be looked after and I hope there will be no difficulty in killing it." When Foraker helped defeat the bill, Archbold sent congratulations: "I enclose for you a certificate of deposit to your favor for $15,000. . . . I need scarcely express our great gratification over the favorable outcome of affairs." When the illegal payments came to light, Foraker was matter-of-fact in his response: "That I was employed as counsel for the Standard Oil Company at the time and presumably compensated for my services was common knowledge. . . . At least I never made any effort to conceal it."[41]

One of the most renowned political scandals involving Standard Oil occurred in 1884, when it was argued that it had successfully bought the election of Ohio senator Henry B. Payne. In 1884, the year that the Anti-Monopoly Party ran its first presidential candidate, Ohio held elections for its state legislature and one U.S. senator. The people of Ohio voted for state legislators based on several issues, including whom they pledged to vote for as U.S. senator. (Until passage of the Seventeenth Amendment to the U.S. Constitution in 1912, U.S. senators were elected by the votes of their state legislatures.) There had been just two Democratic candidates for the senate in Ohio until the popular election for the legislature was complete. The Democrats won a majority, and it was time for the legislators to vote for a U.S. senator. Then, seemingly out of nowhere, a new name appeared that was incredibly popular among the legislators: Henry B. Payne, a former state senator and member of Congress, and also the father of Oliver Payne, Standard Oil's treasurer.

It turned out that Oliver Payne and four other principals of Standard Oil had waged a last-minute campaign to get Henry Payne elected. After a great deal of money changed hands, their campaign was a success. According to Henry Demarest Lloyd in his best-selling 1894 exposé of the trusts, *Wealth Against Commonwealth*, members of Ohio's house and senate were taken one by one by "certain guides to a special room that looked like a bank" because of all the money that was changing hands and "came out with an intense and suddenly developed dislike" of the candidates—except Mr. Payne.[42] At least one state senator testified that he had been given $5,000 for his vote.

There was an immediate public uproar, and investigations were launched in the Ohio house and senate. Both bodies resolved that the election of Henry B. Payne was purchased "by the corrupt use of money" and "by other corrupt means and practices."[43] Republican senator William P. Frye of Maine was one of many legislators who sought an investigation by the U.S. Senate, putting forward this impassioned plea: "When the question comes before it as this has been presented, whether or not the great Standard Oil Company, the greatest monopoly today in the United States of America, a power which makes itself felt in every inch of territory in this whole republic, a power which controls business, railroads, men and things, shall also control here; whether that great body has put its hands upon a legislative body and undertaken to control, has controlled, and has elected a member of the U.S. Senate, that Senate, I say, cannot afford to sit silent and let not its voice be heard."[44] The case was not heard. Senator Payne held his post and dutifully enforced the wishes both of Standard Oil and of the other major trusts.

The uproar over Payne and nine additional U.S. senators whose elections were ultimately investigated for similar forms of bribery contributed significantly to the increasing influence of the Progressive and Populist Movements and public pressure for federal antitrust action.

THE SHERMAN ANTITRUST ACT

A powerful peoples' movement arose to challenge the very existence of Standard Oil and the corporate trusts. It succeeded in making the trusts the leading political issue for Populists, Democrats, and Republicans; in establishing new federal antitrust legislation in 1890; and in the breakup of Standard Oil in 1911.

The nation's farmers were among the most vigilant opponents

of the trusts, for just as Standard Oil shut down the independent producers and refiners of oil, the trusts controlled the producers of wheat, sugar, corn, and other crops. Farmers' alliances began to emerge and grow throughout the 1870s. By 1886 there were two thousand farmers' alliances with a total of some one hundred thousand members. Eighteen eighty-six was known as "the year of the great uprising of labor." It was the year of the Haymarket Massacre in Chicago and of thousands of massive workers' strikes involving hundreds of thousands of people in cities all across the country. It was also the year that the Farmers' Alliance of Cleburne, Texas, met to draw up what would become the first document of the Populist Movement. The "Cleburne Demands" were a clear attack on the concentration of power and wealth in the hands of the trusts and the complicity and participation by the country's elected officials. Among other demands, it called for "such legislation as shall secure to our people freedom from the onerous and shameful abuses that the industrial classes are now suffering at the hands of the arrogant capitalists and powerful corporations."[45]

In 1888 the political platform of the newly formed Union Labor Party—a coalition of the Knights of Labor, farmer organizations, and others—concluded with this declaration: "The paramount issues to be solved in the interests of humanity are the abolition of usury, monopoly, and trusts, and we denounce the Democratic and Republican parties for creating and perpetuating these monstrous evils."[46]

Both the Democrats and the Republicans were ultimately persuaded to join in the admonition of the trusts. The Democratic National Convention platform of 1888 stated: "Judged by Democratic principles, the interests of the people are betrayed when, by unnecessary taxation, trusts and combinations are permitted to exist, which, while unduly enriching the few that combine, rob the body of our citizens. . . ." As for the Republicans, their platform condemned "all combinations of capital, organized in trusts or otherwise, to control arbitrarily the conditions of trade among our citizens" and recommended "such legislation as will prevent the execution of all schemes to oppress the people by undue charges on their supplies, or by unjust rates for the transportation of their products to market."[47]

The National Farmers' Alliance was formed in 1889 with four hundred thousand members, thirty-eight of whom were elected to Congress in 1890.[48] The alliance decided that it needed to form its own political party to directly challenge the Democrats and Republicans. The People's Party—later known as the Populist Party—held its first national convention in 1890. Just two years later, out of a total U.S. population of sixty-three million people, the Populist Party candidate, James Weaver, received more than one million votes for president. The winner, Republican Grover Cleveland, became president riding an antitrust platform. The debate over how far reform would go was at hand.

One of the Populist Party's most famous spokespeople was the powerful orator Mary Ellen Lease, credited for encouraging the farmers of Kansas to "raise less corn and more hell." Expressing the party's position on the trusts with her renowned flair, she told the convention crowd: "Wall Street owns the country. It is no longer a government of the people, by the people, and for the people, but a government of Wall Street, by Wall Street, and for Wall Street."[49]

With the presidential election of 1892 looming, the federal government finally took action with the passage of a new national antitrust law: the Sherman Antitrust Act of 1890.

The Sherman Antitrust Act prohibits contracts or conspiracies in restraint of trade. It also prohibits monopolies and attempts at monopolization. Companies found in violation of this act can be dissolved, and injunctions to prohibit illegal practices can be issued. Violations are punishable by fines and imprisonment. In addition, private citizens directly injured by companies acting in violation of the law can sue the companies in court.

The original target of the Sherman Act was Standard Oil. To quote a typical antitrust textbook, *The Legal Environment of*

Business, "The most famous of the time was the Standard Oil Trust, in reference to which the word *antitrust* was invented. Had the Standard Oil Trust been named the Standard Oil Corporation, the Sherman Act may well have been the Sherman Anticorporation Act."[50]

The Sherman Act remains the most important piece of federal legislation in the United States to protect small businesses and the nation against corporate concentration, power, and abuse. Since it was written more than one hundred years ago, however, far too many people have forgotten its original intent, particularly those whose job it is to implement the law. The law's original authors were guided by the deep and widespread belief that corporations had become so large and powerful that neither the government nor the people could control their actions. At the extreme, they argued, corporate interests drove our nation to pursue imperial power and war. The Sherman Act was offered as one answer to these critical problems that had hamstrung American democracy.

The three men who wrote the Sherman Antitrust Act and guided it toward passage were Republican senators John Sherman of Ohio, George Edmunds of Vermont, and George Hoar of Massachusetts. Senator Sherman, chairman of the Senate Finance Committee, wrote the original bill and spent two years trying to turn it into law. Defending his act on the Senate floor in 1890, he told his colleagues: "If we will not endure a king as a political power, we should not endure a king over the production, transportation, and sale of any of the necessities of life. If we would not submit to an emperor, we should not submit to an autocrat of trade." The problem, he reminded them, was "the inequality of condition, of wealth, and opportunity that has grown within a single generation out of the concentration of capital into vast combinations to control production and to break down competition."[51]

Antitrust law was a reformist approach to this problem, to be sure, and was written in direct response to more radical movements, including those calling for government ownership (or nationalization) of the resources owned and controlled by the trusts. Senator Sherman went on to warn his fellow senators: "The people of the United States, as well as other countries, are feeling the power and grasp of these combinations, and are demanding of every legislature and of Congress a remedy of this evil. . . . You must heed their appeal or be ready for the socialist, the communist, and the nihilist."

The Senate Judiciary Committee took over Sherman's bill, and within one week Senator Edmunds (the chair of the Judiciary Committee) and Senator Hoar (who would become chair after Edmunds the following year) had tweaked the bill and ushered it to passage with a vote of 52 to 1. The House approved the bill shortly thereafter, and on July 2, 1890, President Benjamin Harrison signed it into law. Standard Oil's name so dominated the congressional debate that President William Howard Taft later identified it as the chief reason for the law's passage.[52]

Today's conservative antitrust enforcers argue that the central and virtually exclusive focus of America's antitrust law is to ensure lower prices for consumers. The law's original drafters would have disagreed. They argued strenuously that while ensuring low prices was a valuable goal, it in no way outweighed larger concerns of economic justice and democracy. Senator Edmunds argued, "Although for the time being the sugar trust has perhaps reduced the price of sugar, and the oil trust certainly has reduced the price of oil immensely, that does not alter the wrong of the principle of any trust."[53]

Senator Hoar focused on antitrust law as a tool to attack the concentration of wealth, protect small business, and support economic equality. Hoar explained, "I have given the best study I could to the grave evil of the accumulation in the country of vast fortunes in single hands, or of vast properties in the hands of great corporations—popularly spoken of as trusts—whose powers are wielded by one, or a few persons. This is the most important question before the American people demanding solution in the immediate future."[54] He argued that the Sherman Act ought to be directed at the "organized force of wealth and money." He supported local small businesses, even as the sole supplier of a good, arguing that the person "who merely by superior skill and intelligence . . . got the whole business because nobody could do it as well as he could was not a monopolist." Rather, monopolization involved "the use of means which made it impossible for other persons to engage in fair competition," and "a transaction the direct purpose of which is to extort from the community . . . wealth which ought to be generally diffused over the whole community."[55]

Supreme Court Justice Rufus Peckham's majority opinion in *United States v. Trans-Missouri Freight Association* in 1897 helped frame the early interpretation of the Sherman Act, finding that the " 'corporate aggrandizement' of trusts and combinations is 'against the public interest' even if it generates cost reductions that lower price, because 'it is in the power of the combination to raise [price]' and the trust may 'driv[e] out of business the small dealers and worthy men whose lives have been spent [in that line of commerce].' "[56]

The Sherman Act formalized existing common law that generally declared monopolies illegal, and brought federal cohesion to a series of state laws. In the 1880s, a dozen states, including Texas and Ohio, had begun the process of turning the common law— which was over time being increasingly ignored—into written law, enacting antimonopoly and antitrust laws. Companies like Standard Oil simply avoided the states' piecemeal laws, however, by moving their business from states with antitrust laws to those without. It was clear that the law would not be effectively enforced without a federal statute, with federal means to enforce it.

The Sherman Act is both short and straightforward. While it has seven separate sections, the entire act is just nine hundred words long. Sections 3 through 7 address issues of definition, jurisdiction, and foreign competition. The first two sections are the most critical. Section 1 states: "Every contract, combination in the form of trust or otherwise, or conspiracy, in restraint of trade or commerce among the several States, or with foreign nations, is hereby declared to be illegal." Section 2 states: "Every person who shall monopolize or attempt to monopolize, or combine or conspire with any other person or persons, to monopolize any part of the trade or commerce among the several States, or with foreign nations, shall be deemed guilty of a felony."

The Sherman Act did not outlaw *all* trusts or combinations, only those "in restraint of trade or commerce." The act did not define *monopoly* or what would constitute monopolistic behavior. Nor did it delineate exactly what actions would be considered illegal. Thus, Congress left it to the courts, and later to the new regulatory authority of the Federal Trade Commission and the Department of Justice, to determine which acts and companies would be declared illegal.

What the Sherman Act lacked in specificity, it made up in intent. The law was written in direct response to public concern that large business interests were dominating the government, and was therefore designed to restrain economic wealth from becoming political power. It did not take long for the Sherman Antitrust Act to emerge as the government's most powerful tool against the trusts.

THE PEOPLE VERSUS THE CORPORTIONS

The importance of the Sherman Antirust Act was not lost on the nation's largest corporations, including Standard Oil. For six years after its passage, the companies exerted their influence over the legal process, and as a consequence the act was applied halfheartedly by the government and interpreted harshly by the courts.

Nevertheless, the momentum created by the Sherman Act and the antitrust spirit that guided the 1892 presidential elections gave the Ohio Supreme Court the wherewithal to order the dissolution of the Standard Oil Trust in 1892. Because it was a state order, however, Standard Oil simply packed up and moved to

New Jersey, where it continued its operations unabated. At the time of the Ohio order, Standard Oil controlled 90 percent of the U.S. refining industry. Just three Standard Oil refineries produced more than a quarter of the world's total supply of kerosene. Standard Oil also controlled 80 percent of all marketing of oil products in the United States and a quarter of the country's total output of crude.

The 1896 presidential election presented a critical juncture. The nation was ready for more than antitrust laws; it was ready for antitrust action. The Populists and the Democrats put aside their many differences to unite behind one candidate: William Jennings Bryan, a Nebraska congressman with radical roots and a leader in the antimonopoly movement. The trusts, which were anxious to maintain the status quo in the face of growing public unrest, backed the Republican governor of Ohio, William McKinley.

It was "the people versus the corporations" as the 1896 presidential race introduced the first modern American political campaign. Bryan was the "campaigning candidate." Rather than sit at home and leave the campaigning to others, he took to the road with a whistle-stop tour. Traveling by train, he stopped at towns and delivered rousing political speeches. The corporations were front and center in his attack: "The day will come when trusts will be exterminated; the day will come when corporations will cease to consider themselves greater than the Government which created them."[57]

McKinley, for his part, introduced serious money into the annals of American politics with the most expensive campaign up to that point in history. He outspent Bryan by a shocking sixteen to one.[58] "Businessmen transformed the McKinley campaign into a crusade against trust-busting infidels," wrote Rockefeller's biographer Ron Chernow. Standard Oil alone supplied $250,000 to McKinley's coffers—equal to half of the *total* contributions to the Bryan campaign. Rockefeller personally provided another $2,500. Rockefeller even went so far as to publicly proclaim his support for McKinley—a first for him for any political candidate—asserting, "I can see nothing else for us to do, to serve the Country and our honor."[59]

As usual, Rockefeller got his way. Bryan won twenty-two states and captured nearly 49 percent of the vote, but McKinley won the presidency.

Bryan became one of the most famous orators in American history. In a speech that could easily have been given by a candidate for presidential office in 2008, Bryan decried the role of money in politics: "Monopolies are both corruptive and coercive. By large contributions to campaign funds, they purchase immunity from restraining legislation and from the enforcement of the law. And as they employ an army of laboring men, they can influence elections. . . . They are hurtful from an economic standpoint, they are a corrupting element in politics, and they menace popular government."[60]

McKinley did his financiers proud. During his presidency, companies merged into trusts unabated while their power flourished. Together, McKinley and the trusts then took the United States to war, annexed new lands, and opened the door to American imperialism on behalf of corporate interests. Senators Hoar and Sherman were among those (including, most famously, Mark Twain) who deeply opposed these actions. Hoar and Sherman took leading roles in the first meaningful debate in the United States over American imperialism and the role of corporations.

In 1898 the U.S. Congress declared war on Spain. The United States won the war in a few months. In December 1898, the peace treaty signed with Spain turned Guam, Puerto Rico, and the Philippines over to the United States for $20 million. The reason given for the war was to help Cuba win independence from Spain. Sherman, who was McKinley's secretary of state, strongly opposed the war and resigned his post one week after war was declared. Several years later, the chief of the Bureau of Foreign Commerce of the Department of Commerce admitted what was widely believed at the time: "The Spanish-American

War was but an incident of a general movement of expansion. . . . It was seen to be necessary for us not only to find foreign purchasers for our goods, but to provide the means of making access to foreign markets easy, economical and safe."[61]

Similarly, Senator Henry Cabot Lodge argued in 1895 for war "in the interests of our commerce" stating that "for the sake of our commercial supremacy in the Pacific we should control the Hawaiian islands and maintain our influence in Samoa . . . and when the Nicaraguan canal is built, the island of Cuba . . . will become a necessity."[62]

Standard Oil was certainly among those U.S. companies looking for overseas markets. In fact, it was the first truly multinational American corporation. By 1891, Standard Oil accounted for 90 percent of American exports of kerosene and controlled 70 percent of the world oil market. Oil was second only to cotton as the nation's leading export product.[63] In 1895 Standard Oil bought the California Star Oil Works based in San Francisco, renamed it Standard Oil of California (today's Chevron), and began exporting large quantities of oil to China. The Chinese market, with its 400 million people, was considered a critical market for the United States.

Senator Hoar emerged as one of the most eloquent and outspoken opponents of American imperialism driven by commercial interests. He was no isolationist; rather, he opposed American "expansionism" exercised on behalf of corporate interests and against the Constitution. Hoar firmly opposed what he termed America's growing "lust for empire." In the 1890s, Ida Tarbell, Senator Hoar, and his wife all lived in the same Washington, D.C., boardinghouse on I Street. Tarbell writes with obvious fondness of Hoar and of her participation in Hoar's weekly discussion group. Every Sunday morning, Tarbell and the other boardinghouse residents would listen to the senator, then in his seventies, expound on the issues of the day. Hoar was a fan of the classics and was apt to "spice up" the morning's discussion, which would often stretch on to lunch, with the occasional recitation of Homer or Virgil. Tarbell recalls that Hoar was deeply pained by the nation's growing trend of imperialism as evidenced by the annexation of foreign lands "for commercial purposes only"—a trend that he believed to be "false to all our ideals."[64]

Arguing on behalf of just such U.S. military expansionism in the face of mass public resistance in the Philippines, Senator Albert Beveridge told the Senate in January 1900: "The Philippines are ours forever. . . . No land in America surpasses in fertility the plains and valleys of Luzon. Rice and coffee, sugar and cocoanuts, hemp and tobacco. . . . The wood of the Philippines can supply the furniture of the world for a century to come. . . . Cebu's mountain chains are practically mountains of coal. . . . It has been charged that our conduct of the war has been cruel. Senators, it has been the reverse. . . . Senators must remember that we are not dealing with Americans or Europeans. We are dealing with Orientals."[65]

Senator Hoar's response was a passionate and now famous articulation of anti-imperialism: "But the question with which we now have to deal is whether Congress may conquer and may govern, without their consent and against their will, a foreign nation. . . . [U]nder the Declaration of Independence you cannot govern a foreign territory . . . you cannot subjugate them and govern them against their will, because you think it is for their good, when they do not; because you think you are going to give them the blessings of liberty. You have no right at the cannon's mouth to impose on an unwilling people your Declaration of Independence and your Constitution and your notions of freedom and notions of what is good."[66]

Hoar, with his anti-imperialist views, was in the minority. The annexations proceeded, with American business following close behind. In Cuba, American firms, including United Fruit, American Tobacco, and Bethlehem Steel, dominated the island's key industries within a few short years.[67] In 1900 McKinley and Bryan faced off once again for the office of president of the

United States. Bryan continued his assault on the trusts and now against American imperialism as well. The vote went again to McKinley.

THE BOMBSHELL

Rockefeller had survived the dissolution of his South Improvement Company in 1872, the dissolution of Standard Oil by the state of Ohio in 1882, and his third dissolution, also in Ohio, in 1892. In 1899 Rockefeller yet again changed form rather than function and established the Standard Oil Company of New Jersey as a holding company for the entire operation. New Jersey had just implemented a radical new revision of its business laws to allow corporations to own stock in other corporations—the first such law in the country. A holding company is a corporation that owns enough stock in another corporation to influence its board of directors and therefore to control its policies and management. Yergin describes the Standard Oil Company of New Jersey as "really a bank of the most gigantic character—a bank within an industry, financing the industry against all competitors."[68] Standard Oil of New Jersey controlled all of its component corporate parts, with Rockefeller at the helm.

In 1894 *McClure's Magazine* lured Ida Tarbell back from France to begin what would ultimately become a five-year-long investigation into Standard Oil. She, like much of the nation, had grown repulsed by Rockefeller's ability to shed his skin like the trickiest of snakes and reinvent himself like the most creative of chameleons. When Tarbell's articles began appearing in November 1902, her work "proved to be a bombshell," writes Yergin. "Month after month, she spun the story of machination and manipulation . . . of the single-minded Standard. . . . The articles became the talk of the nation." Samuel McClure told Tarbell, "You are today the most generally famous woman in America. . . . People universally speak of you with such reverence that I am getting sort of afraid of you."[69]

State by state, producer by producer, populist by populist,

court by court, and legislator by legislator, opposition to Rockefeller and Standard Oil grew. Tarbell tied all the facts together, picked up the loose ends, exposed new secrets, and released her findings on a national stage at just the right political moment. It was a devastating indictment at a time when the country was ready for action. Tarbell's writing inspired and armed a public already roused against the trusts to unite around one corporate enemy: Standard Oil.

POWER SHIFT

Theodore Roosevelt assumed office in 1901 following the assassination of President McKinley. Roosevelt was no Bryan, but he did address many of the demands of the Populist and Progressive Movements, including passage in 1907 of the Tillman Act, the first meaningful campaign finance law in the nation, which barred corporations and national banks from making direct donations to candidates for federal office. The Publicity Act, requiring full disclosure of all monies spent and contributed during federal campaigns, followed three years later.

Roosevelt knew that Americans opposed the trusts and their control over government. He argued, "We do not desire to destroy corporations; we do desire to put them fully at the service of the State and the people."[70] Trust-busting emerged as a central tenet of his presidency. He launched forty-five separate antitrust actions against, among others, American Tobacco, DuPont, Union Pacific, and the beef trust. He started with J. P. Morgan by successfully using the Sherman Act to dissolve the nation's first major holding company, the Northern Securities Company, which was formed by Morgan and others to coordinate the activities of the Northern Pacific, Great Northern, and Burlington railroads.

For well over a decade, the Progressive Movement had been calling for a federal Department of Commerce and Labor. In 1903 Roosevelt responded by establishing not only the new department, but also, within it, a Bureau of Corporations to expand the ability of the federal government to take on the trusts. John D. Rockefeller Jr. sent a curt telegram to six senators telling them to stop the Bureau of Corporations: "We are opposed to the antitrust legislation. Our counsel will see you. It must be stopped. John D. Rockefeller."[71] In spite of Rockefeller, Congress did establish the bureau and gave it the authority, money, and staff to launch detailed investigations into the trusts. More important, the bureau had orders to forcibly go about its work investigating the largest and most powerful trusts in the nation. The Bureau of Corporations later became today's Federal Trade Commission.

Tarbell's *McClure* series was published as a book, *The History of Standard Oil,* in 1904. It was an immediate and overwhelming national best seller. She began a speaking tour that took her across the nation and around the world. That same year, after his election, President Roosevelt assigned the new Bureau of Corporations to investigate Standard Oil and the U.S. petroleum industry. Roosevelt said of Standard Oil: "Every measure for honesty in business that has been passed in the last six years has been opposed by these men." Standard Oil's directors were "the biggest criminals in the country."[72]

Rockefeller's power was being weakened on several fronts. For one, Standard Oil was kicked out of some of the nation's most oil-rich states by Populist organizers. James "Boss" Hogg (immortalized in the highly misrepresentative character of the same name on *The Dukes of Hazzard* TV show) was the progressive governor of Texas who railed against corporate interests and money in politics and declared: "Let us have Texas, the Empire State, governed by the people; not Texas, the truck-patch, ruled by corporate lobbyists."[73] Texas was a hotbed of populist organizing, and even today you will find Hogg's picture adorning the Web site of the Progressive Populist Caucus, which calls itself the "democratic wing of the Texas Democratic Party." Hogg had intended to be a farmer, but once he was drawn into politics, he spent his life either in elected office or engaged in political organizing, serving as governor from 1891 to 1895 and remaining politically active until his death in 1906.[74]

At a time when over 50 percent of the state's farmers were impoverished tenant farmers, Hogg sought legislation forcing land corporations to relinquish land to the farmers. He fought against the use of corporate funds in politics, for equality of taxation, and for the suppression of organized lobbying. He demanded steps to make "corporate control of Texas" impossible and open records that would "disclose every official act . . . to the end that everyone shall know that, in Texas, public office is the center of public conscience, and that no graft, no crime, no public wrong, shall ever stain or corrupt our State."[75]

He established the Texas Railroad Commission, which successfully regulated the state's railroads—making Standard Oil's rebate scheme impossible in Texas. As Texas attorney general, Hogg wrote the nation's second antitrust law and put it to work against Standard Oil. While governor, he tried to extradite Rockefeller from New York to stand trial in Texas. All of which ultimately led one Standard Oil director to declare, "After the way Mr. Rockefeller has been treated by the state of Texas, he'll never put another dime in Texas."[76] This was just fine with the people of Texas.

The largely "Standard-free-zone" established in Texas allowed for independent oil companies, such as Gulf and Texaco, to develop outside of Standard Oil's grip in what would emerge as the most oil-rich state in the nation. On January 10, 1901, an oil gusher the likes of which had never been seen in North America shot forth on the little ten-foot mound known as Spindletop in southeastern Texas. With it came the great Texas oil boom. Standard Oil was shut out of this boom and its monopoly power was weakened because of it.

The final nail in Standard Oil's coffin arguably came when Rockefeller tried to venture into another state rich with Populists: Kansas. One cannot blame Standard Oil, for it was simply following the oil, a business motto that would be echoed

ninety-four years later by Dick Cheney, then CEO of the energy
services giant Halliburton: "You've got to go where the oil is. I
don't think about [political volatility] very much."[77] In 1904 oil
suddenly poured forth in great quantities from Kansas, and Standard Oil rushed in to do what it did best: take over.

This time, instead of finding oil producers green to the ways
of Standard Oil, as had happened in Pennsylvania years before,
the company had to face off against the very astute Populists of
Kansas, who sparked a statewide revolt. They invited Tarbell to
come speak to the crowds. She was impressed with what she saw:
"The Populists . . . came out to inveigh with all of their old fer-
vor against the trust. Women's clubs took it up, political parties
took it up."[78] The state passed a law to build a state-owned refinery, which was followed by similar initiatives in states across the
Southwest. While none of the states ultimately took over the refineries, or built their own, these initiatives resulted in even
greater popular demand for Roosevelt to take his trust-busting
campaign directly to John D. Rockefeller's door.

STANDARD OIL COMPANY OF NEW JERSEY V. UNITED STATES

In 1906, in federal circuit court in Saint Louis, Missouri, the
Roosevelt administration brought suit against Standard Oil.
Claiming violations of Sections 1 and 2 of the Sherman Antitrust
Act, the Department of Justice sued the seventy-one corporations
and partnerships and seven individuals, including John D. Rockefeller, of the Standard Oil Trust for conspiring "to restrain the
trade and commerce in petroleum [in the United States] and to
monopolize said commerce." The conspiracy was traced back to
1870, when Rockefeller began the South Improvement Company.
Ultimately, the government argued, the Standard Oil Trust was
able to fix the price of oil and to monopolize interstate commerce
in these products. The government requested that the trust be
broken up so that the companies would operate independently.[79]

By the summer of 1907, there were seven federal and six state
suits against Standard Oil (in Texas, Minnesota, Mississippi,

Tennessee, Ohio, and Missouri), with new legal cases emerging weekly. The Missouri case would become the decisive suit when, in 1909, the federal circuit court ruled unanimously in favor of the federal government and ordered the dissolution of Standard Oil within thirty days. Roosevelt, now out of office, called it "one of the most signal triumphs for decency which has been won in our country."[80]

Standard Oil appealed to the Supreme Court—twice, due to two deaths on the court. The Supreme Court upheld the lower court's ruling finding that the Standard Oil Trust's "intent and purpose [was] to maintain dominancy over the oil industry, not as a result of normal methods of industrial development, but by new means of combination which were resorted to in order that greater power might be added than would otherwise have arisen had normal methods been followed, the whole with the purpose of excluding others from the trade, and thus centralizing in the combination a perpetual control of the movements of petroleum and its products in the channels of interstate commerce." It ordered the dissolution of Standard Oil into thirty-four separate corporate parts.

"The Single Most Important Figure"

Ghoulish is the word that springs to mind when looking at a picture taken of John D. Rockefeller in 1904. He is wearing a dark suit and sitting against a black background. Although he is posing, he looks startled by the camera. His face is stark white and his skin parchment-thin. His eyes bulge from bony sockets. His nose is too skinny and his lips are nonexistent. His ears are pointed, like those of a cat, and his hands are gnarled like claws. He has absolutely no hair. For most of his adult life, Rockefeller suffered from alopecia, a rare skin disease believed to be caused by stress, which leads to the loss of one's hair. By 1901, Rockefeller had fully succumbed to the disease. The man whose actions were so frequently described as monstrous now physically looked the part.

By the time of the Supreme Court ruling, John D. Rockefeller was an utterly embattled man. He was a prisoner in his own home, unable to correspond with outsiders or leave, for fear of being served by subpoenas from one of the dozens of legal cases mounted against him. He missed births, graduations, and funerals. The man who had spent his entire professional life building up the great Standard Oil desperately wanted to shed his public connections to the company (although not his financial benefits from it), but his colleagues would not allow it. Of one of Rockefeller's many attempts to have his title of president removed, vice president Henry Rogers said, "We told him he had to keep it. These cases against us were pending in the courts; and we told him that if any of us had to go to jail, he would have to go with us!"[81]

No one went to jail.

In May 1911 the Supreme Court ruled that Standard Oil was an unlawful trust and had six months to dissolve. This time, Standard Oil could not move to a new state. There were no more corporate models for it to try. The company was broken. At least for the time being.

There were serious deficiencies in the breakup of Standard Oil. Most important was the fact that the ruling went largely unenforced, although later administrations would try to address these problems and expand the authority of the government to protect the nation against monopolies. A significant victory had been won, however, offering critical lessons for us today. People from across the country had joined together to push back against the power of the world's largest corporation. They pushed their elected officials toward radical policies, many of which were implemented, leading to some of the most important labor, antimonopoly, and campaign finance protections currently available to our nation.

The power of corporations over the government was dealt a serious blow, and meaningful policies to circumscribe corporate power and protect workers, the economy, and the nation were put in place. In addition to the Tillman and Publicity Acts, and the creation of the Department of Labor and the Bureau of Corporations, within a few years of the Standard Oil breakup the federal government responded to decades of progressive organizing by passing laws for the eight-hour workday and workman's compensation and against child labor. For the next eighty years, the Sherman Act would be applied to reduce the overall power of corporations, not perfectly, but with effect.

Standard Oil's descendant parts, however, continued to thrive and demonstrated the special place that oil, and oil corporations, would play in U.S. politics for the next one hundred years.

3

Big Oil Bounces Back

From the Breakup to the Near Reconvergence of Standard Oil

*The trouble with this country is that you can't win an
election without the oil bloc, and you can't govern with it.*
—PRESIDENT FRANKLIN ROOSEVELT[1]

ExxonMobil, the most immediate descendant of the Standard
Oil Trust, is today so big that even the Rockefellers can no
longer control it. On October 27, 2006, John D. Rockefeller IV,
great-grandson of the founder of Standard Oil and three-term
U.S. senator from Virginia, was reduced to writing a letter to
the CEO of ExxonMobil, begging him to behave. In the letter,
Rockefeller expressed his outrage at ExxonMobil's nearly
twenty-year-long multimillion-dollar campaign to debunk the
overwhelming scientific consensus on the existence of global
warming. ExxonMobil's "significant and consistent financial
support of this pseudo-scientific, non-peer-reviewed echo chamber" damages the credibility of the United States, argued Rockefeller. "The goal has not been to prevail in the scientific debate,
but to obscure it. This climate change denial confederacy has
exerted an influence out of all proportion to its size or relative
scientific credibility."[2] ExxonMobil had used its money, size,
power, and influence, argued Rockefeller, to tragically alter the

public debate on one of the most pressing issues of our time. Rockefeller, from his seat on the other side of the corporate/ government divide from his great-grandfather, was not enjoying the view.

An apt metaphor for the postbreakup pieces of the Standard Oil Company can be found in the movie *Terminator 2: Judgment Day*. The hero of the film blows up a villain into hundreds of tiny pieces, then looks on in horror as the many parts of the villain's body that have been scattered by the blast turn from flesh, to machine, to liquid metal. Slowly and with painstaking precision, the pools of liquid metal inch back together to reunify, form a whole body, and renew the attack. While *Terminator 2* is fantasy, the gradual reconstruction of Standard Oil has been no less astonishing but all too real.

It took a hundred years, but today the severed pieces of Standard Oil are nearing full reunification. The political power and control exercised by today's oil giants over our government have just one historical precedent: the heyday of Standard Oil. In 1999 government regulators allowed the two largest postbreakup pieces of Standard Oil to merge and form the largest, most profitable company in history: ExxonMobil. In fact, all three of the top U.S. oil companies today are direct descendants of Standard Oil. They are, in order, ExxonMobil, Chevron, and ConocoPhillips. The fifth largest U.S. oil company, Marathon, is also a direct descendant. Moreover, all five of the largest private oil companies in the world, ExxonMobil, the Shell Oil Group (Shell), BP, Chevron, and ConocoPhillips, are made up of former parts of Standard Oil.

While Shell and BP are headquartered today in The Hague and London, respectively, both companies operate large U.S. affiliates. With its rich fields in Alaska, BP America, Inc., is the largest oil and gas producer and one of the largest gasoline retailers in the United States. Shell Oil Company also has extensive U.S. operations. Both companies use their wealth and size to play a significant role in U.S. politics by contributing to U.S.

political campaigns, lobbying U.S. elected officials, and engaging in every level of policy-making.

How did we get from the breakup of Standard Oil in 1911 to the near reunification of the whole company today? The breakup itself largely failed due to the absence of effective government oversight, while the size and cohesion of the postbreakup companies allowed them to maintain their control over the U.S. oil industry. Largely to address these failings, President Woodrow Wilson introduced new laws and, most importantly, a new government agency, the Federal Trade Commission, to tighten the government's control over antitrust violations by U.S. corporations. The radically probusiness administrations of Harding, Coolidge, and Hoover, however, abandoned Wilson's tools and opened the door to Big Oil's global expansion.

Following War World I, the three largest postbreakup companies, Standard Oil of New Jersey, Standard Oil of New York, and Standard Oil of California, took control of the international oil market along with Gulf, Texaco, BP, and Shell. For almost fifty years, these seven companies operated as a global cartel. When tax breaks benefiting foreign over domestic production of oil were implemented in 1950, the companies shifted the majority of their holdings to the international market. U.S. domestic production and refining were then largely left to the relatively smaller U.S. companies known as "the independents." The U.S. government deliberately ignored the obvious antitrust violations of the Seven Sisters in the international arena while more dutifully enforcing antitrust laws at home.

Until quite recently, the primary preoccupation of the major oil companies was to curtail production. For the better part of American and global history, there has simply been too much oil from the perspective of these companies. As a cartel, the Seven Sisters kept production down everywhere, choosing where to produce based on politics as much as economics. The production and pricing decisions made by the companies radically affected the economic well-being of entire nations around the globe.

Whether the companies decided to produce from wells in Iraq, Saudi Arabia, or Venezuela determined the federal budgets available to those nations.

The system worked as long as the developing countries could be played off against one another and while governments favorable to the oil companies' interests were kept in place, both in the United States and abroad. But just as the oil producers of Pennsylvania rebelled against Standard Oil, the oil producers of Mexico, Iran, Venezuela, Libya, Iraq, Kuwait, Saudi Arabia, Nigeria, Algeria, and other nations rebelled against the Seven Sisters. By the mid-1980s, these governments had reclaimed full ownership of the crude oil holdings and facilities from the oil companies operating in their countries. Suddenly the Seven Sisters, which in 1973 earned two-thirds of their profits abroad, on which they paid no domestic taxes, lost their source of income. They turned their attention back to the U.S. market.

With the 1980s came the new mantra, "Merge or die," as the Sisters first set out to buy up the independent U.S. oil companies and then each other. First they needed a pliable U.S. government and a more lenient set of antitrust laws. Since its creation, the Federal Trade Commission (FTC) had remained the primary investigator of the oil industry and threatened action against collusion. While Big Oil had been focusing on its foreign oil holdings, antitrust laws opposing corporate mergers had been strengthened and enforced domestically. For decades many radical and fundamental changes in the U.S. petroleum industry designed to rein in the major oil companies had been proposed and considered by the U.S. Congress. None of these proposals took hold, however. Domestic legislation to subsidize smaller independent companies, support conservation, and invest in alternative energy was pursued in the 1970s, but all of this came crashing to a halt with the election of President Ronald Reagan. Reagan's FTC initiated a new and radically permissive attitude toward corporate mergers that brought about the first major wave of oil company consolidations since the breakup of Standard Oil.

While most aspects of "Reaganomics" have been flatly rejected by subsequent administrations, Reagan's approach to antitrust law has continued unabated through both Democratic and Republican administrations and gone largely unnoticed by the public. As former FTC commissioner for George W. Bush Timothy Muris told me, "There was clearly a Reagan Revolution in antitrust, and my side won."[3] The Clinton and Bush administrations subsequently ushered in the second great wave of petroleum mergers, a nearly reconstituted Standard Oil Trust, and with it a new domestic political landscape that mirrors the Standard Oil era of a century ago.

THE STANDARD OIL BREAKUP: WHAT WENT WRONG

All the companies are still under the same control, or at least working in such close alliance that the effect is precisely the same.

— PRESIDENT THEODORE ROOSEVELT, 1912[4]

The Supreme Court ordered that Standard Oil be dissolved in 1911, and in such a way that the postbreakup companies would have to compete as individual and separate entities. The companies were allowed to contract with one another for "legitimate reasons," but all such actions were to be subject to government scrutiny. This is where the breakup ultimately failed. The court-ordered scrutiny did not happen, and the government abdicated its role as regulator. While Standard Oil was divided into thirty-four smaller entities, for years the companies continued to function essentially as one.

In fact, rather shockingly, Standard Oil was put in control of designing its own dissolution. Rockefeller quite wisely kept virtually half of the entire trust consolidated in just one company: Standard Oil of New Jersey, or "Jersey Standard," the original holding company. Following the breakup, Jersey Standard maintained 26 Broadway in Manhattan as its corporate headquarters and shared the building with the second largest "baby-Standard," Standard Oil of New York, or "SoCoNY." The rest of the companies withdrew to their states of origin, with many retaining their Standard Oil names, such as Standard Oil of Kentucky, Standard Oil of Louisiana, and Standard Oil of Pennsylvania. The companies continued to divide the country as before into eleven separate marketing territories. They sold the same brand names and, according to an FTC report issued a few years later, they did not compete with one another on the prices they charged for their goods.

Rockefeller finally got his wish and was freed from any public connection to the companies. However, he retained personal ownership of more than a quarter of the total shares of the new companies. He held daily meetings at 26 Broadway for the executives of Jersey Standard and SoCoNY. Meanwhile, the rest of his original executives were simply distributed among the new companies. When they ran out of executives, joked one company official, they "had to send out some office boys to head these companies"—begging the question of how truly independent these companies were.[5]

Thus, while it is true that where there had been just one company there were now thirty-four, those thirty-four companies were still run by the same executives, in the same way, and with the same owners as before the dissolution. At the time of the Supreme Court ruling against Standard Oil, J. P. Morgan said, "How the hell is any court going to compel a man to compete with himself."[6]

Meanwhile, the breakup did not take place in a vacuum. Three years before the breakup was finalized, the single most important change in the history of oil consumption appeared on the streets of America: Henry Ford's Model T car. The introduction of the mass-produced car sent the demand for oil skyrocketing. In 1910, one year before the breakup, gasoline sales surpassed those of kerosene for the first time. While in 1900 there were just eight thousand cars on the road, by 1915 there were 2.5 million,

and by 1920 there were 9.2 million. The age of oil had truly arrived, and there was little that the federal government could have
done short of nationalization to keep Standard Oil, in whatever
form, from cashing in.

Within one year of the dissolution, the successor companies'
shares doubled in value. Standard Oil of Indiana's profits tripled,
with its patent of the "thermal cracking" process that doubled
the yield of gasoline from a barrel of crude oil. Rockefeller, with
his enormous holdings in each company, became the richest man
in the world and the first with an income to reach $1 billion. His
wealth was estimated to be twice as large as that of Andrew Car-
negie, the second wealthiest man in the world. The majority of
the rest of the company stocks were divided among a handful of
current and former Standard Oil executives, such that *all* of the
wealthiest families and individuals in the U.S. oil industry from
1901 to 1914 were affiliated with the Standard Oil group.[7] Not
only were their own companies making money, but they also
owned stock in each other's companies—consolidating their control over the industry and their wealth, which in turn allowed
them to continue to exercise great political influence.

The Baby-Standards

Standard Oil of New Jersey (Exxon—ExxonMobil)

Forty-three percent of the entire holdings of Standard Oil remained in Jersey Standard, which later became Exxon and today
is ExxonMobil. Jersey Standard maintained the trust's corporate headquarters and its de facto leader, John D. Archbold.
Archbold had unofficially run the trust for more than a decade,
taking over the day-to-day business from Rockefeller in 1897.
Archbold was even more hated than Rockefeller by people from
the oil regions because Archbold had been one of them before he
turned Judas. After joining the early rebellion against Rockefeller, Archbold had "gone over to Standard" and begun taking
over refineries secretly for the South Improvement Company. In
just a matter of months he acquired almost thirty refineries and

quickly became known as one of the meanest men in the business. This aggressive method carried him to the top of the trust and then to the presidency of Standard Oil of New Jersey.

Jersey Standard remained the mightiest of the postbreakup companies by continuing its role as banker to the others—providing loans for exploration and development. It also maintained control over transportation, refining, and marketing. For the first decade following the breakup, it largely kept its hands clean of the coarse business of oil production, choosing instead to buy its oil from the other baby-Standards. Its constant partner was Standard Oil of New York.

Standard Oil of New York (Mobil—ExxonMobil)

The second largest postbreakup offshoot was the Standard Oil Company of New York, or SoCoNY, which later became Mobil and today is ExxonMobil. At the time of the breakup, it held 9 percent of the trust's net value. SoCoNY was also headquartered at 26 Broadway, and its president, Henry Folger, had worked in Rockefeller's inner circle at Standard Oil for twenty-five years. SoCoNY maintained the extensive overseas marketing presence it held prior to the breakup. Shortly after the breakup, gasoline replaced kerosene as the primary product sold from crude, and the majority of it was sold in the large East Coast cities. SoCoNY's marketing area included all of those cities. While it was the second largest oil company in the nation, SoCoNY was, from its birth, forever known as Jersey Standard's "little sister." The two companies merged into one in 1999, forming ExxonMobil.

Standard Oil of California (Chevron)

After Jersey Standard and SoCoNY, Standard Oil of California, or "SoCal," which is today known as Chevron, was the third largest postbreakup company. Unlike the other two companies, however, SoCal had not begun life as a Standard Oil company. In 1876, just twenty-five years after California became a state, the Star Oil Works, owned by Demetrius Scofield and Fredrick

Taylor, struck oil in the Santa Susana Mountains in southern California. The Pacific Coast Oil Company of San Francisco acquired the company a few years later. While Standard Oil marketed kerosene in California as early as 1879, Rockefeller maintained his disdain for production and left companies like Pacific Coast Oil alone. With the new century, however, came new priorities, and in 1900 Pacific went over to the Standard. Six years later, its name was changed to the Standard Oil Company of California, or SoCal.

At the time of the breakup, California's oil output was larger than that of any foreign nation and accounted for 22 percent of total world production. By 1919, SoCal *alone* accounted for 26 percent of total U.S. oil production—more than any other single company. For most of its early history, however, it was cut off from the U.S. market by the Rocky Mountains and therefore focused its efforts across the Pacific Ocean on China.

The combination of SoCal's oil production and West Coast status gave it a reputation for being more coarse and rough around the edges than its East Coast sisters. Its distance from Washington, D.C., also contributed to SoCal's approach to the federal government, described as, at best, "disdainful" by Anthony Sampson in *The Seven Sisters*. SoCal always worked more closely with its West Coast counterparts (particularly Texaco) than its larger East Coast siblings, and eventually bought and/or merged with the largest West Coast companies, including Gulf Oil in 1984, Texaco in 2001, and Union Oil Company of California (Unocal) in 2005.

Standard Oil of Indiana (Amoco—BP)

Standard Oil of Indiana became one of the most profitable postbreakup companies due to its thermal cracking patent. Indiana used its new capital to develop from just a refining company to one with its own sources of crude.

One of the biggest, most persistent problems for companies in search of oil is that there are always people who want to call the land above the oil "home." While Jersey Standard and SoCoNY eschewed oil production for much of the decade following the breakup, they purchased their crude from other baby-Standards, including Indiana Standard. The latter began working with the Pan American Petroleum Company at the turn of the century and later merged with it in 1954. The merged company was called the American Oil Company, or Amoco. In 1998 BP purchased Amoco.

THE HUASTECS OF MEXICO: For decades, U.S. oil companies dominated Mexico, making it the largest source of foreign oil imported into the United States. Pan American Petroleum, led by Edward Doheny, whose life provided the template for Upton Sinclair's classic novel *Oil!* and Daniel Day-Lewis's character in the 2007 movie *There Will be Blood,* was one of the first and largest companies to enter the country. In the early 1900s it began work in northern Veracruz and nearby regions, then known as the Huastec region for the indigenous people who lived there. Today the area covers the intersection of Veracruz, San Luis Potosi, and Hidalgo. The Huastecs, relatives of the Maya of the Yucatan, had lived in the area as subsistence farmers, growing corn, for centuries prior to the arrival of the oil companies. U.S. visitors to the area regularly referred to it as an Eden for its untouched and endless landscapes of lush tropical rain forest.[8]

The character of the area changed dramatically with the influx of foreign oil companies. In order to gain access to the land and the oil beneath it, agents for the oil companies used every possible manner of persuasion, including murder. "The Mexican literature on the subject brims with well-documented examples of swindles . . . cunning and cruelty" perpetrated by the oil company agents against the Huastecs, according to history professor Myrna Santiago, author of *The Ecology of Oil: Environment, Labor, and the Mexican Revolution, 1900–1938.* Indigenous people who were in line for land inheritance were murdered and their homes burned down.[9] Pushed from their land, the Huastecs

refused to work in the oil fields. With the assistance of local political and military leaders, however, many companies turned to
forced labor. Men were required to work in the oil fields. They
would receive neither food nor wages until after their work was
complete. They were essentially jailed on their worksites as the
roads leading to and from the oil camps were company property,
and workers were not allowed to leave, nor could their families
enter the camps, without the express written permission of the
camp's foreign superintendents.[10]

Millions of acres of land were destroyed by the companies. As
one observer noted, "[W]hat had been a lush monte was now a
gaunt specter of dead trees. The air stunk with the smell of rotten eggs. There was no sign or sound of animal, bird, or insect
life. Nothing stirred in the breeze. The silence was appalling. It
was eerie and frightening."[11]

The taking of the fields and the manner of the expulsion radi-
calized the local people and helped feed the fires of the Mexican
Revolution. In 1938 President Lázaro Cárdenas nationalized
Mexico's oil industry, the world's first oil nationalization, forcing
seventeen foreign oil companies to leave. The oil companies and
their host governments, including Standard Oil of Indiana and
the United States, warned Mexico that its oil industry and its entire economy would collapse within a month. They were wrong.

Continental Oil and Transportation Company
(Conoco—ConocoPhillips)

Back in 1875, the company today known as ConocoPhillips was
little more than a guy on horseback selling kerosene who was
deeply committed to staying free of Standard Oil. Isaac Blake
noticed the demand for kerosene increasing as families began
replacing lone men in the mountains of Utah. He founded the
Continental Oil and Transportation Company to bring kerosene
from East Coast refineries to Utah by rail. The company quickly
spread its services to Colorado, Wyoming, Iowa, Montana, and
California. Horse-drawn tanks delivered kerosene across the

mountains from grocery stores to farms. While the drivers amused themselves "battling serpents," according to the official corporate history, "Continental faced a more formidable foe— John D. Rockefeller and his giant Standard Oil Company."[12]

When Standard Oil moved into California, "Blake pronounced that Continental would drive Rockefeller out of the market. A fierce battle ensued." U. S. Hollister, Continental's vice president at the time, later wrote of the battle with Standard, "We fought in the ring and outside among the spectators, out on the street, and along the country road. It was a fight to the finish." Unable to compete against Rockefeller's railroad rebate scheme, however, Blake was forced to sell out to Standard Oil in 1885. By 1906, Continental, now owned by Standard Oil, controlled a whopping 98.9 percent of the entire Western U.S. kerosene market.[13]

THE OSAGE AND PONCA OF NORTH AMERICA: Following the 1911 breakup, Continental went in search of crude oil in Oklahoma. However, Oklahoma's oil, like that in most of the Midwest, was found largely on Native American land. Of course, this did not stop U.S. oil companies from pursuing and ultimately acquiring the oil. Treaties were rewritten to shift oil-rich land away from tribes. Across the country, tribal people who refused to leave the land were bribed, robbed, threatened, and murdered. In its 1929 merger with Marland Oil Company, the renamed Continental Oil Company, or Conoco, acquired some of the largest crude oil holdings in the world at the time.

Company founder E. W. Marland acquired 200,000 acres of land from the Osage Indians of Oklahoma. He sidestepped U.S. Department of Interior regulations limiting the land purchases of oil companies by establishing a series of different paper corporations. While the oil made the Osage the wealthiest single ethnic group in the United States at the time, they suffered terrible abuse by those who were desperate to acquire their wealth and resources. One history describes the local whites as having "degenerated into an avaricious mob."[14] In the 1920s, dozens of violent murders of Osage with the intent to steal their oil holdings were investigated by the FBI and dubbed the "Osage Massacre." In the end, the vast oil wealth led the Osage to become statistically the most murdered people in the United States.[15]

E. W. Marland's first oil find was on land sacred to the Ponca Indians in Oklahoma. Anxious to drill for the oil that he was sure lay beneath the tribe's cemetery, but aware that he was on sacred land forbidden for white people to even set foot upon, Marland proceeded with caution. The tribesman who owned the land, "Willie-Cries-for-War," arranged a meeting between Marland and the Ponca chief, White Eagle.[16] "After much coaxing and compromise," according to one history, White Eagle was "swayed to [Marland's] way of thinking. The old chief gave [Marland] permission to drill at the burial grounds."[17]

White Eagle may have given his permission, but he did not give his approval. "I remember White Eagle standing near the derrick of the first well when it blew in with a terrific roar," Marland wrote. "He told me in the sign language that I was making 'bad medicine' for him, his people and myself."[18] The chief was correct. The oil production poisoned the tribe's main water source, killing much of the tribe, which later relocated to its original territory in Nebraska.

In 2002 Conoco merged with Phillips Petroleum, a company that also owed its original crude holdings to oil acquired from the Osage Indians, to form ConocoPhillips.

Atlantic Refining Company (Arco—BP)

In 1866 Charles Lockhart and William Warden founded the Atlantic Petroleum Storage Company in Philadelphia, Pennsylvania. After buying a small refinery a few years later, they changed the name to Atlantic Refining. Rockefeller bought Atlantic Refining in 1874, but according to the official company history, kept the purchase "a secret, with Atlantic retaining its identity as a separate company."[19] In 1966 Atlantic Refining purchased the Richfield Oil Company to form Atlantic Richfield Company, or "Arco." In 1998 BP purchased Amoco, and in 2000 BP Amoco purchased Arco, changing its name back to BP.

Ohio Oil Company (Marathon)

The Ohio Oil Company was one of the first oil production companies purchased by Standard Oil. Oil was discovered in northwest Ohio in 1885. Two years later, the Ohio Oil Company was formed as an oil producer. Standard Oil purchased the company in 1889 but left the name unchanged. By the early 1890s, the company produced 50 percent of all the oil drilled in Ohio and Indiana. After the breakup, the company continued to sell oil to Jersey Standard and other postbreakup companies. In 1962 it changed its name to Marathon and in 1997 merged with Ashland Petroleum to form Marathon Ashland Petroleum, today known as Marathon. Ashland was itself the culmination of the merger of three former baby-Standards: Southern Pipe Line Company, Cumberland Pipe Line Company, and Galena Signal Oil Company.

Non–Standard Oil Companies

There were companies outside of the Standard Oil family, which were generally found in states such as Oklahoma and Texas where powerful populist antitrust struggles succeeded in forcing Standard Oil out. These companies enjoyed the backing of other large American capitalists, including Andrew Mellon. The most significant companies were the J. M. Guffey Petroleum and Gulf Refining companies and the Texas Fuel Company.

J. M. Guffey Petroleum Company and Gulf Refining Company (Gulf Oil Company—Chevron)

Patillo Higgins, "a one-armed mechanic and lumber merchant, and a self-educated man," was convinced that oil lay under Spindletop in Beaumont, Texas.[20] He convinced Captain Anthony

Lucas to do the drilling. Lucas, a bald, broad-shouldered bull of man who served in the Austrian navy before immigrating to the United States, set the derrick that brought in the Spindletop gusher. His financing came from John Galey and James Guffey of Pittsburgh, and their financing came from Pittsburgh's Andrew and Richard Mellon. The Guffey Petroleum and Gulf Refining companies (the latter named for the nearness of the Gulf Coast) were founded in 1901. The Mellon family ultimately forced everyone else out and brought the two companies together as the Gulf Oil Corporation in 1907. Andrew Mellon was president, his brother Richard Mellon was treasurer, and their nephew William was vice president.

"Owing to the fact that Mr. Guffey and the Mellon group had a lot of money and I had not," Lucas later explained, "I accepted their offer and sold my interest to them for a satisfactory sum." Lucas went on to have a career in Washington as a consultant engineer and geologist. Guffey and Galey "struggled with trifling drilling projects here and there, largely financed through their waning prestige . . . ," explained Galey's nephew. Both ended their lives deeply in debt and far from their original glory. Higgins tried to sue Lucas but failed. He tried to launch several other oil companies, but these failed as well. He appears to have died both bitter and broke.[21]

The Mellons were as committed as the Texans to keeping their company Rockefeller-free. As Yergin writes in *The Prize*, "The Mellons had no intention of saying 'by your leave' to anyone, least of all to Standard Oil."[22] They determined that production would be the foundation of their business and that they would need to build a fully integrated and independent company. They succeeded. The company had an increasingly powerful advantage in Andrew Mellon, the future U.S. Treasury secretary and ambassador to England.

In 1984, forty-seven years after Andrew Mellon's death, Gulf finally did go over to Standard, however, when Chevron purchased the company.

Texas Fuel Company (Texaco—Chevron)

When Beaumont, Texas, became the home of the Texas oil boom on January 10, 1901, "Buckskin Joe" Cullinan founded the Texas Fuel Company the same year. Buckskin acquired his name because "his aggressive, abrasive personality and his drive to get a job done reminded those who worked for him of the rough leather used for oil field gloves and shoes," according to Yergin.[23] His financing came from Lewis Lapham of New York, who owned U.S. Leather, the centerpiece of the leather trust, and John Gates, a Chicago financier. The company later changed its name to the Texaco Oil Company and then to Texaco. Texaco retained its "Texas upbringing" and was always considered the coarsest and often the meanest of the Seven Sisters. In the words of one Shell executive, "If I were dying in a Texaco filling station, I'd ask to be dragged across the road."[24] Its leading partner became Chevron, and the two companies were often dubbed "the terrible twins."

As with Gulf, Texaco's independence from Standard Oil lasted only for a time. In 2001 the twins merged, forming today's Chevron.

NEW TOOLS: CLAYTON AND THE FEDERAL TRADE COMMISSION

> The concentration of wealth, money, and property in the
> United States under the control and in the hands of a few
> individuals or great corporations has grown to such an
> enormous extent that unless checked it will ultimately
> threaten the perpetuity of our institutions.
> —CLAYTON ANTITRUST ACT CONGRESSIONAL REPORT[25]

The government's failure to follow the Supreme Court's mandate and regulate the breakup of Standard Oil was not lost on President Woodrow Wilson, the first Democratic president in sixteen years. When campaigning for the presidency in 1912, Wilson declared, "The trusts are our masters now, but I for one do not care to live in a country called free even under kind masters. I prefer to live under no masters at all." He argued that the government "has never within my recollection had its suggestions accepted by the trusts. On the contrary the suggestions of the trusts have been accepted by the government."[26] After naming William Jennings Bryan secretary of state, Wilson sought to strengthen the Sherman Antitrust Act by adding specificity, heading off new trusts by restricting mergers, and creating a forceful regulatory body to oversee the antitrust statutes.

The Clayton Antitrust Act and the Federal Trade Commission Act were Wilson's twin solutions to the need for ongoing enforcement and proscriptive action against Standard Oil and the rest of the trusts. With the Sherman Antitrust Act, the Clayton and Federal Trade Commission Acts remain today the most important tools available to the nation to combat corporate concentration.

Congressman Henry Clayton, Democrat of Alabama, and chairman of the House Judiciary Committee, brought Wilson's ideas together in 1914. The purpose of the Clayton Antitrust Act was to stop harmful mergers, "to arrest the creation of trusts . . . in their incipiency and before consummation" and to destroy the holding company, "a common and favorite method of promoting monopoly . . . an abomination and in our judgment . . . a mere incorporated form of the old-fashioned trust."[27]

The Clayton Act has four key provisions. Section 2 prohibits sellers from discriminating in the prices that they offer to different buyers (price discrimination). Section 3 prohibits sellers from requiring buyers who buy one product from the seller to buy other products as well (tying) and from insisting that any buyer who buys from the seller must not buy from the seller's competitors (exclusive dealing). Section 7 prohibits mergers between firms that threaten to substantially reduce competition in any line of commerce. Section 8 prohibits competing firms from having overlapping boards of directors.

The Clayton Act expanded the government's proscriptive

powers. Rather than attacking a monopoly only after it is formed, the new statute gave the government the ability to stop harmful business practices and mergers early in their incipiency and prevent monopolies from ever emerging.[28] This new level of authority required a constantly vigilant government to actively exercise its regulatory authority over business. To enable the government to perform this function, Wilson established the Federal Trade Commission (FTC) with passage of the Federal Trade Commission Act in 1914.

The FTC replaced and expanded upon the authority of the Bureau of Corporations and complemented the enforcement powers of the Department of Justice, which Wilson deemed insufficiently aggressive in pursuing antitrust violations. The FTC was designed as the nation's front line of defense against unlawful business practices and was given oversight as well as investigatory and enforcement authority over the nation's antitrust laws.

The majority of the Federal Trade Commission Act provides for the structure, powers, and procedures of the FTC. As an independent agency, its decision-making authority rests with a board of five commissioners, only three of whom can be from the same political party. From these five a chair is chosen. Historically, the majority of commissioners have been from the president's political party and the president names the chair.

The FTC has the authority to investigate suspect business dealings, hold hearings (rather than trials), and issue administrative orders approved in federal court that require a business to discontinue or modify unlawful acts. Only when these orders are ignored is the firm or individual exposed to criminal sanctions. The Department of Justice (DOJ) shares authority with the FTC for antitrust enforcement. The antitrust division of the DOJ prosecutes violations of the antitrust laws by filing criminal suits that can lead to fines and jail sentences. Where criminal prosecution is not appropriate, the DOJ institutes a civil action seeking a court order forbidding future violations of the law and requiring steps to remedy the anticompetitive effects of past violations.

In 1914 the new FTC immediately picked up where the Bureau of Corporations left off with an in-depth investigation into the failings of the Standard Oil breakup. In a series of reports from 1917 to 1922, the FTC concluded that Standard Oil still dominated the U.S. oil industry. The thirty-four postbreakup companies, referred to as the baby-Standards or the Standard Oil group, controlled the market from the field to the refinery, from pipelines to the sale of finished products. They worked in "a community of interest" much as before the breakup. They did not compete on price, and in fact, the price of gasoline had increased substantially in many markets following the breakup.

The FTC concluded, "The Standard Oil interests occupy the same dominant position in the petroleum industry . . . and usually take the initiative in price changes. The companies, which were separated by the dissolution decree of 1911, do not compete or invade each other's marketing territory to any important extent. This dominant position of the Standard group . . . is due not merely to the magnitude of its various units with respect to production and capital investment, but also because of its solidarity, arising apparently from an interlocking stock ownership resting largely in the hands of a few great capitalists and its great financial resources and credit."[29]

The FTC warned that the Standard companies were already reinstituting the practice of buying up their independent competitors. For example, in 1918 SoCoNY purchased the Magnolia Oil Company of Texas. The following year, Jersey Standard bought a 50 percent stake in baby-Standard Humble Oil Company of Houston. The FTC's solution was to revisit the breakup, recommending "a more effective dissolution of this combination" and "that Congress consider whether a legislative remedy is not desirable for this situation."[30]

The FTC's various reports were not acted upon, however. The first interruption was World War I, when the U.S. government waived any potential antitrust considerations for the operation of the war economy and encouraged U.S. oil companies to expand their crude oil holdings. The second interruption was the 1921 election of radically probusiness president William Harding. It would take another thirty years before the FTC would return to the subject of Big Oil. In the interim, the era of the Seven Sisters began.

THE CORPORATE CARTEL: THE SEVEN SISTERS, 1918–1970

The [Seven Sisters] international oil cartel was perhaps the most significant and successful example of anticompetitive conduct in history, realigning world power, destabilizing economies and toppling governments.

—JONATHAN W. CUNEO, DIRECTOR,
AMERICAN ANTITRUST INSTITUTE[31]

From the conclusion of World War I until the emergence of the Organization of Petroleum Exporting Countries (OPEC) as a dominant political power, the world's oil was owned and controlled by the cartel of the world's seven largest oil companies, or the Seven Sisters: Standard Oil of New Jersey, Standard Oil of New York, Standard Oil of California, Texaco, Gulf, British Petroleum, and Royal Dutch Shell. Through mergers, today, the seven are just four: ExxonMobil, Chevron, BP, and Shell. For more than sixty years, successive U.S. administrations allowed the U.S. members of the cartel to act as a de facto international agency of the U.S. government while dictating the economic development of nations the world over.

1918–1934: Going Global

John D. Rockefeller gave birth to the world's largest oil company, but Walter C. Teagle taught it how to swim. Teagle took over the presidency of Jersey Standard from Archbold in 1917. He carried the company across the Atlantic and Pacific Oceans and into the twentieth century. Teagle's father had owned his own Pennsylvania oil company before secretly selling out to Rockefeller. Teagle worked for his father, found himself in Standard Oil's employ, and remained so for his entire professional career. He became a director of the Standard Oil Trust, then of Jersey Standard, and then its president—a position he would hold for twenty years, until becoming chairman of the board in 1937. Teagle led the company through its first teetering postbreakup steps to its role as global hegemon. The first step was finally to eschew the company's disdain for oil production and get the company solidly into the crude oil business. The second step was to go global.

Teagle was aided by the heavily probusiness Republican administrations of Warren Harding (with whom Teagle regularly played poker), Calvin Coolidge, and Herbert Hoover. Harding's interior secretary, Albert Fall, was found guilty of taking $400,000 in bribes from Harry Sinclair of the Mammoth Oil Company and Edward Doheny of the Pan American Petroleum Company. In exchange for the bribes, the companies received leases for public land that had been set aside as naval petroleum reserves in Elk Hills, California, and the Teapot Dome area of Wyoming. When the bribes and sales came to light, the Teapot Dome Scandal captured the attention of the nation and ultimately led to the forced resignations of Albert Fall and Secretary of the Navy Edwin Denby.

Andrew Mellon served as treasury secretary for all three administrations over the course of eleven years, from 1921 to 1932. Mellon shamelessly used his position to implement economic policies that directly benefited both himself and his financial and corporate cohorts to the detriment of the larger economy. Mellon, heir to a banking fortune, founded the Gulf Oil Corporation, the Aluminum Company of America (Alcoa), the Pittsburgh Coal Company, and the Mellon National Bank, among other companies. Mellon's personal fortune was greatly expanded first by the Spanish-American War of 1898 and then by his terms as treasury secretary.

As treasury secretary, Mellon cut taxes, regulation, and oversight on corporations and the wealthy. He greatly expanded the "depletion allowance," which, begun under President Wilson, permitted companies that owned mineral deposits such as oil and coal to make a 5 percent deduction on their taxable income for the depletion of the deposits left underground. Mellon increased the deduction to a whopping 27.5 percent of the income that companies received from their wells, with no limit on the total amount of money that a company could deduct. Mellon removed the antitrust reins, allowing several mergers, including those by Standard Oil companies, such as Jersey Standard's purchases of Standard Oil of Pennsylvania and the Anglo-American Oil Company with its rich Venezuelan holdings. While increasing the flow of money to the wealthy and the corporations, Mellon reduced government spending, including programs for the poor.

With their power and position growing ever more secure at home under Mellon's close guidance, the oil companies went global in search of crude. World War I was the first large-scale oil war: oil was the source of victory and its reward. At the end of the war, nations found themselves with a short supply of oil and racing to acquire it at its source. The American companies—led by Jersey Standard, Indiana Standard, and Gulf—expanded exploration and production in Mexico and Venezuela. The Russians increased production, led by the Nobel Brothers and Shell. The fall of the Ottoman Empire opened up for the first time the great oil resources of the Middle East.

Having no oil of their own, the British had "gone global" more rapidly than the Americans, having laid claim to the oil of Iran (then Persia) in 1908. Persia's vast oil wealth formed the basis of the Anglo-Persian Oil Company, later called the Anglo-Iranian Oil Company, and later still British Petroleum, then BP. At the outset of World War I, Winston Churchill, then First Lord of the Admiralty of the Royal Navy, railed against the monopoly power of the world's oil corporations. To overcome the control exercised by the oil companies, Churchill argued, the British government would have to get into the oil business itself.

As he told Parliament, "We must become the owners, or at any rate the controllers, at the source of at least a proportion of the supply of natural oil which we require."[32] Parliament agreed, and in 1914 the British government became majority owner of the Anglo-Persian Oil Company.

Royal Dutch Shell was formed by the 1906 merger of Britain's Shell Oil Company with a Dutch oil company that had received a royal charter, known as "Royal Dutch." The merged company, 60 percent held by Royal Dutch and 40 percent by Shell, had founded an oil empire by transporting large oil holdings from Russia to Europe.

Following the war, the British and French took hold of the Middle East's oil as their bounty for victory. Anglo-Persian, Royal Dutch Shell, and Compagnie Française des Petroles—with 30 percent French government ownership (today's Total Oil Company)—agreed to divide the oil resources of the former Ottoman Empire between them. But the Americans wanted in. Backed by the U.S. Department of State, by 1928 Teagle had orchestrated a deal to bring Jersey Standard and SoCoNY into the consortium. When the corporate and government chieftains met in Belgium to write up the deal, however, none of those present knew exactly where the former Ottoman Empire's boundaries lay. Calouste Gulbenkian, an Armenian deal-maker and a partial stakeholder in the arrangement, pulled out a red pencil and drew in what he believed to be the empire's prewar boundaries on a map. The deal, afterward known as the "Red Line Agreement," covered the entire Middle East between the Suez Canal and Iran, with the exception of Kuwait. The oil within the boundaries would belong not to the people of the area but to the foreign oil companies. The companies agreed not to compete with one another but to work only in partnership inside the boundaries and not to pursue oil outside of them.[33]

The partnership between the oil companies went beyond the Middle East. Walter Teagle organized another meeting in 1928—secret at the time but now well known—at Achnacarry

Castle in Scotland. The meeting brought together the heads of the world's largest oil companies: Teagle of Jersey Standard, Henri Deterding of Royal Dutch Shell, and Sir John Cadman of BP. Teagle sought to bring order to the international chaos that he saw swirling across the globe. He was not in a position to buy up his global competitors, so he tried to harmonize their activities. There was too much production, too much oil, and the price was too low. Competition was killing profits. On the other hand, only a handful of companies were controlling the vast majority of the world's oil production; if they could agree among themselves on markets and production levels, order would be achieved. Teagle, Deterding, and Cadman reached an accord known as the "Achnacarry Agreement" that allocated production quotas and markets to each company and set the terms for a uniform selling price for crude. They established two secretariats to oversee daily operations and then invited SoCoNY, SoCal, Gulf, Texaco, and a few other American companies to join them.[34] The corporate cartel was officially forged.

One year later, Walter Teagle's face graced the cover of *Time* magazine. Where Rockefeller was small, thin, and almost ghost-like in appearance, Teagle was tall, broad, and handsome. At 6 feet 2 inches and 230 pounds, Teagle fully embodied the American oilman-turned-international-statesman. He appeared youthful yet strong, eager yet intelligent. The magazine article was about a meeting of the American Petroleum Institute held barely one month after Black Tuesday: the October 29, 1929, stock market crash. While the country was entering the Great Depression, with millions of Americans unable to afford life's basic necessities, the oilmen were worrying that the price of oil was too low. Just as an international oil glut had emerged, huge new oil finds in Oklahoma and Texas had created a flood of oil across the United States. It was the "perennial problem of overproduction" that plagued the industry, wrote *Time*. The article went on to discuss the "national program of oil restriction" of which Teagle was the "pioneer exponent." Teagle and the other oilmen wanted the federal government to set domestic production quotas to reduce the overall amount of crude available on the market so that they could increase the price of gasoline, kerosene, and other products. Within a few years, they got their wish.

A quota on imported oil was first introduced in 1932 for the benefit of the small domestic producers, not the large companies. The following year, the newly elected president, Franklin Delano Roosevelt, established monthly production quotas for every state that were rationed out among each state's producers. The whole system was formalized under the 1935 Connelly Hot Oil Act, which also made illegal the sale of "hot oil," or oil produced in excess of the prorated amounts.

At the same time, Treasury Secretary Mellon's seemingly lifelong appointment came to an inauspicious end. A growing chorus of critics blamed Mellon's "supply side" economic policies for both the onset and the continuation of the Great Depression. Mellon's policies had certainly helped the rich to get richer and the corporations to grow larger but done nothing to spread that wealth to the rest of society. While the economy collapsed, the financial giants that led the country before the Depression, including the Standard Oil group, maintained their positions of power. By 1932, a powerful movement to impeach Mellon, led by Texas congressman Wright Patman, appeared to be nearing success. To avoid the scandal, Mellon agreed to retire from his post as treasury secretary. Far from going into political exile, however, Mellon was appointed U.S. ambassador to Great Britain.

In his new position, Mellon immediately went to work for Gulf Oil in the Middle East. Gulf had not been included in the Red Line Agreement, so Mellon set his sights on Kuwait, a British protectorate outside the Red Line boundary. Non-British companies were barred from oil exploration in Kuwait without London's prior permission. So the newly minted U.S. ambassador to Britain went off to London—and voilà!—Gulf received permission from the British to take Kuwait's oil. Gulf shared the concession with the British through a joint venture that in 1933 received a seventy-four-year concession for ownership and control of Kuwait's oil.[35]

Cut out of Kuwait and the Red Line Agreement, Standard Oil of California struck out on its own. It first found oil in Bahrain and then one year later in the area that would become Saudi Arabia. These turned out to be two of the largest oil fields in history and quickly made SoCal a world player. Within a few years, there was more oil than one company could handle, so SoCal brought Texaco in on both the Bahrain and Saudi Arabian deals. Together they formed the Arab-American Oil Company (Aramco) and the Bahrain Petroleum and California-Arabian Standard Oil Company (Calarabian). SoCal and Texaco also formed a joint marketing company, Caltex, to transport and market their vast oil holdings around the world. Between 1948 and 1950, Texaco alone increased its imports of foreign oil by a whopping 289 percent.[36]

SoCoNY and Jersey Standard had formed a similar joint venture, Stanvac, which sold oil in fifty countries abroad. The name Stanvac derived from SoCoNY's earlier acquisition of the former baby Standard Vacuum Oil Company in 1931. For several years, it went by the name SoCoNY-Vacuum.

1933–1970: On Shakier Ground

The public and many political leaders in the United States and around the world grew increasingly uncomfortable with the power now concentrated in the hands of a few giant oil corporations. Calls for nationalization of domestic resources grew around the world, while in the United States, the decades following the Depression and the Second World War brought numerous attempts at reform, all of which were ultimately thwarted as the corporate cartel expanded its holdings and power and the American Sisters operated as a virtually independent arm of the U.S. government abroad.

President Franklin D. Roosevelt was the first U.S. president to attempt to fundamentally restrict the role of the American Sisters abroad. Big Oil had exercised its financial prowess to try to block FDR's election victories. Writing in 1936, Professor Louise Overacker, the first person to track and report campaign finance in the United States, recorded the huge dollar amounts contributed by the oil industry and went on to conclude of the campaigns against Roosevelt in 1932 and 1936: "The Republicans became more definitely than in the past few campaigns the party of 'big business'. . . . Captains of finance and industry poured their dollars into the fund without stint. . . . The 'haves' rose generously to the defense of a system under which their fortunes had been made."[37]

Elected in 1932 to bring the United States out of the Great Depression, the first Democratic president in twelve years had a decidedly different approach to the oil industry than his predecessors. FDR successfully implemented domestic regulations of the oil industry (not all opposed by Big Oil) and tried, but ultimately failed, to do the same in the international arena. Roosevelt thoroughly appreciated the importance of oil not only to the victory in World War II but also to the stability of the United States. In 1943 he declared that the defense of Saudi Arabia was "vital to the defense of the United States." He did not, however, believe that private companies should be in charge of such a vital relationship, nor did he put his faith in the Saudis. Instead, Roosevelt proposed that the U.S. government should establish a Petroleum Reserve Corporation to acquire 100 percent of Aramco and construct its own refinery in the Persian Gulf. Interior Secretary Harold Ickes, who once wrote that "an honest and scrupulous man in the oil business is so rare as to rank as a museum piece," would be president of the new corporation, and the secretaries of state, war and navy would serve as directors.[38]

Not surprisingly, SoCal and Texaco did not share Roosevelt's enthusiasm for the government takeover of Aramco. Broad support within the U.S. government also did not materialize, and FDR's plan never got off the ground.

Roosevelt was not the only member of the government criticizing Aramco. In 1946 Republican senator Owen Brewster of Maine, chairman of the Senate War Investigating Committee, held hearings and released a searing attack on Aramco. Brewster's report investigated differential pricing and other abuses and found that "the oil companies have shown a singular lack of good faith, an avaricious desire for enormous profits, while at the same time they constantly sought the cloak of U.S. protection and financial assistance to preserve their vast concessions."[39] Brewster's findings did not lead to action against Aramco. On the contrary, that same year the U.S. government instead allowed the company to vastly expand.

As more and more oil was discovered outside the boundaries of the Red Line Agreement in the Middle East, the member companies decided to dissolve the agreement. The end of the agreement freed Jersey Standard and SoCoNY to join SoCal and Texaco in Aramco in 1946. Expressing his deep concern about the antitrust implications of the deal, SoCoNY's chief counsel wrote to the company president: "I cannot believe that a comparatively few companies for any great length of time are going to be permitted to control world oil resources without some sort of regulation."[40] The counsel was proven wrong. The deal was permitted to go through, and no new regulations were imposed.

By this point, the Seven Sisters were operating blatantly as a cartel and were in control of virtually every large source of oil in the world. The FTC launched a formal investigation into the foreign agreements of the oil companies, and in 1952 the Senate released the report "The International Petroleum Cartel," the first full account of the cartel agreements of the Seven Sisters. It found that the Seven Sisters controlled all the principal oil-producing areas outside the United States, all foreign refineries, patents, and refinery technology. The companies actively divided world markets among themselves, shared pipelines and tankers, and willfully maintained artificially high prices for oil to increase their profits.[41] The DOJ resolved to take immediate action and mount an antitrust case against the U.S. Sisters.

The timing was inopportune, however. The CIA was simultaneously working to oust the democratic leader of Iran, Mohammed Mossadeq, placing the American oil companies in line for their first large-scale access to Iran's vast oil wealth (discussed in chapter 8). As Anthony Sampson details in *The Seven Sisters,* the State Department, under America's consummate Cold Warrior Dean Acheson, argued in 1953 against antitrust action: "American oil corporations are, for all practical purposes, instruments of our foreign policy towards these countries." Antitrust action against the companies, the State Department warned, would strengthen the hand of the communists because it would lead other countries to believe that "capitalism is synonymous with predatory exploitation."[42]

Attorney General James McGranery, deeply committed to moving forward with his antitrust case against the companies, wrote his own report, arguing that allowing the Seven Sisters to continue would be profoundly damaging to U.S. national security. "The world petroleum cartel is an authoritarian, dominating power over a great vital world industry, in private hands. . . . [A] decision at this time to terminate the pending investigation would be regarded by the world as a confession that our abhorrence of monopoly and restrictive cartel activities does not extend to the world's most important single industry."[43]

President Harry Truman sided with Acheson and persuaded McGranery to bring civil rather than criminal charges against the companies. The civil action went forward with complaints filed against Jersey Standard, SoCoNY, SoCal, Texaco, and Gulf. Like all large cases brought against the oil giants, this case dragged on for years and resulted in minor action. Years later, Jersey Standard, Texaco, and Gulf agreed to consent decrees, and the cases against SoCoNY and SoCal were dismissed.

In 1953 newly elected president Dwight Eisenhower put the final nail in the antitrust coffin by stressing that enforcement of antitrust actions "may be deemed secondary to the national security interests." The Department of State added, "In the cause of defense and in the fight against communism, the five [U.S.-based] sisters must be brought to Iran."[44] Prime Minister Mossadeq was, in fact, a virulent anticommunist who had come to Washington in search of U.S. support in his efforts to keep his country free of both Soviet communist influence and British imperial control. His pleas, however, fell on deaf ears. Following his successful ouster and the reinstallation of Mohammad Reza Shah Pahlavi, every major U.S. oil company would soon gain a sizable hold on Iran's oil.

Describing the effect of the coup in Iran, Shirin Ebadi, 2003 winner of the Nobel Peace Prize for her tireless work on behalf of human rights in Iran, writes, "In a neat four days, the ailing, adored prime minister was hiding in a cellar and the venal young shah was restored to power. . . . It was a profoundly humiliating moment for Iranians, who watched the U.S. intervene in their politics as if their country were some annexed backwater, its leader to be installed or deposed at the whim of an American president and his CIA advisers."[45]

Now even more firmly ensconced in Saudi Arabia, Iran, and in nations around the globe, the oil companies also gained a new tax write-off that would further direct their attentions outside of the United States. In 1950 the State Department and Aramco came up with an arrangement that became known as the "Golden Gimmick" to deal with taxes on foreign oil production. The impetus came when King Saud of Saudi Arabia demanded an additional 50 percent payment on the vast quantities of crude the Americans were taking from his country. The companies knew that they had to pay the king but did not want to lose any profits as a result. They turned to President Truman for help. Truman agreed that the payments made to King Saud would be regarded as constituting a foreign income tax. Under rules barring double taxation, the companies would not be taxed in the United States. Essentially, the new money paid out to the king would be deducted from the companies' domestic taxes. Other companies and countries soon adopted the tax dodge, and the Golden Gimmick was born.[46]

The Golden Gimmick gave the companies an additional incentive to focus even more of their production abroad. They already had control of the Middle East. By 1960, two-thirds of all oil exports from the Gulf were handled by the five American companies.[47] All seven companies expanded their reach further into the North Sea, Angola, Nigeria, Ecuador, Peru, Indonesia, Canada, and beyond—such that between 1960 and 1966, the Seven Sisters' share of oil production outside of North America and the communist countries increased from 72 to 76 percent.[48] All seven companies, with the support of their home governments, worked aggressively to keep in place foreign governments that supported the companies' continued access to the nations' oil. The companies also spent their earnings lavishly at home, contributing heavily to electoral campaigns to ensure that their home governments remained supportive of their activities. One U.S. administration after another dutifully responded, deliberately turning a blind eye to the obvious antitrust violations of these international oil collaborations.

As the American Sisters shifted the majority of their holdings to the international market, they generally left domestic production and refining to the smaller U.S. companies, such as Getty, Sunoco, Superior, and Pennzoil. The U.S. government maintained active antitrust enforcement at home. Independent oil companies sought to secure their domestic market from the American Sisters by successfully lobbying President Dwight Eisenhower to implement more significant quotas on foreign oil imported to the United States. In 1959 import quotas were imposed allowing only 13 percent of oil consumption to come from abroad. At the same time, new finds in Alaska brought a wealth of domestic oil resources on line. Arco became a major player when it discovered the largest oil field in North America in Prudhoe Bay, on Alaska's North Slope, in 1968. It purchased Sinclair Oil the following year.

While the Seven Sisters made their money from crude, they still marketed their gasoline all across the United States. Following the breakup, however, none of the baby-Standards were permitted to use the Standard name to market their brands nationally. By the 1960s, with the advent of the national highway system, television, and modern advertising techniques, the companies were ready to take their brands national, and a series of name changes took place. In 1966 Standard Oil of New York took the name Mobil, as in "mobility." In 1971 Jersey Standard, which for decades had been marketing its gasoline on the East Coast as Esso, became Exxon, a word that means nothing at all but tested well "linguistically, psychologically, and for design potential."[49] In 1984 Standard Oil of California became Chevron, from the Anglo-French word referring to the V-shaped stripes that symbolize protection and military rank.

Mobil tried to establish itself as the "sophisticated and scientific sister." In 1971 it began underwriting PBS's brand-new TV show *Masterpiece Theater*. At the same time, Mobil began running weekly "advertorials"—paid advertisements that look like editorials—every Thursday on the Op-Ed page of the *New York Times*.

Overseas, Mobil, far from alone among the Sisters, had a very different character. It would take some thirty years for the full story to come out, but Mobil's Indonesian operations, begun the same year as its *Masterpiece Theater* support, demonstrate not only the brutal governments that were supported by the oil companies, but present once again the deadly reality of energy production for those living at its source.

JOHN AND JANE DOE OF ACEH: In the mid-1960s, Mobil went in search of new oil and natural gas in Indonesia. It signed a contract with one of the most infamously brutal dictators in world history, General Mohammed Suharto, to explore and produce in Indonesia's Aceh region, a province of about four million people on the northern tip of Sumatra Island. Production in Aceh began in 1971. A lawsuit brought against the company thirty years later and currently under litigation charges that from the outset soldiers under Mobil's and then ExxonMobil's control who guard its facilities have engaged in massive human rights violations against the local population.[50]

According to the suit, the soldiers regularly engaged in "serious human rights abuses, including genocide, murder, torture, crimes against humanity, sexual violence, and kidnapping."[51] Agnieszka Fryszman, the Acehnese's head lawyer in Washington, argues that Mobil "essentially privatized" the Indonesian soldiers "in spite of their well-documented history of abusing Indonesian citizens."[52] Mobil and then ExxonMobil, according to the suit, knowingly employed the brutal military troops to protect its operations, and then aided and abetted the human rights violations through financial and other material support to the security forces acting as either their employees or agents.[53]

Literally dozens of brutal stories of rape, torture, murder, and abuse are detailed in the suit. A typical example is that of "Plaintiff John Doe II," whose complaint alleges that in August 2000 he was riding his motorbike and was stopped by "soldiers assigned to ExxonMobil's TNI Unit 113," the military security force hired to guard ExxonMobil's facility. The soldiers put his motorbike in their truck and then "beat him severely on his head and body." They tied his hands behind his back, blindfolded him, and threw him into their truck until he emerged at Rancong Camp. He claims that he was detained there and tortured for three months, all while blindfolded. He was tortured by the soldiers "using electricity all over his body, including his genitals." After three months, the "soldiers took off his blindfold, took him outside the building where he had been detained and showed him a large pit where there was a large pile of human heads. The soldiers threatened to kill him and add his head to the pile." He was ultimately released, only to have the soldiers return later to burn down his house.

Local and international human rights groups regularly brought such charges to the company. The reports of abuse and murder also appeared regularly in the media. Amnesty International USA began to campaign actively against these practices and to dialogue with Mobil on these issues in 1998. When the company remained unmoved and took no action to halt the alleged abuse, the International Labor Rights Fund, a Washington, D.C.–based advocacy group and law practice, brought the suit in 2001 to the U.S. district court for the District of Columbia on behalf of the Indonesian victims.

According to the International Labor Rights Fund, ExxonMobil's primary defense in the case "appears to be that the human rights violations may very well be occurring, but the company did not specifically intend this result, and therefore cannot be held liable."[54] ExxonMobil, which still operates in Aceh, has told reporters that it "categorically denies any suggestion or implication that it or its affiliate companies were in any way involved with alleged human rights abuses by security forces in Aceh" and that there is no basis for the case in U.S. courts.[55] While ExxonMobil has spent six years trying to have the case thrown out, in the most recent court ruling, in January 2007, ExxonMobil's motions to dismiss were denied.

Unfortunately, the story of ExxonMobil in Aceh is far from an isolated incident. Nigeria's encounter with oil companies, particularly with Shell and Chevron, provides a strikingly similar case in point.

THE PEOPLE OF THE NIGER DELTA: In 1956 Royal Dutch Shell discovered crude oil at Oloibiri, a village in the Niger Delta, and commercial production began in 1958. Nigeria achieved independence from the British two years later. Nigerians argue, however, that colonial rule was quickly replaced by corporate rule as Shell participated forcefully in the nation's politics, ensuring that only governments that supported its operations would remain in power.[56] As the exploitation of oil resources grew, Nigeria became increasingly reliant on oil, and its once extensive agricultural sector faded into virtual nonexistence. As Nigeria's export earnings grew, the power of the oil companies grew accordingly, with successive regimes (most often military dictatorships) more accountable to the oil companies that financed their rule than to the people of their nation.

Decades of abuse have been recorded, but Shell's Nigerian operations became global news in 1995 with the killing of the "Ogoni 9." In 1990 the Ogoni, indigenous people who have lived in the Niger Delta for millennia as farmers and fishers, organized to resist Shell's operations on their land. The Ogoni resistance was brutally suppressed, with some thirty villages laid to waste by Nigerian forces and thousands of Ogoni killed and injured.[57] Nigerian Lieutenant Colonel Paul Okuntimo later stated that he was paid by Shell to "sanitize" the Ogoni.[58] Shell admitted that it invited the Nigerian authorities to help put down the "disturbance" in its Ogoni production area, although maintaining that the soldiers it paid were not responsible for Ogoni deaths or injuries.[59] Ken Saro-Wiwa and eight other Ogoni activists were later hung, on charges by the Nigerian government of murdering four Ogoni chiefs. The United Nations General Assembly formally condemned the executions and encouraged member states to impose sanctions against Nigeria, supporting the widely accepted belief both then and now that the only "crime" committed by the Ogoni 9 was their leadership roles in the nonviolent struggle against Shell and the Nigerian government.[60]

Chevron also began operating in Nigeria in the 1960s and today extracts some half a million barrels of oil per day there. Nigerians have alleged abuse at Chevron's hands for decades, and in 1999 Nigerian plaintiffs succeeded in bringing a case against Chevron in U.S. court. According to the plaintiffs' attorneys, a group of Nigerians went to Chevron's offshore Parabe platform to demand that company officials meet with community elders on shore in response to environmental and human rights abuses. The local people claim not to have carried weapons. After three days of negotiations, the protestors agreed to leave the platform the next morning and informed Chevron of their intentions. In the early morning of May 28, 1998, the day the protestors planned to leave, Chevron-leased helicopters carrying soldiers and Chevron representatives approached the platform. The soldiers opened fire on the protestors, killing two and wounding and later torturing others.[61]

Seven months later, on January 4, 1999, in apparent retaliation for the Parabe incident, plaintiffs claim that Chevron-leased helicopters carrying Chevron representatives flew over the fishing villages of Opia and Ikenyan and opened fire. Soldiers in Chevron-leased boats followed the helicopters in, attacking the villages. The assaults left at least seven people dead, many others injured and missing, and both villages almost completely burned to the ground.[62]

Although Chevron does not deny that the killings and destruction took place, the company argues that its Nigerian subsidiary, not the parent company, is to blame and that the Nigerians were not peaceful. Chevron says the attacks on the villages were "in response to a violent insurrection" in which Chevron "was literally caught in the crossfire."[63]

In the most recent ruling in the case, in 2007, a U.S. district court judge found evidence that Chevron's personnel "were directly involved in the attacks" and that Chevron transported and paid the Nigerian government's security forces to these attacks, knowing that they were "prone to use excessive force." The judge concluded that the evidence would allow a jury to find not only that Chevron knew the attacks would happen and assisted in them, but also that Chevron actually agreed to the military's plan.[64] A jury trial is scheduled for September 2008 in San Francisco.

COUNTRY BY COUNTRY, REGION BY region, the Seven Sisters took control of the world's oil. The money from the oil companies supported the governments that in turn supported their work, often some of the most notoriously corrupt governments in the world. Oil production pushed out other forms of economic development, increasing the role of oil in the countries' economies. The companies controlled production levels for each country and determined the value of every barrel of oil sold in the world, effectively dictating to governments how much income they would receive for their oil. Thus, as oil grew in importance and value, the oil companies were determining not only the size of government budgets but also the very growth of national economies.

The companies made their production decisions based as much on politics as on economics. Exxon Mideast Coordinator Howard Page told a U.S. Senate commission that the oil companies actively punished uncooperative countries with production cuts while raising production elsewhere to reward good behavior.[65] These decisions radically impacted the economic well-being of the host nations and the power of the host governments. Whether the companies decided to produce from wells in Iraq, Saudi Arabia, or Venezuela determined the federal budget available to those nations. The companies were also notorious for withholding exploration and production data from the host governments, generating constant concern that the companies were not honestly meeting their contractual obligations and that the governments were not being paid appropriately for their oil resources. The oil companies' ultimate strength lay in their ability to play the host governments off against one another in negotiations over royalty rates, production levels, and other contract terms. As long as the host governments were competing with each other to attract the oil companies, and the oil companies stood together, the companies had the upper hand.

THE OIL COUNTRIES CARTEL: OPEC, 1970–1982

The system worked as long as the U.S. government ignored the blatant antitrust violations of the companies operating as a global cartel to constrain competition, and as long as the oil-producing countries were powerless to change the terms of trade. The patience of the oil-rich countries ran out long before that of the U.S. government. By the 1950s and 1960s, revolutionary movements had spread throughout the world, and former British and French colonies achieved hard-fought independence. These newly independent nations increasingly banded together with other developing countries to demand greater global equality. In the midst of this growing Third World unity, the oil companies made a fatal blunder.

In 1960 the oil companies once again faced a global oil glut. Jersey Standard, always the leader, announced that it would cut the price of Middle East oil by 10 cents per barrel. The rest of the companies followed suit. "This historic decision," wrote Sampson in *The Seven Sisters*, "which so drastically diminished the income of the chief Middle East countries, was taken inside the boardroom of a private corporation." The decision provided the proverbial "straw that broke the camel's back" to galvanize the oil-rich countries. One month later, a meeting was convened in Baghdad attended by representatives of Saudi Arabia, Iran, Kuwait, and Venezuela, at which they decided to form a "cartel to confront the cartel"—the Organization of Petroleum Exporting Countries (OPEC). OPEC would allow the oil-producing countries to stand together in their negotiations with the oil company cartel to achieve better terms for their oil.

The Seven Sisters were aghast and on the whole simply refused to acknowledge either OPEC or its negotiating power. The formation of OPEC did, however, provide yet another argument for maintaining the corporate cartel. Newly elected president John F. Kennedy turned to John Jay McCloy for advice about OPEC in 1961. McCloy, a former assistant secretary of war during World War II, onetime president of the World Bank and Chase Manhattan Bank, and a longtime presidential adviser, was also an antitrust lawyer employed by the Seven Sisters. McCloy warned Kennedy that OPEC's creation made it necessary to allow the oil companies to continue their collusion. Over the following decade, he made the same argument to successive attorneys general, each of whom followed his advice.[66]

For most of the 1960s, neither the oil companies nor the U.S. government had reason to be overly concerned about OPEC, as the member countries were having difficulty finding their organizational footing. Domestically the United States was embroiled in the civil rights, women's rights, and antiwar movements. Lyndon B. Johnson was the first president from Texas and, while a Democrat, had received considerable support from the oil industry. In turn, he offered continued domestic and international support to the industry.

Three forces conspired to radically alter the existing order and make both the oil companies and the U.S. government take greater notice of OPEC. In 1970 the United States hit its own peak of oil production. From that point on, it was far more reliant on imports to meet domestic consumption, and U.S. companies were less able to use their domestic production as a hedge against changes in international supply. Moreover, demand for oil was higher in 1970 than the oil companies had predicted, and they had not produced enough oil to meet it. Thus, for the first time since OPEC was formed, it found itself in a sellers' market, with demand for oil outstripping available supply. In the face of these conditions, Libya took a monumental step: it nationalized the holdings of the foreign oil companies operating in the country—the first oil nationalization since Mexico in 1938.

Changes to the oil industry came fast and furiously. The following year, six new members joined OPEC: Qatar, Indonesia, Libya, United Arab Emirates, Algeria, and Nigeria. Within a few years, a string of new nationalizations took place. The tables were ready to be turned. OPEC now controlled enough production and had enough cohesion to set the price of a barrel of oil and enforce it through production quotas. The companies would now have to accept the price dictated by OPEC. The first major exercise of OPEC's new power came with the Arab-Israeli war of 1973.

The 1970s Oil Crises

With the onset of the Arab-Israeli war, the OPEC countries knew that for the first time they were in a position to wield oil as a weapon. The U.S. government backed Israel in the war, and the oil-exporting governments retaliated. In May 1973, King Faisal of Saudi Arabia told the American press, "America's complete support for Zionism and against the Arabs makes it extremely difficult for us to continue to supply the United States with oil, or even to remain friends with the United States." Texaco, So-Cal, Mobil, and Exxon still owned Aramco at this point. The companies, afraid of losing their access to the Saudis' oil, chose sides. Texaco, SoCal, and Mobil publicly demanded that the U.S. government change its Middle East policy to oppose Israel.[67] President Richard Nixon disagreed.

The Arab-Israeli war began on October 6, 1973. One week later, the Arab nations of OPEC agreed to a full oil embargo against the United States. In December OPEC set the price of oil at $11.65 per barrel ($56.03 in 2008 dollars), a 468 percent increase over the price in 1970. The embargo hurt the American and global economy, but not the oil companies. In the case of Saudi Arabia, in particular, it was the U.S. oil companies that actually implemented the embargo. When the Saudis told Aramco not to send oil to the United States, the oil companies acceded. In addition, rather than accept lower profits, the American oil companies passed along their higher costs to the American consumer by increasing prices.

From October 1973 to February 1975, prices for gasoline in the United States increased 30 percent and for home heating oil more than 40 percent. At the same time, oil company profits skyrocketed. Not only did the companies profit from the higher gas prices, but they also made out like bandits from the increased value of their crude oil holdings. The U.S. Treasury Department found that the twenty-two largest U.S. oil companies averaged higher earnings in 1973 than in any of the preceding ten years. In 1974 Standard Oil Company of Indiana's profits were up 90 percent, Exxon's were up 29 percent, Mobil's were up 22 percent, and Texaco's were up 23 percent.[68] The embargo ended just three months after it began, on March 18, 1974, with the cooling off of active hostilities between the Arab nations and Israel.

It is not an exaggeration to say that it became an American obsession to do away with OPEC, with much of the effort led by presidents Nixon and Ford's national security adviser and secretary of state, Henry Kissinger. "The primary goal of the Nixon and Ford administrations was to break OPEC," writes Rachel Bronson in *Thicker than Oil: America's Uneasy Partnership with Saudi Arabia*.[69] Kissinger had a three-pronged approach: military intervention, conservation, and finding oil outside of OPEC. Kissinger initially advocated using U.S. airborne forces to seize the oil fields of Saudi Arabia, Kuwait, and Abu Dhabi.[70] When that plan was rejected, conservation took the fore and Kissinger organized the International Energy Agency (IEA) to facilitate collaboration among the world's largest oil-consuming nations. In February 1975, the members of the IEA agreed to cut their joint consumption of oil by 6 million barrels per day.[71]

Kissinger's efforts dovetailed nicely with the burgeoning environmental movement, which organized on behalf of one of the most important pieces of environmental legislation of the last thirty years: the Energy Policy and Conservation Act. Signed by President Gerald Ford in 1975, the law mandated a doubling of the average fuel efficiency for new automobiles by 1985. The government also made new investments in public transportation, wind power, and solar energy. To encourage the nation, President Jimmy Carter put solar panels on the White House and donned a sweater while turning down the White House thermostat in winter. These and other conservation efforts worked: the United States was 25 percent more energy-efficient and 32 percent more oil-efficient in 1985 than in 1973.[72]

While Kissinger set out against OPEC, the American public rightly directed its own anger at Big Oil. The public knew it had been manipulated by the oil companies and demanded action. At least ten major lawsuits were filed against the largest oil companies during this time, on charges of collusion and various forms of price-fixing, price-gouging, and discrimination. The companies rode out most of them until the plaintiffs were forced to drop the cases from lack of time and resources. Congress, the Federal Trade Commission, and a succession of presidents responded with investigations and a series of radical proposals for a fundamental reorganization of the American oil industry.

In 1974 seven executives of the nation's largest oil companies stood before the U.S. Senate and the nation and declared their innocence. They insisted that they had not used the 1970s oil crisis to their companies' advantage. For three days, the executives of Exxon, Texaco, Gulf, Mobil, SoCal, Standard Oil of Indiana, and Shell appeared before the U.S. Senate Subcommittee on Investigations. Senator James B. Allen, Democrat of Alabama, captured the prevailing attitude when he asked the executives, "Would it be improper to ask if the oil companies are enjoying a feast in the midst of famine?"[73]

Democratic committee chairman Senator Henry Jackson of Washington grilled each of the executives at the hearing. He also introduced a bill to enforce the "federal chartering" of the oil companies, allowing the appointment of a government nominee on each board to ensure that they acted in the public's interest.

Senator Adlai Stevenson III and Congressman John Moss (the chief sponsor of both the Freedom of Information Act and the Clean Air Act) introduced a bill to create a Federal Oil and Gas Corporation (FOGCO). Had FOGCO become law, it would have established a corporation owned by the federal government that would develop and sell natural gas and oil from federal lands. The company would have exploration and production rights to half of the oil and gas offered for lease by federal authorities, while private companies would have access to the other half. FOGCO would give price, supply, and delivery preferences to state and local governments and to independent refiners.

Michael Pertschuk was chief counsel to the Senate Commerce Committee and helped write the FOGCO legislation. When I interviewed Pertschuk in 2007, he explained that while he did not think Congress would pass FOGCO, "it was intended as the beginning of a serious dialogue on whether oil corporations should be given free rein in such an important area."[74] Sounding every bit the turn-of-the-century populist, Ralph Nader, the 1970s preeminent consumer advocate, said of FOGCO at the time, "Among the flurry of legislative proposals in Congress on the energy problem, one stands out as a constructive and lasting solution to the monopolistic grip that the giant oil companies have on the nation, small businesses and consumers."[75]

The FTC launched a landmark investigation in 1973, charging collusive activity among the nation's eight largest oil companies: Exxon, Texaco, Gulf Oil, SoCal, Standard Oil of Indiana, Shell Oil, Atlantic Richfield, and Mobil. For the first time, it sought to break the eight oil companies into separate production, pipeline, refining, and marketing operations. Democrat Philip A. Hart, chairman of the Senate Antitrust and Monopoly Subcommittee, introduced a bill to achieve the same outcome. While it did not pass, in 1975 forty senators voted for Hart's bill, which had been expanded to include the fifteen largest U.S. oil companies.[76]

Also in 1975, Senator Frank Church of Idaho, chairman of the Senate Committee on Foreign Relations Subcommittee on Multinational Corporations, released a damning report, "Multinational Oil Corporations and U.S. Foreign Policy," which argued, "In a democracy, important questions of policy with respect to a vital commodity like oil, the life blood of an industrial society, cannot be left to private companies acting in accord with private interests and a closed circle of government officials."[77]

That same year, a poll found that while 81 percent of Americans rejected the idea that the government should own all major industries, 44 percent believed that it would be a good thing for the government to take over ownership of oil and other natural resources.[78]

The FTC's Last Hurrah

In 1976 President Jimmy Carter appointed Michael Pertschuk chairman of the FTC. Pertschuk had spent fifteen years as a staff person in the U.S. Senate and as a consumer advocate before taking his post at the FTC. In addition to coauthoring the FOGCO legislation as chief counsel to the Senate Commerce Committee, Pertschuk drafted legislation requiring health warning labels on cigarette packages and banning broadcast advertising of tobacco products. He was not, however, Carter's only candidate for the FTC chair.

Hamilton Jordan headed President-elect Jimmy Carter's transition team and guided the process of filling the top positions of the new administration. "Jordan gave Carter two names: Bella Abzug and I," Pertschuk recalled in an interview with me. "Carter answered, 'We can't name Bella Abzug chair of the FTC!' so he named me instead." Bella Abzug was a three-term congresswoman; a renowned labor, civil rights, and women's rights attorney; a leading peace activist; and variously referred to as both a socialist and a communist—although she identified as neither—who was considered so controversial at the time that one study estimated that her sponsorship of a bill would *cost* it 20 to 30 votes. "It certainly made me look like a much safer choice," added Pertschuk. "Looking back on it now, it really shows just how much times have changed. I don't think anyone knows that story."

Pertschuk served as FTC chairman throughout the Carter administration and was the last consumer advocate to hold the post. He argued that the FTC should be "the greatest public interest law firm in the country" and unleashed the agency to pursue antitrust violations aggressively.[79] Echoing the founders of antitrust law, in 1978 Pertschuk warned, "Unrestrained conglomeration could conceivably result in the concentration of an enormous aggregation of economic, social and political power in the hands of a small number of corporate leaders, responsible in a formal sense to stockholders but in a real sense only to themselves. . . . This vision of a relatively few companies dominating the private sector is not so far from reality."[80]

Pertschuk pursued the FTC's case against the oil companies throughout his entire term. The companies fought back using their substantially greater financial and personnel resources to wait out the government. It is a tactic they had already perfected and continue to implement successfully today. The *New York Times* described the "glacial pace" at which the oil companies responded to the FTC's requests for information and the "constant skirmishing with the attorneys . . . over procedural issues." The oil companies' "batteries of lawyers have challenged the FTC staff on jurisdictional issues, the scope of the discovery, subpoena, and other matters. They have brought collateral challenges to the case in the Federal courts, and appeals are pending in three circuits."[81] Michael Spiegel, an antitrust lawyer who ultimately won one of the only successful lawsuits against the U.S. petroleum industry for collusive price-fixing, told me in an interview, "The oil industry just ran these guys ragged until the government was forced to drop the case. It was a disgrace that the industry could do that to the government. But an industry with unlimited funds can just run a case into the ground."[82]

The end of Pertschuk's tenure and the beginning of the Reagan administration marked the end of an era at the FTC. Within the first year of the new administration, President Reagan's FTC simply dismissed the case against the oil companies. It then began a concerted effort to eliminate the antitrust capacity of the FTC altogether. Reagan's FTC was responding to the oil industry's desire to reconsolidate its power in the wake of the nationalizations of the companies' foreign oil holdings. The nationalizations were the most important change in the composition of the world oil market since the formation of Standard Oil. Across the world, the oil-rich nations were taking back their oil from the Seven Sisters.

Nationalization

In an incredibly short period of time, control over arguably the most valuable resource in the world changed hands from the oil companies to the oil countries. From Libya's nationalization in 1970 to Iran's nationalization following its revolution in 1979, to Saudi Arabia's full takeover of Aramco (now Saudi Aramco) by the mid-1980s—over the course of fifteen years, these nations as well as Iraq, Venezuela, Kuwait, Nigeria, Algeria, Qatar, and the United Arab Emirates, among others, fully nationalized the holdings of the major oil companies. In 1972 the Seven Sisters produced more than 90 percent of the Middle East's oil and 77 percent of the supply outside the United States, Eastern Europe, and China.[83] But from 1977 to 1984, the companies' oil reserves dropped by an astounding two-thirds.[84]

These companies, which had made the vast majority of their income from their crude oil holdings—and paid no taxes on it—were suddenly desperate to find new sources of crude. Their profits fell precipitously, as did their overall financial and political power. Texaco's profits plunged 88 percent from 1980 to 1985, and Mobil's fell by more than 60 percent.[85] The companies were desperate to recover all that they had lost, and quickly. It is impossible to overstate the significance of the nationalizations to the oil companies, the host countries, and the world economy.

Oil Nationalization Day is celebrated in Iran every March 20. National Expropriation Day is celebrated on March 18 in Mexico with festivals and parades, complete with dancing, cheering, and rousing speeches. Similar tributes take place all around the world, often linked directly to celebrations of independence from colonial rule. The recovery of their oil resources remains a pivotal and defining moment for these nations, marking both political and financial independence.

A letter to the editors of *Time* magazine in July 1979 reflects the harsh attitude of some Americans at the time. "OPEC has declared war on the Western world. An infinitesimal percent of the earth's population is directing the destruction of the economic foundation of the world. Odd and even selling days are not the answer. The basic solution is that the OPEC cartel must be broken, and now," wrote David N. Rosner of Miami.

It is telling that one of the most popular television series of the era was *Dynasty,* which ran for eight years, from 1981 to 1989. While it is best known for the battles between its female protagonists, Alexis Carrington and Krystal Jennings, the central story line is of two warring oil empires, Denver Carrington and Colby Oil Company. The pilot episode aired January 12, 1981. Titled "Oil," it begins with the violent nationalization of Denver Carrington's oil in an unnamed "Middle Eastern" country. Given the timing of the show, I surmise that the country is most likely Iran.

Watching today, the episode is painfully comic as it reveals the general ignorance about the Middle East at the time. Dark-skinned men in camouflage uniforms speaking a sort of Spanish-gibberish represent "the Middle Easterners." They blow up Carrington's oil derrick while his American employees are held back at gunpoint. One blond, blue-eyed Texan fights back to try to save the derrick, only to be beaten and thrown into the back of a truck. The Americans are then pushed onto a plane that will carry them out of the country, while an angry crowd that looks more like the cast of a 1970s version of *West Side Story* than the population of a Middle Eastern nation is barely held at bay by a barbed-wire fence. They're yelling and waving signs in English expressing their rage: "American Dogs Go Home!" "Down with American Greed!" "It's Our Oil, Americans Get Out!"

The Texan oil worker returns to meet with his boss, Blake Carrington, who is equally enraged: "You make a deal with these people, you think they'd keep their end of it!" To which he adds of the U.S. government, "If they'd just given those folks the F15s they'd asked for, they might not have been so quick to throw us out of there." Later in the episode, Carrington's daughter jokingly berates him for driving his gas-guzzling limo. "Daddy, don't you know there's an energy crises going on?" she asks. "What are you," Carrington replies, "a spy for Ralph Nader?"

While the show's portrayal of these events is humorous, it nonetheless demonstrates how great a part of the popular discourse the oil nationalizations and the 1970s energy crises were.

The oil companies were in fact more to blame than the Iranians for the second energy crisis to hit the United States. In 1979 the Iranian revolution was followed by the nationalization and then an embargo of the nation's oil. The second oil shock was even worse than the first for American consumers, many of whom still remember the long lines for gasoline. However, the period was equally profitable for U.S. oil companies. The price per barrel of oil more than doubled from 1979 to 1981, rising from approximately $44 to $104 per barrel, in 2008 dollars. Gas prices at the pump increased an unprecedented 150 percent. The embargo cut global supply by less than 5 percent, however. What caused the oil shock was not the embargo but rather the panic buying by the oil companies.

Afraid that other countries would follow the Iranians in the embargo, the oil companies stockpiled oil. Their collective stockpiling reduced global supply even further and caused prices to skyrocket. In reality, imports of oil into the United States were 8 percent higher and gasoline inventories 6 percent higher in 1979 than in 1978, but the oil companies were sitting on the supply. Consequently, the combined net earnings of Exxon, Mobil, SoCal, Gulf, and Texaco increased by 70 percent between 1978 and 1979, from $6.6 billion to $11.2 billion, while 1980 was the most lucrative year in the industry's history up to that point.[86]

The companies then made a catastrophic mistake. They each released their stockpiled oil at the same time, leading to a vast oil glut. The glut was exacerbated by the global recession brought on by the second oil shock, which reduced demand for oil everywhere. In the 1980s the prices of oil and gas reached their lowest levels in decades, and the profits of the major oil companies collapsed.

It is important to note that, by and large, the oil companies were not shut out of the oil-rich countries following the nationalizations. Rather, the now state-owned oil operations contracted with the major oil companies to sell their oil abroad using marketing contracts and to provide technical service where needed using limited service contracts. The oil companies were denied control over production and price, however, as well as ownership of the reserves. The latter was critical, because the value of oil company stock is largely determined by the oil reserves they hold, referred to as "booked reserves." To shore up their stocks, profits, and shrinking political power, the companies needed to act fast.

They set out to hunt for oil not in the field but rather on Wall Street, by buying up other oil companies. They also sought to start making money from what were previously low-income activities for them: the domestic refining and selling of gasoline. First, however, they would need to get past domestic antitrust laws. To accomplish this task they turned to their new friend in government, President Ronald Reagan, whom they had heavily supported in his 1980 campaign against Walter Mondale.

The Reagan administration pursued an economic model not seen since Treasury Secretary Mellon's days in office, and the great 1980s merger wave followed. As Hobart Rowen, the *Washington Post*'s director of business and economic news coverage, observed in 1984, "The oil merger trend, any way you look at it, is dubious from the public-interest point of view. Yet it may be difficult to stop because the new antitrust philosophy (if it can be dignified by that phrase) is that bigness per se is no longer a no-no. Having many years ago broken up Standard Oil in what may be its most famous antitrust case, the federal government now seems willing to stand by while the monopoly gets put back together again."[87]

THE GREAT OIL COMPANY MERGER WAVES, 1980–TODAY

*These mergers are almost obscene. . . . They have absolutely
no redeeming social or economic value. They don't make
sense as a matter of national energy or antitrust policy.*
                    —SENATOR HOWARD METZENBAUM, 1984[88]

The Anti-Antitrust: Reagan's FTC

*The optimum size of the FTC is undoubtedly much smaller
than its current size; whether it's greater than zero is an open
empirical question.*

                    REAGAN ADMINISTRATION APPOINTEE
                                    TO THE FTC[89]

Michael Pertschuk remained at the FTC as a commissioner during the first few years of the Reagan administration. Upon his
departure, Pertschuk wrote that Reagan's FTC "has been consumed with a single-minded determination to undo the past—not
just the immediate past—but the very foundation of antitrust
and consumer protection law laid down by Congress."[90] The
FTC under Reagan initiated a new and radically permissive attitude toward corporate mergers that brought about the first major
wave of oil company consolidations since the breakup of Standard Oil. As antitrust law professor Herman Schwartz told me,
the Reagan team "never met a merger they didn't like."[91]

"I joined the Reagan Revolution as a radical ideologue," wrote
David Stockman. "I learned the traumatic lesson that no such
revolution is possible."[92] James "Jim" C. Miller III, Reagan's
chairman of the FTC from 1981 to 1985, learned no such lesson.
A close ally of Stockman, Miller took over as head of Reagan's
Office of Management and Budget in 1986 when Stockman left
the job discredited, dejected, and done with politics. Prior to joining the Reagan administration, Jim Miller was codirector of the
ultraconservative American Enterprise Institute's Center for the

Study of Government Regulation, where he argued for the privatization of the U.S. Postal Service and for deregulation of workplace safety laws, environmental and consumer protections, airline transportation, and virtually every other area of government intervention. He shared Stockman's radical ideology and succeeded in instituting the Reagan Revolution at the FTC—a revolution from which the institution has yet to recover fully.

The FTC exercises its antitrust enforcement through its Bureau of Competition. Stockman first tried to eliminate the Bureau of Competition altogether, which would have effectively done away with the FTC's antitrust jurisdiction. Stockman argued on behalf of the cut before a House committee, explaining that it was "an integral part of the Administration's efforts to redirect regulatory policy in order to reduce the burdens that misguided efforts have imposed upon the American economy."[93] William Baxter, Reagan's appointee to head the DOJ's Antitrust Bureau, also argued that his should be the only government agency charged with antitrust enforcement. "There were a lot of people in the administration, including Bill Baxter, whose position was that the FTC should not exist," Jim Miller later told me in an interview. "Although Baxter did say magnanimously several times since that 'as long as Jim Miller's the chairman of the FTC, we're okay.' "[94]

While Congress saved the Bureau of Competition, Jim Miller succeeded in gutting the FTC's budget by about half. Not surprisingly, the annual number of antitrust complaints filed by the government declined precipitously during his tenure, from an average of 9.8 during the Carter years to 5.4 during the Reagan administration. Likewise, the number of cases on the docket declined as well, from fifty in the last year of the Carter presidency to fifteen in the last year of the Reagan administration.[95]

Miller, an economist trained at the University of Chicago, was neither an antitrust specialist nor even a lawyer. In fact, he was both the first nonlawyer and the first economist to serve as chairman of the FTC. He argued that antitrust's "traditional concern" with corporate concentration was at best misguided and that the policies implemented to weed out monopolies before they could form were simply inefficient. Efficiency would replace democracy as an overriding concern of the agency. *Consumers*—a term used to refer to the buyers' interest in low prices to the exclusion of virtually every other concern, such as product safety—took precedence over *competitors* or smaller businesses.

Miller's entire approach to antitrust was radically different from that of either its founders or his predecessors at the FTC. His approach to consumer protection is demonstrative. At his first press conference as FTC chairman, Miller argued that "imperfect products" should be available on the market because "consumers have different preferences for risk avoidance" and "those who have a low aversion to risk—relative to money—will be most likely to purchase cheap, unreliable products."[96] Miller's words sound particularly shocking today, when toys are being recalled from store shelves by the millions across the nation; Congress is investigating whether an estrogenlike compound, bisphenol-A, found in plastic baby bottles, tin cans, and dozens of everyday products is known by manufacturers to cause reproductive disorders; the consumer rights organization Public Citizen lists 181 prescription drugs available on the market that are unsafe or ineffective; and pet foods have been found to be contaminated with poisons.

Miller compiled a team of like-minded anti-antitrust advocates. He selected longtime colleague Robert Tollison as director of the FTC's Bureau of Economics. Tollison described how the FTC would allow "a lot of mergers to go through. . . . Then if there are anticompetitive problems, we can try to unscramble the eggs. . . . [P]olicing ex post is much more appealing to me."[97] This meant that the FTC could let workers lose their jobs, investors their money, and competitors their businesses as a result of unhealthy mergers because the government could step in and retroactively pick up the pieces.

"We seem to have answered once and for all in the negative

the question of whether antitrust is the proper means of dealing with social and political—real or imaginary—problems created by mergers," J. Paul McGrath, U.S. assistant attorney general, observed without regret in 1984. Other laws would have to address the impact of mergers on consumers, on workers, and on society as a whole, he explained.[98]

The FTC and the DOJ then wrote new guidelines that made it easier for companies to merge. The guidelines, implemented in 1982, were remarkably successful, and the first great merger wave in one hundred years quickly followed. Soon "business leaders put together mergers they would never have even considered before," according to antitrust law professor Herman Schwartz, chief counsel to the Senate Antitrust and Monopoly Subcommittee from 1979 to 1980. "The number of huge mergers broke records and often with government help," Schwartz told me. Far from being a passive player, "the government would help design and facilitate the combinations."[99]

At the same time, Reagan appointed anti-antitrust enforcers such as Robert Bork, William Rehnquist, and Antonin Scalia to judicial benches across the nation and to the highest court, ensuring that the Reagan Revolution in antitrust would be enforced for decades to come.

All the big companies began eyeing each other. "It's like a square dance with everybody lining up on different sides of the floor," observed William F. Randol, an analyst for the First Boston Corporation.[100] In reference to the $5.1 billion combination of Santa Fe and Southern Pacific railroads, the biggest merger of 1983, the president of Sante Fe Industries commented, "Fifteen years ago, if we had tried that deal the antitrust busters would have come down so hard on us it never would have gone through."[101]

The 1980s Oil Company Mergers

It would not take long before the $5.1 billion Santa Fe and Southern Pacific merger would seem almost trivial, for a wave of massive oil company mergers soon followed. Most mergers of this era involved larger oil companies purchasing smaller independent firms. The largest merger, however, was the first between two of the Seven Sisters, when Chevron purchased Gulf Oil for a record-breaking $13.3 billion in 1985. Two of the most dramatic mergers were Texaco's merger with Getty Oil and Mobil's merger with Superior Oil. Among the many others were Occidental Oil's acquisition of Cities Service Company and MidConCorp; U.S. Steel Corporation's purchase of Marathon and the Texas Oil & Gas Corporation; BP's acquisition of Standard Oil of Ohio; Amoco's acquisition of Dome Petroleum of Canada; and, in the last year of the decade, Exxon's acquisition of Texaco-Canada.

Many congressional attempts to block the mergers failed, as did efforts by public interest groups. One concrete victory was achieved through a California legal action against the Texaco-Getty merger, whereby states earned the legal right to participate in the FTC's deliberations over oil company mergers. Nevertheless, the FTC facilitated and permitted each successive merger. Pertschuk told a reporter in 1984, "They obviously think they can get away with it now. . . . There is no question that these types of acquisitions by one oil company of another would have been unthinkable as recently as five years ago."[102]

The Texaco-Getty Merger

The first merger between two large oil companies took place in 1984, when Texaco acquired Getty Oil Corporation for over $10 billion. It was the largest merger in U.S. corporate history at the time, and it nearly put Texaco out of business.

In 1982 Texaco was the third-largest oil company in the United States with revenues of $48 billion. But it was in trouble, having lost its primary source of oil in Saudi Arabia. "If Texaco reserves continue to drop at their current rate," warned the *Financial Times,* "one of the mightiest of the Seven Sisters dominating the world oil industry would soon be out of business."[103] Getty Oil was the fourteenth-largest company in the United

States with $12.3 billion, and Pennzoil was a hardly noticed competitor, with just $2.3 billion.[104]

Getty Oil, already the product of several oil company mergers, was owned first by George Getty and then, upon his death in 1930, by his son, Jean Paul. By 1957, Jean Paul Getty was deemed the richest American by *Fortune* magazine. The largest piece of his fortune was his 80 percent ownership of Getty Oil and its nearly two hundred affiliated companies. He remained Getty Oil's president until his death in 1976, whereupon Gordon Getty, the youngest of his three surviving sons, inherited 13 percent of the company.

Gordon had little connection to the company other than the $28 million a year that his dividends paid him, which helped earn him *Forbes* magazine's title as the richest American in 1983.[105] When a sudden death in the company put Gordon in control of a majority of Getty Oil's shares in 1982, he decided that he wanted to sell.

Getty's board of directors did not want to sell. They found an ally in Gordon's brother, J. Paul Getty Jr., who represented the rest of the family members who were opposed to a sale. The family members even tried to acquire a restraining order against Gordon to prevent him from selling. The family also filed a lawsuit against Gordon in the name of J. Paul's fifteen-year-old son, Tara Gabriel Galaxy Gramophone Getty. These efforts, however, were to little avail.

Learning of the internal unrest, Pennzoil chairman J. Hugh Liedtke thought Getty Oil seemed the perfect candidate for a takeover. Liedtke contacted Gordon, and the two put together a $5.2 billion deal to buy up Getty Oil's stock jointly for $112.50 per share. After much wrangling, arm-twisting, and conniving, the Getty board of directors realized it had little choice but to accede to the deal with Pennzoil and agreed to support it "in principle."

Before the ink was dry, however, Texaco chairman John K. McKinley learned of the Pennzoil bid and quickly stepped in to top it. McKinley offered the board $125 per share. In a hastily scheduled telephone conference call, the board approved the new, higher offer. The Texaco deal went through, and the Pennzoil deal was off. Pennzoil immediately sued, arguing that it had signed a deal with the board prior to Texaco's sneak attack, and the board should have to honor the Pennzoil deal. A Texas jury agreed and ruled in favor of Pennzoil in 1985. It awarded the company $12 billion in damages, the largest damage award in history at the time. With a net worth of just $13.5 billion, Texaco filed for bankruptcy in 1987. The jury did not reverse the merger, however, and the Texaco-Getty merger stuck.

The purchase immediately doubled Texaco's oil reserves and moved the company into a virtual tie with Mobil in sales, behind Exxon. Texaco acquired Getty's 1.2 billion barrels of oil reserves and 2.4 trillion cubic feet of natural gas. Bankruptcy protection, meanwhile, saved Texaco from economic collapse.

California's state attorney general had sought to block the merger. Before Texaco's purchase, Getty was a major supplier of inexpensive oil to small independent refineries. These refineries sold gasoline at cheaper rates to independent gasoline stations, which in turn sold less expensive gas to motorists than did the major oil companies. Texaco's acquisition of Getty, the attorney general argued, would threaten this arrangement by giving Texaco excessive control over petroleum markets in California, forcing independent companies out of business and raising prices for consumers. The California State Supreme Court ruled that California and other states, for the first time, should be allowed to be involved in FTC decision-making concerning mergers. However, it did not agree to block the merger, nor did the FTC.

Pertschuk, in one of his last actions as FTC commissioner, issued the lone vote against the merger. He said that allowing the Texaco-Getty merger "compounds the hands-off antitrust standard of the Reagan administration and effectively invites the major oil companies to race to acquire the reserve-rich middle tier firms." He quite accurately predicted that the long-term impact would be "tighter control of the oil industry by the major companies . . . and higher prices for consumers."[106]

The Chevron-Gulf Merger

One month after the Texaco-Getty merger, Gulf Oil finally went over to Standard when it was purchased by Chevron. It was the first merger between members of the exclusive Seven Sisters. It was also the largest merger in corporate history at the time, whereby the fourth-largest oil company in the nation was purchased by the fifth-largest company. Chevron had lost its major oil reserves to the nationalizations, particularly to the nationalization of Aramco, and was in need of crude. Overnight, the merger nearly doubled Chevron's worldwide crude reserves to about 4 billion barrels and increased its natural gas reserves by three-quarters. The merger also made Chevron the number one refiner and gasoline retailer in the United States, giving it thirty-four refineries and close to thirty thousand service stations worldwide.[107]

Chevron added exploration and production projects where it was already operating, such as in the Gulf of Mexico, Canada, and the North Sea, as well as in West Africa, where Gulf's reserves suddenly advanced the company to a leading position. Chevron also acquired Gulf's other assets, including the Pittsburg & Midway Coal Mining Company and Warren Petroleum, a manufacturer and a seller of natural gas liquids, respectively. The FTC hardly blinked.

In response to the Getty, Texaco, Gulf, and Chevron mergers, senators J. Bennett Johnston, Democrat of Louisiana, Howard Metzenbaum, Democrat of Ohio, and New Hampshire Republican Warren Rudman led an antimerger movement in Congress. "We're seeing a madhouse," Senator Rudman told his colleagues, with business leaders "starting to play Monopoly with real money."[108] The senators tried to implement, among other measures, a six-month moratorium to delay all mergers among the fifty top oil companies. The Senate Judiciary Committee held hearings, while other antimerger legislation was also introduced in the House. Additional measures were introduced specifically to bar the Chevron-Gulf merger.[109] "I'm still sympathetic to the industry," Senator Johnston explained in 1984. "This just happens not to be in the national interest, in my view. The horse is going to be out of the barn and the eggs scrambled in the next few months, and unless we act now to stop not just this merger but this trend, the oil business is going to be fundamentally restructured, and I think not in the interest of the country."[110] Veto threats and a lack of support from the Reagan White House ensured that all of these measures failed.

Family Feud: The Mobil-Superior Takeover

> *This would never have happened if he had just been civil to his sister.*
>
> —AN ACQUAINTANCE OF HOWARD KECK[111]

As soon as Reagan took office, Mobil went in search of mergers to acquire more crude oil. It tried two hostile takeovers, first of Marathon in 1981 and then of Conoco in 1982. Mobil was blocked in both cases by state-level antitrust actions. Undeterred, Mobil set its sites on the Superior Oil Company of Houston.

Willametta Keck Day, daughter of William Keck, the founder of the Superior Oil Company, hated her older brother, Howard. As the story goes, they were just children when Howard fed her pet ostrich an orange. The ostrich died, and Willametta never forgave her brother. Their childhood fight developed into a decades-long feud that played itself out on a very public stage over the fate of their father's Superior Oil Company: Willametta wanted to sell; Howard did not.

William Keck was the son of a Pennsylvania oil worker. In the late 1880s, while in his teens, William left Pennsylvania and his family for the California oil boom. He worked the oil fields and eventually made his way up to become a drilling contractor. In

1921 he founded the Superior Oil Company. Large finds in Texas and Louisiana made the company rich in crude. In the 1930s, Superior discovered the first commercial oil field in the offshore waters of the Gulf of Mexico. Keck moved his headquarters to Houston in the early 1960s. By 1984, Superior operated more than sixty platforms in the Gulf. Keck prided himself on his company's independence and tended to partner only with other independent companies. He ran the company for more than forty years until turning it over to his son, Howard, in 1963, dying one year later.

Howard took over from his father and ran the company for nearly twenty years. But for Willametta, there was little love lost between her and her father, and by corollary, his company. "We were not raised as a close family," she later said. "The Old Man gave up his life to Superior Oil."[112]

In the merger wave of the early 1980s, Superior was an extremely attractive target. It was the biggest independent oil and gas producer in the United States. Superior was crude-rich at a time when Mobil needed oil. Purchasing the company would add 1 billion barrels of oil to Mobil's reserves.[113]

Howard hoped that his seat on the board, his control of almost 20 percent of the company's stock, and the support of the company's management would protect him from having to sell the company. Willametta only owned 3 percent of the stock, but she had a strong ally in T. Boone Pickens, the head of Mesa Petroleum and the king of the 1980s hostile takeover. Pickens purchased a small stake in Superior and was ready to back up Willametta and cash in on the $6 billion sale.

Howard tried to put in place several devices that would have made Superior almost invulnerable to a hostile bid. To stop her brother, Willametta went public. She reportedly spent $2 million on an advertising campaign that included the purchase of full-page ads in the *New York Times,* tantalizing shareholders with the wealth they would achieve if they voted against her brother.

Willametta explained that it was "good common sense on my

part. I was thinking of estate planning. I thought I should do something before I'm scattered."[114] In fact, the "Old Man" had left his children quite well off, with a $1.6 billion trust fund, 10 percent of which was paid out annually and divided between the brother and sister. In response to her brother's resistance to sell, Willametta reportedly told Howard, "You're a dumb son of a bitch and you ought to get off the board and sell the company."[115]

In the end, Willametta won. Howard resigned from the board in 1984, clearing the way for Mobil's bid. Mobil bought Superior for $5.7 billion and Howard and Willametta each received $1 billion. Willametta died one year later. Neither the money, nor the sale, nor even Willametta's death ended Howard's problems, however. His son, Howard Jr., decided that he deserved a larger share of the family's financial pie. Father and son engaged in a legal dispute that resulted in Howard Sr.'s two daughters choosing sides, his wife divorcing him, and Howard Sr. claiming that Howard Jr. was not his biological son (a claim later proved false).[116]

Mobil's takeover of Superior kept the company firmly ensconced as the nation's number two oil company after Exxon.

Reagan's supply-side economics, like Andrew Mellon's, succeeded in putting more wealth in the hands of the already wealthy and more power in the hands of the already powerful. However, the promised "trickle down" to the rest of society never occurred. David Stockman, the head of Reagan's Office of Management and Budget, ultimately left the administration in disgrace largely due to the devastating failure of these policies.

As the result of placing corporate interests above all other concerns and cutting out government programs to support lower income groups, small businesses, and others, the bottom fell out of the economy. According to the U.S. Census Bureau, between 1980 and 1990, the wealthiest Americans gained an additional 20 percent of the total national income pie, while the poorest lost more than 10 percent, with incomes falling in absolute terms.

While the public ultimately condemned "Reaganomics," Reagan's antitrust policies have escaped the same public scrutiny and have carried on with a vengeance in subsequent administrations.

The 1990s and Twenty-first Century Merger Tsunamis

There was clearly a Reagan revolution in antitrust and my side won.
—FTC COMMISSIONER TIMOTHY MURIS, 2007[117]

While the 1980s brought a merger wave, what came next is best described as a veritable merger tsunami. More than 2,600 mergers occurred in the U.S. petroleum industry from the 1990s to 2004, and more have followed since.[118] In 1999 the single largest merger in corporate history occurred between the two largest Standard Oil spin-off companies: Exxon and Mobil. The 1990s also saw the megamergers of BP and Amoco and then of BP Amoco and Arco. The new century began with the merger of "the terrible twins": Chevron and Texaco. Then came the merger of giants Conoco and Phillips and Chevron's purchase of Unocal. In 2003 Devon Energy and Ocean Energy merged to become the largest independent oil and gas producer in the United States. In 2006 Anadarko Petroleum purchased Kerr-McGee and Western Gas Resources.

These and the thousands of other oil industry mergers were overseen by very different administrations but with remarkably consistent antitrust policies. President Bill Clinton's antitrust policies were part and parcel of his efforts to expand the rights and privileges of multinational corporations abroad through corporate globalization or "free trade" policy. His FTC chairman explicitly saw his antitrust policies as a continuation of those in the preceding George H. W. Bush administration. President George W. Bush shared Clinton's free trade agenda but combined it with a more militarist, imperialist, and unilateralist approach.

The mergers that occurred under these three administrations vastly expanded the power, influence, and reach of the megacorporations. But compared with earlier periods, the mergers occurred with hardly a ripple of resistance from Congress and far less analytic coverage in the mainstream media. The few congressional hearings that took place seemed more like corporate cheerleading sessions than serious questioning. Also during this period, the United States fought two wars on behalf of Big Oil, both in Iraq, and the industry's political contributions reached proportions equal to those of the Standard Oil era.

Meanwhile, the public responded, and resistance to the mergers was part of the growing anticorporate globalization movement that captured headlines in a string of massive protests, including the fifty-thousand-person protest against a World Trade Organization in Seattle, Washington, in 1999. Public interest, human rights, environmental, and consumers' groups reached out to shareholders and the media and protested against proposed mergers at oil corporation meetings, but ultimately without success.

The two men most directly responsible for the mergers were FTC chairmen Robert Pitofsky and Timothy Muris. In an interview with Pitofsky, Clinton's FTC chairman, I asked him about a number of recent anticompetitive effects in the oil industry that have followed the merger waves of the 1980s and 1990s. He told me that he had not really followed these developments since he left office, and then called George W. Bush's FTC commissioner, Timothy Muris, for help. Muris, in turn, sent me a 150-page monograph entitled "A Dozen Facts You Should Know about Antitrust and the Oil Industry." It was a good firsthand demonstration of the closeness of these two men, who seem worlds apart on paper.

Bob Pitofsky was FTC chairman from 1995 to 2001, covering all but the first two years of President Clinton's terms. He had served earlier as FTC commissioner under Chairman Pertschuk. Timothy Muris succeeded Pitofsky as FTC chair under President

George W. Bush. Having worked hand-in-hand with Reagan's chairman, Jim Miller, for almost the entire 1980s, he went on to serve as an economic adviser to Bush's presidential campaign and to the Bush-Cheney transition team. He stayed in his post as FTC chair until 2004. Today, Muris is cochair of the antitrust practice division at the O'Melveny & Myers law firm in Washington, D.C. His corporate clients have included ExxonMobil, which he represented in an antitrust suit brought against the company by the FTC.[119] Pitofsky teaches at Georgetown University Law School.

Timothy Muris is a true believer in the Reagan Revolution. In 1974, when he was just twenty-four years old and on his way to Washington for his first government job at the FTC, most Americans were still reeling from the trauma of Watergate. "In 1974, the proportion of the electorate who described themselves as Republican fell to 20 percent," point out John Micklethwait and Adrian Wooldridge in *The Right Nation*. "Most Americans thought of the Republican Party as untrustworthy, incompetent and closely allied with big business. Asked to name something good about the party, two-thirds of voters couldn't think of anything at all. The Republican National Convention ran advertisements asking rather desperately, 'When has it been easy to be a Republican?' "[120]

Bucking the trend was young Timothy Muris, who had been a party activist since he was a teenager. In 1970 he worked for Reagan's gubernatorial campaign in his hometown of San Diego, and he remains a party faithful, pitching for presidential candidate John McCain at the time of our interview in 2007. While Muris was working at the FTC, he took a few graduate economics classes at George Washington University, including a class taught by Jim Miller. By 1981, Muris's and Miller's careers would follow a virtually identical trajectory.

Bob Pitofsky's first job after serving in the military was at the DOJ. After that, he went to the Wall Street law firm Dewey Ballantine and then taught law at New York University. After three years at the FTC, he returned to academia. While he has continued to practice law, the FTC and the academy have largely shaped his career.

While Muris and Pitofsky differ on some points of policy and would not have decided all of the same cases in the same ways, the outcomes of their terms were remarkably similar. Under Chairman Pitofsky, from 1998 to 1999, the overall value of U.S. mergers increased tenfold compared with their value from 1990 to 1992, from $151 billion to a whopping $1.7 trillion. There were roughly 4,700 mergers in 1999, up from about 1,500 just five years earlier.[121] "Despite the huge number of mergers proposed and consummated, virtually none of these mergers were challenged and litigated on antitrust grounds," reported antitrust law experts Robert Litan and Carl Shapiro in 2001. "In no year were more than six percent of proposed mergers subjected to a full investigation; in no year were more than one-half of one percent of proposed mergers challenged in Court."[122] During the height of this merger tsunami, from 1998 to 2000, Pitofsky's FTC challenged just 0.7 percent of proposed mergers. The identical ratio, 0.7 percent, held throughout Chairman Muris's tenure, from 2002 through 2004.[123]

The new wave of megamergers would put the 1980s mergers to shame. They began with Marathon's 1997 purchase of Ashland, creating the fifth-largest oil company in the United States, and have not stopped.

The BP-Amoco-Arco Mergers

In 1998 BP purchased Amoco for $53 billion. With it, BP acquired one of the largest oil companies in the United States and the largest natural gas producer in North America with exploration in twenty countries and production in fourteen countries. The new company, BP Amoco, became the largest producer of both oil and natural gas in the United States and launched BP Amoco to become Britain's largest corporation.

When the merger was announced, leading consumer advocates James Love and Robert Weisman issued a joint statement calling on the Clinton administration to provide a public forum on the issue of concentration in the oil sector: "We fear the BP-Amoco merger, announced today, will hurt consumers . . . [and] spur a round of anticompetitive mergers in the oil industry and dangerous concentration of economic and political power."[124]

Two years later, BP Amoco purchased Arco for $27.6 billion. The FTC had first blocked the merger, but then allowed it to proceed after requiring that Arco sell its Alaska holdings to Phillips Petroleum.

BP is the fourth-largest corporation in the world today, and the third-largest global oil company. Were it based in the United States instead of Britain, it would be the third-largest company in America.

The Exxon-Mobil Merger

The final year of the Clinton administration brought the most important and largest merger in corporate history: Exxon's $81 billion purchase of Mobil. Exxon was certainly hurt by its loss of crude during the nationalizations of the 1970s, but its oil holdings were more diversified than most, and the company did not take part in the 1980s merger wave in the same way as the other baby-Standards. By the 1990s, however, it was feeling the crunch: it needed not only more crude but more control over the domestic market, and Mobil had become its chief competitor in every area of operation—from exploration to production to refining to marketing.

Connecticut's attorney general Richard Blumenthal expressed to Congress his strong opposition to the merger, which he found would result in the top four oil companies in the country controlling 73 percent of the retail market in half the metropolitan areas in the Northeast and mid-Atlantic region.[125]

Jeffrey E. Garten, dean of the Yale School of Management, who was undersecretary of commerce for international trade in the first Clinton administration, warned Congress and the public of the dire implications of the Exxon-Mobil merger and the overall merger wave for democracy. Writing in the *New York Times* in 1999, his words are strikingly prescient:

The real problem could be the unchecked political influence
of the new global goliaths. . . . Many mega-companies
could be beyond the law, too. Their deep pockets can buy
teams of lawyers that can stymie prosecutors for years.
And if they lose in court, they can afford to pay huge
fines without damaging their operations. Moreover, no
one should be surprised that mega-companies navigate
our scandalously porous campaign financing system to
influence tax policy, environmental standards . . . and
other issues of national policy. Yes, companies have
always lobbied, but these huge corporations often have
more pull. Because there are fewer of them, their influence
can be more focused, and in some cases, the country may
be highly dependent on their survival.[126]

Garten's fears would come to fruition. Nonetheless, after requiring some divestitures the FTC approved the merger by a vote of 4
to 0. The merger created an economic behemoth that has used its
subsequent wealth and power to fundamentally alter the course
of history.

In April 1999, Albert Foer, president of the American Antitrust
Institute, wrote to FTC chairman Pitofsky, warning of overconcen-
tration in the oil industry: "Coming on top of BP's recent acquisition of Amoco, Exxon's pending acquisition of Mobil, and a flurry
of other petroleum industry acquisitions and joint ventures, the BP
Amoco acquisition of Arco puts the question squarely before the
Commission: when will the Government draw the line?"[127]

Today ExxonMobil is, after Wal-Mart, the second-largest
corporation in the United States and the world, and the world's
most profitable corporation many times over.

The Chevron-Texaco Merger
As with Exxon and Mobil, few people were surprised that Chevron and Texaco wanted to merge; it was only a question of
whether the feds would allow it to happen, especially on the

heels of so many other megamergers. But after more than one hundred years of "independence," Texaco became part of the Standard Oil fold when its 2001 merger with Chevron was given the green light. Chevron first tried to purchase Texaco in 1999, but the company CEOs could not agree on a deal and the $37.5 billion offer fell through. By 2001, however, Exxon had merged with Mobil and BP had purchased both Amoco and Arco. Chevron and Texaco decided that they either had to join forces or get left behind. This time, Texaco accepted a smaller bid of $36 billion, and the acquisition was complete.

Companies knew that they now had to search farther afield for oil, in riskier, more environmentally destructive, and more expensive enterprises. In the case of Chevron and Texaco, the two wanted to move more aggressively into "lucrative but highly risky deepwater offshore projects in West Africa, Brazil and the Caspian Sea."[128] They needed their combined resources to do so. "What the oil companies have found out is that as you go deeper and deeper into the offshore projects, that you are a pioneer and, therefore, mistakes will be made," explained Mehdi Varzi, the director of research at Dresdner Kleinwort Benson at the time of the merger. "To exploit those reserves, you need the acreage and you need the money."[129]

Commenting at the time on the merger, Wenonah Hauter of the research and consumer advocacy organization Public Citizen said, "We're not pleased to see it. We think this doesn't bode well for consumers, because we'll have fewer competitors. And in the long run, there's the additional problem of the increased political power of these larger, wealthier companies."[130]

The merged company briefly went by the name ChevronTexaco, but reverted back to Chevron in 2005, the same year it purchased the Union Oil Company of California (Unocal) for $18.2 billion. The Unocal purchase brought ChevronTexaco 1.7 billion new barrels of crude, increasing its total reserves by about 15 percent. Unocal had significant holdings in the U.S. Gulf Coast, in the Caspian Sea, and in Asia-Pacific.

The mergers propelled Chevron to the powerful position of second-largest oil company in the United States, third-largest U.S. corporation, and seventh-largest company in the world.

The Conoco-Phillips Merger

Separately, Conoco and Phillips were midsized companies. Together, their $15.2 billion 2002 merger thrust them into their current position as the third-largest oil company in the United States. "The deal is the latest step in the relentless consolidation of the oil and gas industry," the *New York Times* reported at the time. "For Phillips and Conoco, both proudly independent, the merger comes as an acknowledgement that they can no longer afford to go it alone."[131] Phillips had recently grown in size with its own megamergers: the 2000 acquisition of Arco's large crude holdings in Alaska for $7 billion and its 2001 purchase of Tosco—the largest independent refiner and marketer of petroleum products in the United States at the time, also for $7 billion. ConocoPhillips became the nation's largest gasoline retailer, combining pump brands like Conoco, Phillips 66, Union 76, and Circle K. In 2006 ConocoPhillips purchased Burlington Resources, a Fortune 500 oil company with major fields in Algeria, Canada, and China, solidifying its third-place position.

The Shell-Pennzoil Merger

Shell officially joined the Standard Oil fold when it purchased Pennzoil for a mere $1.8 billion in 2002. Houston-based Pennzoil was the product of the previous mergers of four baby-Standard companies: Eureka Pipe Line Company, South Penn Oil Company, National Transit Company, and South West Pennsylvania Pipe Lines. Pennzoil had also merged with Quaker State and was the leading producer of motor oil in the United States. It was also owner or franchisee of more than 2,150 Jiffy Lube service centers. The acquisition gave Shell, which also produced Havoline brand motor oil, three of the top five U.S. motor oil brands. In 1996 Shell and Texaco had formed a joint venture with their

Equilon and Motiva brands. Shell had also purchased gas stations formerly owned by Texaco.

All of this has helped make Royal Dutch Shell, based in the Netherlands, the second-largest oil company in the world and the third-largest global corporation. Like BP, were Shell based in the United States, it would be the third-largest American corporation.

Valero

Formed in 1980, Valero Energy Corporation does not produce oil but rather refines and sells it. It has built itself through a string of aggressive acquisitions of existing refineries and retail stations, including some that were spin-offs from the mergers of other companies. While each large merger went forward, the FTC required that some of the companies sell refineries, gas stations, pipelines, and other side businesses as a condition of the merger. Valero's most important spin-off acquisition, in 2000, was of Exxon's Benicia, California, refinery, located near San Francisco, its 270-store retail distribution chain, and eighty company-operated retail sites. This acquisition marked Valero's entry into the retail business when it debuted the Valero retail brand. It 2001 it purchased Ultramar Diamond Shamrock, making it one of the nation's top three refining and marketing companies. In 2005 Valero purchased Premcor Inc. for $8 billion and acquired its four refineries in Port Arthur, Texas; Memphis, Tennessee; Delaware City, Delaware; and Lima, Ohio.

Today, Valero is the fourth-largest oil company in the United States.

FROM ITS VERY CONCEPTION TO the present day, the oil industry has been plagued with massive anticompetitive, undemocratic, socially, economically, and politically destructive practices. All the while, it has been coddled, subsidized, protected, and preserved by the U.S. government. We have come all but full circle from the Standard Oil of Rockefeller to the ExxonMobil of to-day. For decades the oil companies have been permitted to collude and wreak havoc on the governments and people of the world, only to return home and direct their collusive energies against the United States and its people. In 2007 the *Wall Street Journal* declared, "The federal government has nearly stepped out of the antitrust enforcement business, leaving companies to mate as they wish."[132] The impacts of the merger waves are being felt in critical ways today. From Chevron's purchase of Getty, to BP's purchase of Amoco, to Exxon's massive merger with Mobil, antitrust experts warned over and over again that concentration in the oil industry would lead to an erosion of democracy, market manipulation, reduced supply, higher gas prices, and other forms of both market and political abuse. They were right.

4

Driving the Price of Crude

*The commodities futures markets have become an orgy of
speculation, a carnival of greed.*
—SENATOR CARL LEVIN, 2008[1]

*Despite the recent record jump in oil prices, the outlook
suggests that oil prices will continue to rise steadily over
the next five years, almost doubling from current levels.*
—JEFF RUBIN, CHIEF ECONOMIST, CIBC WORLD
MARKETS, APRIL 2008[2]

The merger tsunamis of the last twenty-five years enabled the
newly minted ExxonMobil, Chevron, ConocoPhillips, BP,
Shell, Marathon, and other leading oil corporations to increase
their oil holdings by pooling the reserves of each postmerger company. The mergers expanded their capital, allowing the companies to explore for and produce oil in far more expensive terrains
and using costlier techniques. The increased capital also allowed
the oil companies to regain and solidify their economic and political clout both in the United States and around the world.

In the United States, the oil companies bought up and pushed
out competitors in the refining and marketing sectors, turning
these into highly profitable enterprises for the companies. Glob-
ally, Big Oil has pulled in unprecedented profits from its sizable

crude oil holdings. However, the companies have thus far been unable to regain the ownership and control of the world's oil supply that they exercised during the Seven Sisters era. Nor have they been able to unilaterally set the price of oil for the rest of the world as they once did.

But Big Oil has not sat idly by watching from the sidelines.

Today the price of a barrel of oil is largely determined by the actions of energy futures traders, including those working for and on behalf of Big Oil. The oil companies, together with the nation's largest banks, Enron, and other like-minded players, lobbied successfully to remove government oversight and regulation from much of this trading, such that oil futures have become one of the hottest but least regulated trading properties in the world. Analysts estimate that as much as half the price of a barrel of oil is due exclusively to the actions of energy traders.

Thus, while many factors alter the daily price of crude, the most important and most overlooked factor driving the meteoric rise in oil prices today is the deregulation of energy trading. Deregulation has created as ripe an opportunity for price manipulation of crude oil as it did for Enron's manipulation of the entire West Coast electricity market in 2000. While much has changed since Enron's collapse, the deregulatory trick it used to manipulate the market— referred to as the "Enron Loophole"—remains firmly in place today, facilitating the blistering pace of crude oil futures trades.

As the price for its oil rises, Big Oil's profits grow accordingly. And while global oil consumption continues its own steady climb, there is little reason for Big Oil to stand in the way of this seemingly limitless oil price bonanza.

A METEORIC RISE

The price of oil still is out of whack with normal supply and demand fundamentals.

—PHIL FLYNN, OIL ANALYST, ALARON TRADING CORPORATION, 2008[3]

On New Year's Day 2008, oil reached $100 per barrel for the first time in history. Adjusted for inflation, the price was actually higher in 1981 at the height of the second oil shock, when oil reached $104 per barrel in 2008 dollars ($44 in 1981). Nonetheless, the psychological impact of crossing the $100 divide was felt powerfully across the nation and around the world. It did not take long for oil to reach the highest price ever paid for a barrel of oil in modern history when on March 5, 2008, the price surpassed $104 per barrel and just kept on climbing. In 1981 the high price of oil led to a massive, debilitating global recession. Today both the United States and the world are on the brink of just such an economic peril.

Not only is the price per barrel of oil breaking records, but so too is the rapid pace at which the price is rising. The price of oil has been rising for twenty years, but virtually nothing in history compares to the rate of increase we are experiencing today. In the twelve years from 1988 to 2000, the price doubled from $18 to an average of $36 per barrel. In just the five years from 2000 and 2005, the price doubled again, rising to $60 per barrel. But the prices in 2007 and 2008 would exceed them all. In just fourteen months, from January 2007 to March 2008, the price doubled again, increasing from $55 to $110 per barrel. And the price keeps rising. Such a rapid rise in price has only happened twice before in modern history: during the 1973 and 1979 energy crises—periods of intentional market manipulation specifically enacted to increase the price of crude for the benefit of producers.

Among the many factors impacting the price of a barrel of oil are war in the Middle East, conflict in Africa, hurricanes, and refinery shutdowns. These factors can and often do account for daily price fluctuations, but they have always been there. Strife in oil-rich nations, especially in the Middle East and Africa, is more often the rule than the exception. The weather always changes, and production mishaps are a matter of course in the oil industry. These factors certainly affect the price of oil, but they cannot account for the meteoric rise in prices over the last eight years.

More recently, the rapid decline in the value of the U.S. dollar has been blamed for the rise in the price of oil. There is some validity to this argument. By definition, the weaker the dollar is, the less a dollar buys, which would in turn encourage sellers to increase the price charged for oil. The weak dollar also encourages investors to turn away from other U.S. investments, such as Treasury bonds, and toward oil—which sends the price of oil higher, which in turn weakens the U.S. economy, which sends the dollar lower. The weak dollar, however, can only account for a small portion of the increase in the price of oil.[4] From 1995 to 2002, the dollar rose in value by about 40 percent and then began what was until quite recently a very gradual decline, and thus cannot account for the long-term trend of dramatically rising oil prices.[5] Moreover, while from approximately April 2007 to April 2008, the dollar lost approximately 10 percent of its value, oil prices increased by a whopping 85 percent. Something else is clearly affecting price.

What about the fundamentals of demand and supply? The public is increasingly aware that conventional oil is nearing its peak of global production, which means that from that point on it will steadily become scarcer until it runs out completely. Thus, many people accept the rapid price increase of crude oil as a natural reflection of supply and demand fundamentals, assuming that supply must be down, demand must be up, so price is, as a direct consequence, high. The reality is quite different.

Demand for oil—driven largely by the United States, China, and India—will certainly outstrip supply at some point, and quite possibly within the very near future, but we have not reached that point yet. Today the available supply of oil surpasses global demand and has done so for many years.

In the United States, domestic stocks of crude oil—that is, the amount of oil sitting in storage tanks—reached the highest levels in almost a decade in mid-2007 and have since remained at or above average. Yet the price of crude climbs ever higher.

BP Statistical Review of World Energy 2007, the most trusted source for global energy statistics, reports that in every year since 2003, the global supply of oil has exceeded demand by some 15 to 50 million tons. With 1 metric ton of oil filling approximately 7 barrels, these production excesses translate to hundreds of millions of barrels per year. The built-up excess supply is sitting in storage tanks all around the world, serving almost no other function than to garner profits for oil companies and energy traders who have been accurately betting that the oil will be worth more tomorrow than it is worth today.

"During the last 24 months, the world has added over 200 million barrels to petroleum inventories around the globe. How is that supply not keeping up with demand?" asked Citigroup energy analyst Kyle Cooper in 2005. "Demand has grown significantly. Supply has met and exceeded demand by 200 million barrels. . . . I don't see how anybody in their right mind can say this [high oil prices] is based on [demand and supply] fundamentals."[6]

"The relationship between U.S. [crude oil] inventory levels and prices has been shredded, has become irrelevant," concluded global oil economist Jan Stuart of UBS Securities.[7] Similarly, Senator Carl Levin, chairman of the Senate Permanent Investigations Subcommittee, said at a 2007 hearing, "It seemingly defies the laws of supply and demand to have an astronomical increase in the price of oil at the same time the U.S. inventory of oil has stayed above average."[8]

Big Oil's Oil
One often overlooked piece of the high-oil-price puzzle lies with Big Oil itself. According to their 2007 annual reports, ExxonMobil, Chevron, ConocoPhillips, Marathon, Shell, and BP today hold approximately 40 billion barrels of oil reserves

among them.* Were these six companies one country, Big Oil would rank among the top ten most oil-rich nations in the world. Ranked above Big Oil are Saudi Arabia, Canada, Iran, Iraq, Kuwait, UAE, Venezuela, and Russia. Big Oil is tied in ninth place with Libya and has larger reserves than Nigeria, Kazakhstan, the United States, China, Qatar, Mexico, Algeria, Brazil, Angola, Norway, and Azerbaijan—the rest of the countries rounding out the world's top twenty. Big Oil's reserves are, in fact, larger than those of the United States and China combined.

ExxonMobil has the largest reserves of any non-government-owned oil company in the world, with approximately 11 billion barrels, equivalent to Brazil's oil reserves. BP reports over 10 billion barrels of reserves; Chevron over 7.5 billion; ConocoPhillips over 5.7 billion; Shell approximately 4.9 billion; and Marathon, in distant fifth place, reports just over 1 billion barrels. Daily, the companies produce more oil than Saudi Arabia—about 13 per cent of the world's total oil supply for 2006.†

The companies' control of their own oil, combined with their political and financial power, undoubtedly translates into influence over how much they charge and pay for crude oil. The vast majority of physical oil changes hands through long-term contracts. ExxonMobil signs a contract to sell a certain quantity of oil over a specified amount of time for a given price to a government or company such as Japan or American Airlines. Exxon-Mobil also purchases crude from national governments such as Saudi Arabia or Iraq. These are private commercial contracts; we know essentially nothing about them. Big Oil has worked hard to ensure that as many of these trades as possible remain beyond public scrutiny and government regulation. But we can be sure

---

* This calculation, compiled from the companies' 2007 shareholder reports, includes the companies' tar sands reserves.
† The total combined reserves of the oil companies were virtually unchanged between 2006 and 2007 at approximately 40 billion. The most recent available data for country reserves is 2006.

that an element of independent price-setting enters into every contract that the oil companies negotiate.

What has made the last twenty-five years unique, however, is that neither Big Oil nor the Organization of Petroleum Exporting Countries (OPEC) unilaterally tells the world how much oil will cost. The market has taken over this function.

Standard Oil once set the price of a barrel of crude oil for the United States. From approximately 1928 to 1973, the Seven Sisters—Exxon, Mobil, Chevron, Texaco, Gulf, Shell, and BP—owned the majority of the world's oil. Operating as a cartel, they agreed upon a set price for crude that they would make available to the world's buyers. The Seven Sisters lost this role when the largest oil-producing nations nationalized their oil reserves and formed OPEC, their own cartel. For the next ten years, from 1973 to 1983, the OPEC nations owned the majority of the world's oil and used their cartel to set the price for the world's buyers. OPEC's price-setting ability was destroyed by three concurring events: the rapid decline in demand for oil following the 1970s oil crises; increased production of oil in non-OPEC countries, which decreased OPEC's hold on the world oil supply; and the 1983 introduction of the futures market for oil at the New York Mercantile Exchange (NYMEX).

Big Oil never stopped trying to regain its price-setting authority. The companies engaged in the megamergers of the last twenty-five years to increase their reserves, expand their capital, and increase their powers of persuasion with governments both at home and abroad. But Big Oil has not regained the crude oil holdings it held before the nationalizations and the formation of OPEC, nor has any other group of oil interests arisen to take its place.

Big Oil produces approximately 13 percent of the world's oil, while OPEC produces about 40 percent. Although both are still dominant players, neither unilaterally sets the global price of oil as they once did. The rest of the world's production is now dominated by a few state oil companies—led primarily by Russia and China—that do not have a history of working together in their production or price-setting decisions.

Today, energy traders, including those who work for and on behalf of Big Oil, set the market price for a barrel of oil. These energy traders are the missing link in the rising price of crude. Thanks to the deregulatory efforts of Big Oil, Enron, and the nation's largest banks, increasing numbers of their trades are taking place completely outside the purview of government regulators. Economists and energy analysts conservatively estimate that 20 to 25 percent of the increase in the price of crude oil is directly attributable to the actions of energy traders.[9] Less conservative estimates, such as those offered by Fadel Gheit, a veteran oil analyst at Oppenheimer & Company in New York, puts the "speculative premium" at half the value of a barrel of oil.[10] In other words, if energy traders were not trying to push the price of crude oil up in order to make money off the trade, crude would cost 20 to 50 percent less than it does today.

A disturbingly large number of these traders perfected their art working for Enron, masterfully manipulating the Enron Loophole (about which more later). Rather than go to jail, as did many of Enron's executives, Enron's energy traders are now hard at work displaying their skills and exercising their loophole on the crude oil futures market.

And for those worried about high oil prices, futures trader James Cordier warns, "Get ready. It's going to get worse before it gets better."[11]

THE PAST AND PRESENT OF FUTURES MARKETS

Predatory parasites, thieves, [and] gamblers [who live] like lords and ride in high-powered automobiles and live in great residences.

—FUTURES MARKET SPECULATORS, AS DESCRIBED AT A
1922 CONGRESSIONAL HEARING[12]

Where the New York Stock Exchange facilitates companies and individuals making money from the trade in corporate *stocks*, the New York Mercantile Exchange (NYMEX) helps companies and individuals make money from the trade in commodities traditionally sold by *merchants*, such as sugar and cotton and, more recently, electricity, natural gas, gasoline, and crude oil. NYMEX was both the creator and original home of the first publicly traded crude oil futures contract.

Located in the World Financial Center building on New York City's lower West Side, NYMEX sits just a few blocks from Wall Street and the New York Stock Exchange. Think of NYMEX as a very well endowed financial middleman. It is the guarantor of every trade that takes place under its domain. It ultimately acts as the seller to every buyer and the buyer to every seller. It does not take positions in the market, nor does it advise people on what positions to take. It guarantees that every contract will be honored and provides rules of conduct, a model form of contract, rules for disclosure, and, most importantly, a physical location where exchanges take place.

The trading floor is the historic heart of NYMEX and a world unto itself, with its own language, dress code, and rituals. Approximately one thousand contracts are bought and sold on the floor every minute. Traders stand in rings or pits wearing brightly colored identification badges. Runners go back and forth through the narrow, crowded aisles carrying customers' orders from the clerks who receive them by telephone to the brokers in the trading ring, and then carry confirmations of the trades back to the telephone clerks. Sellers cry out offers while the buyers yell out bids. In order to be heard and seen, the traders yell, gesture wildly, and jump in the air. If two of them can both hear and see each other and agree on a price and quantity, then the cry of "Sold!" or "Done!" will echo out from the floor. Each seller must then immediately record the completed transaction on a card and fling it into the center of the trading ring within one minute of the completion of the transaction. If the card misses its mark or is late, the trade does not count. The pit card clocker sits in the center of the trading ring wearing protective eye goggles to guard against the flying cards. The clocker time-stamps each card, which is then rushed to the data entry room, where operators key the data into the central computer system. NYMEX employees nearby, dressed in bright yellow jackets, use handheld computers to transmit the trades to the media and private data collection services in real time.[13]

The opening bell rings at 10 A.M. and trading ends at 2:30 P.M. "It's like if you spent four hours on a football field or a basketball court," energy trader Eric Bolling explained to a reporter. Another trader had a double hernia operation that he blamed on trading; the larger of the two hernias was on the left side, where he was pushed most often. Certain world events can intensify the already chaotic trading floor. Bolling, for example, described how he lost a shirtsleeve on the trading floor during the first U.S. invasion of Iraq.[14]

When the physical floor closes, trading continues on the NYMEX electronic exchange, which facilitates online trading. In fact, the traders' antics are becoming antiquated as the online trading world replaces NYMEX's physical floor. Approximately 122 million of the 313 million trades taking place on NYMEX's virtual and physical floors in 2007 were trades in crude oil futures contracts. A futures contract is an agreement to make or take delivery of a product in the future, at a price set in the present. There are essentially three reasons to enter into a futures contract: to lock in a set price for a good you want delivered in the future, to make sure you have the money to pay for a good you are buying in the future, or simply to make money.

Hedges

Rather than face the chance that prices will get higher in the future, the buyer of a futures contract—let's say a small independent oil refinery—knows that it has a guaranteed supply of crude oil coming, and the price for that oil will not change between today and the time of delivery. The price is set regardless of what happens in the market in the future, including a rise in price. The seller—let's say Chevron—knows that it has a guaranteed buyer at a set price. The price is set whether the refinery could find a better deal from another oil company or the market price for crude declines by the time of delivery. In this example, the futures market locked in the current price for future delivery and reduced the risk associated with a volatile market. This is called a hedge, literally a "means to protect against losses."

Less than 1 percent of crude oil and gasoline (or any other product) physically changes hands through futures contracts. Instead, most crude and gasoline changes hands through regular commercial contracts between the buyer and seller. The remaining oil and gas changes hands on the spot market.

For almost as long as oil has been traded, there has been a spot market, which is literally a location where actual oil is traded "on the spot." The first spot was Rotterdam, a port city in the Netherlands, where oil from the Middle East arrived (and still arrives) for European delivery. Singapore and Dubai are key spots. The main spot in the United States is Cushing, Oklahoma, located just about dead center in the middle of the country. On its face, Cushing appears to be just like any other sleepy town in the flatlands of central Oklahoma: downtown has just one bar, the Buckhorn, and the movie theater near City Hall sells tickets for $1.50, $2.00 on weekends.[15] What makes Cushing unique is that whereas most small towns in Oklahoma are surrounded by rolling fields of wheat and corn, Cushing is surrounded by rows of giant oil storage tanks, miles of pipeline, and truck depots that appear to outnumber the town's nine thousand residents, one thousand of whom reside in the local prison. Visitors entering Cushing are met with a giant sign constructed of old oil pipes, which reads "CUSHING OKLA. PIPELINE CROSSROADS OF THE WORLD." It is the key junction where physical oil changes hands in the United States.

The spot market is generally used to address short-term supply or demand needs of companies. If a company temporarily has more supply than it can refine into gasoline, for example, it will offer some for sale in the spot market. Likewise, if a company suddenly comes up short in a given month, it will purchase oil on the spot, on a cargo-by-cargo, shipment-by-shipment basis. The spot market price for crude oil is the amount charged for an immediate, onetime delivery of crude.

While physical crude changes hands on the spot market, money changes hands on the futures market. Rather than trade the good and the money "on the spot," the deal is pushed into the future. The astronomical and ever-rising number of trades now taking place on the futures market makes it the primary determinant of the global price of a barrel of oil today.

Oil companies, refineries, public utilities, and other users of goods have traditionally used futures markets to ensure that they will have the money to cover the cost of the price changes associated with these volatile markets. Let's say that I buy gasoline for the city of San Francisco. I have a commercial contract with the Chevron refinery in Richmond, California. Chevron agrees to deliver 1,000 gallons of gasoline to me in four months. The amount I pay to Chevron will then be determined by the market price for gas at the time of delivery. When I sign the contract in January, I am very concerned about whether the price of gas will rise by the time I have to pay for it in May. To ensure that I'll have the money if the price rises, I simultaneously hire an energy trader to purchase a gasoline futures contract. The amount of gasoline the trader buys with the futures contract is identical to the amount of gas I bought with the commercial contract for physical delivery. When May rolls around, if the price of gasoline has gone up, the energy trader will sell the futures contract at a profit, and I will use the profit to pay Chevron for the physical gasoline. Thus, the futures contract provides risk insurance. The city will have the extra money it needs to pay Chevron if the price of gas rises.

The hedge is ultimately a zero-sum transaction used in markets with volatile prices. In this example, the buyer was protected from prices rising at the time of delivery. Similarly, the hedge can be used to protect the seller from prices dropping at the time of delivery. "Because of the hedging ability the dual market provides," Andrew Scott, head of Chevron's oil trading operation in Stamford, Connecticut, explained in 1991, "if George Bush says we're going to war or we're signing a peace treaty, I'm protected if the price moves $5 to $10 a barrel."[16]

Speculators

Now here's where it gets interesting. Futures markets always attract *speculators*—those who set out to make money from market fluctuations. Anyone involved in a trade to make money, rather than to hedge, is a speculator. A speculative transaction is one in which the trader has absolutely no desire to take hold of a barrel of oil or a gallon of gasoline at the end of the trade. Instead, the speculator enters the trade to bet on which direction the market will go. The speculator buys futures contracts with the full intention of selling them prior to the physical delivery date and cashing out the deal. The crude oil or gasoline in a futures contract may change owners literally hundreds, if not thousands, of times. The speculator makes money from the sales, resales, and purchases of the futures contracts, not the actual selling of the crude oil or gasoline.

Speculators are theoretically good for the market because they provide a steady cash flow. But they also increase and thrive off volatility—prices that constantly move rather than remain stable. The greater the volatility, the greater the profit made when, for example, the speculator buys low and sells high. But greater volatility also means greater risk. Thus, speculators usually have a lot of money to burn and come with large bankrolls. They tend to be banks, large corporations, or the misleadingly named "hedge funds." Hedge funds combine lots of investors' money. They enter the market to make money, not to hedge prices. Pension funds are increasingly moving into the futures markets for crude oil, gasoline, and other energy commodities, often with disastrous results.

Over the years, market speculators have earned bad reputations. They have a disturbing tendency to make money out of other people's misery. Simply put, the more prices spike or dive, the more money speculators make. These sharp changes also lead directly to catastrophe in many people's lives. Thus, enormous profits were made by those who played their cards right in the crude oil and gasoline futures markets when hurricanes Katrina and Rita hit, when the United States invaded Iraq, and when terrorists attacked the United States on September 11, 2001. Each of these events caused a sudden large drop in supply, which pushed the value of crude and gasoline up and increased the value of the futures contracts held by the energy traders.

Another reason for their bad reputations is that the temptation is always ripe for speculators to try to make prices move in a particular direction, rather than just sit idly by and hope that their guesses prove correct. When the market for home mortgages, grain, gasoline, or electricity is manipulated, people's lives are thrown into turmoil throughout the economy. Speculators then profit from the suffering they have helped to create. Take Enron as an example: the company not only made money from the California energy crisis, but actually created the crisis through the actions of its energy traders. Of course, Enron did not invent market manipulation or profiting from the suffering of others. The temptation has always been there, as have the devastating real-world consequences.

After a series of disastrous price manipulations hit NYMEX and its sister trading facility in Chicago in the 1920s, the federal government began to regulate the futures market, seeking to prevent fraud, abuse, and manipulation. But as with all other areas of government regulation, for as long as the government has sought to oversee futures trades, the traders have been trying to get the government off their backs.

Regulating Futures Markets

Grain merchants created the futures contract in 1865 at the Chicago Board of Trade. A few years later, New York dairy merchants formed the Butter and Cheese Exchange of New York. By 1882, the Butter and Cheese Exchange had outgrown its name and become the New York Mercantile Exchange. This was the early heyday of the corporate trusts, when corporate America's concentrated wealth and dominant power ruled over the U.S. government. The government allowed these companies to operate with a free and open hand, and the futures markets were no exception. Thus, the government did not regulate either operation. As the markets expanded into virtually every agricultural commodity and added futures trading, the speculators took over and market manipulation soon followed.

"[T]he frequent picture of commodity exchanges was one of unbridled speculation, recurrent market manipulations, and spectacular price fluctuations," reported an investigation of the early futures markets by the Senate Committee on Agriculture, Nutrition, and Forestry in 1982.[17] The speculators—generally large companies and banks—got rich, while farmers and everyone who relied on them went bankrupt, and the entire national economy was routinely imperiled. The futures markets quickly became part and parcel of the larger problem of corporate trusts. The "shenanigans that took place year in and year out [in the futures markets] . . . fed into the populist resentment against the trusts, banks, and other large corporate interests toward the end of the century," reports historian Dan Morgan in *Merchants of Grain*.[18]

Following World War I, grain speculators cornered the Chicago Board of Trade futures market, buying up enough grain to restrict supply and send the price skyrocketing. When they then sold off their grain to take their profit, the bubble was burst, and the price of grain plummeted, contributing significantly to one of the greatest crashes in U.S. farm history. Farmers across the country were thrown into poverty. But this was also a time of tremendous organized resistance, so the nation's farmers joined together and demanded action. Some called for the complete closure of the futures markets. Congress responded with regulation. The result was the Grain Futures Act of 1922 and the subsequent Commodity Exchange Act of 1936, which established much of the legal framework for the regulation of futures markets in effect today.

In 1974 Congress created the Commodity Futures Trading Commission (CFTC) as the government agency tasked with regulating futures markets. The CFTC's authority was weak, however. It immediately proved inadequate to the task at hand with the Great Potato Default of 1976. From World War II on, the Maine potato emerged as the mainstay of NYMEX. A full 80 percent of NYMEX's membership was in the potato business as late as 1976, when potato speculators overran NYMEX and promptly defaulted on $4 million worth of contracts. NYMEX was unable to make good on one thousand contracts for nearly 50 million pounds of potatoes in May 1976. The default cost Maine farmers $2 million and the NYMEX a great deal of its reputation.[19] Some openly questioned whether the speculators, J. R. Simplot, the "Idaho Potato King," and his associate P. J. Taggares, had actually intended to break the exchange.[20] If so, they almost succeeded. It was the biggest default in commodity futures history at the time. When the NYMEX was unable to provide either payments to the Maine potato farmers or potatoes to the buyers, the entire raison d'être of the exchange was thrown into question.

The potato default once again reminded the nation that manipulation goes hand in hand with futures markets, and the CFTC's regulatory oversight over NYMEX was tightened. Just five years later, the exchange that had nearly been taken down by the potato moved into a far more important and volatile commodity: oil.

The Futures Market for Crude Oil

*I always believed that energy futures would ultimately
succeed and replace the OPEC pricing mechanism.*
—MICHEL MARKS, FORMER CHAIRMAN, NYMEX[21]

In January 1981, within days of taking office, President Ronald
Reagan took the U.S. government out of the business of subsidizing small oil refineries and setting price and allocation controls
for gasoline and crude oil. The end of federal regulation opened
the door to energy futures trading. Just eight months later, in
October 1981, gasoline futures were introduced on the NYMEX,
and crude oil futures arrived two years later.

At first Big Oil was skeptical and even resistant to the introduction of crude oil futures contracts. The companies surely hoped
that eventually they would regain control of enough crude to set
prices unilaterally. They were also most likely not enthusiastic
about making the process of setting the price of oil so thoroughly
public. Whatever the reasons for their initial resistance, the realization that the futures market had the potential to eliminate
OPEC's authority over oil prices must have ultimately persuaded
Big Oil to play along. "The crude oil futures contract would reso-
lutely undermine OPEC's price-setting powers," writes Daniel Yergin in *The Prize*.[22] Consequently, Big Oil kept its hand in the
development of the futures market from the outset.

NYMEX chairman Michel Marks was the force behind the
creation of the modern crude oil futures contract. According to
Marks, NYMEX began developing relationships with "key oil
industry players" in 1982 while preparing the crude oil contract.
NYMEX had also established a petroleum advisory committee
composed of industry experts and representatives.[23] The *Financial Times* of London reported on the heavy involvement of the
oil industry in the development of the crude oil futures contract:
"Most observers agree that it is the support of the oil industry
which has enabled NYMEX to dominate the energy futures

market." As Marks told the paper, "I don't know much about oil; to make money is our function as a broker. So I seek the advice of professionals in the industry." He emphasized a "continuing dialogue between the oil industry and the exchange" as the central feature of NYMEX's development policy.[24]

NYMEX's first demonstration that it had replaced OPEC as the setter of global crude oil prices came in 1984. In October, OPEC tried to raise the price of crude oil by lowering production quotas. NYMEX traders did not budge, and the price for crude oil did not waver on the trading floor. OPEC officials continued to declare that prices would rise. Instead, the cost of oil futures on NYMEX fell. By December, futures prices were 5 percent lower than at the time of the original OPEC announcement. OPEC was simply unable to set the price of oil. "The Merc [NYMEX] has become the new benchmark for oil," commented Gary M. Becker in 1984, director of the Paine Webber Energy Futures Group.[25] Within three weeks, crude oil futures achieved the most rapidly expanding growth of any previous energy contract. Within a year, newspapers reported that "all five major oil companies" were participating in the futures trade.[26] Trading grew by 500 percent after the first year and by over 2,500 percent by 1988.[27]

All the major oil companies participated in the futures market, though some more than others. BP, which lost a full 40 percent of its reserves due to the OPEC nationalizations (particularly in Iran), was the first to see futures trading as a unique opportunity to turn a profit. It quickly established futures trading as a separate profit-making enterprise for the company and has led the way in speculative trading ever since.[28] Mobil and Texaco were reportedly larger speculative players than Exxon and Chevron in the early days.[29] This may well be due to the fact that they were economically weaker companies, which is also why Exxon and Chevron later bought them up.

While Big Oil celebrated the elimination of OPEC's price-setting powers, the companies' main problem with the futures market was the transparency of it all, including those pesky government regulators standing between the companies and their oil trades. By the early 1990s, Big Oil had had enough and went in search of a way to get the government and the public out of their trades. To do so, Big Oil teamed up with an expert: Enron.

DEREGULATION

Let's say you like idea of trading in crude oil futures, and you even like the idea of these trades ultimately determining the overall price of crude. But let's also say you would rather that the federal government and the public did not watch the deals you conducted. What would you do? You would use your economic and political influence to get the federal government to agree to weaken its own oversight capabilities over your trades. That is exactly what the major oil companies, banks, and Enron did.

Mobil, Conoco, Phillips, BP North America, Enron, Koch Industries, Coastal Corporation, Phibro Energy, and J. Aron & Company began the process of deregulating energy futures trading with a joint letter delivered to the Commodity Futures Trading Commission (CFTC) in November 1992.[30]

Koch Industries is one of the nation's largest privately held oil production and trading companies and a top contributor to both ultraconservative causes and Republican political candidates. Phibro Energy is an oil futures trading company, now a subsidiary of Citigroup. J. Aron & Company is Goldman Sachs's trading unit. If Coastal Corporation sounds familiar, it is most likely because company founder and CEO Oscar Wyatt pled guilty in 2007 to funneling $200,000 in illegal kickbacks to Saddam Hussein as part of the oil-for-food scandal. Wyatt made the payments in 2001, just before selling his Coastal Corporation to the El Paso Corporation. One witness testified that Hussein personally told Wyatt that he was among Iraq's few friends during the years of sanctions. Fearing a twenty-year jail sentence and even potential charges of treason, the eighty-three-year-old Wyatt stopped his trial by pleading guilty to one count of fraud and conspiracy.[31]

The signatories to the joint CFTC letter call themselves the "Energy Group," and the letter is a formal petition to the CFTC to remove from its purview certain key energy futures contracts, allowing them to take place off the NYMEX or any other regulated exchange. Mobil, Conoco, Enron, and any large company would henceforth be allowed to trade energy futures contracts among themselves without government regulation.[32]

Exxon, the American Petroleum Institute (the oil industry's preeminent lobbying organization), J. P. Morgan, Morgan Stanley, and Chase Manhattan Bank all submitted their own individual letters to the CFTC in support of the Energy Group's application.[33]

The Energy Group's request was highly controversial. It came on the heels of a 1990 district court ruling that Exxon, Conoco, BP, and Shell had conspired to lower the market price of crude oil sold in Europe by using crude oil futures contracts. The companies sought lower crude prices in order to reduce the taxes they paid for European oil production. The court found that the oil companies pulled off the conspiracy by evading government regulation through using a different name for the contracts— "forward" rather than "futures" contracts. Whatever the oil companies chose to call the deals, the court argued, they were in fact futures contracts and therefore belonged under the CFTC's regulatory authority.[34]

All the companies ultimately settled the charges against them. Then, in 1992, some of the companies formed the Energy Group, turned to the CFTC, and asked it to rule that these trades be called "swaps," not crude oil futures contracts, and that the trades be exempted from the CFTC's oversight. The CFTC agreed.

In May 2007, Tyson Slocum, energy program director at Public Citizen and a leading authority on the inner workings of the

U.S. oil industry, described in congressional testimony the outcry of opposition that immediately met the CFTC's energy trading deregulation. Congressman Glen English, then chairman of the House committee with jurisdiction over the CFTC, protested, "In my eighteen years in Congress [the deregulation] is the most irresponsible decision I have come across." He argued that the ruling prevented the CFTC from doing its job even in cases of outright fraud. CFTC commissioner Sheila Bair dissented from the decision, arguing that the deregulation set "a dangerous precedent." A U.S. General Accounting Office report issued a year later urged Congress to increase regulatory oversight over these contracts, and a congressional inquiry found that CFTC's own staff analysts and economists believed that they had not had an adequate opportunity to review the rule before it was passed.[35]

Why would a government agency choose to reduce its own regulatory authority? The answer lies in the same deregulatory wave that struck the Federal Trade Commission (FTC) in the 1980s, and at the feet of the CFTC's chairwoman at the time, Wendy Gramm.

"I guess I'm the regulatory czarina," joked Wendy Gramm in 1985.[36] Until Enron largely ended her political career, she was riding high on President Reagan's deregulatory wave. With a Ph.D. in economics, Gramm worked closely with all of Reagan's key corporate champions. She was the director of the FTC's Bureau of Economics, where she worked side by side with FTC chairman James Miller. She briefly went over to the Office of Management and Budget, where she worked with Reagan's supply-side economics guru David Stockman. She then took the helm of the administration's most important deregulatory arm as executive director of Reagan's Presidential Task Force on Regulatory Relief. But the position that really stuck for Gramm was as chairwoman of the CFTC. She was appointed in 1988 and held the position throughout the George H. W. Bush administration. With the election of Bill Clinton in 1992, however, Gramm's days at the CFTC were numbered.

On the final day of the Bush administration, January 21, 1993, Wendy Gramm enacted the Energy Group's request. The CFTC approved the rule exempting key energy futures contracts from government regulation and returned a giant chunk of the energy market to the grand old days of unregulated futures trading. Six days later, Gramm resigned. Barely one month after resigning, she joined Enron's board of directors.

The Enron Loophole

At 10:00 P.M. on December 12, 2000, the Supreme Court appointed George W. Bush president of the United States. Two days later, in the final days of a lame duck session of Congress, Senator Phil Gramm took over where his wife had left off.

Texas Republican senator Phil Gramm is one of the all-time top recipients of oil and gas industry campaign contributions in U.S. history. All the giants supported Gramm, but Enron led the pack. In fact, after George W. Bush and Texas senator Kay Bailey Hutchison, no elected official received more in campaign contributions from Enron than did Phil Gramm.[37] Enron's Ken Lay even served as the regional chairman of Gramm's unsuccessful campaign for the Republican presidential nomination in 1996. Phil's wife, Wendy Gramm, served on Enron's board from 1993 until 2002 and sat on Enron's audit committee. She was therefore one of the directors responsible for Enron's financial reporting. It was the revelation of Enron's illegal accounting methods that ultimately broke the company and led to its financial collapse. It is estimated that Wendy Gramm was paid nearly $2 million in salary, attendance fees, stock options, and dividends for her service on Enron's board.[38] Under the haze of his wife's and his own Enron scandals, Gramm retired from twenty-four years in the Senate in 2002 and went on to become a vice president at UBS bank.

In 1999 the Energy Group organized again to retain and expand the CFTC rule. Without any congressional hearings or debate, or any public notice, on December 12, 2000, Phil Gramm slipped what would forever be referred to as the "Enron Loop-hole" into the 262-page Commodity Futures Modernization Act, of which he was a sponsor. The act was then belatedly but quite suddenly attached to the 11,000-page omnibus appropriations bill that was passed into law by Congress and signed by President Clinton.

Gramm codified his wife's earlier rules into federal law and then went further. Instead of just exempting certain energy futures *contracts*, including swaps and over-the-counter trades, from federal regulation, the Commodity Futures Modernization Act allowed energy traders to establish their own *exchanges* on which to trade these contracts and then exempted the exchanges in their entirety from government regulation. Instead of using the regulated NYMEX, they could trade between themselves or on other exchanges without being subject to government regulation.

The loophole was implemented over the express and emphatic opposition of the President's Working Group on Financial Markets, which included Treasury Secretary Lawrence Summers, Federal Reserve Chairman Alan Greenspan, Chairman of the Securities and Exchange Commission Arthur Levitt, and CFTC Chairman William Rainer. The Working Group released a report one year before Gramm slipped the loophole into his bill, arguing against just such deregulation.[39]

Among those lobbying on behalf of the loophole was the Energy Group, which in 1999 included Mobil, BP America, Enron, J. Aron & Company, Koch Industries, Phibro, and the Sempra Energy Trading Corporation.[40]

There were two immediate beneficiaries of the loophole: the Intercontinental Exchange and Enron. In May 2000, just months before the Commodity Futures Modernization Act became law, several oil companies and banks came together in Atlanta to form their own futures exchange. The resulting Intercontinental Exchange (with the appropriately ominous acronym ICE) is their own privately held futures exchange specializing in the very trades that Wendy Gramm deemed outside the CFTC's jurisdiction and that Phil Gramm codified into federal law as immune from government oversight: "over-the-counter" energy trades.

ICE was founded and is now largely owned by BP, Shell, TotalFinaElf, Goldman Sachs, and Morgan Stanley, among others.[41] While ICE also trades agricultural and other energy commodities, it was intended as a trading platform for crude oil. By the end of its first year, almost 70 percent of all futures contracts traded on the ICE were for crude oil. By 2006, the percentage had grown to nearly 80 percent, and the number of crude oil futures contracts traded on the ICE surpassed the number traded on the NYMEX.

Intercontinental Exchange Over the-Counter (ICE OTC) is thus an energy futures exchange operating completely outside of U.S. government regulation, just as the original Chicago Board of Trade and the Butter and Cheese Exchange of New York operated more than one hundred years ago. As the exchange states on its Web site: "ICE operates its OTC electronic platform as an exempt commercial market under the Commodity Exchange Act and regulations of the Commodity Futures Trading Commission, or CFTC."

A special investigation by the Senate concluded in 2007 that "the Enron Loophole . . . that exempts key energy commodities from government oversight . . . [has] resulted in the irrational situation in which one key U.S. energy exchange, the NYMEX, is subject to extensive regulatory oversight and obligations to ensure fair and orderly trading and to prevent excessive speculation, while another key energy exchange, ICE, operates with no regulatory oversight, no obligation to ensure its products are traded in a fair and orderly manner, and no obligation to prevent excessive speculation."[42]

Anyone uncertain as to the potential risk inherent in the deregulation of energy futures need look no further than the second major beneficiary of the Enron Loophole: Enron.

Enron's West Coast Pillage

It was the traders' job to make money, not to benefit the people of California.

—FORMER ENRON EXECUTIVE[43]

When the Enron Loophole was codified in 2000, Enron had already established the expertise and infrastructure to move all of its electricity and other energy futures trades to unregulated exchanges, including its very own online energy futures exchange, the aptly named Enron Online. The California and West Coast energy crisis was its first grand accomplishment.

From 2000 to 2002, Enron's energy traders intentionally and successfully drove up the price of electricity in California and across the West Coast through manipulation of the energy market. "Yes, we moved markets," bragged one Enron trader. "We wanted that sucker up, it went up." The attitude was "Play by your own rules," explained another Enron trader. "We all did it. We talked about it openly. It was the schoolyard we lived in. The energy markets were new, immature, unsupervised. We took pride in getting around the rules. It was a game."[44]

The company utilized eleven strategies in all, with ominous names like "Death Star" and "Fat Boy," designed to manipulate the energy markets by creating a false scarcity in electricity to drive up prices. Because Enron's trades were taking place on its own unregulated exchange, no one knew the full extent of what Enron was up to until it was far too late.

One internal Enron memo from 1999 demonstrates the company's ruthless approach to gaming California's energy market: "The Contemplated Transaction, though questionable on business, political, and social grounds, does not appear to be prohibited under current law. Moreover, even if the Contemplated Transaction is illegal under current law, it is highly unlikely that any prosecution would be successful, for want of necessary evidence."[45]

The evidence would be "wanting" because the transactions were taking place completely outside of the purview of government regulation thanks to the Enron Loophole.

As a result of the false scarcity of electricity and the rising prices created by Enron, people throughout the West encountered rolling blackouts—the first in California since World War II—and high electricity bills that many could not afford to pay. The blackouts closed down schools and businesses and threatened the health of the young, elderly, and infirm, who lost access to electricity and air-conditioning as temperatures exceeded 100 degrees Fahrenheit. Across the West, businesses closed down because their owners were unable to pay their energy bills, tens of thousands of people lost their jobs, California alone lost tens of billions of dollars, and the state's two largest public utilities declared bankruptcy. In 1999 Californians paid $7.4 billion for wholesale electricity; one year later, these costs rose 277 percent to $27.1 billion.[46]

Meanwhile, Enron raked in the profits. In just four months in the summer of 2000, Enron's West Coast energy traders brought in $200 million—roughly *four times* the profit they had made in all of 1999.[47]

"The 'Enron loophole' almost immediately caused havoc in energy markets," concluded Michael Greenberger, CFTC division director from 1997 to 1999, in a 2007 Senate hearing. "It is now beyond doubt that manipulation of futures and derivatives contracts pursuant to that loophole dramatically increased the market price of electricity in the Western United States during 2001–2002." Greenberger's assessment of the CFTC's actions was particularly harsh: "Only after [the internal Enron] memos were uncovered in April–May 2002 did the CFTC begin serious investigations into these markets. Prior to that time, that agency's leadership was assuring Congress and the public (as it is today in the case of soaring gas prices) that the rising price of electricity was purely a matter of market fundamentals."[48]

The Bush administration certainly was in no mood to step in

to stop Enron. Both the company and its top officers were George W. Bush's single greatest career campaign contributor.[49] Energy Secretary Spencer Abraham dismissed claims of Enron price manipulation as "myths." Vice President Cheney decried "politicians who want to go out and blame somebody and allege that there is some kind of conspiracy."[50] The CFTC persistently declared that supply and demand, not market manipulation, was driving the rising cost of electricity. At times the resistance to uncovering Enron's schemes seemed nearly as intense from outside the company as from within.

Fortunately, the so-called conspiracy theorists were not easily dissuaded. Week in and week out, month after month, protestors came out in San Francisco, San Diego, Los Angeles, Sacramento, Portland, and Seattle to decry Enron's intentional manipulation of the West Coast electricity market. As police dragged one protestor, Joel Tena, out of a California Public Utilities Commission hearing in 2001, Tena expressed the frustration of people across the state: "You no longer represent the public! You represent big business! You are cronies for the corporations!" Fellow protestor Lellingby Boyce, a retired Oakland schoolteacher, got the hearing attendees to join her in song. Among its lyrics: "It's clear to us consumers we're the jokers getting screwed. I'm reading now by candlelight, wrapped in blankets day and night."[51]

During another 2001 protest, Mary Bull, a small woman in a giant handmade papier-mâché penny costume, stood in front of San Francisco's federal building, "NOT ONE PENNY MORE!" boldly written across the penny's midsection. Human rights activist Medea Benjamin of the San Francisco–based organization Global Exchange joined with protestors at California governor Gray Davis's office demanding that private companies be taken out of the equation altogether: "We've got 10,000 signatures from people who are refusing to pay the electric rate hikes. Our message is simple: no rate hikes, no bailouts. We need public power now."[52] Eva Skoufis joined the protests because her energy bill for the coin laundry she ran in San Francisco tripled in just a matter of months. Having moved from Greece in 1968, Skoufis was furious as she told a reporter, "I came from one dictatorship. Now I face a capitalistic dictatorship. I want to believe that democracy in this country works."[53]

The pundits scoffed at the protestors. Reciting a refrain commonly used nowadays in response to rising gasoline and oil prices, they declared that it was pure market fundamentals driving the energy crisis, not greedy corporations. *Washington Post* columnist Charles Krauthammer wrote that, while childish Californians "think that the rolling blackouts are a conspiracy by the power companies to raise rates" and "politicians are thundering, fingers are wagging, and complicated theories are being hatched," the problem is simply that "demand is up and supply is down."[54]

As prices rose and the protests continued, the press dug deeper. Elected officials increasingly demanded that federal regulators take action. There was a complete lack of publicly available information as to exactly what Enron was up to. Thanks to deregulation, only by launching a formal investigation could even government regulators get their hands on the necessary information. Finally, two years after the manipulations began, the Bush administration launched an investigation and uncovered Enron's intentional and merciless effort to reduce the supply and raise the price of electricity.

Enron not only gamed the West Coast energy market, but it also conned its stockholders by fraudulently inflating the value of the company. When its various scams came to light in 2001, the company declared bankruptcy and has since all but shut its doors. All that is left is the Enron Creditors Recovery Corporation, a shell company settling claims and litigation. More than 5,500 Enron employees lost their jobs, while more than 20,000 remain in legal proceedings trying to recover lost pensions.[55]

Enron's former executives have not been spared. Among four of the most prominent executives, two are in federal prisons, and two have died. Former CEO Jeffrey Skilling is serving a prison term of twenty-four years and four months in Waseca, Minnesota.

Skilling is appealing his conviction of nineteen counts of fraud, conspiracy, insider trading, and lying to auditors. Former CFO Andrew Fastow is in a federal prison in Louisiana, about 200 miles from Houston. He is serving a six-year prison term after pleading guilty to two counts of conspiracy. Kenneth Lay, Enron's founder and president, died of a heart attack just weeks after a jury convicted him of conspiracy and fraud. He was expected to face twenty-five years or more in prison. Vice Chairman J. Cliff Baxter was found in his black Mercedes sedan with a gunshot wound to his head and a .38-caliber revolver at his side, having committed suicide on January 25, 2002, before any trial against him began.

Enron's former energy traders have faired much better. Not only were they not sent to prison, but their skills have translated readily from the electricity trade to the crude oil, gasoline, and natural gas trades. Alas, while much has changed since Enron's demise, the Enron Loophole remains completely untouched. And nobody knows how to work the loophole better than Enron's former energy traders.

FROM ELECTRICITY TO OIL—ENRON KEEPS TRADING

These are markets that can and are being manipulated easily. They need to be regulated in the same way that gambling casinos are regulated.

—MICHAEL GREENBERGER, CFTC DIVISION
DIRECTOR, 1997–1999[56]

Chevron hopes the building will one day be known as "1500 Louisiana." But everyone in Houston still calls it "the Enron building." It is a huge, garish, 1.2-million-square-foot, forty-story, glass-towered building looming over Houston's downtown. An elevated circular walkway made of concrete and glass hovers menacingly above the sidewalks and roadway. The walkway connects 1500 Louisiana directly to Enron's infamous former main building—the one that had the now iconic giant crooked glass *E* perched on its lawn. Enron built the new building for $260 million, complete with an 11,000-square-foot cafeteria, but went bankrupt before ever moving in.[57] The building sat empty until Chevron arrived in 2004, flush with cash from two straight years of the highest profits in its own 125-year corporate history, driven largely by the skyrocketing price of crude oil. Chevron not only bought Enron's building, but also hired many former Enron energy traders.[58]

Since the introduction of the Enron Loophole, trading in oil and gas is booming—growing twice as fast as during Enron's reign.[59] Energy traders are hot commodities, pulling in on average salaries of $5 million to $15 million, some even larger than those of the CEOs who hire them. Houston, in turn, is the lead recruiting base for traders, as "it is home to many . . . traders trained by the former Enron Corp.," writes the *Wall Street Journal*'s Ann Davis.[60]

Enron's former energy traders are working for oil companies like Chevron and at the nation's largest banks, and operating their own multibillion-dollar hedge funds. UBS bank, where Phil Gramm became a vice president after leaving the Senate, purchased Enron's entire online-trading unit, replete with 630 employees, in February 2002, just months after Enron's collapse.[61] Barclay's Bank of London hired twenty-six former Enron traders in 2004.[62] Garnering the number one spot on *Trader Monthly* magazine's "Top 100 Traders for 2006" was John Arnold, age thirty-three, a former Enron energy trader who made an estimated $1.5 billion to $2 billion in 2006 in personal income on his natural gas trades alone. It is "the largest sum, we believe, [any trader] has ever earned in one year," gushed the magazine's editors.

While energy trading has taken off on the regulated NYMEX, it has skyrocketed on the unregulated ICE, with ICE replacing NYMEX in 2006 as the home to the majority of crude oil futures trades. The volume of energy futures trading on

NYMEX increased by some 160 percent from 2000 (the year the Enron Loophole was introduced) to 2006. The number of these trades more than doubled, from approximately 73 million to more than 190 million. The number of crude oil futures contracts increased by more than 90 percent, from 37 million in 2001 to more than 70 million in 2006.[63] Economist Philip Verleger estimates that as much as $60 billion was invested in NYMEX crude oil futures contracts from 2004 to 2006 alone.[64]

Energy trading on ICE ballooned by more than 270 percent from 2000 to 2006, increasing from about 25 million trades to well over 90 million. The number of crude oil futures contracts traded on ICE increased by a staggering 322 percent between 2000 and 2006, and by 140 percent from 2005 and 2006 alone. In 2006, while roughly 71 million crude oil futures contracts were traded on NYMEX, 73 million traded hands on ICE.[65]

"This explosion in unregulated trading volume means that more trading is done behind closed doors out of reach of federal regulators," argues Public Citizen's Slocum, "increasing the chances of oil companies and financial firms to engage in anti-competitive practices."[66]

"Growth in our industry is certainly exceeding the ability of the regulators to get their heads around it," admits the chairman and CEO of ICE, Jeffrey Sprecher.[67]

ICE has increased its profits in every year since it opened, and 2007 was no exception. Its third-quarter 2007 profits were a full 60 percent higher than its third-quarter profits in 2006. ICE attributes this profit explosion to its over-the-counter unregulated operations.[68]

The impact of all of this trading, both regulated and not, is to increase the demand for crude and to drive the price ever higher. The market is blind to the intent of a purchase. It makes no difference if the barrel is sold for future or immediate delivery, or if the buyer will ever use the barrel. Nor does it matter if the buyer is a refinery in Richmond, the government of Japan, a Marathon energy trader, a banker in Buffalo, or a retiree in San Diego whose pension is invested by a hedge fund. Each barrel sold is a barrel added to demand. The more the demand rises, the more the price rises. The higher the price rises, the more speculators pour into the market. The more speculators, the more demand, and around and around—or rather—up and up we go. But the price increase has absolutely nothing to do with actual supply and therefore is not a reflection of supply and demand fundamentals.

"Are investment funds adding to the price of crude oil? Yes," argues James Cordier, president of Liberty Trading Group, a futures trader in Tampa, Florida. "People do not invest in commodities to bet on prices to go down."[69]

Cordier's assessment is representative of the view held by the majority of industry experts. Tim Evans, senior analyst at IFR Energy Services, finds, "What you have on the financial side is a bunch of money being thrown at the energy futures market. It's just pulling in more and more cash. That's the side of the market where we have runaway demand, not on the physical side."[70]

"The answer to the puzzle posed by rising prices and inventories, industry analysts say, lies not only in supply constraints such as the war in Iraq and civil unrest in Nigeria and the broad upswing in demand caused by industrialization of China and India. Increasingly, they say, prices also are being guided by a continuing rush of investor funds in commodities investments," reports the *Wall Street Journal*.[71]

"It's all about futures speculators shooting for irrational price objectives, as well as trying to out-think other players—sort of like a twisted game of chess," one energy trader told *Natural Gas Week*. "[T]he basic facts are clear, this market is purely and simply being controlled by over-speculation."[72]

"Factors other than supply and demand are now impacting the price," contends oil-and-gas trader Stephen Schork, who publishes the *Schork Report* on energy markets. "We now have to factor in how the speculators are going to affect the market, because they have different priorities in managing their portfolios."[73]

Combining the expertise of these and other analysts, including leading oil economist Philip Verleger, the Senate Permanent Subcommittee on Investigations concluded in 2006 that speculative purchases of oil futures alone accounted for more than a quarter of the price of a barrel of crude.[74] Other analysts believe the figure is much higher. Commenting on oil reaching $104 per barrel in March 2008, George Littell, an analyst with Groppe, Long & Littell in Houston, said, "This has gone beyond reason," and argued that oil should be trading in the range of $60 per barrel, $44 less than the current price.[75] Similarly, Fadel Gheit, managing director and senior oil analyst at Oppenheimer & Co., told a Senate hearing in December 2007 that the price of oil is "inflated by as much as 100%."[76]

Regulation of this trading even on the NYMEX is becoming more difficult as trades move off the physical trading floor and online. In September 2006, 80 percent of NYMEX crude oil futures trades were taking place on the trading floor. By March 2007, the percentage ratio had reversed, with 80 percent of trades taking place online.[77] Simply keeping up with the pace of trades is extremely difficult for the understaffed and underfunded CFTC. Moreover, online trades are proving inherently more difficult to regulate than trades on the physical floor because it is often difficult to clearly identify the trader behind each trade, the number of trades each trader is engaged in, and how the trades relate to one another.

Moreover, more of the trades are now taking place off the regulated exchanges altogether, either at the ICE or as unregulated swaps between major traders. And more of the trading is pure speculation. Data compiled by the CFTC demonstrates that from approximately 2000 to 2006, the amount of energy trading due to speculation nearly tripled.[78] All of which opens the door to manipulation.

The players ready to walk through that open door are oil companies, banks, and hedge funds.

Big Oil Goes Speculating

With the possible exception of ExxonMobil, all the major oil companies participate directly in speculative energy trading—although they would rather we did not know it. Speculators are once again developing a bad reputation. So if the speculators are largely to blame for the rising price of oil, who are they? The answer to this question is difficult to come by, primarily because of how a *speculator* is defined. The CFTC defines a speculator as someone who "does not produce or use the commodity, but risks his or her own capital trading futures in that commodity in hopes of making a profit on price changes."[79] Put another way, speculators do not use the commodity as part of their business. Any commercial entity with any involvement in the oil industry is not, by definition, a speculator. Therefore, oil companies—and banks, many of which are increasingly moving into the commercial oil business—are always given the benefit of the doubt and are, by definition, let off the speculative hook. How convenient! But it is not only convenient, it is also a ruse to avoid the traditional limits and controls placed on speculative—but not commercial—trades.

The reality is that anyone who buys more in futures contracts than he or she intends to use of the physical contract is inherently taking part in speculation—whatever that person chooses to call it. Big Oil's tax filings, moreover, reveal that each company (again with the possible exception of ExxonMobil) engages in, to use ConocoPhillips's words, "energy trading not directly related to our physical business." The companies report conducting trades and earning profits from swaps and over-the-counter trades as well as on the ICE and the NYMEX.

Shell, Marathon, and BP North America have also been caught trying to use the futures market to manipulate prices. In 2004 Shell agreed to pay nearly $40 million to settle two separate charges of energy market manipulation. In 2005 a Shell subsidiary paid $4 million to settle allegations that it provided false information during a federal investigation into market manipulation. And in 2006 the CFTC issued a civil penalty against Shell for "non-competitive transactions" in U.S. crude oil futures markets.[80]

Marathon was charged in June 2007 with attempting to manipulate the price of crude oil illegally and agreed to pay $1 million to settle the charges. Marathon also agreed to cooperate with federal regulators in their ongoing investigation into manipulation of oil markets. Federal regulators warned other companies trying to game the system, "It would be in their best interest to come to us before Uncle Sam comes knocking."[81]

Four months later, an employee of BP was charged with attempting to manipulate the price of gasoline illegally on the NYMEX. Paul Kelly, who worked for BP's North American branch in New York City, agreed to pay $400,000 to settle the charges against him.[82] Shortly after that, BP North America was found guilty by a district court in Illinois of cornering the U.S. propane market "for the purpose of dictating prices . . . in order to obtain a significant trading profit." BP was ordered to pay more than $3 million to settle the charges.[83]

While Big Oil is involved in speculative trading, it does not yet appear to be as major a direct participant in these markets as investment banks and hedge funds. Big Oil does not need to take on as great a risk as these other players, given that it can sit back and enjoy the fruits of its deregulatory lobbying by allowing others to push up the price while the oil companies reap the profits. ExxonMobil, already the most profitable corporation in the world many times over, may have the least to gain by participating in futures speculation. When you earn $40 billion in pure profit, there is little need to enter into risky futures trading speculation. In addition, when your company profits from the speculation whether you actively involve your company in it or not, there is also little need to get involved. ExxonMobil is also notoriously stodgy in its business practices. Change comes to it very slowly, mostly because it is just so darn good at doing what it has always done and sees little need to change. Thus, ExxonMobil is alone in explicitly stating in its 10K SEC tax filing that it does not engage in speculative trading.

Banks as Crude Oil Speculators

The proprietary trading desks of [Goldman Sachs, Bank of America, or Morgan Stanley] and other large investment banks are actually 'hedge funds in drag,' just as Enron was.
—PETER C. FUSARO AND GARY M. VASEY,
INTERNATIONAL RESEARCH CENTER FOR ENERGY AND
ECONOMIC DEVELOPMENT, 2005[84]

Big banks and Big Oil have a lot in common: they have heavily interlocking boards; they lobby together; and they contribute money to many of the same political candidates. They share energy traders, such as Richard Bronks, cohead of global commodities at Goldman Sachs and former energy trader for BP, and Julian Barrowcliffe, a trader at Bank of America, also a former BP trader. They also share corporate titans. For example, John D. Rockefeller Sr.'s grandson David Rockefeller served as arguably one of the most powerful and influential American bankers in history as CEO and chairman of the board of Chase Manhattan Bank from 1969 until his retirement in 1981. It was said of David Rockefeller that he was "the only man for whom the presidency of the United State would be a step down.[85] Big banks and Big Oil also increasingly share the nuts and bolts of the oil business.

As participants in the Energy Group discussed above, the nation's largest investment banks joined Big Oil in the push to remove much of the trading in energy futures from government oversight. The banks have since become some of the largest beneficiaries of this deregulation, particularly as many move directly into the oil business themselves. Moreover, as the banks have lost billions of dollars in the sub-prime mortgage debacle (largely caused by deregulation and market speculation), they are moving more aggressively into energy trading.

The industry leaders are the investment banks Morgan Stanley and Goldman Sachs. While figures are somewhat difficult to come by, Morgan Stanley reported earnings of about $1.5 billion in 2004 and as high as $1.8 billion in 2005—about 6.5 percent of the bank's total revenue—from energy trading alone.[86] The bank's longtime commodities chief, Neal Shear, reportedly made $35 million in total compensation in 2006.[87] Goldman Sachs also reported energy trading earnings of approximately $1.5 billion in 2004, while its overall earnings from commodities trading reached an estimated $3 billion in 2006. Goldman Sachs estimates that pension funds and mutual funds have invested a total of approximately $85 billion in commodity index funds, and that investments in its own Goldman Sachs Commodity Index have tripled over the past few years to $55 billion.[88]

In 2007 Lehman Brothers announced a doubling of its staff devoted to commodity trading, while J. P. Morgan added forty-five new staffers.[89] Citigroup's trading unit, Phibro, generated close to 10 percent of the bank's total net income in 2007. The longtime head of the unit, Andrew Hall, personally took in $125 million in 2005, around five times the amount earned by Charles Prince, who was then Citigroup's chief executive.[90] The banks are also giving their commodities traders more money to play with by risking more of the banks' money. In 2007 Morgan Stanley increased the amount of money it is willing to lose on any given day of trading, its so-called value at risk, by $3 million, raising it to $36 million. Lehman increased its risk to $8 million a day, from $7 million in the previous quarter.[91]

The banks are literally starting to look more and more like oil companies as they purchase pipelines, storage fields, and even their own oil fields. J. P. Morgan Chase owns pipelines and storage facilities. Goldman Sachs owns pipelines, terminals, an oil refinery in Kansas, and natural gas wells in Pennsylvania, West Virginia, Texas, Oklahoma, and offshore Louisiana. It is also part owner of Cobalt International Energy, a new oil exploration firm run by former Unocal executives.[92] Lehman Brothers just purchased Eagle Energy Partners, a Houston-based energy services company. "We believe there to be enormous market opportunities in the commodities space in the coming years," announced the bank in a press release. "The combination of Eagle's remarkable contacts and knowledge in the physical and financial markets for gas and power, married with Lehman Brothers' capital markets expertise, will be a powerful contributor to this effort."[93]

Just as Chevron moved into Enron's building at 1500 Louisiana in Houston and became a more aggressive energy trader, Morgan Stanley now operates from Texaco's former headquarters in Purchase, New York, as it moves directly into the oil business. United Airlines recently turned to Morgan Stanley for its oil supply. "Now, employees of the bank scour the world for jet fuel for the airline," reports the *Wall Street Journal*. "They charter barges, lease pipelines and schedule tanker trucks, delivering more than a billion gallons a year to United's hubs. They even send inspectors to make sure no one tampers with the stuff."[94]

Morgan Stanley is part owner of twenty-six oil and gas fields and is a major provider to wholesalers of heating oil in the northeastern United States. It has custody of a quarter of America's strategic reserve of home heating oil. And it is the second-most-active U.S. seller of electric power, ahead of scores of utilities, according to Federal Energy Regulatory Commission rankings.[95]

The banks are becoming more like oil companies for several reasons. One is their desire for information, which raises the specter of insider trading. As Morgan Stanley's John Shapiro explains, "Being in the physical business tells us when markets are oversupplied or undersupplied. . . . We're right there seeing terminals filling up and emptying. Or we're there saying 'I need 500,000 barrels' when someone else says 'I don't have it.' "[96]

Becoming commercial providers of oil also makes the banks

eligible to take full advantage of the loopholes implemented by
Wendy and Phil Gramm. The loopholes were restricted to large
commercial traders—meaning those involved in the commercial
trade of energy products. Wendy Gramm's loophole exempted
trades between large commercial companies making bilateral
energy futures trades. Thus the banks can increasingly take advantage of unregulated exchanges like the ICE and unregulated
trades like swaps.

Hedge Fund Speculation

Hedge funds are the relative newcomers to the world of energy
trading. A hedge fund pools investment dollars and then takes
big risks with the goal of generating big profits. These funds use
what are termed by the industry "aggressive strategies," strategies that are denied to mutual funds, for example. Hedge funds
both crave and create volatility through their trading tactics.
"They like the opaque and financially immature energy complex.
They are here to stay," reports leading energy consultant Peter
Fusaro.[97]

The man who has spent his life predicting the movement of oil
markets, T. Boone Pickens, has not been left behind. One year
before former Enron energy trader John Arnold topped him, T.
Boone Pickens was recognized by *Trader Monthly* magazine for
garnering "the largest one-year sum ever earned." T. Boone made
more than $1.5 billion in 2005 from crude oil futures trades
through his $5 billion hedge fund, BP Capital. Pickens's returns
on his trading were over 700 percent.

As recently as 2003, there were only ten or so hedge funds
actively trading energy commodities. Today, there are more than
550.[98] Many attribute the dramatic increase to the rush of former Enron energy traders into the market. "When Enron and
other energy merchants collapsed, the first wave of energy trading talent was picked up by very astute hedge funds and banks in
2002 and 2003," writes Peter Fusaro. "We are now in year four
of higher and more volatile energy prices."[99]

While T. Boone Pickens represents the potential windfalls available to hedge funds, Brian Hunter, described as "among the top natural gas traders in the world" in 2005, represents the inherent potential loss, not only to an individual, but to the entire economy.[100] Brian Hunter lost $6 billion in one week of trading in energy futures. He took his hedge fund, Amaranth Advisors, down with him, along with pension funds that had invested in Amaranth and lost millions of dollars. Before he crashed, he single-handedly drove the price of home heating in the United States out of the reach of millions of Americans. His tool was the Enron Loophole, and his exchange of choice was the ICE.

Amaranth Advisors

Brian Hunter was the industry darling after he "cleaned up on the double-whammy of Hurricanes Katrina and Rita." Hunter had bet that natural gas prices would skyrocket after the hurricane season, and he was right. With the next hurricane season, he bet wrong, and lost $6 billion in one week in September 2006. It was enough of a loss to break the $9 billion Amaranth Advisors LLC hedge fund for which he worked.

The news coverage was understandably harsh: "From Hero to Zero in Two Years." "If there were a Bad Trade Hall of Fame, Brian Hunter would have just secured himself a prominent spot." "The Houdini Award goes to Amaranth Advisors and its founder, Nicholas Maounis, for overseeing the evaporation of $6 billion in less than one week at the hands of a 32-year-old Ferrari-driving energy trader." "The Better-Than-Barings Blow-Up Award"—in reference to Nicholas Leeson, a young trader at Barings Bank in Singapore who "blew up Barings" when he burned through a mere $1.3 billion in trading losses.[101]

While the headlines might have been funny, the financial loss was painfully serious. Pension funds have been moving aggressively into energy futures trading as the returns continue to rise. Among those burned by Hunter's loss were the members of the San Diego County Employees Retirement Association, which had placed $175 million in Amaranth. By using massive trades to bet on natural gas prices, Amaranth raised relative 2006 winter prices for the whole natural gas market, causing consumers to pay radically inflated prices. A public gas company in Georgia estimates that it paid $18 million more than it would have without Amaranth's excessive speculation. An industry association told the Senate that Amaranth's trading in winter gas likely cost consumers billions of dollars.[102]

In August 2006 the NYMEX penalized Amaranth for excessive speculation, which is illegal under the Commodity and Exchange Act. In response, Amaranth simply moved its trades over to the unregulated ICE.

When the CFTC failed to act against Amaranth, the Federal Energy Regulatory Commission (FERC), which typically regulates the physical movement of energy commodities, stepped in. The FERC charged Amaranth and Hunter with successfully manipulating gas prices by manipulating the price of gas futures on the NYMEX. It has brought approximately $300 million in charges. The CFTC eventually stepped in as well, but with a far weaker charge, accusing Amaranth and Hunter of "trying" to manipulate the price of natural gas futures contracts on NYMEX.

Of course, neither regulatory body can do anything about Amaranth's ICE trades.

CONCLUSION

The price of a barrel of oil should be high in order to account for and pay for the environmental, public health, social, and political costs of oil. However, the world needs to prepare for higher oil and gasoline prices with greater investment in clean energy alternatives and public transportation. The world does not need the shock therapy of rapidly rising, volatile prices under the unregulated manipulation of energy traders—with the profits captured not by the governments that need to make these vital investments, but by the already overstuffed pockets of Big Oil.

Big Oil has a great deal. The companies pushed for the deregulation of energy trading, and that trading has now catapulted the price of crude oil through the roof, with truly no end in sight. The companies can now sit back and watch the energy traders go wild.

We know that price manipulation is already taking place on the regulated exchanges, but we have essentially no idea of what is happening on the unregulated ICE or in the bilateral trades between large firms. The less government regulation there is over all of this trade, the less we know what is going on—from the volume of trade to the amount of money involved, to who the large traders are, to the nature of their trades. From what we have observed of these markets, however, it is safe to assume that unsound, unsustainable, and fraudulent trades are regular occurrences.

Whether fraudulent or legal, when the traders move the price of electricity, home heating fuel, and oil to meet their needs, real people lose access to vital services, while national and global economics that run on these crucial resources are thrown into turmoil. It turns out that the energy trader who pushed the price of crude oil to $100 per barrel on New Year's Day 2008 did so intentionally to earn a place in history. "The lone trader was apparently looking for vanity bragging rights," reported the *New York Times*. One oil analyst commented of the trader, "He's probably going to frame the ticket and sell it on eBay for $100,000."[103]

While the Enron traders who intentionally manipulated the California energy market were certainly brutal and even criminal in their tactics, they were also correct to say that it was their job to make money. It is the job of elected officials, government regulators, and the public to ensure the well-being of the people. Government officials largely abdicated that role when they allowed key trades to go unregulated through the Enron Loophole.

There are growing calls for reform and fundamental change

in the crude futures market. The Senate Permanent Subcommittee on Investigation has called for the closing of the Enron Loophole, regulation of the ICE, and more active regulation of the NYMEX. Legislation has been introduced to achieve these ends.

India's petroleum minister, M. S. Srinivasan, has gone further, calling for a halt to crude oil futures trading altogether—arguing that if crude were eliminated from the commodities traded on the NYMEX, the world would "see a drastic reduction in the price" of crude.[104] Developing countries such as India might remember more clearly the last time the price of crude oil was run up above $100 per barrel, in the 1979 oil crisis. The result was a global recession from which developing countries in particular fought long and hard to recover. Today many argue that the United States has already entered a recession, while the world teeters on the brink. The high price of crude oil is a key contributing factor to this economic peril.

Deregulation of the trade in crude has also, of course, had winners. It has led to an unprecedented rise in the price of oil, yielding similarly unprecedented profits for Big Oil on the global market. The price of oil is a key determinant of the price of gasoline, as is Big Oil. In the United States, Big Oil used the mergers of the last twenty-five years to take control of the refining and marketing of gasoline, with the result that today the companies exercise significant control over the skyrocketing price of gasoline charged to consumers at the pump. Just as the rapid run-up in the price of oil has had catastrophic economic impacts, so too has the rapidly rising price of gasoline. Just as the price of oil is being artificially manipulated, so too is the price of gas.

5

PAYING THE PRICE

Consolidation, High Gas Prices, and Contempt

If concentration in the oil industry continues to increase,
higher [gasoline] prices can be expected.
—U.S. SENATE PERMANENT SUBCOMMITTEE
ON INVESTIGATIONS, 2002[1]

The rising price of crude oil has helped push gasoline prices in the United States to the highest levels in modern history. For an economy still unprepared for a rapid transition away from fossil fuels, the effect has been to help push the United States into a recession. While the price of crude is the principal determinant of gasoline prices, it is still just one among several. As Big Oil's control over crude oil waned following the 1970s oil nationalizations, the companies turned their attention to other enterprises—principally the refining and marketing of gasoline. Through mergers, mass consolidation, and the determined elimination of competitors, Big Oil has taken firm control over the price of gasoline in the United States. Today the profits from rising gasoline prices are going into the already overstuffed pockets of Big Oil, allowing the companies to pursue their chosen policies to the great detriment of small business, worker safety, public health, the environment, and the larger economy.

A prestigious group of ranking Republican and Democratic U.S. senators introduced legislation in mid-2006 to address the havoc in gasoline prices brought on by the wave of oil company mergers in the previous twenty-five years. "With the high fuel prices the American consumer is enduring, it is time for an examination of what oil and gas industry consolidations have done to prices," said Republican senator from Pennsylvania Arlen Specter, then chairman of the Senate Judiciary Committee. "We have allowed too many companies to merge together and reduce competition." California's senior senator, Democrat Dianne Feinstein, concurred: "What you have today is an oligopoly in the oil and gas industry, and I think it's disastrous for the American people. It is time that Congress takes a closer look at the mergers and market consolidation that the federal government has allowed over the last decade. . . . Oil and gas companies must not be allowed to manipulate the market at the expense of consumers." Wisconsin Democrat Senator Herb Kohl, now chairman of the Senate Judiciary's Subcommittee on Antitrust, Business Rights, and Competition, added, "[T]here is a failure of competition in our oil and gas markets, and a failure of antitrust enforcement."[2]

The senators' legislation, like virtually every attempt at federal legislation to address Big Oil's manipulation of the domestic petroleum market, did not become law. It is nonetheless part of a much larger movement. Protests have taken place across the country, organized by truckers, gas station owners, people living near and working in refineries, and everyday consumers of gasoline. Lawsuits alleging price-gouging, market manipulation, collusion, conspiracy, and other abuses by Big Oil have been filed. Big Oil's CEOs have been brought in time and again to testify before national hearings. Hundreds of laws have been introduced, and many have even been passed at the state level. But as the states' attorneys general who testify regularly before Congress make clear, without federal legislation and action, the states are unable to get to the heart of the problem: Big Oil. Several have called for a moratorium on oil company mergers. California's assistant attorney general for antitrust, Tom Greene, stressed "the necessity for aggressive, affirmative antitrust enforcement," at a Senate hearing.[3] New Jersey's attorney general Richard Blumenthal has gone further, calling for the mandatory breakup of all oil companies that have engaged in predatory and anticompetitive acts.[4]

As a result of the merger wave of the last twenty-five years, thousands of independent oil refineries and gas stations across the United States have been swallowed or crushed by today's oil giants. The six largest oil companies operating in the United States today—ExxonMobil, Chevron, ConocoPhillips, BP, Shell, and Valero—control almost 60 percent of the U.S. refining market. That is nearly twice as much as the six largest companies controlled just twelve years ago.[5] These same companies, with the exception of Valero, control more than 60 percent of the nation's gas stations, compared with 27 percent in 1991.[6]

Due to consolidation, Big Oil now exercises greater control over how much oil gets refined into gasoline, how much gasoline is available at the pump, and how much the gasoline costs. Big Oil is using this power to charge us increasingly exorbitant gasoline prices. The extra money that you are paying for gas is not going to fund better public transportation, more affordable, fuel-efficient cars, or meaningful investments in alternative fuels. Nor is it going to gas station owners or toward making the companies' refineries safer for workers and communities. Rather, Big Oil is using this money to increase its political influence, making its activities more difficult to regulate.

John D. Rockefeller built Standard Oil by taking over virtually the entire process of refining and selling kerosene in the United States. One hundred and thirty years later, the spawn of Standard are trying to follow suit with gasoline. From the 1920s through the 1970s, the major U.S. oil companies largely abandoned the refining and selling—referred to as "marketing"—of gasoline in the United States as major profit centers in favor of overseas crude production. The domestic U.S. market was filled with a large number of independent refiners and sellers. The nationalizations of the major oil companies' foreign oil reserves in the 1970s forced them to change course and renew their focus on the domestic downstream market of refining and marketing.

Ever since the 1980s, Big Oil has bought out competitors, merged with former rivals, and consolidated its control to turn refining and selling into highly profitable activities. They have restricted the supply and availability of gasoline, eliminated competitors, and skimped on costs. There has not been a single new refinery built in the United States in more than a generation. Those that remain are dangerous to the workers they employ and the communities within which they operate. In 1981 there were 324 refineries in the United States, owned by 189 different companies.[7] Today there are fewer than half as many refineries, 149, owned by less than a third as many companies—just 50.[8] The companies have, in turn, closed gas stations and ceased to build new ones. Nearly 50,000 gas stations have been shut down in the United States in the last twenty-five years, bringing about the near disappearance of the small, independently owned gas station.[9]

Just as Rockefeller's methods of consolidation and control were illegal, so too, many now argue, are the activities of his oil company descendants. But just as they did over one hundred years ago against Standard Oil, today's victims of Big Oil have also begun to rise up in revolt.

GAS PRICES ON THE RISE

We are beyond frustrated. We are angry. We want answers as to why prices at the pump continue to escalate in the absence of new seasonal, weather or world events.

> —GOVERNOR M. JODI RELL,
> REPUBLICAN OF CONNECTICUT[10]

On New Year's Day 2008, gasoline prices in the United States averaged nearly $3.16 per gallon—then the highest national average in at least twenty-five years—and the price just kept rising. By the first week of April, for example, the national average was $3.38. Of course, national averages hide enormous differences. On April 3 a Shell gas station in downtown San Francisco charged $4.11 for premium gasoline. At the same time, a Gasco station in Hamilton, New Jersey, charged just $2.98 per gallon for regular gas. When prices for diesel topped $4.00 in some places, truck drivers responded with a nationwide protest. On April 1, convoys slowed to 20 miles per hour on the New Jersey Turnpike, and trucks traveling from Florida to Chicago turned off their engines in a one-day work stoppage.

The rising gasoline prices of 2008 are part of a ten-year trend during which prices have been on a steep upward climb, from a modern low of $1.07 per gallon in 1998 ($1.39 adjusted for inflation) to $2.86 per gallon in 2007, to $3.16 in the first three months of 2008. While the pace of rising gas prices has not been as meteoric as that of crude oil (crude oil prices have more than quadrupled since 2000; gasoline prices have doubled over the same period), it is one of the fastest in history, rivaling that of the first 1970s oil crisis. From October 1973 to February 1975, prices at the pump rose an average of 30 percent. Similarly, from March 2006 to March 2008, the price rose an average of 34 percent.

The only time in modern American history when the price of gas has risen more precipitously was from 1979 to 1981, when it rose by a whopping 150 percent, while the nation faced gasoline shortages and long lines at the pump. Big Oil learned its lesson with the second oil crisis, which resulted in a massive national and global commitment to energy conservation, which succeeded, for a time, in significantly reducing oil and gasoline consumption. Never again would Big Oil allow shortages on such a massive scale, or such a rapid and dramatic run-up in prices. Thus far, it has succeeded.

Big Oil would, of course, prefer us to believe that the companies have no control over the price of gasoline, which they argue has just one determinant—the price of oil, which, they also argue, they do not control. While oil is undoubtedly the largest factor determining the price of gasoline, it is still just one factor among many. The other factors are the costs and profits associated with refining oil into gasoline, transporting and marketing it, and taxes. The U.S. Department of Energy estimates the percentage of every dollar we spend on a gallon of gasoline that goes to each of these variables. For every dollar we spent filling up our gas tanks in 2007, we paid an average of about 52 cents for the crude oil, 21 cents for the refining, 11 cents for the marketing, and 16 cents in taxes. Because both refining and marketing have increasingly been consolidated into the hands of Big Oil, over 30 percent of the price of gasoline at the pump can fall fully under the companies' control. Moreover, Big Oil exercises its influence over price every step of the way—from the field to the refinery, to the pump, to the State House.

CRUDE OIL AND THE PRICE OF GASOLINE
Prices

The price of gasoline certainly trends with the price of crude oil, but the trend is neither uniform nor universal. As the U.S. Senate's Permanent Subcommittee on Investigations concluded, gas prices "do not necessarily reflect crude oil prices."[11]

Let's look at the effect that the changing price of crude had on the price of gasoline over a random four-week period. In the first week of March 2008, gas prices averaged $3.21 per gallon, while crude sold at approximately $103 per barrel. The following week, crude oil leaped to $109 per barrel, and gas prices rose accordingly by an average of 6 cents to $3.27 per gallon. The next week, oil prices fell dramatically to $105 per barrel. Gas prices, on the other hand, kept rising, increasing by a whopping 60 cents to reach $3.33 per gallon. While oil eventually dropped back down to $100 per barrel by the first week of April, gasoline prices continued a steady upward climb, reaching an average of $3.38 per gallon—at the time, the highest monthly average in the last twenty-five years. If history is a guide, eventually gasoline prices can be expected to come back down, but this trend is a hallmark of the industry. Referred to as a "rockets and feathers pricing pattern," while gas prices immediately shoot up with an increase in the price of crude, they take their own sweet time retreating after the price of crude has gone down.

Just as gasoline prices can stay up while the price of crude falls, the opposite also occurs, with gasoline prices falling while crude prices increase. For example, in April 2007, crude oil cost $63.98 per barrel and gasoline $2.95 per gallon. In May, the price of crude fell while the price of gasoline climbed: to $63.45 and $3.15, respectively. One year earlier, in May 2006, crude was far more expensive, selling at $70 per barrel—almost $7 higher than in May 2007. The price of gas in May 2006, however, was $2.90 per gallon, or 25 cents lower than in May 2007.

The 2007 gasoline price outraged motorists, who responded by organizing a National Gas Out, refusing to buy gasoline on May 15. A week later, the motorists were joined by gas station owners, who shut down their pumps for one day to protest the high profits Big Oil was making at their expense. The boycotts may well have worked, for in June 2007, while the price of crude increased by more than $5, gas prices fell by 10 cents. According to one industry analyst, the reason why gasoline prices stayed down while crude prices increased was because of "record-high refinery margins"—oil companies were making higher-than-average profits refining crude into gasoline and could therefore afford to leave gasoline prices alone.[12]

The price of oil, therefore, is clearly not the only factor impacting the price of gasoline.

ExxonMobil, Chevron, ConocoPhillips, Shell, BP, and Marathon together produce more crude on a daily basis than does Saudi Arabia—some 10.5 million barrels compared with 9.2 million barrels per day. Therefore, both the independent and collective production and marketing decisions of the oil companies are factors driving the available supply and price of crude oil.

Most of the companies also engage directly in the futures market for crude oil that is now the primary determinant of the price of crude. The companies also make internal profit-and-loss decisions for their oil. Each of the major oil companies, moreover, is vertically integrated—that is, the same company owns each leg of production from the field to the refinery to the gas pump, and can therefore make profit-and-loss decisions all along this chain. For example, if the crude comes from a Chevron oil field, is refined in a Chevron refinery, and is sold at a Chevron-owned gas station, then a great deal of the decision-making over costs and profit is directly in Chevron's hands. The fewer competitors it has along the way, the greater is Chevron's control.

While Big Oil does not have the level of control over the price of crude that it maintained during the Seven Sisters era, it has sought to find other avenues of control and profit within the refining and marketing sectors of the oil industry. "A steady flow of extreme consolidation has led to tight markets, particularly for the refining and marketing of gasoline, allowing oil companies to control the market to the disadvantage of smaller producers, consumers, and the economy," stated the U.S. Senate's Permanent Subcommittee on Investigations in its 2002 report "Gas Prices: How Are They Really Set?" The result of a series of hearings and a lengthy investigation, this report remains one of the most comprehensive studies of the U.S. petroleum industry of the last thirty years. In 2007 the American Antitrust Institute concurred: "Perhaps the most important feature of the domestic petroleum industry over the last 20 years has been the significant level of consolidation at the refining and marketing level."[13] Increased control over refining and marketing has allowed Big Oil to take more thorough control of some 30 percent of the price of every gallon of gasoline.

The Supplies of Crude and Gasoline

Oil companies would like us to believe that gasoline prices rise not only in relation to the price of crude, but in relation to its supply as well. The basic economic principles of supply and demand lead us to assume that if supplies of crude are low, then the supply of gasoline would also be low, and gasoline prices would, in turn, be high. For example, there is a general belief that since we are at war in Iraq, the United States is no longer importing oil from Iraq, reducing the overall supply of crude for the nation. This perceived loss of supply is often cited as a reason why gasoline prices have been so high over the past several years in particular.

In fact, U.S. companies have *increased* their imports of Iraqi oil since the U.S. invasion of Iraq in March 2002. Within a few months of the invasion, according to the U.S. Department of Energy, about half of Iraq's crude oil exports began coming to the United States and have continued to do so with little interruption. Overall, Iraq's oil production has remained largely steady either at or near prewar production levels of 2.5 million barrels of oil since shortly after the invasion. Most recently Iraq began exporting an even higher percentage of its oil than before the invasion. U.S. imports of Iraqi oil have exceeded 2002 import levels in every subsequent year. ExxonMobil, Chevron, Marathon, ConocoPhillips, BP, Shell, and others buy the oil from the Iraqi government and refine it at their U.S. refineries. In May 2007, for example, Chevron alone imported 1.1 million barrels of oil from Iraq to its Richmond, California, refinery.[14]

Even excluding oil going to the government's Strategic Petroleum Reserve, the overall supply of crude oil stocks (the amount of crude sitting in storage facilities) in the United States increased from about 285,000 barrels in 2000, to a high of approximately 355,000 barrels in mid-2007, to about 319,000 barrels as I write in mid-2008. Apparently contradicting the laws of supply and demand, while overall the supply of crude increased from 2000 to 2008, the price of gasoline increased as well.[15]

The reason is simple: while crude oil supplies in the United States increased over the last eight years, the amount of *gasoline* declined precipitously. From a high of 161,000 barrels in 2001 and 2002, the supply of gasoline has declined to 105,000 barrels today.[16] In other words, more oil is available in the United States, but less of it is being refined into gasoline. The oil companies appear to be creating an "artificial scarcity," which is illegal under antitrust law.

Husband and wife Michael and Rebecca Siegel have launched one of the many suits against Big Oil, arguing that the companies have intentionally created an artificial scarcity in gasoline. The Siegels are suing, among others, ExxonMobil, Marathon, Shell, and BP for "falsely advertising gasoline's scarceness and excessively marking up the price of gasoline." Their case, brought in Illinois in 2005, for which they are seeking class-action status on behalf of all affected Illinois consumers, goes on to charge the companies with "engaging in a scheme to control and increase the price of gasoline to consumers by controlling inventory, production, and exports, limiting the supply, restricting purchase, and using zone pricing."[17] In the most recent ruling in the case, in May 2007, the judge denied the companies' request to dismiss the lawsuit and found, "Facts consistent with these allegations could establish that defendants unjustly enriched themselves or acted deceptively or unfairly."[18]

The price of gasoline is set by the profit and loss decisions of oil companies. Big Oil is able to exert this control over prices because of the consolidation of the oil industry.

MAKING IT PAY: REFINERY CONCENTRATION

In the 1970s, the major oil companies made the bulk of their profits from their upstream operations: exploring for and producing crude oil. As late as 1972, the Seven Sisters produced 91 percent of the Middle East's crude oil and 77 percent of the supply outside the United States and the former Soviet Union.[19] Domestically, the federal government limited company profits by regulating gas prices from 1971 to 1981 and heavily subsidizing smaller refiners through the 1973 Crude Oil Entitlement Program.

Given that the major oil companies paid hardly any taxes on their foreign earnings and that there were relatively insignificant opportunities for large profits in the domestic mid- and downstream markets, they were generally willing to leave these operations to other companies or to use them as mere conduits to bring their more profitable product—crude—to their consumers as gasoline. Midstream operations are pipelines and other infrastructure used to transport products from the field to refineries. Downstream operations are the refining of crude into finished products, transporting those products from refineries to storage terminals, and marketing (or selling) the products through wholesalers and gas stations.

When the big oil companies' foreign crude oil holdings were nationalized, they needed to find new sources of crude as well as new profit centers. President Ronald Reagan's election came along just in time. During his first year in office, 1981, Reagan ended gas price regulations, allowing companies to largely determine the price of gasoline. He ended the Crude Oil Entitlement Program, leaving most independent refineries unable to compete with the larger and increasingly vertically integrated oil companies. These refiners either shut down or sold out. Reagan's Federal Trade Commission under chairman James Miller provided an open-door policy for oil company mergers, which have continued unabated to this day.

As the major oil companies moved into the downstream markets, the independents were pushed out. While a Chevron refinery typically produces the Chevron brand of gasoline, which is then sold at Chevron gas stations, independent refiners generally produce unbranded gasoline—a generic or "no name" gasoline that is sold at independent gas stations. Stations that are "independent" from the refiner and the major oil companies can purchase gasoline from any refinery and sell it for any price. The unbranded or generic gas station generally competes with Chevron and the other big-name brands by selling gasoline at a lower price. Fewer independent refiners, therefore, mean fewer independent gas stations and less cheap gas. Fewer independent stations also mean that the name brands face less competition and therefore can maintain higher gasoline prices.

"The presence of competitors other than a few major brands is critical to price competition in local markets," argued the Senate's Permanent Subcommittee on Investigations.[20]

The consolidation of refineries began in the 1980s, but excess refining remained a problem for the major oil companies into the 1990s. The more refining that takes place, the more gasoline there is for sale, and theoretically the less expensive gasoline should be at the pump. The 1980s and much of the 1990s were periods of oil and gasoline gluts; increasing amounts of both were available on the market. The main reason is that the oil companies no longer owned the world's oil and therefore were no longer controlling how much oil was pumped out of the ground and put onto the world market. Since they could no longer control the supply of crude on the market, the companies took control of how much oil was refined into gasoline by taking over the refineries, reducing supply, and, in the words of one Texaco document cited below, finding ways to "increase demand for gasoline."

The oil industry stated its concerns in internal company memos, several of which were made public in the report of the 2002 U.S. Senate Permanent Subcommittee on Investigations. An internal Texaco document from 1996 reveals the industry's concerns about the surplus supply of gasoline and the need to control it: "As observed over the last few years and as projected into the future, the most critical factor facing the refining industry on the West Coast is the surplus refining capacity, and the surplus gas production capacity. The same situation exists for the entire U.S. refining industry. Supply significantly exceeds demand year-round. Significant events need to occur to assist in reducing supplies and/or increasing the demand for gasoline."[21]

Chevron relayed similar concerns expressed by the oil industry's leading association, the American Petroleum Institute (API), in an internal company memo: "A senior energy analyst at the recent API convention warned that if the US petroleum industry doesn't reduce its refining capacity, it will never see any substantial increase in refining margins."[22]

The major oil companies actively worked to ensure that refineries that closed down stayed closed. In 1995 the Powerine Oil Company Refinery in Santa Fe Springs, California, closed. An internal Mobil document states quite matter-of-factly, "Needless to say, we would all like to see Powerine stay down. Full court press is warranted in this case."[23] "We were protecting our investment," ExxonMobil executive James S. Carter explained to the Permanent Subcommittee on Investigations in 2002. "We thought that was the best way to level the playing field."[24] Despite documented attempts by Powerine to work in conjunction with major oil companies to restart the refinery, the companies said no, and the refinery remains closed.[25]

It took about twenty years, but Big Oil largely attained its goal, and the results are phenomenal: demand for gasoline has increased, the number of refineries has decreased, the supply of gasoline has decreased, and refining and marketing have become major profit centers for Big Oil. Greater refinery consolidation in the hands of Big Oil has allowed the companies to increasingly control the amount of crude refined into gasoline, to increase the price they charge for wholesale gasoline, and to increase gasoline prices.

In 1991 companies received an average return of slightly less than 2 percent on their investment in refining and marketing. In 2005, after almost 920,000 barrels of oil per day of capacity owned by smaller independent refiners were shut down, the return on investment was a full twelve times larger, at 24 percent.[26] By 2001, according to the American Petroleum Institute, the return on investment in refining and marketing was even higher than the return on oil and gas production.[27]

Refiners measure this success as "refining margins"—the difference between the cost to the refiner to acquire crude oil and the price at which the refiner sells the finished product. In 1999, U.S. oil refiners received nearly a 20 percent margin for every gallon they refined from crude oil. By 2005, they were earning nearly a 50 percent margin.[28]

A comprehensive study of the refining sector by the RAND Corporation, a conservative, probusiness think tank, describes how the industry implemented a strategy to restrict overall gasoline supply in order to increase its profits: "Low profits in the 1980s and 1990s were blamed in part on overcapacity in the sector. Since the mid-1990s, economic performance industry-wide has recovered and reached record levels in 2001. On the other hand, for consumers, the elimination of spare capacity generates upward pressure on prices at the pump."

RAND found that the industry responded to overcapacity by reducing capacity. "Increasing capacity and output . . . is now frowned upon," explained the report. Instead, the industry favored a "more discriminating approach to investment and supplying the market that emphasized maximizing margins and returns on investment rather than product output or market share." Companies decided to stick with their old plants rather than build new ones, relying on "existing plants and equipment to the greatest possible extent, even if that ultimately meant curtailing output of certain refined products. . . ." According to the report, the plan paid off: "For operating companies, the elimination of excess capacity represents a significant business accomplishment."[29]

The profitability of the major oil companies' refining and marketing operations is written all over their midyear earnings statements for 2007:

> ExxonMobil: "Earnings per share were up 6% from the second quarter of 2006. Lower natural gas realizations were mostly offset by higher refining, marketing and chemical margins. Downstream earnings were $3,393 million, up $908 million from the second quarter of 2006, driven by higher refining and marketing margins."

Chevron: "Earnings and cash flows were strong in the second quarter. . . . Downstream earnings improved $300 million on higher margins for refined products."

ConocoPhillips: "Refining and marketing net income was $2,358 million in the second quarter, up from $1,136 million in the previous quarter and $1,708 million in the second quarter of 2006. The increase from the previous quarter was due to higher worldwide realized refining and marketing margins."

Valero: "The company posted its best ever quarterly profits. . . . The environment for refining margins was terrific in the second quarter, and we continued to benefit from our complex, geographically diverse refining system. . . . Gasoline and diesel demand in the U.S. has been excellent, and growing worldwide demand has increased competition for refined products."

Shell: "Earnings benefited from higher refining margins, improved marketing margins and a divestment gain."

BP: "Compared with 2006, both the second quarter and half-year results benefited from significantly stronger refining margins, particularly in the US; marketing margins were also stronger."

Eliminating the competition has made both refining and marketing more profitable, as has keeping the total number of refineries down while running existing refineries at full bore, with little concern for the environmental, health, or safety implications. The companies have slightly expanded the capacity of their existing refineries, but the additional capacity has hardly kept pace with demand. According to the Department of Energy, while refinery capacity increased by a little more than 2 percent from 1977 to 2002, demand for gasoline increased by almost 30 percent.[30]

The companies have also shut down refineries because they find it more profitable to operate fewer refineries at very high levels of production. The FTC reports that these levels are at twenty-five-year highs, with utilization rates exceeding 90 percent since the mid-1990s. In 1998 utilization rates hit an all-time high with an average of 96 percent. "Refiners are running near capacity because [the companies] have little incentive to build more. For starters, they make more money when supplies are tight," explained Peter Coy, associate business editor at *Business Week*.[31] In 2007 the rate averaged 90 percent. While running each refinery to the hilt increases the companies' profits, it makes the refineries less safe and far more vulnerable to accidents and shutdowns.

The high utilization rates are combined with "just-in-time" inventories, meaning that refineries do not store extra gasoline. In 1981 the amount of gasoline in storage in the United States equaled about forty days' worth of consumption. Today the storage has been halved to about twenty days' worth of consumption. As reported by the Permanent Subcommittee on Investigations, "In the past several years most refiners have aggressively reduced amounts of gasoline held in inventory. . . . ExxonMobil, the largest oil company, has established a goal of reducing its crude oil and refined products in inventory by 15 percent. . . . Prior to its merger with Texaco, Chevron had reduced its inventories of mid- and premium-grade gasoline by nearly two-thirds over the previous decade." The report concludes, "Low inventories are widely regarded as a key factor contributing to the increased volatility of gasoline prices."[32]

The U.S. government's General Accounting Office (GAO) agrees. In an exhaustive 2004 study of the effect of mergers and market concentration in the U.S. petroleum industry, the GAO found that the leading factors affecting the volatility of gas prices include "limited refinery capacity," "inventory levels relative to demand," "supply disruptions," and "market consolidation."[33]

Historically, the industry "overrefined" in the winter, refining more gas than was demanded at the pump. Refiners then stored the gas until it was needed in the spring and summer when demand always rose. The increased demand was met without a price spike by using the inventory refined in the winter. Inventory was also adequate to compensate for unexpected disruptions, mechanical or weather-related, at refineries.[34] Today's just-in-time inventories and full-bore production combine to lead to greater volatility and higher prices for the simple reason that there is not any excess product, and the supply of gas is almost always tight—even during predictably higher demand periods, such as the summer driving months.

As the FTC reports, "Relatively high refinery capacity utilization rates ordinarily imply that refineries will have less supply available to send to areas in which refined product prices have risen suddenly due to a disruption in supply."[35] Therefore, if there is a storm in New Orleans and refineries in the Gulf are closed, or if there is a small malfunction at a refinery in Oregon and it has to close for a day, or if a pipeline cracks in Alaska, there is no extra gasoline anywhere—simply because the oil companies have found it more profitable to produce and store less gasoline. Moreover, the refineries are pumping at such high utilization rates that the number of accidents and outages increases, which also increases supply volatility and prices.

The FTC identified five separate occasions in 2000 and 2001 when gas prices suddenly spiked on the West Coast because of unplanned refinery outages. During the summer of 2003, a pipeline problem in the Southeast caused gas prices in Arizona to spike to more than $4.00 per gallon. Another pipeline problem in the spring of 2004 caused a gasoline price spike and supply shortages in Nevada.[36] There is less supply, prices are more volatile, and prices just keep rising.

In a study of West Coast gas spikes, the GAO found a direct relationship between increased refinery utilization rates and increased prices: for every 1 percent increase in refinery utilization rates, gasoline prices went up by about 0.1 to 0.2 cent per gallon.[37]

Increased gasoline prices are not the only reason to be concerned about increased utilization rates and ever more consolidated, powerful oil companies. Full-bore utilization, lax regulation, and an omnipotent industry create breeding grounds for pollution and threaten the health and lives of workers and those who live near the nation's aging refineries.

THE COSTS TO PUBLIC HEALTH, WORKERS, AND COMMUNITIES

The 1970 Clean Air Act and subsequent enforcement rules introduced new laws to make refineries cleaner and safer. The laws were needed because refineries are notorious polluters and their operations are extremely hazardous. However, all existing refineries were grandfathered in: any refinery built prior to the law's passage did not have to retool to meet the higher standards. Only brand-new refineries were required to utilize widely available pollution-reducing and safety technology to meet the new, tougher standards.

Rather than spend money on building new and better refineries, the oil companies have made do with getting as much as possible out of their existing old, dirty, and unsafe refineries. Thus no new refinery has been built in the United States since 1976, and the industry has no plans to start building anytime soon. "Increases in domestic production will come from continued expansion of existing refineries because expansion at existing sites is generally more economic than new refinery construction," concludes the National Petroleum Council, an industry group composed of the CEOs of ExxonMobil, Chevron, ConocoPhillips, Shell, BP, and every other major oil corporation operating in the United States.[38]

Oil refineries pumped more than 250 million tons of carbon dioxide into the air in 2004 and, along with chemical plants, constitute the second greatest stationary source of greenhouse gases.[39] Refineries are also the largest stationary source in the United States of volatile organic compounds (VOCs). VOCs are air pollutants and include known carcinogens and reproductive toxins that cause leukemia, lymphatic tissue cancers, birth defects, bronchitis, and emphysema. They evaporate easily, hence the term *volatile*. The "bad boy" of VOCs, in the words of the former secretary of the California Environmental Protection Agency, Terry Tamminen, is benzene, a known carcinogen "with a growing body of evidence showing that health harms from inhaling it are significant even at very low levels."[40]

"Benzene is a highly volatile chemical and is readily absorbed by breathing, ingestion or contact with the skin," reports the California Department of Toxic Substances. "Short-term exposures to high concentrations of benzene may result in death following depression of the central nervous system or fatal disturbances of heart rhythm. Long-term, low-level exposures to benzene can result in blood disorders such as aplastic anemia and leukemia." [41]

Think that this does not affect you? Think again. Nearly one in three Americans lives within thirty miles of an oil refinery.[42] In 1995 the EPA concluded that all who live in this range are being exposed to benzene concentrations in excess of the Clean Air Act's acceptable risk threshold.

The 149 refineries in the United States are spread out over thirty-three states. The highest concentrations of refineries are in Texas, California, and Louisiana—which have twenty-five, twenty-one, and nineteen refineries, respectively. These three states alone account for 40 percent of all the nation's refineries. Alaska and New Jersey are tied with six each. Wyoming, Washington, Utah, Pennsylvania, Oklahoma, Ohio, Montana, Florida, and Alabama each have four or five refineries. Arkansas, Colorado, Delaware, Georgia, Hawaii, Indiana, Kansas, Kentucky, Michigan, Minnesota, Mississippi, Nevada, New Mexico, North Dakota, Oregon, Tennessee, Virginia, West Virginia, and Wisconsin each have one, two, or three.

Most refineries in the United States are between fifty and

seventy-five years old, and many are even older. Far too many are dangerous, dirty, and polluting enterprises, but they could be improved with the necessary investment and effort. However, Big Oil is not using its new megaprofits to substantially improve refineries; rather, the companies are using their profits to fight regulation and roll back existing standards.

Worker Lives Sacrificed

I personally believe that BP, with its corporate culture of
greed over profits, murdered my parents.
—EVA ROWE, WHOSE MOTHER AND FATHER DIED AT A
BP REFINERY IN 2005[43]

A massive explosion rocked BP's Texas City refinery on March 23, 2005. It was the worst workplace accident in the nation in fifteen years. Fifteen workers were killed and 180 injured when a truck backfire accidentally ignited a flammable vapor cloud. The U.S. Chemical Safety Board, an independent federal agency, investigated the blast and released a devastating indictment of BP and Amoco, which owned the refinery before it merged with BP in 1999. The board faulted the companies, which were swimming in profits, for relentless cost-cutting, for refusing to upgrade the aging refinery and overproduction. The board also warned that such dangerous operations were not limited to the Texas City refinery or to BP, but could be industrywide.[44]

The "Texas City disaster was caused by organizational and safety deficiencies at all levels of the BP Corporation," the report found. "The combination of cost-cutting, production pressures, and failure to invest caused a progressive deterioration of safety at the refinery." These practices, begun by Amoco in the 1990s, "left the Texas City refinery vulnerable to catastrophe." BP continued the process, targeting budget cuts of 25 percent in 1999 and another 25 percent in 2005, "even though much of the refinery's infrastructure and process equipment were in disrepair."

The report also found fault in BP for downsizing operator training and staffing.[45]

The 25 percent across-the-board budget cuts applied to each
of BP's five U.S. refineries, which are located in Texas, Indiana,
Ohio, California, and Washington. A subsequent investigation
by the Chemical Safety Board found a pervasive "complacency
towards serious safety risks" at all the refineries. In 1992 the Occupational Health and Safety Administration (OSHA) had cited
as unsafe equipment similar to that which caused the vapor release at the Texas City refinery in 2005, but withdrew the cita-
tion as part of a settlement agreement with the company.
Concerned that mergers and other changes had led these same
failures to exist at other refineries, the U.S. Chemical Safety
Board called on OSHA to increase inspection and enforcement
at all U.S. oil refineries and to "require these corporations to
evaluate the safety impact of mergers, reorganizations, downsizing, and budget cuts."[46]

The death and injury toll at the Texas City refinery uncovered
a filthy secret of the industry: nobody is keeping track of how
many workers are actually hurt and killed at our nation's oil refineries. Industry lobbying has succeeded in restricting which
workers are actually considered worthy of being counted by
regulatory agencies. Only "employees" of companies are counted
when they are injured or killed at work. Contractors, who make
up at least half of refinery workers and who generally get some of
the most dangerous jobs, are not counted. Because the workers
who died at BP's Texas City refinery were contractors, the company's official death rate was exactly the same the day after the
explosion as the day before.

For more than a decade, government task forces have recommended that OSHA require employers to include contract workers in site-based safety records. Under intense industry lobbying,
the regulators have thus far resisted. "The more dangerous an
occupation, the less likely a company would want to hire those
people directly—they want to boost their own safety rates and

decrease their liability," retired Bureau of Labor Statistics economist Guy Toscano explained to the *Houston Chronicle*. Thus,
while OSHA reports seventy-six employee deaths at U.S. oil refineries from 1992 to 2002, most observers of refinery practices
suspect that the number is far greater. For example, the *Chronicle* conducted an extensive review of media accounts and other
public information and found that, while the U.S. Bureau of Labor Statistics reported no refinery deaths in 2002 or 2003, "at
least nine people were asphyxiated, burned or fell to their deaths
at our nation's refineries during those years."[47]

The government only began counting injuries at these refineries in 2003. Over just the two-year period from 2003 to 2005,
the Bureau of Labor Statistics reported almost three thousand
employee injuries at oil refineries. By adding contractors, who
account for about half the workforce, we can extrapolate that
these numbers are likely to be at least double: more than 150
deaths over ten years and nearly six thousand injuries in two.

The failure to report all the injuries and deaths virtually guarantees that the most dangerous refineries will evade government
regulators. Former OSHA administrator Patrick Tyson stated
that without this data, "If the site gets picked up [by OSHA], it's
going to be almost a fluke."[48]

In those instances when worker deaths have been recorded,
companies have won additional changes in OSHA reporting to
avoid liability. In 1990 OSHA began to accede to employer demands that it replace the word *willful* with *unclassified* in citations
involving workplace deaths. Lawyers who specialize in defending
corporations against OSHA invented the latter term. The reclassifi-
cation turns a death from one that could lead to criminal liability
for the company to one with a giant get-out-of-jail-free card.[49]

A *New York Times* investigation found that "major corporations, and their lawyers, have been increasingly successful in
persuading the agency to eliminate the word 'willful.'" OSHA
has done so even for companies that have repeatedly shown a
deliberate disregard for safety laws, resulting in multiple deaths.

In the case of just one company, Shell, eleven worker deaths at its U.S. refineries since 1994 occurred under conditions of repeated violations, accidents, documented cases of delays in necessary maintenance, and neglected pledges of safety improvements. Nonetheless, lawyers convinced OSHA to term the deaths *unclassified* instead of *willful*: the company was fined, but there was no admission of wrongdoing and no referral to prosecutors.

"When you are talking settlement, essentially the rules go away," Robert C. Gombar, a lawyer for Shell, told the *Times* in the wake of two of the explosions. His firm, McDermott, Will & Emery in Washington, advertises that it "pioneered" the use of unclassified violations to avoid "unnecessary complication presented by harmful labels."[50]

Since the creation of OSHA thirty-two years ago, the agency has reported more than two hundred thousand workplace-related deaths. However, OSHA has referred only 151 cases to the Justice Department for criminal prosecution as "willful violation" of OSHA laws. Federal prosecutors have declined to pursue two-thirds of these cases, and only eight of them have resulted in prison sentences for company officials.[51]

Communities in the Crossfire

> *Oil refineries are inherently dirty, but [Communities for a Better Environment] research finds that in the short-term their operations could be required to drastically reduce unnecessarily sloppy, wasteful, and toxic emissions. Smaller businesses with less influence would rarely be allowed to belch out the huge masses of toxic chemicals on neighbors on a regular basis, when prevention is readily available.*
> —COMMUNITIES FOR A BETTER ENVIRONMENT[52]

> *Emissions reductions and an improved environment benefit society in many ways. However, the magnitude and uncertainty of environmental requirements and their*

*enforcement increases cost and adversely affects domestic
refinery investment.*

—NATIONAL PETROLEUM COUNCIL[53]

Chevron's Richmond Refinery in Richmond, California, is one
of the oldest and largest refineries in the United States. "From
the beginning, among West Coast refineries, it was the colossus,"
reads its corporate history. Built in 1902, the refinery sits on
nearly 3,000 acres of land. To refine its capacity of 87.6 million
barrels of crude oil per year—240,000 barrels per day—the refinery produces over 2 million pounds of waste per year.[54]

The Richmond refinery shows its age. The most recent findings
of the U.S. Environmental Protection Agency (EPA) report almost
three hundred pollutant spills from the refinery in just three years,
from 2001 to 2003. These are highly toxic, often cancerous,
chemicals spilling directly into residential communities of families, children, the elderly, and the sick. The EPA lists the refinery in
"significant noncompliance" for air pollution standards.[55] But this
is nothing new. In 2001 the refinery released almost 25,000
pounds of known carcinogens into the surrounding community.
From 1989 to 1995, there were more than three hundred reported
accidents at the refinery, including major fires, spills, leaks, explosions, toxic gas releases, flaring, and air contamination.[56]

San Francisco is sixteen miles away from the Chevron refinery.
In January 2007, most residents of the area (I among them)
thought the refinery had exploded. On the news we heard the giant *boom!* and watched a yellow ball of fire and a black cloud of
smoke explode into the air. A leaking corroded pipe "that should
have been detached two decades ago," according to investigators,
was to blame. The five-alarm fire burned for nine hours, and the
100-foot flames could be seen with the naked eye in San Francisco. Almost three thousand people in nearby neighborhoods
received telephone calls instructing them to stay inside with their
doors and windows shut to avoid breathing the toxic fumes.

Later that year, in August, another giant explosion rocked

Chevron's largest U.S. refinery, in Jackson County, Mississippi. The fire burned near the heart of the Pascagoula Refinery and 200-foot flames were visible for miles down the Mississippi coast. Afterward, Chevron offered free car washes to dislodge the thick layer of black soot that had settled on nearby cars from the fire. The cause of the explosion has yet to be identified.

Another old equipment part was cited as the cause of one of the worst explosions in the Richmond refinery's history. According to Chevron, a leaking valve that "was initially installed more than 30 years ago" ignited a massive explosion in March 1999.[57] An 18,000-pound plume of sulfur dioxide smoke was released in the explosion. Ten thousand residents were told to remain inside for several hours, while those in the closest neighborhoods were evacuated. "A column of thick, acrid, foul-smelling smoke rose high in the air, cloaked the refinery and then began to drift slowly to the southeast," according to one report. "The cloud killed trees and took the fur off squirrels," reported a resident. Hundreds of people flooded local hospitals complaining of breathing difficulties and vomiting. "Will Taylor, a man in his 40s, described how instant waves of nausea brought him and his co-workers to their knees, retching and gasping for breath. 'My eyes burned. My nose ran. With each breath I got sick to my stomach.' A strong chemical taste stayed in his mouth and he felt poorly for days." "I lost my voice for six weeks," reported another resident. "And I threw up a lot. Everybody did."[58]

It takes about forty minutes on public transportation to get from San Francisco to Richmond. Richmond is the last stop on the line and has a population of about a hundred thousand people, 82 percent of whom are listed as minorities by the U.S. Census. Seventeen thousand people, including those in two public housing projects, live within just three miles of the Chevron refinery.[59] The majority of these residents are low-income African-American families who moved to Richmond from the South in the 1940s in search of work. Within one mile of and abutting the refinery are businesses, houses, an elementary school, and playgrounds.

Nationally, it is estimated that race, even more than income level, is the crucial factor shared by communities most exposed to toxic chemicals like those released by the Richmond refinery, with communities of color disproportionately bearing the burden of our national "cancer alleys."[60]

Dr. Henry Clark was born in Richmond in 1944. Except for stints in San Francisco and Minnesota while he earned a Ph.D. in comparative religious education and counseling, he has lived in Richmond his entire life. In an interview, he told me that the only reason he left was because "during the Civil Rights and Black Power Movements we were told to get an education and come back to help your community. This is what I did." Today Dr. Clark lives and works just a few blocks from the Chevron refinery, but during his childhood it was literally his backyard. He was raised with the omnipresent toxic smell of VOCs. He would wait before going to school on days when the rotten egg smell was too strong to bear. He experienced regular shock waves from the refinery's periodic explosions. "They felt like earthquakes," he says.[61]

Dr. Clark realized early on that it was not a coincidence that the Chevron refinery was located in a community of color where most people lived below the poverty line. It was even less of a coincidence that the refinery operated in such open disregard for those who lived on the other side of its fence. In 1986 he joined with others in the community to form Richmond's first organized group to take on the refinery, the West County Toxics Coalition. Today he is its executive director. "We've been organizing to try to get Chevron to invest their profits in pollution prevention equipment and to reduce the impact on our community," Dr. Clark explained. "There's asthma in our community, skin rashes, there's cancer, and this company makes a profit at our expense and laughs all the way to the bank."

The mayor of Richmond, Gayle McLaughlin, recently wrote in the local newspaper of the refinery's impact on the health of the community. She observed that the children in Richmond who suffer from asthma "are hospitalized for this condition at twice the rate of children throughout Contra Costa County," in which Richmond is located. "Time and again," she wrote, "the Richmond City Council has heard testimony from residents about the impact of refinery emissions on their lives: burning eyes, shortness of breath, foul smells, residues on cars and windows. One senior citizen from Atchison Village talked about entire days when she is unable to leave her home, even to work in her garden, because of the noxious fumes that permeate the air in her neighborhood." [62]

In 1992 the California Department of Toxic Substances Control reported on the groundwater of areas directly abutting the refinery, including homes, an elementary school, and a playground. The department found the groundwater impacted by VOCs, including benzene, ethylbenzene, toluene, and xylenes. On the long list of additional harmful compounds, the report lists metals like chromium, lead, nickel, and vanadium. According to the report, lead causes damage to the nervous system and blood and is a reproductive toxin. Vanadium and nickel are both toxic substances, and nickel can be cancer-causing. [63]

Families at the two public housing units near the refinery, Triangle Court and Las Deltas, describe having little choice about where they live. At the same time, they know that the emissions from the Chevron refinery have sickened their children. Nakia Saucer and Ugochi Nwadike, who each have four children, describe how their children have chronic asthma, skin rashes, recurring nosebleeds, headaches, and coughing attacks.

"I don't smoke cigarettes, I don't drink alcohol, and I have no history of asthma," said Nwadike, a native of Nigeria who recently earned a nursing degree at San Francisco State University. "The poison from the refinery is killing these children." [64]

In addition to the Chevron refinery, three more oil refineries are located in Contra Costa County and another lies just north in Solano County. Recent county health reports confirm that death rates from cardiovascular and respiratory diseases are higher in Contra Costa County than statewide rates and are rising. Among the fifteen most populous counties in California, Contra Costa ranked second in incidence rates for breast, ovarian, and prostate cancers. Richmond's rate of hospitalization for female reproductive cancers is more than double the county's overall rate.[65] These statistics are all the more startling given that, due to California's high concentration of refineries and other toxic polluters, eleven of the nation's twenty-five worst counties for ozone contamination are in California. In 1996 the estimated risk of a person getting cancer in California as the result of lifetime exposure to outdoor air pollutants was 310 times higher than federal Clean Air Act goals. In 2002 the risk of cancer in California was 25 percent higher than the national average.[66]

Community organizations led by West County Toxics Coalition and Communities for a Better Environment have put constant pressure on the state and local governments to enforce existing pollution control laws against Chevron. Occasionally the government responds with civil lawsuits against the company, virtually all of which are resolved through negotiated fines as opposed to substantive changes in practice or upgrades. In 2004, for example, Chevron paid a total of about $330,000 in negotiated fines to settle two lawsuits. The Contra Costa district attorney brought the suits for more than seventy reported violations at the Richmond refinery in two years, from 2000 to 2002.[67] In 2001 Chevron was fined $242,500 for failing to repair leaking pipe connectors in a timely manner. The amount of this negotiated fine was based on 241 separate leaks in just *three months* in 1998. These leaks spew toxic fumes into the air and can lead to explosions. In fact, most refinery toxic air pollution nationally is from leaks in equipment, not smokestacks. Technology to prevent these leaks has been widely available for decades, but companies refuse to invest in it.

In response to the above-mentioned 2001 settlement with Chevron, Suma Peesapati, staff attorney at Communities for a Better Environment, noted, "When polluters know they can settle with the government for a small amount, it greatly compromises the integrity of our environmental laws."[68]

Small fines and nonenforcement are the rule, not the exception. For example, a fifty-year-old oil spill from a Mobil refinery in New York left an estimated 8 million barrels of oil to soak the ground beneath streets, homes, and businesses in Brooklyn's Greenpoint neighborhood. The oil continues to pollute groundwater, a nearby creek, and the air through the release of potentially toxic vapors. A 1990 agreement between Mobil and the state government required the company to recover the spilled oil, but it specified no deadline and required no remediation of either the creek or the polluted soil under Greenpoint. Seventeen years of relative inaction by the company led the new state attorney general to take the company to court.

Just a few days before I met Dr. Clark in Richmond to interview him, there had been a spate of shootings in the city, leaving twelve men injured and three dead. Richmond is accustomed to shootings, but this many in one day and during broad daylight was unique. As we arrived at his office, Dr. Clark pointed toward the park across the street and the corners surrounding the building. He described the shootings that had happened there. I followed his eyes as he nodded toward a city bus approaching us. "People were using the bus as cover while the bullets were flying," he said. The neighborhood is not wealthy, but it is well kept, residential, and dotted with small community buildings—all of which were closed.

As I began to interview Dr. Clark, I was reminded of an e-mail exchange I'd had two years earlier with a woman in Baghdad. I was doing research for my book *The Bush Agenda* and wanted to learn details of the availability of water and electricity in her neighborhood—services that the Bechtel Corporation and other U.S. companies had been paid to perform but had failed to provide. She patiently answered my questions, but by the third or fourth e-mail she wrote, "We are dying here. I cannot leave my house without fear of being shot. Our children are dying. I am tired of talking about the electricity."

When I mentioned this exchange to Dr. Clark, he responded, "Chevron took us to war for oil. They refine their Iraqi oil here. Nobody wants to stay in Richmond. Everyone tries to leave. Businesses won't stay. People won't stay. It is a toxic waste site. It is unhealthy to breathe the air or drink the water. It's unsafe. So, those who are here struggle. The kids struggle. And drugs, guns, and gangs are the natural result. It's like living in a war zone."

The same cost-benefit analysis for refiners in Richmond is used at refineries across the nation: it costs less money to use less sophisticated equipment, to neglect upkeep and repairs, and to run refineries at high levels of utilization than it costs to take care of the subsequent pollution, accidents, shut-downs, and explosions.

The technology and best practices are readily available to make refineries safer and cleaner, if not exactly safe or clean. But Big Oil's executives and its lobbying organizations take every possible opportunity to fight for fewer environmental and safety requirements, less oversight, and less regulation. More often than not, they succeed. As Red Cavaney, president and CEO of the American Petroleum Institute, told the U.S. House Energy Committee in 2006, "The permitting process required to construct new refineries or modify existing facilities is very complex and time-consuming. . . . In order to further increase U.S. refining capacity, government policies are needed to create a climate more conducive to investments in refining capacity."[69]

Would less regulation bring an expansion in capacity at refineries or lower gasoline prices? Probably not. Thus far Big Oil has been more interested in shutting down refineries than building new ones, while the companies' proposals for their existing refineries have been not to expand output but rather to retool the refineries to burn dirtier forms of crude oil, such as the oil found in the tar sands of Alberta and the shale regions of the midwestern United States. As for lower gasoline prices, Big Oil has not only solidified its hold over the nation's refineries, but has also gained control of the nation's gas stations and thus firmed its grip on gas prices. To date, the oil companies have proved their unwillingness to use this influence to reduce the price of gasoline, and there is little reason to believe that their attitude will change in the future.

DEATH OF THE INDEPENDENTS: CONCENTRATION AT THE PUMP

Somebody out there is making money at these prices, but not me.

HARVEY POLLACK, OWNER,
TOWNE MARKET MOBIL[70]

While the number of cars on the road in the United States has more than doubled over the last twenty-five years, the number of gas stations has declined by one-third, from approximately 216,000 in 1981 to 166,000 today.[71] The remaining stations are in fewer hands, allowing the companies that own them to exercise greater control over what they sell and how much they sell it for.

There are many brands of gasoline, but only a few companies own them. Big Oil knows that we have loyalty to specific brands. The companies also know that while the different brands of gasoline are virtually identical, we associate them with different levels of quality. When they merge or buy each other up, the companies usually maintain the old brand names, even though the money, decision-making, and influence are in the hands of just one company. The incessant pace of oil company mergers has led many smaller brands to disappear from the market, while a shrinking number of oil corporations own those that remain.

Among the brands that have been lost through mergers over the years are Thrifty (now BP), Superior (now ExxonMobil), Ashland (now Marathon), Scot (now BP), and Tosco (now Conoco-

Phillips). ConocoPhillips owns the Conoco, Phillips 66, and Union 76 brands and Circle K Convenience Stores. When you fill up at Amoco or Arco, you are buying your gas from BP. Whether you are at a Diamond Shamrock, Shamrock, Ultramar, Total, or Beacon gas station, you are ultimately purchasing Valero's gas. Marathon owns the Marathon and Speedway brands and is 50 percent owner of Pilot Travel Centers. Chevron owns the Chevron and Texaco brands, just as ExxonMobil owns the Exxon and Mobil brands. Shell prefers to market most of its gas under its own name, eliminating the brand names of companies that it takes over, such as Motiva and Equilon.

Two-thirds of all gas stations sell brand-name gasoline. About one-quarter of these are directly owned and operated by the oil companies.[72] The rest of the stations that sell brand-name gasoline, known as "branded dealers," are either owned independently or run as franchises. The remaining third of all gas stations are known as the "independents"—those that are not associated with any major brand.

Big Oil simply tells its company-owned gas stations what price to sell gasoline. It is illegal for oil companies to set prices at gas stations they do not own, but Big Oil has found several ways to get around the law—by controlling the prices charged at its branded stations through the wholesale price for gasoline, suggested retail prices, and zone pricing.

The wholesale price is the price at which the gas station purchases its gasoline from the oil company. Big Oil sets the wholesale price of all gasoline sold to its branded dealers. The U.S. General Accounting Office concluded that mergers have led directly to higher wholesale gasoline prices.[73] Higher wholesale prices translate into higher gasoline prices for customers at the pump and bigger profits for Big Oil.

Setting the wholesale price allows Big Oil to establish a sort of vise around the price that branded gas stations can charge and a lock on the profits derived from higher retail gasoline prices. The price we pay at the pump includes the wholesale price plus a small margin, usually between 3 and 10 cents per gallon, depending on the station.[74] These pennies per gallon are the *only* profit that the gas station owner receives. Were the gas station to sell its gasoline below the wholesale price, it would lose money on every sale. Were the station to charge more than a few cents above the wholesale price, it would be out of step with the company-owned stations in its area, and no one would buy its gas.

Beyond merely setting the wholesale price, it is common practice for Big Oil to "suggest" a retail gasoline price to all dealers selling its gasoline. In an attempt to avoid charges of price-fixing, these suggestions are usually given verbally by oil company representatives, who are sent out to counsel stations about how much they should charge for gas.[75] Big Oil determines this price by first starting with the recommended retail price, then adding a fixed margin that the gas station owner gets to pocket, and then arriving at its preferred wholesale price.

The 3 to 10 cents per gallon that goes to the gas station owner generally remains constant *regardless* of the retail price. If, for example, a branded dealer sells Exxon gasoline for $2.50 per gallon in February and $3.50 per gallon in March, the dealer takes in the exact same margin in March as he or she did in February. When gas prices rise, Big Oil, not the gas station owner, captures the profit.

Several branded dealers told the Senate Select Committee on Investigations that if they tried to increase their margins over what was "recommended" by the oil company, the increase would be reflected in their next wholesale price, "calling into question," concluded the Senate report, "the degree to which the price is actually recommended."[76] "Arco allows you to have a six-cent profit," dealer Charlie Mulcahy told the *Los Angeles Times* in 2005. If he were to raise pump prices by two cents per gallon, Mulcahy told the paper, and Arco "didn't want me to have that eight-cent margin, then the next day my dealer tank wagon [wholesale] price would go up two cents,'"[77] effectively erasing Mulcahy's attempt to increase his own share of the profits.

How does Big Oil come up with its prices, and why do gasoline prices vary so significantly among gas stations within a few blocks of each other? Oil companies set wholesale and company-owned gas station prices using "zone pricing," which involves grouping gas stations into geographic zones. Zones can vary widely in size, from one gas station to an entire town. Even though the gasoline is the same and the costs comparable, Big Oil routinely charges different wholesale prices to gas stations that are in the same geographic area—often within blocks of each other—but in different zones, which leads to different retail prices.

Antitrust law makes it illegal for companies to sell wholesale products at different prices to "similarly situated retailers." To get around the law, the oil companies have developed extremely complex systems to differentiate between retailers in the same area—but they have kept the systems secret. Complex computer models and techniques are used to design zones. Location, traffic volume, population, demand, and competition are reportedly all considered. But do not ask the gas station owner what zone he or she is in or how the zone is determined. The owners do not know—nor does just about anyone outside of the oil companies. The companies regard information about the configuration of their zones, the criteria used to establish them, and the prices charged within and between them as highly proprietary information.

Patrick Meadowcroft is an independent gas station owner who, in his twenty-five years in the business, has run Exxon, Chevron, and Gulf stations. He told a Senate committee hearing in 2005, "I'd like to clarify some common misunderstandings about how gasoline prices work. Everyone knows that prices at the pump have been going up, but not everyone understands that gas station owners don't set prices independently. We set our prices based on what we pay for the gas we sell. We make a very small margin on gas, and rely largely on other products that you buy at the gas station—everything from a can of oil to a cup of coffee. When you pay more to fill up your tank, it's because the station owner paid more to fill up his station's tank."[78]

For the independent owner or company-lessee, in fact, gasoline is one of the least profitable items sold at a gas station. Nationwide, gasoline only provides about 25 percent of the owner's earnings at any given gas station, and the owner must pay substantial fees and taxes out of that amount. While the oil company makes money from the gasoline sold at a gas station, the gas station owner largely makes money from the convenience store. Cigarettes and tobacco are the biggest sellers, accounting for a full one-third of all nongasoline sales, followed by soda, then beer and alcohol, and finally fast food.[79] So if you really want to help out a gas station owner, you should skip the gas and head straight to the convenience store.

Seeing the e-mails circulating for the May 15, 2007, National Gas Out for consumers, gas station owners decided to make their own statement against Big Oil. Henry Pollack, owner of Towne Market Mobil in the Milwaukee suburb of Mequon, wrapped his Mobil gas pumps in yellow tape and shut down his station for twenty-four hours. He explained to reporters that he has essentially no say in what he charges for gas, makes 8 cents per gallon from it, and earns most of his money from his convenience store. When Maria McClory, a nearby resident, heard about the protest on a local television station, she got in her car and drove down to Pollack's to buy diet soda. "I just wanted to support them and thank them for making a statement," she said.[80]

Jeff Curro, who has sold gas for twenty years at his Shell station in Brookfield, Wisconsin, also turned off his pumps. Curro said that he usually has only about a 3-cent-per-gallon profit margin. "The way I see it is, I'm doing all the work of providing the labor, the wages, the electricity, the lighting, the maintenance of the pumps, the repairs and the insurance, which is quite substantial," Curro said. "I'm doing all the work, and somebody else is getting fat on me."[81]

The oil companies are able to get away with controlling the price of gasoline because there are few competitors selling gasoline at a lower price. Big Oil has achieved this end by forcing out independent gas stations and refineries. Many independent gas stations that once pushed prices down in their local markets have totally disappeared. The Senate Select Committee on Investigations found that in California, for example, after Arco (now BP) purchased the Thrifty chain of independent gasoline stations, prices increased in the areas formerly served by the Thrifty stations.

The major oil companies generally do not replace the independent stations with their own brand-name stations. Rather, they are reducing the number of gas stations altogether. From 1984 to 1997, the major oil companies reduced their branded outlets by 63 percent. "In other words," the U.S. Department of Energy concludes, "as a result of consolidating and refocusing their gasoline marketing efforts, the majors have closed gasoline stations at a rate more than twice as fast as the national average."[82] In total, nearly fifty thousand gas stations have been shut down in the United States in the last twenty-five years.[83]

When one San Francisco Shell gas station owner felt that Shell was trying to force him out of business, he protested by raising his prices to over $4.50 per gallon (a very high price in May 2007). "I got fed up," Bob Oyster told a reporter. "It makes a statement, and I guess when people see that price they also see the Shell sign right next to it." Shell was making it increasingly difficult for Oyster to earn a living from his station. For example, Shell dictated where Oyster could purchase his supply. Oyster explained that he could buy gasoline for up to 20 cents per gallon less if the company would "just let me buy my gas where I want to. . . . They won't let me do that. . . . They don't care. Shell would rather put us out of business." Over a period of ten years, Shell also increased Oyster's rent from $1,000 to $13,000 a month. Oyster sued, and a court ordered that, based on real estate values, the rent should be $6,000 a month, but Shell simply came back with a new demand of $13,000. Rather than fight another court battle, Oyster is shutting down the station. "I'm getting nothing for the station," he says. "I just give them the keys and walk away. They told me they were probably just going to fence it and bulldoze it anyway."

"The dealer can no longer be competitive," said Dennis De-Cota, executive director of the California Service Station and Automotive Repair Association. Responding to Bob Oyster's protest, DeCota said, "The companies are squeezing these guys out. Bob's tired of it, and a lot of us are. It's just wrong."[84]

There are not only fewer gas stations, but also less cheap gasoline. In the past, when a Chevron or Exxon refinery had met its own refining needs, it would produce unbranded or generic gasoline to sell to independent gas stations. Today Big Oil refines just enough gasoline to serve its own ends, chooses to sell excess capacity in bulk to hypermarkets like Wal-Mart or Costco, or increases the wholesale price charged for unbranded gasoline. The result is that the independents are unable to compete.

Many independent gas stations believe that Big Oil is intentionally pricing them out of business by charging higher wholesale prices for generic gas than for branded gasoline. "No Gas Until Prices Drop" read the sign in front of the Rockett Express gas station in Fallston, North Carolina, in April 2006. Rockett shut down its pumps to protest the 11 cents more per gallon it was paying for its generic gas than its brand-name competitors paid down the road. In San Diego, at least three independent stations closed in protest. They said they were quoted a price of 40 cents per gallon more than their brand-name competitors.[85] As Patrick Meadowcroft explained to the U.S. Senate, "As an independent station, our cost to *purchase* fuel is 20 to 40 cents more than the cost at which a branded competitor is *selling* its fuel."[86]

Unable to afford Big Oil's unbranded gasoline, small independent gas stations are forced to look elsewhere. However, there are now fewer places to look, because the major oil companies are not only refining less generic gas, but—just as they have done with independent gas stations—have also bought up and shut down independent refineries. "[S]ince the 1990s," concluded the GAO, "the availability of unbranded gasoline from refiners has decreased substantially."[87] Hence the independents disappear and the price of gas rises.

Oil companies change the price of gasoline based on what they believe we will pay; they spike prices when they believe we will pay more, and reduce prices when they believe we will not. They exercise control directly over the price of crude. Their even greater control over refining allows them to control the supply of gasoline. Pushing out much of their lower-priced competition at both the refining and marketing levels allows them to set high prices without fear of being undercut. The major companies also tend to make pricing decisions in concert and therefore do not underprice each other. While it is illegal under antitrust law for the oil companies to collude with each other in this way, courts have found all the major U.S. oil companies guilty of price collusion at some point in the last forty years.[88]

CONCLUSION

Regulatory and antitrust action must be taken against the U.S. oil industry (topics to which I return in chapter 9). Ultimately, however, gasoline prices in the United States are not too high: the real problem is that too great a percentage of the price of gas is taken by Big Oil as profit. Gasoline prices are overly—and most likely illegally—manipulated by Big Oil, rising more quickly than the economy is able to adjust. The benefits of these rising prices are being captured by Big Oil in the form of profits and power rather than by governments in the form of taxes and regulation. As with the price of crude, were the price of gasoline to adequately account for the environmental, public health, worker protection, and other costs associated with refining and selling gasoline, the price would (and should) be much higher.

Other nations apply large taxes to gasoline in order to account for externalities such as the environmental and public health costs of oil and gasoline production, to discourage the use of automobiles, and to acquire government funds with which to fund alternatives, such as public transportation and clean-energy vehicles. The United States ranked second to last in a 2005 study of the gasoline taxes charged by the twenty-three wealthiest nations in the world (Mexico had the lowest taxes).[89] While U.S. taxes averaged 46 cents per gallon, average gasoline taxes in Turkey were more than $5.00 per gallon. Gasoline taxes averaged $4.22 in Britain, just over $4.00 in Germany, and $2.15 in Japan. Repeated attempts to increase gasoline taxes in the United States have been aggressively and successfully fought off by, among others, Big Oil. The American Petroleum Institute, for example, has referred to such proposals as "extremely regressive."[90] Big Oil prefers that any increase in the price of gasoline be captured in its pockets alone.

The problem is not high gasoline prices per se, but that we are not reaping the benefits of those prices to support alternative modes of travel such as public transportation, electric cars, more pedestrian-friendly cities, corridors for high-speed rail, and the like. Such investments would make demand for gasoline more elastic—more responsive to price because there would be more options for consumers to turn to. Today in the United States, if the price of gasoline rises and you do not live in a city with good public transportation, your work is too far away to walk, you are unable to carry your three children to school on your bike, you cannot afford a new electric or hybrid car, and there are no independent gas stations around that offer cheaper gas, you will generally have no alternative but to buy the higher-priced gas.

In March 2008, for the first time in a decade, Americans reduced their consumption of gasoline.[91] While only 1 percent, it was a reduction nonetheless. At the same time, public transit ridership reached a fifty-year high.[92] Tragically, cities across the U.S. simultaneously *reduced* access to these very services as they too were hit by higher gasoline prices and shrinking city budgets, while the federal government refused to step in with new funding.[93] Thus, just as many Americans made their first foray into public transportation, they faced reduced service, higher fares, and greater inconvenience.

Big Oil is not using its profits from crude, refining, and marketing to make its refineries safer, cleaner, or more efficient. Rather, it is using its profits to manipulate public policy decisions to the companies' extreme benefit and to the detriment of the larger society. The government has, in turn, largely abdicated its regulatory role, permitting mass manipulation and abuse. The next chapter exposes exactly how Big Oil exercises its influence over our democracy and how people are fighting back.

6

Lobbyists, Lawyers, and Elections

How Big Oil Kills Democracy

[Big Oil] is like some big muscle-bound brute coming into a room and stripping off his T-shirt and flexing his muscles. All of us 90-pound weaklings are going to look at that and say, "Oh god, no!"

—JUDY DUGAN, FOUNDATION FOR TAXPAYER AND
CONSUMER RIGHTS[1]

Money is like manure. You have to spread it around or it smells.

—J. PAUL GETTY, GETTY OIL[2]

Big Oil has simple needs. It wants to explore for, produce, refine, and sell oil and gas wherever possible without restriction. It wants laws that allow it to expand all of its operations. It wants to prevent laws that stand in its way and roll back those that already exist. Big Oil wants friends in office and enemies out of office. It wants friendly regulators in government and unfriendly regulators out of government. Big Oil does not want to pay taxes, fees, or fines. It does not want to be slowed down or financially burdened by government bureaucracy, environmental laws, protections for public health or worker safety, or concerns for human rights.

Big Oil has a simple formula for getting its needs met: get bigger, get richer, and spend, spend, spend. The mergers of the last twenty-five years—secured through Big Oil's wallet—have taken financial giants and turned them into economic behemoths, allowing Big Oil to dominate the political process and drown out the voices of those who seek to constrain, regulate, oversee, or erase its footprint. The more money the oil corporations have, the more power they wield, and the more they are able to achieve their goals.

Big Oil wields its power from small towns to state capitals to the federal government and beyond. It buys lobbyists, lawyers, elections, and spin. It hides behind front groups and creates an omnipresent force infecting everyone from congressional staff members to government bureaucrats, to elected officials, to the public at large.

The George W. Bush administration was the prize that Big Oil had been working toward for one hundred years. No other candidate for federal office has received as much financial support from the oil and gas industry as has George W. Bush. Each of the major oil companies set its own record for campaign contributions in 2000 and got what it paid for. When Bush named at least thirty former energy industry executives, lobbyists, and lawyers to influential jobs in his administration, they could stop lobbying and start legislating. The oil companies gained long-sought access to national lands to drill for oil, billions in tax breaks and new subsidies, easing of environmental regulations, and a seat at every negotiating table.

But their control was not absolute. The 2006 midterm elections showed the cracks in Big Oil's armor when voters rebelled and kicked out the party that has received three-fourths of the oil industry's money over the last twenty years. However, Big Oil's influence did not die with the shift in congressional power, for even one-quarter of its $209 million in campaign giving wields plenty of influence. The Democrats' big talk during the elections yielded little legislative change, and every major candidate for president in 2008 received money from Big Oil at some point in his or her career.

Big Oil has turned our democracy into a farce.

BIG OIL VERSUS CALIFORNIA

It was a political operation the likes of which I for one have never seen.

—YUSEF ROBB, COMMUNICATIONS DIRECTOR,
PROP 87 CAMPAIGN[3]

It was the most expensive ballot measure ever fought in U.S. political history. On its face, it was not a particularly radical idea. California's Proposition 87 on the November 2006 state ballot would have implemented a small fee per barrel of oil drilled within the state and directed the funds to investments in clean, renewable, alternative energy sources. The measure had a unique and impressive lineup of public health, environmental, alternative energy, labor, and government supporters—including the American Lung and American Nurses Associations, the Sierra Club and National Wildlife Federation, Bill Clinton, and Al Gore. When Prop 87 was first introduced in July 2006, more than 60 percent of Californians polled said it was a great idea. But at the voting booth in November, the measure was defeated 55 to 45 percent. What took place in the intervening five months is the story of how Big Oil flexes its muscle. And while the amount of money spent was unique, Big Oil's battle plan was not. It is the same model repeatedly used by the industry to ensure that its political agenda is enacted in state, federal, and international arenas.

Money lies at the heart of the story: a seemingly bottomless pit of financial reserves that the oil industry successfully unleashed on the state. For every dollar the supporters of Prop 87 spent, the oil companies spent two and were always prepared to spend more. In total, oil companies spent over $100 million to defeat Prop 87—a local issue in a single state—and they succeeded. To put this amount in context, consider that John Kerry and John Edwards spent $240 million on their entire 2004 presidential campaign. And while you never saw their names in the "paid for" line of any commercial or printed on the back of any campaign flyer, it was Chevron, ExxonMobil, Shell, and Occidental that led the charge against the measure. Advocates of Prop 87 certainly expected oil company opposition, but few anticipated the full extent of the assault.

California is one of the most politically progressive states in the nation. Kerry beat Bush by 10 percentage points there, entire cities ban large chain stores, Humboldt County passed a measure in 2006 banning out-of-county corporations from participating in local political campaigns, and five times more hybrid cars were sold there than in any other state in the nation in 2006. California also sits on about 3.5 billion barrels of oil—the third largest proved oil reserves in the nation.

The interests of the oil czars who own and pump this oil tend to clash with the views of the majority of California's residents. Nonetheless, fifteen bills opposed by Big Oil before California's state legislature were successfully defeated in 2006. While one might expect Big Oil to have a dominant grip on Republican stronghold states such as Texas or Louisiana—the number one and two oil-producing states in the nation, respectively—it is shocking to see that power translate just as readily to the heavily left-leaning, generally Democratic-controlled state of California.

Of course, California does have a Republican governor. Arnold Schwarzenegger and his wife, Maria Shriver, drove a Hummer the few blocks from their home to the polling place where they cast their votes for Schwarzenegger in California's 2003 gubernatorial recall election. His campaign was fueled by millions of oil industry dollars, the largest source of which was California's own Chevron Oil Corporation. But just as California is not a typical state, Schwarzenegger would not have a typical Republican administration. At his side was a true environmental activist, Terry Tamminen.

Terry Tamminen is a bright, energetic, deeply committed man who says he never intended to work for the government. For six years he was executive director of Santa Monica BayKeepers, a national network of clean water advocates led by Robert F. Kennedy Jr., Maria Shriver's cousin. Between Kennedy and Shriver, it did not take long for Tamminen and Schwarzenegger to meet. "When my friend Arnold decided to run for governor," Tamminen told me, "I decided to help him write a powerful environmental action plan."[4] When Schwarzenegger won, Tamminen was ready to head home. On his way out the door he told Schwarzenegger that he might be in for a tough fight, but at least "you've got a great plan to execute." Tamminen then turned on his thickest Schwarzenegger accent to share the governor's five-word response with me: "No I don't. You do." And that is how green activist Terry Tamminen became California's environmental secretary.

Tamminen lasted just three years and left before Schwarzenegger's 2006 successful reelection campaign. He was adequately soured on the state of our democracy and ready to move on. A few months later, his book *Lives Per Gallon: The True Cost of Our Oil Addiction* was published. It is a no-holds-barred exposé of the many ways Big Oil and Big Auto collude to fight regulation, sidestep the law, defraud the public, and poison our air, water, earth, and bodies along the way. The book calls for aggressive lawsuits against both industries, modeled after those against the tobacco industry in the 1990s. In a candid interview, Tamminen described to me how oil industry dollars translate into policy action in California's state capital.

The Tamminen/Schwarzenegger environmental action plan sought to reduce air pollution in the state by 50 percent by 2010. While bold in comparison with the laws of other states, such a reduction would merely bring California into compliance with

existing state and federal health standards. To reach the 50 percent goal, the state's leading polluters, including Big Oil, would
need to reduce their deadly emissions.

Tamminen had reason to believe he would get the oil industry's support, given that Schwarzenegger was a popular governor
whom the industry helped to elect and wanted to keep in power.
The oil companies, however, had a different idea about what
Schwarzenegger's election meant for them. They had supported
Schwarzenegger's campaign, and the new governor would now
do the industry's bidding.

Tamminen told the oil companies that the state had to reduce
its pollution, which would require that they reduce emissions
from their oil production and/or their refineries. He asked for the
oil industry's help in meeting the governor's goals. What were
they willing to do to help the governor and to help the state?
"Their collective answer was, 'What are you going to do for
us?'" Tamminen recalled. In return for agreeing to some reductions from their existing refineries, "they wanted relief from
regulatory requirements on those and any future refineries that
would have made their air pollution even worse." In other words,
in order to agree to one set of emission reductions, they wanted
the state to allow them to pollute even more.

Tamminen tried a different approach. He proposed that instead of requiring the oil industry to reduce its own pollution,
the state would add a small (2-cent) tax to wholesale gasoline
sales (gasoline sold by the refiner to the gas station) that would
fund alternative methods of reducing pollution. The oil companies said they would not oppose such a measure, but in return
they asked for the same elimination of existing environmental
laws on their oil refineries. They also wanted to expand their refineries without being subject to new environmental reviews.
Both measures would, of course, have the effect of increasing
deadly air pollutants.

"We could have tried to implement the tax over their objections," Tamminen said, "but it would have been much harder."

New taxes in California require a two-thirds majority vote, as opposed to the simple majorities required in most states. "So we would have had to have Republicans on board, and we couldn't have done that without the oil companies. So in essence, without the oil companies, it wouldn't have passed." This was the bottom line that drove Tamminen to leave the government. "It is extremely difficult for government officials to fight wealthy corporations determined to use almost any means to stall or stop meaningful regulation," Tamminen explains. "I can testify that it is nearly impossible to perform that function [of a government regulator] sitting on the other side of the petroleum-powered smoke screen."

When the state government gave up on the idea of taxing oil corporations, Californians tried to do it on their own with a citizen ballot initiative, Proposition 87. Over one million signatures were collected across the state—enough to qualify the measure for California's November 2006 ballot. The voters could then decide if they wished to have the state implement the proposition.

Proposition 87

Prop 87 would have introduced a severance tax on oil produced in California. Virtually every state in the nation imposes a tax on corporations when they sever natural resources such as minerals, coal, timber, or salt from the ground. All oil-producing states except California impose a severance tax on oil production, generating millions of dollars in revenue for the states every year.

Four of the largest oil companies in the world would have borne the full brunt of the Prop 87 tax. California pumps approximately 612,000 barrels of oil per day. Chevron, which has its world headquarters in San Ramon, California, pumps about 33 percent of the state's oil. ExxonMobil and Royal Dutch Shell (based in Houston and Geneva, respectively) pump another 30 percent through the joint venture Aera Energy. Occidental Oil

Corporation (based in Los Angeles) produces another 13 percent. Combined, these four companies produce three-fourths of California's oil. Sold at an average price of $58 per barrel in 2006, this oil earned these companies roughly $27 million *a day* in combined revenue that year.

The state of California receives nothing from the companies for this oil. Under Prop 87, California would have levied a 6 percent fee on the value of oil produced in the state when oil topped $60 per barrel, excluding the oil of smaller producers. All of the oil companies combined would have paid approximately $400 million a year for ten years (at 2006 oil prices). The estimated $4 billion that was to be raised by Prop 87 over its ten-year life span was earmarked for consumer rebates for hybrid vehicles, grants to scientists and universities, subsidies to industries for developing nonpolluting alternatives to oil, and incentives for increased solar, wind, and other renewable energy use.

The oil companies wanted not only to defeat Prop 87, but also to ward off the array of new legislative measures popping up at the state and federal levels that sought to increase taxes and funding for alternatives, reduce subsidies, and investigate price-gouging. Big Oil "is trying to signal to anyone else contemplating similar measures that if you're going to take on the industry, you are going to have to spend a ton of money," explained John Matsusaka, director of the Initiative and Referendum Institute at the University of Southern California.[5] And send a message they did. Prop 87 communications director Yusef Robb described the effect of this spending to me in an interview: "Anything that we did was doubled, exceeded, and outmatched by the oil companies. The oil companies proved that they have infinite wealth from which to draw in defeating any threat."[6]

The leader of the pack, according to Tamminen, was Chevron's Sacramento lobbyist, Jack Coffey. "It was Chevron's home turf," Tamminen explained, "so the others followed Coffey's lead."

The heart of the campaign was a full-throttle media blitz in every city and county across the state. "If we ran one TV ad, they ran two *and* a radio ad *and* a newspaper ad," said Robb. While the Prop 87 campaign had Robb and at times as many as two other press secretaries, its opponents had six full-time press secretaries, one sitting in every major media market in California: San Diego, Los Angeles, Orange County, Bakersfield, Sacramento, and San Francisco, Robb told me. This allowed the opponents of Prop 87 to respond immediately to any political development or story wherever and whenever it happened, frame it to their liking, hold a press conference, file a report, address a query, and be all wrapped up before Robb had stepped off the plane.

The media campaign was not only aggressive and well funded, but also persuasive. ExxonMobil, Chevron, Shell, and Occidental executives did not appear at press conferences and were rarely quoted in news stories. No oil company logos appeared on advertisements or mailers. Instead, groups well financed by the oil industry did its public bidding. "When we launched a campaign against Big Oil," Robb explained, "the people of California did not understand that Big Oil was our opponent. It was cloaked behind front groups, consultants, and lobbyists, and the cloak was secured by the lack of media scrutiny." Media inquiries made to the oil companies were diverted to the campaign's front group, Californians Against Higher Taxes, virtually 100 percent funded by oil company money, or to the California Chamber of Commerce. The Chamber of Commerce is a huge recipient of oil industry largesse on the local, state, and national levels, and its boards of directors are littered with past and present oil industry executives. Local chamber affiliates held regular press conferences and small business forums across the state that were covered by the local media as "grass roots" events having nothing to do with Chevron, ExxonMobil, or the statewide opposition campaign.

Led by Chevron, the oil companies poured money into trade associations, business alliances, and antienvironmental and

antiregulatory groups—particularly those with large member-
ships. These groups are then easily tapped when the industry
needs them to take a stand on a particular issue. The groups hold
their own local events, send out their own mailers, make their
own appearances on local talk radio, and no one is ever the wiser
to their Big Oil connections. Big Oil "sways these associations to
take a stand on oil-related issues because their contributions are
so large," Tamminen explained. "You're going to do what the
guy who pays more than others tells you to. Chances are you're
going to follow the policy that he wants followed."

The mantra repeated in every ad, every mailer, and by every
spokesperson focused on the one thing that scares Californians
even more than global warming: higher gas prices. Those who
campaigned against Prop 87 argued that prices would go up because costs would rise and oil companies would be forced to abandon California. This claim was supported by an "independent"
expert analysis provided by LECG, an economic consulting firm
(the letters are not an acronym). It turned out that LECG was paid
over $94,000 by the opponents of Prop 87 to write the report and
share the results with the public.[7] With painfully few exceptions,
LECG's findings were reported without any hint as to who had
paid for the study. ExxonMobil perfected this scheme when it
spent millions of dollars paying seemingly unbiased front groups
to produce analyses disproving the existence of global warming.
"Follow the money," Robb advised. "Virtually everybody who
stood up against Prop 87 was paid by the oil companies."

Economists challenged the claim that gas prices would rise
and the companies would be forced to leave the state as specious.
The tax was simply too small to have any meaningful impact on
the expenditures of these megacorporations. The idea that the
companies would leave California was even more ludicrous. For
the oil industry, an extra $1-million-per-year expenditure in
California is nothing compared with the costs of working in hostile nations from Nigeria to Colombia or spending billions to
extract oil from the tar sands of Canada. Alaska imposes some

of the highest severance and other taxes on oil production in the nation, yet gasoline at the pump is cheaper there than in California, and the oil companies fight desperately for the right to produce in Alaska's Artic National Wildlife Refuge. "Misinformation was the industry's number one tactic to defeat Prop 87," argued Tamminen.

In the fight against Big Oil, California still had one ace up its sleeve: Hollywood. Brad Pitt, Leonardo DiCaprio, and Julia Roberts held press conferences in support of Prop 87, which provided the campaign with the "free media" it needed to counter the paid ads of Big Oil. The public interest groups and individuals supporting Prop 87 raised several million dollars for the campaign—no small achievement for these groups. But for the big cash, Prop 87 turned to movie producer Stephen Bing, heir to a real estate fortune and one of the biggest financers of Democratic and environmental causes in the nation. Bing provided $50 million to the Prop 87 campaign. But for every dollar Bing ponied up and every "free media" moment provided by celebrities and political dignitaries, the oil companies matched it, surpassed it, and made clear that they would continue to do so without end.

On Election Day the number one issue that Californians said guided their overwhelming "no" votes against Prop 87 was the fear of rising gas prices.

BIG OIL VERSUS THE NATION
How Big Oil Spreads Its Money Around

Just as with the Prop 87 campaign, Big Oil's dominance of the national political process ultimately derives from its money—money spent on campaigns, lobbyists, and lawyers. The unparalleled cash on hand of the nation's large and ever-growing oil companies translates into vast and direct political control. With over $40 billion in 2007 profits, ExxonMobil reigns supreme in national political spending, dwarfing virtually all contenders. The Center for Responsive Politics (CRP), a nonpartisan, nonprofit research organization, provides the most comprehensive public record of political spending using Federal Election Commission data—and is hence the source for all such figures throughout this book. According to the CRP, ExxonMobil spent almost $5.5 million on presidential and congressional elections from 1998 to 2006. Chevron spent almost $4 million, and BP spent over $3.2 million. These enormous sums of money have earned each company a spot among the highest contributors to political campaigns in the nation. This money gives each company enormous pull over its chosen candidates.

But elections are only the beginning. Big Oil turns on the big guns when the electioneering is over and the policy-making begins. The millions of dollars that the companies spend on elections are utterly dwarfed by the tens of millions of dollars that they spend day in and day out on lobbying the federal government. From 1998 to 2006, ExxonMobil alone spent more than $80 million lobbying the federal government, over *fourteen times* more than it spent on political campaigns. Chevron's $50 million spent on lobbying was twelve and half times more than its campaign giving, while BP spent $34 million, ten times more than on campaign expenditures. National elections are important but only happen once every two years, at most. Policies, on the other hand, are made every single day, and Big Oil's money always secures it a prominent seat at every table.

Federal Elections

Overall, the oil and gas industry ranks among the top ten highest all-time spenders on federal election campaigns, donating over $209 million since 1990 (the earliest date, in most cases, for which the CRP provides data). This money goes a long way. Elections in the United States are monstrously expensive and are only getting more so. The average price of winning a Senate seat increased by 81 percent between 2000 and 2006, rising from just over $5.3 million to more than $9.6 million. In the House, the price increased by almost 50 percent, rising from $840,000 to $1.25 million over the same time period. Those running for office are therefore deeply in need of those with money. As money becomes more concentrated among a shrinking group of extremely profitable companies and wealthy individuals, their relative influence over the electoral process grows.

Every member of Congress is affected by the rising cost of campaigns, even those who are in noncompetitive seats or not up for reelection. Marcy Kaptur, Democratic congresswoman of Ohio, has represented her district, which includes Toledo and stretches along the southwestern edge of Lake Erie, for more than twenty-five years. As the senior woman in the House, she has what is known as a "safe seat"—she is well liked in her district and wins elections with a comfortable margin. One might assume that she is less beholden to the election purse. Not so. However, Kaptur's position allows her to be uniquely frank about the corrosive influence of money on all elected officials. She has described how members of Congress are now expected to raise hundreds of thousands of dollars for their colleagues "if you are going to move forward." "When you go to a [party] caucus meeting," Kaptur explains, "you are now graded and publicly embarrassed about how much money you've raised compared to the rest of your colleagues, and it's that way on both sides of the aisle. . . .[Members] bid for committee positions based on how much money they've raised."[8]

Congresswoman Kaptur has received little if any money from the oil and gas industry, and certainly none from Big Oil, in the last two decades. This is not particularly surprising, not only because Kaptur is a strongly populist politician who gets most of her financial support from labor unions, but also because on the whole, Big Oil supports Republicans rather than Democrats. Since 1990, a full three-fourths of the oil and gas industry's combined $209 million in contributions has gone to the Republican Party. The Republican bias of the largest oil companies is even starker. ExxonMobil, the 900-pound gorilla in every room, gives about 90 percent of its federal campaign money to Republicans. There has not been a single Democrat on its top twenty list of all-time recipients since at least 1990. Chevron is only slightly more balanced, due to its largely Democratic home state of California, giving around 80 percent of its contributions to Republicans. Chevron's top twenty list of recipients includes two Democrats: California's senator Dianne Feinstein, who ranks in third place, and oil-rich Louisiana's senator John Breaux, who ranks fourteenth.

The campaign giving of the oil companies follows a set pattern: the companies give to officials from their home states, states where they have production and refining operations, states where they would like to have operations, and to those on key congressional committees or in leadership positions. The companies hope the influence these officials wield at both the state and federal level will protect them from taxation, regulation, and oversight and allow them to expand their operations.

ExxonMobil, ConocoPhillips, Marathon, BP North America, and Shell Oil Company (Shell's U.S. affiliate) are all headquartered in Texas, where they have production and refining operations and would like to have more. Their campaign giving is concentrated in this state. Likewise, Chevron, Occidental, and Valero, which are headquartered in California and have production and refining operations there, give generously in their home state.

Chevron produces oil and gas in California, Louisiana, Texas, New Mexico, Alaska, Colorado, and Wyoming and operates refineries in California, Mississippi, New Jersey, Hawaii, and Utah. Its campaign funding reflects all of these locations, with significant contributions to representatives such as Don Young of Alaska, Wayne Allard of Colorado, Tom DeLay, Kay Bailey Hutchison, and Phil Gramm of Texas, Craig Thomas of Wyoming, and Jim McCrery of Louisiana. But California is the site of Chevron's world headquarters as well as of half its domestic production and two of its six refineries—making it the primary focus of Chevron's campaign giving. While Chevron's overall campaign spending heavily favors Republicans, just about every member of California's congressional delegation has at some point received money from the company or its employees.

This spending has generally (although not universally) translated into an overall lack of congressional support for local communities that are struggling against Chevron and a reticence about challenging the company head-on. Congressman George Miller is a particularly disappointing example. Miller is usually a critically important friend of the environment, workers, and human rights, but he has also received direct (although, not substantial) campaign contributions from Chevron over the years. He represents Richmond, just seventeen miles north of San Francisco, and from the perspective of many who struggle against the refineries there, has turned a blind eye to their plight, allowing Chevron to go about its business with inadequate oversight.

Chevron's best friend in office was also its number one recipient of campaign giving: Republican congressman Richard Pombo. Pombo represented San Ramon, the location of Chevron's world headquarters, for fourteen years. Chevron's money was well spent. From his perch as chairman of the House Resources Committee, Pombo did more than just about any other politician to support the interests of Chevron and Big Oil, earning himself the number one spot on the League of Conservation Voters' "Dirty Dozen" members of Congress list for 2006. "From proposals to sell off national parks to legislation that rewards the oil companies with huge tax breaks," the league explained, "Rep. Pombo uses his position to advance the interests of greedy developers and big oil companies." In an editorial, the *St. Petersburg Times* of Florida called him "the oil industry's errand boy in the U.S. House."[9] Pombo introduced a bill to lift the twenty-five-year ban on offshore drilling, allowing oil and gas drilling within 100 miles of shore along the entire U.S. coastline. His bill would even have sold off fifteen national parks to private developers. Pombo was Chevron's pitch-perfect colleague in arms, until he was swept away in the Jack Abramoff scandal and the great 2006 peoples' rebellion (more on that later).

ExxonMobil's giving follows a similar pattern, particularly in its home state. Its top three campaign recipients since 1990 are all from Texas and are, in order: George W. Bush, Senator Kay Bailey Hutchison, and Senator Phil Gramm (of Enron Loophole fame). Number four on ExxonMobil's list is Senator Don Young of oil-rich Alaska. All four recipients are notorious and uncompromising supporters of ExxonMobil and the oil and gas industry more broadly. Like Chevron, over the years ExxonMobil and its employees have spread their wealth through the entire state delegations of Texas and Alaska, giving to both Democrats and Republicans.

Money Means Influence

Does campaign giving necessarily ensure that candidates will do the bidding of Big Oil after they are elected? More than three in four Americans think so: 84 percent of those polled said that members of Congress would be more likely to "listen to those who give money to their political party." Only one in four believe that members are likely to give "the opinion of someone like them special consideration."[10]

These popular views are supported by separate analyses conducted by the Center for American Progress (CAP) and Oil Change International, both progressive research and advocacy organizations. CAP investigated the connection between money and votes for HR 2776, the Renewable Energy and Energy Conservation Tax Act of 2007. The bill sought to eliminate $16 billion in oil and gas industry tax breaks and to increase funding for clean energy alternatives. CAP found an astounding correlation between oil and gas industry campaign funding and legislators' votes. Members of Congress who voted against the bill received on average *four times* more money in campaign contributions from the industry than those who voted for the bill, approximately $110,000 and $26,000, respectively, from 1989 to 2006.[11] However, with Democrats in the majority, there were more $26,000 recipients than $110,000 ones, and the bill passed the House by 30 votes, 221 to 189. Big Oil was not yet done, though. Under the weight of millions of dollars of oil industry lobbying, the bill stalled in conference committee.

Oil Change International applied a similar analysis to seven different key votes in the House and six in the Senate on issues such as increasing automotive fuel economy standards, reducing greenhouse gas emissions, increasing investments in alternative energy, and eliminating tax subsidies to the oil and gas industry from 2005 to 2008. As with HR 2776, House and Senate members who voted against these proposals received over four times more oil money than those who voted in the public interest. Overall, the twenty-five members of Congress who took the most oil money between 2000 and 2007 voted for legislation supporting Big Oil on average 86 percent of the time. Of these twenty-five representatives, twenty-three were Republicans. The ten senators who took the most oil money between 2000 and 2007 voted for Big Oil on average 98 percent of the time. All of these senators were Republicans.[12]

For the best evidence that oil money leads directly to oil influence, we need only look to the number one recipient of oil and gas industry largess: George Walker Bush. In the last two decades, no candidate for any U.S. office has received more money from this industry than Bush, and probably no other president who has been more subservient to its needs. The 2000 presidential election was the most expensive election for the oil and gas industry to date. The tag team of Bush and Cheney shattered all previous fund-raising records, and Big Oil shattered all its own records as well.

For the industry as a whole, the 2000 campaign was far and away the most expensive campaign in the last twenty years. The oil and gas industry donated *thirteen times* more money to George Bush and Dick Cheney than it did to Al Gore and Joseph Lieberman, nearly $2 million compared with just over $140,000. Overall, the industry spent $34 million on the 2000 elections— nearly $10 million more than the next most expensive campaign, the 2004 elections. Almost 80 percent of this money went to Republican candidates.

George W. Bush is Chevron's number two all-time campaign recipient (after Richard Pombo). In 2000, on the eve of its merger with Texaco, Chevron gave more than any other oil company to federal campaigns: $1.6 million. ExxonMobil and BP were close on Chevron's heels, giving $1.4 million and $1.3 million apiece.

Hidden Costs

These figures, however, represent only direct contributions to federal candidates from individuals associated with oil companies, political action committees funded by the companies, and soft money contributions to the national political parties. Beyond this money lies an entire labyrinth of funding that is virtually impossible to trace fully. There are, for example, the Bush-Cheney Pioneers, who, after meeting the legal limit for personal donations, convinced their wealthiest friends to do the same, each raising over $100,000 for the candidates in 2000. In 2004 Bush and Cheney introduced campaign "Rangers," who bundled $200,000 apiece. We only know what Bush and Cheney choose to reveal about who these people are and how much money they have provided to the candidates.

Then there are donations to party conventions, the 2000 recount, and inaugural parties. Again, we only learn who gives to these multimillion-dollar funds when and if the parties feel like sharing the information. For example, while the Bush-Cheney 2001 Presidential Inaugural Committee reported that it took in a record $40 million in private contributions, only $28.8 million of that amount was broken down by individual donor. These include $100,000 donations made by BP Amoco, Conoco's CEO Archie Dunham, Chevron's CEO David O'Reilly, ExxonMobil's vice president James J. Rouse, Hunt Oil's Ray Hunt, and Occidental's vice president of Federal Relations Gerald McPhee. Chevron's Sacramento lobbyist Jack Coffey and Conoco's Tassie Nicandros gave $5,000 each.[13]

Even this list of spending only touches the surface. The Center for Public Integrity, one of the most important campaign funding watchdog groups in the nation, has reported on campaign giving to state and local party committees: "What is not well understood by the American people is the substantially lawless extent to which the political parties launder hundreds of millions of dollars throughout [these committees]. There are certain 'Cayman Island' states that have no limits on contributions and no public disclosure, and dubious donors can easily slide their big checks into those states, knowing a transfer can be made to another place." The center tracked some of these expenditures and found that, in the 2000 elections, donors they thought had given hundreds of thousands of dollars to a political party had actually written millions of dollars in checks to state party committees nationwide.[14]

"Campaign finance anarchy reigns," according to the center, "and the two major political parties thrive in the chaos. They can cavort and collude with powerful vested interests that want something from government, with very little if any accountability. The amounts of money will increase, and accessibility by ordinary, well-intended, serious folks will become even more limited."[15] The bottom line is that those with big money have big influence, and we do not even know how to track it, much less control it.

The Real Money: Lobbying

It's just the unfortunate fact of life we're up against. When all is said and done, there's no more powerful industry then Big Oil when it comes to environmental concerns.

— GENE KARPINSKI, PRESIDENT,
LEAGUE OF CONSERVATION VOTERS[16]

Even if Big Oil has contributed twice as much to campaigns than we know about, that amount still thoroughly pales in comparison with what the companies spend on lobbying. Big Oil has at least two things working against it when it comes to elections: there are limits on how much can be spent, and the money is, for the most part, publicly reported. Companies can and most likely do find ways around these limitations, but they are still constrained in a way that is completely foreign to the limitless land of lobbying. Furthermore, it has been a long time since Big Oil had a positive public image, if it ever did. The money given to candidates and political parties is generally widely reported in the media, albeit not to the extent that most of us would prefer, and few candidates want to walk around with a giant ExxonMobil logo stuck to their lapel in the public mind if they can avoid it.

Finally, let's be frank. Elections are not where the real action is. In 2004, 96 percent of incumbent senators and 98 percent of incumbent House members who ran were reelected. Since 1990, the rate of reelection has not gone below 77 percent in the Senate or 94 percent in the House. The money it costs candidates to run acts essentially as a barrier to significant change. If only a relatively few seats actually change hands, a company that wants to influence the everyday decisions of elected officials must do so while those individuals are in office, not just when they are campaigning.

Lobbying is not only limitless, but it takes place almost completely off the public's radar. Only those residing in the inner corridors of the nation's capital, walking the halls of Congress or sitting in their offices on K Street, know what it means for one company to spend an average of $9 million every year to lobby the federal government alone. The combined yearly lobbying expenditures of ExxonMobil, Chevron, Shell, BP, Marathon, and ConocoPhillips are over $26 million. Combined, these six companies spent $240 million lobbying the federal government from 1998 to 2006—more than the *entire oil and gas industry* spent on federal election campaigns from 1990 to 2006.

What does this money buy? At the most fundamental level, this money has bought Big Oil its very existence. In their merger years, each oil company's lobbying expenditures spiked dramatically.

The companies' lobbyists printed glossy information packets and detailed studies. They blanketed Capitol Hill, federal agencies, and the White House. They held one-on-one meetings with elected officials and met with congressional and White House staff, agency bureaucrats, and anyone else who would listen.

The amount of money they spent is astounding. In 1998 and 1999, Exxon and Mobil spent almost $23 million lobbying the federal government. This two-year total is four times greater than ExxonMobil's total federal campaign expenditures over the eight years from 1998 to 2006. Chevron and Texaco spent a combined $8 million lobbying the federal government in 2000 and 2001—the year their merger was approved. After the merger, Chevron surpassed this lobbying record only once, when it successfully pursued its merger with Unocal in 2005, spending over $8.5 million. BP Amoco, Arco, and British Petroleum (before it changed its name to BP) spent $18.5 million on federal lobbying from 1998 to 2000, facilitating the 1998 merger of British Petroleum with Amoco followed by the Arco merger two years later. The same pattern exists for each company: a sharp increase in lobbying money spent to grease the wheels for megamergers.

Overall, these hundreds of millions of lobbying dollars mean that the oil industry is omnipresent in Washington. The money pays for hours of time from squadrons of the most well-connected lobbyists, both in-house and at the nation's most expensive lobbying firms. It pays for costly lobbying campaigns, including commercials, Web sites, and pricey publications complete with exhaustive research and expensive data.

While both companies and lobbyists are prohibited from paying for trips for elected officials or their staff, well-financed lobbyists can afford to tag along on government-sponsored congressional trips. According to a *Wall Street Journal* investigative report, such trips happen more often then you would think: some 3,140 were reported from 2000 through 2006. In 2005 alone there were 658 official foreign trips by congressional delegations, compared with 220 a decade earlier. Republicans led most of the trips and made up the bulk of the attendees. While it is illegal to do so, lobbyists have often been found paying for expensive dinners and other outings along the way. According to the report, "for the corporations that host lawmakers, the benefits are clear. While no one alleges any quid pro quo for the meals, veteran staffers who have been on such trips say they can influence congressional business. The meals help smooth the way for favorable votes. They also give companies advance access to information.[17]

This oil industry presence, both at home and abroad, completely outweighs the efforts of those working to support consumers, the environment, public health, or worker and human rights. Every time a bill comes up for consideration, a tax is proposed, a law is debated, or a fine is considered, the oil industry is there in full force—always. Gene Karpinski, president of the League of Conservation Voters, described an example of this presence to me: "You've got an eight-day-long Commerce Committee hearing covering environmental issues. There will be two hundred people in that room each day, and half a dozen will be from the environmental community. The rest, if they are not [congressional] staffers, are representatives of the oil industry."

During the 1990s, I worked in Washington, D.C., as a legislative assistant for two Democratic members of Congress: John Conyers Jr. of Michigan, chairman of the House Judiciary Committee, and Elijah Cummings of Maryland, a senior member of the House Committee on Oversight and Government Reform. I heard from industry groups approximately three times more often than from environmental, human rights, public health, or consumer organizations. I received faxes, letters, e-mails, expensive publications, lengthy analyses of bills before Congress, and visits. I attended their congressional briefings, which were almost always accompanied by a meal or drinks to encourage staff to show up. Unlike other staff members, I was never invited on outings to discuss policy while playing golf or taking in a sunrise in

Tahiti. I would estimate, however, that given congressmen Conyers's and Cummings's progressive political views (and mine), I received probably a third as much lobbying by industry as the average staff person—if that much.

But I was not your average staff person: I was better informed and far more studious than most. I say this not to brag but to ensure that no one reading this book harbors any illusions about the policy expertise or the independence of the average congressional staff person. These men and women make key policy decisions every single day. Most are in their twenties, greatly overworked, and may have to cover policy issues of which they knew absolutely nothing prior to being hired. The issues involved in oil and gas are uniquely complex for anyone untrained in the industry, including both staff and elected officials. Many staff people are easily swayed by the information placed before them because it saves the time and effort of seeking alternative voices. Many of them simply succumb to the constant pressure of the industry, as do their bosses. Finally, far too many also have their feet halfway out the door on their way to more lucrative positions working for or on behalf of the very same companies that are lobbying them. The omnipresence of Big Oil makes a big impact by always providing information, always hinting at post-government-service jobs, and always applying pressure.

For elected officials, part of the pressure is the likely impact of their actions on their next election. Speaking about legislation before the California State House in 2006, State Senator Joe Dunn expressed his frustration with the oil industry's "enormous voice." Too many elected officials, he felt, "were too concerned about what this industry might do in the campaign this fall" to pass necessary legislation.[18]

In-house lobbyists, lobbying firms, and groups such as the American Petroleum Institute and the U.S. Chamber of Commerce represent the oil companies. Many of the lobbyists are former members of Congress, cabinet secretaries, and ex-White House, congressional, or agency staff people. They have personal relationships with the existing staff, know how the Hill works, and know how to do their companies bidding.

ExxonMobil's outside lobbying firm of choice over the past few years, for example, is the Nickles Group. Don Nickles served as the Republican senator from Oklahoma for twenty-four years before retiring in 2005, the same year he founded his lobbying firm. Nickles was a key member of the Republican leadership, chairman of the Senate Budget Committee, and a ranking member of the Energy and Natural Resources Committee. He was a dutiful friend of Big Oil, and Big Oil was a dutiful friend in return. Since 1989 (the earliest year data is available), ConocoPhillips was his number one donor, BP was number three, ExxonMobil number five, and Chevron number six (number seven was the National Beer Wholesalers Association). These four Big Oil companies gave Nickles a total of $140,000 in direct campaign contributions—almost nothing in comparison with what they gave him when he started lobbying. In 2006 and 2007, according to the Federal Lobbyist Disclosure Database, the Nickles Group received $450,000 from ExxonMobil alone. The relationships of elected officials to Big Oil can have as much to do with their expected payout when their government service is done as with the campaign contributions they receive while in office.

Among Chevron's in-house lobbyists is Richard Karp, policy coordinator in Chevron's Policy, Government and Public Affairs group, where he helps to "identify, address, and manage emerging global public policy issues that could significantly impact the company's businesses, future endeavors, stakeholder relations, or global reputation," according to his bio.[19] Karp, a former CIA intelligence officer, previously served as the Washington representative for the American Petroleum Institute. Before that, he was director for International Energy at the National Security Council, where he worked for then National Security Advisor Condoleezza Rice. Rice served on Chevron's board of directors from 1991 to 2001 and chaired its Public Policy Committee. A

Chevron supertanker was named in her honor, the SS *Condo-leezza Rice.*[20]

Big Oil likes the anonymity of lobbying. Those being lobbied certainly know that Big Oil is doing the talking, but the public at large is generally unaware of these activities. While it garners a lot of media attention when it occurs, it is the rare ExxonMobil executive who testifies before a congressional hearing or conducts an interview with reporters. Far more often, when the industry needs a public face or when it wants Congress to believe that its interests have universal support, two key groups take the stage: the American Petroleum Institute and the U.S. Chamber of Commerce.

The American Petroleum Institute

Since its founding almost a hundred years ago, the American Petroleum Institute (API) has been the leading trade group representing the interests of the oil and gas industry. It has four hundred corporate members, seven hundred committees and task forces, and its board is composed of the CEOs of every major oil company. Following in the footsteps of Walter Teagle, former Exxon-Mobil CEO Lee Raymond served nearly twenty years as an API board member, including two terms as chairman. Upon Raymond's retirement, API honored him with its 2006 Gold Medal for Distinguished Achievement. When he was Halliburton's CEO, Dick Cheney served on API's board and on its Public Policy Committee. API's 2006 annual budget exceeded $112 million, and it annually spends around $3 million on federal lobbying.

API employs lobbyists, economists, statisticians, policy analysts, and technical experts. It conducts its own research and also pays other groups to do research and release reports. Starting with the negotiations leading to the Kyoto Protocol climate treaty in 1997, API has promoted the idea that lingering uncertainties in climate science justify delaying restrictions on emissions of carbon dioxide and other heat-trapping smokestack and tailpipe gases. It funds studies to debunk the existence of climate change, including one of the reports most often cited by the Bush administration: "Lessons and Limits of Climate History: Was the 20th Century Climate Unusual?" This 2003 study by the George C. Marshall Institute, a nonprofit research organization, examined "the repeated claim that 20th century climate was unusual compared to that of the last 1,000 years"—and concluded that it was not.[21] The institute received some $90,000 from Exxon-Mobil in 2002, and its president, William O'Keefe, formerly served as API's chief operating officer.[22] When the report was published in the journal *Climate Science,* three journal editors resigned in protest.[23]

If you want to know the oil industry's government agenda, you need only talk to API's chief economist and leading spokesperson, John Felmy. Trained as an economist at the University of Maryland, Felmy has spent his entire career in Washington. He speaks at virtually every government hearing on behalf of the industry, writes position papers, talks to students, speaks to the media, and lets people like me in on API's political agenda.

API's primary job on behalf of its oil company members, as Felmy described it for me in an interview, is quite straightforward: to eliminate barriers to oil production.[24] The barriers Felmy has on his radar include outright moratoriums on oil production in areas such as public land in the western United States, off the shores of the East and West Coasts and parts of the Gulf of Mexico, "Alaska, of course," and Iran. API would like to see access for the development of shale oil in the West. API would also like to see a full accounting of just how much oil and gas is sitting under public lands, although Felmy admits that there is strong resistance to such an idea because "many argue that this would be the first step to development on those lands."

Felmy spoke against "policies that really restrict our ability to develop foreign resources as efficiently as we could," such as "outright unilateral sanctions—for example Iran or other countries" against which the United States exercises full sanctions (discussed in detail in chapter 8). Iran's oil reserves, the third largest in the world, are effectively cut off to U.S. oil companies and oil services providers. API would like to see that situation change because it "basically just puts the U.S. at a disadvantage while other foreign countries allow their companies to be able to develop resources there."

There are other, subtler barriers to production, primarily environmental protections and government bureaucracy. Felmy argues that the permitting process for drilling or expanding refineries is onerous: it involves costly and time-consuming environmental impact statements, analysis, and hurdles such as increasing emissions standards—including the discussion of new ozone standards to protect against global warming—and wildlife restrictions. There are disagreements among the different agencies on granting permits, and the process is backlogged. "There's really a host of these types of hurdles that you've got to go through, which can slow down the ability to look for energy and then actually develop it," Felmy explained. "What we're thinking about is the ability to streamline the permitting process to be able to remove unnecessary, unwise impediments."

Felmy has every reason to believe that API's agenda will be met, as it has had an excellent track record in this regard. In one particularly glaring example, made public through a Freedom of Information Act request by the Natural Resources Defense Council, an official from API sent an e-mail on March 20, 2001, to Joseph Kelliher, then a Department of Energy policy adviser, proposing language for a new Bush administration policy on energy regulations. API called it "a suggested executive order to ensure that energy implications are considered and acted on in rulemakings and other executive actions." The e-mail recommended a new directive requiring U.S. government agencies to consider whether environmental or other regulations would cause "inordinate complications in energy production and supply." On May 18, President Bush issued Executive Order 13211, directing all U.S. government agencies to assess whether regulations would have "any adverse effects on energy supply, distribution or use." API proposed that the order apply to "any substantive action by an agency that promulgates or is expected to lead to the promulgation of a rule, regulation or policy, including, but not limited to, notices of inquiry, advance notices of proposed rule-making, notices of proposed rule-making, and guidance documents." The Bush executive order applies to "any action by an agency . . . that promulgates or is expected to lead to the promulgation of a final rule or regulation, including notices of inquiry, advance notices of proposed rule-making, and notices of proposed rule-making."[25] In essence, the effect of the Executive Order is to ensure that no government regulations are made without first taking into account the impact on API's membership.

The U.S. Chamber of Commerce

The U.S. Chamber of Commerce, with its $150 million annual budget, is hands down the greatest lobbying force before the federal government and most likely before most state houses across the nation.[26] The Center for Responsive Politics reports that since 1998 the chamber has spent $338 million on federal lobbying. That amount is nearly five times greater than the lobbying expenditures of ExxonMobil; more than $100,000 greater than the *combined* lobbying of ExxonMobil, Chevron, Shell, BP, Marathon, and ConocoPhillips; and twice as great as that of the second greatest lobbying force, the American Medical Association.

The chamber has more than three million members, and its twenty-eight hundred affiliated chapters give it a presence in nearly every state and congressional district.[27] Unlike API, the chamber represents all business sectors, although the interests of big business over small business strongly prevail, particularly at the national political level. Reflecting the growing economic clout of Big Oil, energy now dominates the chamber's legislative agenda, which is part and parcel of that set out by Felmy. The chamber lobbied heavily in opposition to HR 2776, the Renewable Energy and Energy Conservation Tax Act, which would have cut Big Oil's subsidies and tax breaks. The chamber also lobbies aggressively against all meaningful legislation to address climate change. In a recent article, Thomas Donohue, the chamber's president and CEO, warned, "Now, with the emergence of climate change as a major issue, we face the risk of digging our country into an even deeper hole when it comes to potentially crippling restrictions on our ability to acquire, produce, and use energy."[28] Former FTC chairman Timothy Muris's paper "A Dozen Facts You Should Know about Antitrust and the U.S. Oil Industry" appeared front and center in the "Issues" section of the Chamber's Web site throughout 2007 and 2008. The chamber lobbies against antitrust enforcement and gasoline price-gouging legislation and in favor of regulatory rollbacks, tax breaks, and subsidies for the industry.

To focus its energy-lobbying efforts, the chamber founded the Institute for 20th Century Energy in 2007. According to *National Journal,* this $20 million to $40 million effort has key oil company backing. ExxonMobil "played a pivotal role in jump-starting the project," and "several other oil giants are expected to join."[29]

The Good Guys

As I have said, there is simply no comparison between the financial reach of the oil industry and that of organizations working on behalf of consumers, the environment, public health, alternative energy, antitrust enforcement, and human rights. Most of the organizations that work on behalf of these groups and interests are prohibited from participating in political campaigns and all but prohibited from lobbying. They are generally nonprofit advocacy groups taxed as 501(c)3 organizations. To maintain their nonprofit status, they are allowed to educate the public and elected officials but not to participate in direct political giving and can spend no more than 20 percent of their total yearly budget on lobbying. Their budgets are miniscule in comparison with those of the oil industry.

In 2006 ExxonMobil spent more than $15.5 million on federal lobbying alone. The entire annual budget of Oil Change

International, whose vote analysis is cited above, is approximately $350,000. The American Antitrust Institute, the only organization that approaches antitrust policy from a public, as opposed to a purely corporate, perspective, has an annual budget of about $400,000. Chevron's spending of nearly $7.5 million on federal lobbying in 2006 was seven and a half times larger than the entire $1 million budget of Amazon Watch, which organizes the "ChevronToxico" campaign. Even the Sierra Club, one of the largest environmental organizations in the world with its 1.3 million members, had a 2006 budget of just less than $30 million.

A few organizations set aside resources to establish a 501(c)4, which may engage in political activities as long as these do not become its primary purpose. Again, these budgets are miniscule in comparison with those of the oil industry. Others form political action committees (PACs), which can raise and spend limited "hard money" contributions for the express purpose of electing or defeating candidates. Unions are the only PACs representing progressive issues that are ever found among the top campaign contributors. Otherwise, industry PACs dominate. Public interest organizations have influence and can make their presence known. Their power lies in the number of people they reach, the number of voters they organize and influence, and the "people power" they can bring to action. But as elections become increasingly expensive and as the lobbying of the oil industry saturates every pore of our government, more often than not the voice of the people is lost.

THE REVOLVING DOOR

> *There is something about oil that makes high officials lie.*
> —KEVIN PHILLIPS, *AMERICAN THEOCRACY*[30]

One of Big Oil's most powerful tools is its ability to use big salaries and campaign spending to influence people's careers. Big Oil lures government regulators away from their jobs and into its employ, while ensuring that its own people get key government posts. The largest oil company mergers and the major regulatory decisions on the key issues of our day—including gasoline price-gouging, access to our nation's public lands, taxation, global warming, environmental and public health, and even the decision to go to war—have all been overseen by legislators and government officials who either began their careers with or went on to work for or on behalf of Big Oil. There is a startling overlap between the legislative agenda set out by the oil corporations and their lobbying bodies and the actions taken by their former and soon-to-be employees serving in government. While there are many ethics and conflict-of-interest rules set out by state-level bar associations, state governments, and the federal government, most apply for just one to two years and are filled with caveats and loopholes.[31]

Big Oil's Lawyers

Big Oil spends a lot of money on lawyers. At all stages, the use and production of oil is an intrinsically destructive process that raises issues of pollution, environmental harm, health risks, and worker safety. The oil companies must contend with the rights of the people who live in and near their sites of operation. Then there are government regulators watching for price-fixing, collusion, conspiracy, fraud, and other corporate crimes. Big Oil gets sued a lot, and its greatest defense is its financial might—its ability to outspend any and all challengers (whether it's a single gasoline consumer in Illinois or the federal government) and ride cases out for five, ten, or even twenty years until its challengers throw up their hands for lack of funds or are scared away from launching a suit. Its other great defense is its lawyers. Chevron alone has three hundred in-house lawyers and an annual budget of $100 million for farming out litigation to private firms. It employs some 450 law firms globally, while 80 percent of its legal work goes to just forty upper tier firms, and 50 percent of that to a select group of five "principal legal partners."[32]

One of Big Oil's most important needs over the last twenty

years was the need to merge. The Federal Trade Commission (FTC) and Department of Justice (DOJ) antitrust lawyers, both inside and outside of the federal government, have often proved to be among the oil industry's most reliable allies.

Granting Mergers and Stifling Oversight: the Federal Trade Commission and the Department of Justice

The FTC and the DOJ have overseen the near reunification of the Standard Oil Trust. We would all like to believe that as Exxon, Mobil, Conoco, Phillips, Tosco, Chevron, Getty, Gulf, Texaco, BP, Amoco, Arco, Unocal, Marathon, Ashland, Burlington, Valero, Shell, and the rest of the companies seeking mergers made their cases before federal regulators, the government's lawyers decided without bias that it was in the public interest to allow these giants to merge and become the behemoth oil companies they are today. But we are forced to ask how disinterested regulators genuinely can be when lucrative jobs with or representing the very oil corporations they are supposed to be regulating play such central roles in so many of their careers.

O'Melveny & Myers and Jones Day are two of the key law firms representing the nation's largest oil companies that also have a penchant for lawyers with FTC and DOJ experience. Both firms are over one hundred years old and rank among the most prominent corporate antitrust law firms in the nation. O'Melveny is the smaller of the two—about half the size of Jones Day. O'Melveny has some twelve hundred lawyers operating in thirteen offices. It is predominantly a California law firm, but also has offices around the nation and the world. Jones Day has twenty-three hundred lawyers in thirty offices across the United States and around the world. Jones Day boasts "more than 250 of the Fortune 500 among our clients," and that "surveys repeatedly cite Jones Day as among the law firms most frequently engaged by U.S. corporations."

O'MELVENY & MYERS: O'Melveny & Myers likes to represent Goliath in his fights against David. When Enron CEO Jeff Skilling needed representation in both his civil and criminal cases, O'Melveny & Myers was his firm. When Burmese villagers sued Union Oil Company of California (Unocal) alleging its complicity in acts of slavery, forced labor, torture, rape, murder, and crimes against humanity, O'Melveny & Myers represented Unocal.[33] The case was settled just weeks before Unocal was purchased by Chevron. Although the prodemocracy movement fighting against the military junta that rules Burma has called for an end to foreign investment in the nation, Chevron remains a direct business partner of the junta, one of the largest foreign investors in Burma, and the only remaining major U.S. corporation with a significant presence there.[34]

O'Melveny & Myers has a particularly close relationship with ExxonMobil, as well as Exxon and Mobil prior to the merger. One of the cofounders of the firm's original Washington, D.C., office, David Gray Boutte, went to Mobil in 1980 and became executive director of Mobil International. The firm has also represented ExxonMobil in numerous cases over the years, including against thousands of people exposed to asbestos, including those who worked at ExxonMobil refineries, who had joined a class-action lawsuit against ExxonMobil and other corporate defendants. But the firm's most notorious case representing Exxon is the case it won before the U.S. Supreme Court in 2008, when 32,677 Alaskans sued Exxon in the wake of the *Exxon Valdez* disaster.

Just past midnight on March 24, 1989, the super-tanker *Exxon Valdez*, en route to Los Angeles carrying its capacity 53 million gallons of oil, veered severely off course traveling through the Valdez Narrows of Prince William Sound, Alaska. With its captain drunk belowdecks, the *Valdez* struck Bligh Reef, ripping a hole through eight of its eleven cargo tanks and pouring more than 11 million gallons of crude oil across 600 linear miles—larger than the distance between Washington, D.C., and Atlanta.

The *Valdez* remains the biggest oil spill in U.S. history. It was and remains both an ecological and economic disaster. But it was hardly an isolated incident. Just two weeks earlier, the *Exxon*

Houston tanker ran aground in Hawaii, spilling an estimated 25,200 gallons of crude.[35] One month after the *Valdez*, the *Exxon Philadelphia*, carrying 22 million gallons of Alaskan crude, lost power and drifted off the Washington coast for nearly seven hours, narrowly skirting another spill.[36] In June, three large spills occurred within twelve hours of each other: the *World Prodigy* tanker spilled 420,000 gallons of oil after going off course in Narragansett, Rhode Island; in Texas, a barge leaked about 250,000 gallons of oil when it collided with a cargo ship; and the *Presidence Rivera* tanker spilled roughly 800,000 gallons of oil into the Delaware River after straying from its shipping lane and hitting a rock.[37] The "freewheeling" attitude of the industry was well known and highly criticized, while the *Valdez* disaster was both anticipated and largely avoidable.

Much of the case against Exxon would ultimately focus on the captain's drinking. Just a week after the accident, Exxon CEO Lawrence Rawl acknowledged that the corporation had known about the captain's drinking, had ordered him into rehab, and then had allowed him back at the helm despite numerous reports that he relapsed. As Rawl would put it at the time, "The judgment to put him back on the ship . . . was a bad judgment."[38] But this was not merely a case of one drunken sailor.

There was never any doubt among Alaskans, the government, or even the industry that carrying oil out of the narrow and treacherous waterways of Prince William Sound would likely be catastrophic. In fact, from the time oil was discovered at Prudhoe Bay, Alaska, in 1968, locals argued the Alaska Pipeline should run not to Valdez, but rather through Canada, thus avoiding the inherent dangers of maritime transport altogether.[39] In 1977, Alaska representative Keith Specking asked an oil industry spokesman how they would respond to a scenario of a fully loaded tanker going aground on Bligh Reef, ripping open its holds, and spilling its cargo of crude oil. The spokesman replied with assurances that as highly unlikely as it was, there would be the best technology and equipment to quickly clean up the spill.[40]

For the sixteen years between the 1973 passage of the Trans-Alaska Pipeline System Authorization Act and the *Exxon Valdez* disaster, the state of Alaska and the Alyeska Pipeline Service Company, the consortium of oil companies including Exxon that built and managed the pipeline, remained in a pitched legislative and litigated battle over the inadequacy (from the state's perspective) of the consortium's oil spill contingency plans and tanker safety regulations. In a 1989 congressional hearing, just over a month after the disaster, Alaska's commissioner of environmental conservation, Dennis Kelso, forcefully argued that the devastation of the spill was caused in part by Alyeska's "decade long efforts to scuttle any meaningful oil spill contingency plan" and Exxon's failure to adequately prepare for a spill that was not only likely, but probable.[41]

The 1989 congressional hearings addressed many other inadequacies, from the technology and equipment used by the Coast Guard to track the passage of tankers in the Valdez Narrows, to the industry's increased use of smaller crews and the corresponding problem of increased sleep deprivation, to inadequate training and oversight of crew members, to the failure of earlier attempts by Congress and previous administration's to restrict the usage of single-hulled tankers such as the *Valdez* altogether in favor of more secure (although also more expensive) double-hulled tankers.[42] In the wake of the *Valdez*, Congress finally passed legislation phasing out the use of all single-hulled ships, although it does not take effect until 2015.

From 1989, O'Melveny & Myers was among the firms representing Exxon in its numerous cases arising from the spill.[43] Nearly twenty years later, the firm served as lead counsel before the U.S. Supreme Court defending Exxon in a case stemming from a 1994 court ruling that punitive damages "necessary in this case to achieve punishment and deterrence" should be imposed against Exxon in the amount of $5 billion, the amount intended to be the equivalent of about a year's average profits for the company.[44] Exxon's appeal, for which O'Melveny was also the lead counsel, reached the Ninth Circuit Court of Appeals in 1999.[45] Since then, according to law professor William Rodgers, Exxon followed a "scorched-earth" litigation plan, filing more than sixty petitions and appeals, seeking twenty-three time extensions and filing more than a thousand motions, briefs, requests, and demands.[46] In 2001, the damages were reduced to $2.5 billion and then in 2008, in a massive victory for both O'Melveny and Exxon, the U.S. Supreme Court reduced the damages to a mere $507.5 million.

Over the course of the nineteen-year litigation battle, more than three thousand of the claimants died, as well as the original cocounsel, Richard Gerry, who died at the age of eighty in 2004. Alaska Representative Les Gara said the 2008 Supreme Court decision was the result of twenty years of "Bush and Reagan appointees and a conservative movement that doesn't believe in corporate responsibility." Plaintiff Mary Jacobs of Kodiak said, "This is just saying that the oil companies aren't accountable. . . . Punitive damages is what keeps some businesses in line from taking risks, and the cost of operations just got less."[47]

O'Melveny & Myers explains on its Web site that it has advocated "groundbreaking punitive damages strategies and have reduced our clients' exposure to punitive damages awards dramatically. In the *Exxon Valdez* litigation, we pioneered the concept of 'limited fund class action' to reduce the scope of punitive damages."[48]

The firm's work on behalf of ExxonMobil and its other oil industry clients go beyond punitive damage litigation to include the firm's leading antitrust division.

Richard Parker and former FTC chairman Timothy Muris cochair the antitrust practice division at O'Melveny & Myers. Parker joined the firm almost straight out of law school and his corporate clients have included ExxonMobil, which he represented in a class action lawsuit. He had been working at O'Melveny & Myers for more than twenty years—twelve as a partner—when in February 1998 he left for a three-year stint at the FTC. As director of the FTC's Bureau of Competition, Parker oversaw Exxon's $81 billion purchase of Mobil: a merger of the two largest oil companies in the United States and the two largest postbreakup pieces of Standard Oil. Parker also oversaw BP Amoco's $27.6 billion purchase of Arco. Parker left the FTC in December 2000 and was back at O'Melveny & Myers within two months.[49]

Chairman Muris left the FTC in August 2004 after overseeing two enormous oil company mergers: Chevron's $36 billion purchase of Texaco, which created the second-largest oil company in the nation, and Conoco's $15 billion purchase of Phillips, which brought two midsized oil companies together to create the nation's third-largest oil company. In September, Muris joined O'Melveny & Myers, where, by December 2005, he was representing ExxonMobil before the FTC.[50]

Muris brought his chief of staff, Christine Wilson, and his primary oil adviser, Bilal Sayyed, from the FTC with him to O'Melveny & Myers. Christine Wilson had counseled oil and gas company clients while in private practice prior to her brief stint at the FTC, which lasted less than two years. Now a partner at O'Melveny & Myers, Wilson represents oil and gas industry clients including the Marathon Oil Company, which she has represented before the FTC.[51]

Bilal Sayyed was also in private practice representing corporate clients, including before the FTC, prior to his four-year term at the agency from 2001 to 2004. At the FTC, he coordinated all of Chairman Muris's "petroleum matters," including merger investigations, the FTC's gasoline price monitoring program, and reports and research on the industry, such as the FTC's critical 2004 investigation into petroleum industry mergers.[52] In the report, the FTC concluded that all was well in the U.S. petroleum industry, that the mergers had not led to anticompetitive problems, and that the FTC had not made a single error in judgment in allowing the wave of oil industry mergers to proceed. Upon arriving at O'Melveny & Myers, Sayyed joined with Muris to represent ExxonMobil in the FTC's post-Katrina gasoline price-gouging investigation begun in late 2005.[53]

In fall 2005, gas prices across America surged in the aftermath of Hurricane Katrina. Outraged motorists flooded hotlines with reports of price-gouging. The average price of gasoline in the nation rose by nearly 80 cents in just a few months, from almost $2.20 per gallon in June to almost $3.00 per gallon in September. The issue was not only the steep rise in prices following the storm but also the fact that the prices never went back down. Since the storm, the average price of gas has not yet returned to its pre-Katrina level. While gas prices may well have increased legitimately in the days or even weeks immediately following the storm, the oil companies appeared to be taking advantage of a onetime necessity by keeping gas prices high indefinitely. In September 2005 the governors of Oregon, Wisconsin, Michigan, Illinois, New Mexico, Iowa, Montana, and Washington demanded that the Bush administration investigate "excessive profits being made by oil companies who are taking advantage of this national crisis."[54] The Congress concurred and ordered the FTC to launch a formal investigation.

The FTC's report was released in May 2006. It concluded that while there were instances of price-gouging by certain refineries and retailers (no companies were named), no illegal activity was identified. "What we found ought to give people confidence," Phill Broyles, assistant director of the FTC's Bureau of Competition, told reporters. "While prices might be higher than they like, it isn't the result of anything nefarious by the oil companies."[55] Rather, it was the result of "profit maximization strategies" that did not require further investigation. The FTC concluded that federal price-gouging statutes were unnecessary and would run counter to consumers' needs.

Few journalists reported that the FTC's former chairman Timothy Muris and his chief petroleum adviser, Bilal Sayyed, now represented ExxonMobil before the FTC in its price-gouging investigation. Nor was it reported that then FTC chair Deborah

Platt Majoras and Commissioner J. Thomas Rosch had both previously served as oil industry lawyers. Commissioner Rosch had represented Tosco (the largest independent oil refiner and gas marketer in the United States until it was bought by Phillips Petroleum in 2001—today ConocoPhillips), while Chairwoman Majoras had represented Chevron.[56]

Deborah Platt Majoras replaced Timothy Muris as chair of the FTC in July 2004. Consumer and environmental groups and members of Congress roundly opposed Majoras' nomination. President Bush resorted to slipping Majoras into office while Congress was out of session as a "recess appointment," a process that is supposed to be reserved for emergencies that cannot wait for the Congress to return. Majoras had worked at the Jones Day law firm representing Chevron less than one year prior to joining the FTC and only two years prior to the gas price-gouging investigation that cleared Chevron, ExxonMobil, ConocoPhillips, and every other oil company of illegal activity. In March 2008, Majoras left the FTC—the nation's leading consumer protection agency—to become vice president and general counsel to Procter & Gamble Co., the largest consumer products company in the United States.

JONES DAY: The Jones Day law firm specializes in representing companies against class-action lawsuits. It represented R. J. Reynolds Tobacco in the smoking-related class-action suits and IBM in a class-action suit in which former IBM employees charged that they developed cancer after being exposed to acetone, benzene, and other chemicals while working for IBM in the 1960s, 1970s, and 1980s.

Jones Day has a particularly close relationship with Chevron. It represented the company in two of the most notorious human rights and environmental destruction cases that have ever been brought against any oil company: *Bowoto v. Chevron*, for the alleged crimes in Nigeria discussed in chapter 2, and *Aguinda v. Chevron*, in Ecuador.

Representing Chevron in *Bowoto v. Chevron* is Jones Day lawyer Noel Francisco. Before joining the firm, Francisco represented George W. Bush in the Florida recount, then served as associate counsel to President Bush from 2001 to 2003, and then as deputy assistant attorney general in the DOJ's Office of Legal Counsel from 2003 to 2005.[57]

Jones Day also represents Chevron in a $6 billion lawsuit in which five indigenous groups and eighty Ecuadorian communities are demanding recompense for the destruction of their homes, health, environment, and livelihoods.[58] The lawsuit, *Aguinda v. Chevron,* argues that from 1964 to 1992 Texaco built and operated oil exploration and production facilities in the northern region of the Ecuadorian Amazon. Indigenous communities were removed from their land to make way for the oil facilities, and more than 1 million hectares of ancient rain forest were cleared. According to the suit, rather than install the standard environmental controls of the time for reinjecting toxic drilling waters back into the ground, Texaco dumped 18.5 billion gallons of toxic waste directly into the rain forest—a spill roughly thirty times larger than the amount spilled in the *Exxon Valdez* disaster. The result, the plaintiffs argue, is an exploding health crisis years later among the region's indigenous and farmer communities, including shockingly high incidences of leukemia and lymphoma, as well as cervical, stomach, larynx, liver, and bile duct cancer.[59] Chevron says that it complied with Ecuadorian law at the time and has since mitigated any environmental harm.

The case is currently at trial in Ecuador. If Chevron loses in Ecuador, Jones Day's plan is essentially to argue that what happens in Ecuador stays in Ecuador. Federal judges in the United States are not bound to enforce foreign judgments, and Chevron will not say for sure that it will pay any judgment imposed in the case: "What happens in Lago [Ecuador] doesn't necessarily decide the issue of who pays," says Thomas Cullen Jr., a Jones Day partner who represents Chevron in the case.[60]

Jones Day also partakes in the revolving door. Charles James is their poster boy. Today, James is a vice president and general counsel for Chevron. *Inside Counsel* magazine reports that "when James isn't working, he usually can be found driving around the Bay Area on his Harley" or in his thirteenth Porsche, a steel gray Carrera 4S.[61] From 1979 to 1992, James moved back and forth between Republican administrations and private practice—from the FTC, where he helped write the agency's more lenient merger guidelines, to Jones Day, to the DOJ, and then back to Jones Day. He sat out the Clinton administration as the chair of Jones Day's Antitrust and Trade Regulation Practice. With the presidency of George W. Bush, James was soon back to the DOJ in June 2001 for a sixteen-month stint as assistant attorney general in charge of antitrust issues.

During James's confirmation hearing before the Senate Judiciary Committee in May 2001, Senator Patrick Leahy quipped, "Mr. James, you have been so successful in advising an impressive list of corporate clients that some have joked that [if appointed] you will have to recuse yourself from doing your job. You have represented the corporate 'Who's Who' of who wants to merge."[62]

James describes two main influences that helped form his views on antitrust: "one is [a] sort of bedrock conservatism that causes me to question the wisdom of replacing free-market competition with regulation. My views were also formed with my counterpart Tim Muris and [former FTC chairman] Jim Miller."[63] James, as the DOJ's antitrust chief, worked so closely with FTC chairman Muris that the two raised red flags when it was discovered that they were dividing antitrust enforcement responsibility between the FTC and DOJ in what were widely described as "secret meetings," including by then FTC commissioner Mozelle Thompson, who publicly criticized the meetings for not including agency staff or commissioners.[64]

Chevron's merger with Texaco was approved by the FTC in September 2001. The lead lawyer responsible for the government review of the merger was Sean Royall, who spent a little more than two years working for the FTC as deputy director of the Bureau of Competition.[65] Royall went on to become cochair of Gibson, Dunn, & Crutcher's Antitrust and Trade Regulation Practice Group, where his corporate clients have included Phillips Petroleum and Paramount Petroleum.[66]

Charles James left the DOJ a year after the Chevron-Texaco merger to take his self-described "job of a lifetime" as vice president and general counsel of Chevron.[67] At Chevron, James led the company's successful bid to acquire Unocal in 2005. James was assisted in the Unocal merger by two Jones Day lawyers: Kathryn Fenton, who had spent two years at the FTC as an attorney-adviser to Chairman Miller, and Joe Sims, who spent two years at the DOJ as deputy assistant attorney general for antitrust.[68]

Over at the FTC was Jeffrey Schmidt, deputy director of the Bureau of Competition. Schmidt, formerly a managing partner at Pillsbury Winthrop, had successfully represented Chevron in 1999 in a case brought by gas station owners in Virginia alleging fraud.[69] Schmidt began working at the FTC in February 2005. Four months later, the FTC approved Chevron's $18 billion purchase of Unocal. Today, Schmidt is the director of the FTC Bureau of Competition amid press reports that he may soon return to private practice.[70]

Marathon's bid to purchase Ashland Oil in 1998 succeeded under the expert guidance of two former FTC trial attorneys who had sought out the more lucrative environment of Jones Day: Tom Smith and Robert Jones. Smith has represented many oil and gas companies at Jones Day, including Chevron, Koch Industries, Total S.A. in its acquisition of Elf Aquitaine, and Valero in its acquisition of Premcor.[71] Michael McFalls is another former FTC attorney who has gone on to Jones Day. From 1997 through 2000, McFalls served as attorney-adviser to Chairman Pitofsky and worked on several mergers, including BP-Arco and Exxon-Mobil. McFalls also helped develop and draft the

FTC's more lenient antitrust guidelines. At Jones Day, McFalls counsels numerous corporate clients, including Chevron.[72]

ChevronToxico

Leila Salazar is one of Charles James's and Jones Day's most important and formidable adversaries. For four years, Salazar was the organizer of Clean Up Ecuador, a part of the ChevronToxico Campaign at the small, California-based nonprofit organization Amazon Watch. Salazar has done more than just about any single organizer to try to hold Chevron—and before it, Texaco—to account for one of the greatest oil-related disasters in history. It is virtually impossible for indigenous people in Ecuador to make the American public aware of the crimes committed by U.S. firms in their communities. They need American allies to accomplish this task. Leila Salazar is one of their foremost allies.

As Salazar described to me in an interview, her grandparents first immigrated to the United States from Mexico to work in the grape fields of Delano, in California's Central Valley, but later returned to Mexico.[73] Her parents then immigrated in the 1960s and raised Leila in Oceanside, in northern San Diego County. Salazar became an environmental activist while in high school and went on to major in environmental studies and political science at the University of California in Santa Barbara.

Salazar's first journey to the Amazon in 1995 at age twenty-one changed her life. She went to Ecuador as an intern at the Jatun Sacha Biological Station ("big forest" in Quichua). Within hours of arriving in Ecuador, Salazar was on a public bus traveling through the Amazon to Jatun Sacha when her bus was forced to make an emergency stop. Oil was gushing from a broken pipeline, blocking the road, flooding the forest, and filling a nearby river. It was a good indication of the omnipresence of oil—and accidents—in the Amazon. Salazar, becoming increasingly invested in the people and the environment of Ecuador, returned to Jatun Sacha every summer while in college. After graduating, she spent one year with Green Corps, a nongovernmental environmental equivalent to the Peace Corps, and then the Fields School for Environmental Organizing. In 1999 she went to work for the human rights organization Global Exchange, and in 2002 she went to Amazon Watch.

Salazar's job was to increase public awareness of the actions of Texaco in Ecuador and of the lawsuit against the company. In November 1993, a class-action lawsuit, *Aguinda v. Texaco*, was filed by citizens of Ecuador in the Southern District Court of New York alleging large-scale environmental abuse. The case spent nine years winding through the courts until a 2002 ruling that the case should be dismissed in the U.S. but relocated to Ecuador, where it is currently being tried.[74] Salazar described how Texaco hired the most expensive PR firms and "entire law firms" who "produced reams of documents to just slow everything down" while the company "spent and spent and spent." Salazar argues that Texaco's success in having the case tried in Ecuador was due in large part to the lack of public awareness or media scrutiny of Texaco's actions before the court. She believes that the company would not have been able to get away with its delay tactics and other "questionable behavior" before the court if its PR team had been challenged by a broad "PR campaign" on the part of the plaintiffs.

All of those supporting the Ecuadorians in the case were deeply troubled by the 2001 merger of Texaco and Chevron. They feared not only that the merged company would have significantly greater financial resources, but also that all the effort that had gone into raising awareness of Texaco's actions would be lost when its name disappeared. For a time, the new company went by the name of ChevronTexaco, but it soon dropped the latter name. Leila is among those who believe this decision had a great deal to do with the Ecuador case—which is to date the largest lawsuit ever brought against an oil company. The name change forced the campaigners to start over again and explain that Texaco was now Chevron.

The case against Chevron in Ecuador was filed shortly after Salazar arrived on the job. She immediately went to Ecuador to meet with the indigenous federations to devise a joint plan of action. Explaining her involvement in the case, Salazar told me, "Chevron's our company, it's in our backyard. It was our responsibility to hold them to account."

Amazon Watch has an annual budget of approximately $1 million, compared with Chevron's $100 million annual budget just for outside representation. Salazar knew they could never compete with Chevron financially. Instead, they launched a grass-roots campaign to reach out to the public. Salazar partnered with international human rights organizations such as Project Underground and Amnesty International, and local communities struggling against Chevron, including Communities for a Better Environment and West County Toxics Coalition. They reached out to Chevron's shareholders (to pass shareholder resolutions), its workers, and its neighbors in San Ramon. They tried to get California's state pension fund to divest from Chevron. There is nothing like a protest at Chevron's headquarters or a march through San Ramon to get the press to take notice of an issue that it is generally failing to cover. The campaign's tools were the stories of those affected by Chevron, the scientific facts of the spill, and Chevron's refusal to pay compensation even as its profits skyrocketed.

Salazar's greatest frustration was with what she described as "Chevron's lies." "There was a press release on February 2, 2005, that I will never forget," Salazar told me. "Chevron [Texaco] hired a doctor who said that oil contact does not cause cancer. Even the EPA [Environmental Protection Agency], not a radical group, says that oil contamination causes cancer. This is what money buys. You can pay anyone to say what you want them to say. If you have the money, people will take it. I like to say we have the truth on our side and I try to be fair. So, how can they just lie?"[75] In response to ChevronTexaco's press offensive, fifty scientists and doctors from across Latin America, North America, and Europe released a letter to "Texaco and its consultants," published in *The International Journal of Occupational*

Health, condemning both the method and the content of ChevronTexaco's "paid consultants" findings and warning that their inaccuracies could seriously mislead and threaten the public.[76]

The coalition considered organizing a consumer boycott of Chevron, but quickly realized it would face problems common to campaigns against Big Oil: there are few alternative oil companies to send consumers to; there are inadequate alternative means of transportation for the majority of people to turn to; and the oil companies often appear to be too big for a consumer boycott to have a meaningful effect.

When I asked Salazar what sort of support she has received from California's elected officials, she answered in two words: "Richard Pombo." In other words, as long as a congressman like Pombo represented San Ramon, there was no chance of receiving support. Amazon Watch brought indigenous leaders to California and Washington, D.C., as often as possible. They met with Congresswoman Pelosi and Senator Boxer, who were willing to help with visas but not much else. "The Democrats who care about the environment did not want to challenge Chevron," Salazar said. As for seeking help from the Bush administration, "we just didn't bother."

THE BUSH ADMINISTRATION'S OPEN-DOOR POLICY

Big Oil spent big bucks to get fellow oilmen George W. Bush and Dick Cheney into office in 2000 and to keep them there in 2004. In return, Big Oil's people were able to stop lobbying and start legislating—by moving directly into key government positions themselves. From these choice positions they helped the administration and the Congress implement the legislative agenda of the oil industry.

The Council on Environmental Quality

The particularly unique and special relationship between the White House and Big Oil has been a major factor in

*hindering progress toward a host of important issues, but
particularly on addressing climate change.*

—GENE KARPINSKI, PRESIDENT, LEAGUE OF
CONSERVATION VOTERS[77]

To demonstrate the importance of environmental protection to the nation, Congress established the Council on Environmental Quality (CEQ) within the Office of the President in 1969. It functions as the foremost environmental and natural resource advisory group to the president and coordinates all federal environmental efforts.

The Senate must confirm all cabinet secretaries, which brings significantly more media and public attention to the heads of agencies than to their subordinates. Thus, while the head of the CEQ, James Connaughton, has oil industry ties—he was a lobbyist for Arco (now BP)—it is his second in command who has the "oiliest" connections.

Bush appointed Philip Cooney as the CEQ's chief of staff. Cooney was an American Petroleum Institute lobbyist and its "climate team leader" prior to working for the White House. Rick Piltz, a scientist who coordinated the government's climate research, resigned in 2005 and went public with documents exposing Cooney's work at the CEQ. Piltz reported that Cooney had been editing the reports of other government agencies before they were publicly released in order to downplay the effects of global warming. For example, in a section on the need for research into how global warming might affect droughts and flooding, Cooney simply eliminated a paragraph describing the projected reduction of mountain glaciers and snowpack. "Each administration has a policy position on climate change," Mr. Piltz wrote. "But I have not seen a situation like the one that has developed under this administration during the past four years, in which politicization by the White House has fed back directly into the science program. . . ."[78] Cooney was forced to step down in the ensuing public scandal, so he left the government and immediately went to work at ExxonMobil.[79]

The Department of the Interior

Congress established the Department of the Interior in 1849 to act as the nation's premier protective body for public land, water, and wildlife conservation, the administration of Native American land, and the national park system. The Interior Department protects our natural heritage, managing the coastal waters surrounding the United States and almost a fifth of all of the nation's land: approximately 500 million acres, including more than 50 million acres belonging to Native Americans. Valuable natural resources including everything from trees to wildlife to oil and natural gas—all of which belong to the American public—abound within these waters and acres of land.

The United States is unique among the world's nations in that the rights to minerals found belowground belong to whoever owns the land aboveground. Thus anyone who owns a piece of land that sits above an oil field owns the oil beneath it. In virtually every other nation in the world, oil and other minerals, no matter whose property they lie beneath, are held in common by the nation's people and generally administered by the state. But America's national lands and coastal waters are the only places in the United States where the natural resources belong to the public. Ever since the public has sought to increase protection of this land and close off portions to natural resource exploitation, oil companies have been trying to gain greater access.

Secretary Gale Norton

Former Bush-appointed Interior Secretary Gale Norton and Deputy Secretary J. Stephen Griles have done more than most government officials to ensure that oil companies have had their desires met. Today, Gale Norton is general counsel for Shell Oil's oil shale development program in Colorado and other western states. Twenty-five years ago, she was a lawyer at the Mountain

States Legal Foundation, which was created by Ronald Reagan's interior secretary, James Watt. The foundation received significant funding from the oil industry and pursued an agenda that opposed windfall profit taxes for oil companies and supported the "wise use" agenda of opening more public lands to oil and gas exploration. In between these jobs, Norton held several positions, including two terms as attorney general of the state of Colorado. Norton was President George W. Bush's interior secretary from his first election until 2006, when she resigned under the deep tarnish of the Jack Abramoff influence-peddling scandal discussed below. While she was not accused of any direct wrongdoing, both her immediate subordinate, J. Stephen Griles, and her former associate Italia Federici pled guilty to charges arising from the case.

From the perspective of Big Oil, Norton's reign was arguably second only to that of her mentor James Watt as the best Interior Department in the history of the United States. Under Norton, the Interior Department's top priorities were to increase domestic oil and gas production, offer more incentives to drillers in the U.S. Gulf Coast, and open the Arctic National Wildlife Refuge and other wilderness areas to drilling. The department reduced spending on enforcement, cut back on auditors, and sped up approvals for drilling applications. In 2001 alone, the Interior Department opened 4 million new acres of public land to oil, natural gas, and coal mining.[80]

In a classic case of putting the fox in charge of the hen house, Norton appointed as her special assistant for Alaska, Camden Toohey, who had been the executive director of Arctic Power, the chief lobbying group in the campaign to open the Arctic National Wildlife Refuge to oil drilling. Toohey left Interior in 2006 to take a job at Shell. Toohey (and Norton) were soon joined at Shell by Elizabeth Stolpe, who until February 2007 had worked at the White House CEQ. Prior to her White House gig, Stolpe had been an in-house lobbyist for Koch Industries, the nation's largest private oil and gas company.[81]

Norton succeeded in opening vast tracts of public land to oil industry exploration and development—transforming Colorado in the process. Once gorgeous and increasingly rare mountain vistas and landscapes became industrial zones under Norton's tenure. Colorado now has 32,000 active oil and natural gas wells, but plans call for at least 40,000 *additional* wells to be drilled in the next decade. The Wilderness Society predicts that, at the current rate of opening public lands, 125,000 new wells can be expected to be drilled across the western United States. The expansion has been so aggressive that many conservative Republicans across Colorado have formed heretofore unheard-of alliances with left-leaning environmentalists in the hope of preserving some of the last great natural expanses in the United States.[82] Today, thanks in no small part to Norton, nearly 35 percent of the oil and 39 percent of the natural gas produced in the United States come from federal land and federal offshore areas.

Norton fast-tracked the permitting process of leases on federal land. She also vastly expanded access for oil shale development—one of the most environmentally destructive forms of oil extraction. In November 2006, the Interior Department awarded Shell new leases for oil shale development in Colorado. Two months later, Norton was hired by Shell as general counsel to the unit working on oil shale development.[83]

Deputy Secretary J. Stephen Griles

Norton certainly cashed in on her deregulatory efforts at Interior, but her actions look like those of an amateur in comparison to the expert machinations of her immediate subordinate at Interior, J. Stephen Griles. That is, until those machinations landed Griles in jail.

Over the course of his career, according to the Federal Lobbyist Disclosure Database, Griles has lobbied on behalf of Chevron, Sunoco, Unocal, Occidental Petroleum, and the American Petroleum Institute, among others. Like Norton, Griles was an early

Watt devotee who began his government career as deputy director of Surface Mining in Watt's Interior Department. Griles gutted strip-mining regulations and was a relentless advocate of allowing U.S. oil companies greater access to the western United States. He also pushed (unsuccessfully) to overturn the moratorium on offshore oil drilling on the Pacific Coast.[84] Griles left the Reagan administration to cash in on his successful deregulatory efforts. He launched his own D.C. lobbying firm, J. Stephen Griles and Associates, where he represented the nation's largest oil and mining companies before the federal government. In 2000 Griles took on a side gig with the lobbying firm National Environmental Strategies, where he lobbied for Chevron on behalf of its merger with Texaco.[85] Griles then headed off to the Interior Department in 2001, the same year the merger was approved.

Bush tapped Griles for the number two spot at Interior and gave him the keys to the nation's oil and mineral holdings. As deputy secretary, Griles wasted little time getting to work on behalf of his former—and soon to be again—oil company clients. We have a unique look into Griles's activities at Interior due to the many investigations launched against him, including one federal inspector general's report from 2004 describing Griles's tenure at Interior as "an ethical quagmire."[86]

On at least sixteen occasions, Griles arranged meetings between himself, his former industry clients, and other administration officials to discuss the rollback of air pollution standards for oil refineries, power plants, and industrial boilers. Griles's logs show that in just two years, from 2001 to 2003, he met on at least thirty-two occasions with other administration officials to discuss pending regulatory matters that were a concern to his former clients. These meetings flout federal ethics rules that prohibit executive branch officials from participating in any "particular matter" that could advance their own financial interests or that involves former employers or clients.[87] Griles pressed the EPA to support a plan, developed by six other former clients, to drill for oil in Wyoming and Montana. He pushed for rollbacks in environmental standards for air and water and tried to exempt the oil industry from royalty payments.

Griles was a lead actor in the Cheney Energy Task Force, serving as the Interior Department's chief representative. As such, he played a lead role in mapping out the U.S. oil industry's interests in Iraq's oil fields and developing some of the most destructive national energy bills in the nation's history, giving more than $14 billion worth of subsidies, tax breaks, and other benefits to the oil industry. After passing billions of dollars over to the industry, Griles left the Bush administration in January 2005 to once again cash in. Former White House National Energy Policy director Andrew Lundquist and former congressman George Nethercutt joined Griles to form Lundquist, Nethercutt, and Griles. The lobbying firm's clients included the American Petroleum Institute and BP.

The incestuous links between Griles, the Bush administration, and the nation's oil companies only get worse. The Associated Press reported that Griles bought a nearly $1 million vacation home with his girlfriend, Sue Ellen Woodridge, and Donald R. Duncan. Such a purchase would not have turned heads had Donald Duncan not been ConocoPhillips's top Washington lobbyist and had Woodridge not been the nation's lead environmental prosecutor at the DOJ. Nine months after the purchase, Woodridge signed two proposed consent decrees with ConocoPhillips: one giving the company as much as two to three more years to install $525 million in pollution controls at nine refineries and the other dealing with a Superfund toxic waste cleanup.[88]

It was only a matter of time before this all came crashing to a halt. In March 2007, Griles pled guilty to felony charges of obstruction of justice by lying on four separate occasions about his connections to Jack Abramoff. Abramoff got his Native American clients to pay him tens of millions of dollars to lobby the Interior Department. Part of his pitch was that he had serious pull at the department, especially with Griles.[89] Griles was sentenced to ten months in prison in mid-2007 and began serving his sentence that September. He faces another three years of probation following his release. Italia Federici, who had founded the Council of Republicans for Environmental Advocacy with Gale Norton in 1997, pled guilty to income tax evasion and obstructing justice for her role as conduit between Griles and Abramoff.[90]

Patricia Lynn Scarlett replaced Griles as deputy secretary of the interior. She served briefly as secretary following Gale Norton's resignation. Before she joined the Bush administration, Scarlett was president and CEO of the Reason Foundation, a classic industry front group. Reason Foundation funders in 1999 included the American Petroleum Institute, ExxonMobil, Chevron, Arco, BP Amoco, and Shell. The group promotes "New Environmentalism" based on principles of "privatization and individual stewardship, decreased regulation, and the power of free markets."[91]

Interior's Oil Royalty Scheme

In exchange for access to drill for oil and natural gas on public lands, companies are supposed to pay the American people a royalty. This is a set fee of generally 12 to 16 percent of a company's sales earned from the resource. Oil companies have succeeded in escaping many of these fees. When public and congressional scrutiny turned toward the Interior Department's crippled royalty-collection system in 2006, the Bush administration turned to the American Petroleum Institute. David Deal, API's general counsel of thirty years, was named by Interior to head a task force to evaluate the failed system. The investigation was initiated in response to a "mistake" expected to yield the petroleum industry an estimated $10 billion or more over five years.

In 1998 and 1999, the Clinton Interior Department waived royalty payments on eleven hundred offshore leases signed with every major oil corporation. At the time the leases were signed, the price of oil was between $9 and $15 per barrel. The companies were supposed to start paying royalties when oil topped

$34 per barrel. Reportedly, however, the leasing officials mistakenly omitted the $34 clause for two years. Midlevel officials at Interior spotted the omission in 2000 and quietly made sure to include the clause in all subsequent leases. But no one tried to fix the leases that had already been signed, and almost no one talked about them until oil prices started to climb above $34 per barrel in 2004. This is when the oil companies reportedly began pressing the Bush administration to clarify how it would treat the leases, trying to ensure that they would not have to pay any royalties.

When the public got wind of the situation in 2006 and congressional hearings began, the Bush administration first claimed ignorance and then blamed the Clinton administration. But when it came to light that the Interior Department was talking to oil companies in 2004 about the payments, an investigation was launched. The investigation was led by Deal, the API's former lobbyist. As a result of the scandal, several Interior Department regulators quietly left the administration, while Bush asked the oil companies to start paying their royalty fees voluntarily. Needless to say, the oil companies have not lined up to do so. In the interim, these leases are yielding oil worth $100+ per barrel, and an estimated $10 billion is going to oil companies that could and should have gone to the American public.

While few would argue that the federal government adequately pursued royalty fees under the Clinton administration, its enforcement record far surpasses that of the Bush administration. The Interior Department generated an average of about $176 million annually in the 1990s from royalty payments, with a peak of $331 million in 2000, according to data from the Congressional Budget Office and the Interior Department. But from 2001 through 2005, a period when oil prices quadrupled in value over those in the 1990s, the Interior Department brought in less than a third of the money, an average of about $46 million a year.[92]

One senior auditor, Bobby Maxwell, left the Interior Department and has since become a whistleblower against the Bush administration. Maxwell had been a senior auditor at Interior for more than twenty years when he left the department in 2002 out of frustration at the Bush administration's lax enforcement. Maxwell and his auditing team spent months painstakingly detailing a scheme by the Kerr-McGee oil company to intentionally bilk the U.S. public out of as much as $12 million in royalty fees. Kerr-McGee, a large independent oil company active in the Gulf of Mexico, was purchased in 2006 by Anadarko Petroleum, based in Houston. Maxwell brought his findings to his superiors at the Bush Interior Department, who told him to drop it. "The word came down from the top not to issue this order," Mr. Maxwell said. "There have always been people who don't want to pursue things. But now it's grown into a major illness. It's dysfunctional."[93]

Maxwell retired to pursue the case as a whistleblower under the False Claims Act. He filed the suit in June 2004. Kerr-McGee tried and failed to have the suit dismissed. Eight major oil companies including ExxonMobil and Chevron weighed in on Kerr-McGee's side. A federal jury in Denver agreed with Maxwell and ruled that Kerr-McGee had underpaid the government by $7.5 million, but the judge reversed the jury on technical grounds, ruling that Maxwell was not entitled to invoke the False Claims Act.

Every major oil company has at some time been charged with intentionally bilking the nation of its royalty payments and has chosen to settle the case. For example, a former oil trader at Arco, J. Benjamin Johnson Jr., filed a False Claims Act suit in 1995 contending that all the major oil companies had used elaborate swapping schemes to cheat on royalties owed to private and state landowners, as well as the federal government. The DOJ joined the suit in 1998. Chevron and Shell hired their favorite oil industry lobbyist, J. Steven Griles, to testify as an expert witness on their behalf. Mobil was the first to settle, paying more than $40 million in 1998. Chevron paid $95 million. Shell paid $110 million. Phillips paid $8 million. By 2002, fifteen oil companies had paid a total of almost $440 million in settlements.[94]

ExxonMobil was found guilty of intentionally underpaying royalties from natural gas wells in Alabama in 2000. An Alabama jury awarded the state $3.5 billion in damages. In 1996 in Texas, a lawsuit was filed against the thirteen largest oil corporations for underpaying royalties on oil extracted from land owned by the federal government and several Native American tribes. The companies settled out of court for $400 million. In California the state and the city of Long Beach brought suit against Exxon and other corporations for avoiding royalties by underpricing oil extracted from public lands. The case dragged on for twenty years until the companies agreed to settle the case for $325 million in 1999.[95]

Tax Abuse

It is in the arcana of the federal tax code that oil industry lobbyists, among other corporate lobbyists, have succeeded in achieving some of the most lucrative policies implemented by the Bush administration. In early 2002, Congress passed and Bush signed legislation hugely expanding corporate tax breaks, then extended and expanded those tax breaks in 2003. They remain in place today. At the same time, proposals to crack down on even the most abusive corporate tax-sheltering activities were blocked by Republican congressional leaders and the White House. As a result of these government actions and inactions, corporate income taxes in fiscal 2002 and 2003 fell to their lowest sustained share of the economy since World War II (with the exception of a single year during the early Reagan administration).[96]

In the most comprehensive report of its kind, the Center for Tax Justice (CTJ) and the Institute on Taxation and Economic Policy (ITEP) conducted an extensive analysis of the 2004 tax returns of 275 of the Fortune 500 companies. The report, "Corporate Income Taxes in the Bush Years," finds that in the first three years of the Bush administration, federal corporate tax collections for all corporations fell to their lowest sustained level in six decades. "The sharp increase in the number of tax-avoiding companies reflects the results of aggressive corporate lobbying and a White House and a Congress eager to do the lobbyists' bidding," said Robert McIntyre, director of CTJ and coauthor of the report. The oil industry was one of the top beneficiaries.

Corporations are "supposed" to pay 35 percent of their earnings in federal taxes. But once tax breaks and loopholes are accounted for, the oil industry as a whole paid a mere 13.3 percent effective tax rate from 2001 to 2003. ExxonMobil ranked seventh among all 275 companies in corporate tax breaks, receiving more than $4 billion in tax breaks from 2001 to 2003. In fact, in 2002 ExxonMobil's effective tax rate was just 5.3 percent. That's less than the average effective tax rate for all Americans, which was approximately 9 percent in 2005.[97] ConocoPhillips received tax breaks of almost $2 billion, reducing its federal income tax by an incredible 72 percent from 2001 to 2003. Valero's tax breaks were the most impressive: in 2002 the company had an effective tax rate of *negative* 36.3 percent. Valero not only paid zero taxes that year, but it actually received money back from the federal government. Marathon had the highest effective tax rate of 21.7 percent in 2002.

But federal taxes are just a part of the story. Chevron was not included in this study, but we are offered a unique insight into Chevron's local efforts at tax abuse, and those trying to hold it to account, in Richmond, California.

Company Town

I may be the mayor, but in this city, Chevron has the power.
—GAYLE McLAUGHLIN, MAYOR, RICHMOND,
CALIFORNIA, 2007[98]

I have tried to interview numerous government officials for this book, but most have declined. When I contacted the office of the mayor of Richmond seeking an interview, after leaving e-mails, voice messages, and speaking to the same assistant on several occasions, I assumed I was getting the runaround. I was therefore surprised when Mayor McLaughlin personally called me back to set up an interview. When she picked me up at the Richmond BART station in her car, drove me to her small but comfortable apartment, and made us coffee in her kitchen while we talked, I knew I was not dealing with your average politician.

City Council and Green Party member Gayle McLaughlin ran for mayor of Richmond in 2006. She refused all corporate money. Home to one of the largest and oldest refineries in the nation, Richmond is a company town. For nearly a hundred years, Chevron—originally headquartered just across the bay in San Francisco and now only slightly farther away in San Ramon— has wielded enormous influence over the city. Once the sole and largest employer in town, Chevron's refinery employs only about 5 percent of the town's workers today. Chevron once provided the majority of the city's budget through its taxes; today its taxes account for closer to 30 percent of the budget.[99]

City residents have struggled to gain an upper hand over the refinery. Mayor McLaughlin explained how they tried and failed to get Chevron to install state-of-the-art pollution controls, to reduce toxic flaring as other refineries have done, and to reduce air and water pollution. This deeply impoverished, crime-ridden city has been trying to get Chevron to pay its fair share of taxes and to provide greater worker protections, but its efforts have been stymied by Chevron's financial weight. Chevron contributes heavily to the campaigns of local politicians, and its allies have dominated Richmond's government for decades. According to McLauglin, Chevron controls the local Chamber of Commerce—the current chairperson, Jim Brumfield, is a Chevron executive—and the local Industry Council. It donates checks for $5,000 and $10,000 to libraries and local civic groups, while fighting to get its property taxes reduced by $5 million a year. McLaughlin explained that her challenger in the mayoral race, then-sitting mayor Irma Anderson, a Democrat, was heavily backed by Chevron, as were the majority of the City Council. "Chevron has bought elections in this town for years," McLaughlin told me.

McLaughlin had already been surprised by her City Council victory. She frankly did not expect to win her mayoral seat given the force leveled against her, principally by Chevron. "Chevron's power is through its money," McLaughlin explained. "It's not as though their arguments make particular sense to anyone. They have the money to buy elected officials and candidates, put out the glossy mailers, buy advertising and media, and to distort the truth.

"There were two things in that [2006 electoral] campaign which Chevron bitterly opposed," McLaughlin recalled. "Me and Measure T." Measure T would have introduced a new manufacturer's tax in Richmond. The primary target was Chevron, which would have paid an additional $8 million a year in new taxes. The measure would also have eliminated a minor tax break given to small landlords. Between Chevron, the Chamber of Commerce, and the Industry Council, two to three mailers appeared in mailboxes every day declaring, "Gayle Should Fail with Her Terrible T!" Through a media onslaught, the opponents of McLaughlin and Measure T sent fear through poverty-stricken Richmond that rental rates would skyrocket if Measure T passed. Of course it was Chevron—not the Tenants Union—that opposed Measure T. The onslaught killed Measure T, but Gayle won. A citizens' ballot is now working its way through the city that would maintain the landlord tax break while increasing taxes on Chevron by $16 million per year. Stay tuned.

McLaughlin's message of holding Chevron accountable for its abuses of the environment, public health, workers, and environmental justice (a term that refers to the disproportionate effect on people of color of environmental harm such as exposure to pollution-causing industries) resonated with voters who were sick of business as usual. "The community at large understands that Chevron has caused more harm than good to this city," according to McLaughlin. The City Council is still dominated by recipients of Chevron's largesse, however, and Mayor McLaughlin's ability to exercise power over Chevron has been limited.

One problem that she continually confronts is Chevron's unwillingness to share basic information with the government. For example, McLaughlin said that high levels of mercury have been found in the bay near the refinery. It is known that mercury is a by-product of Chevron's production, but Chevron refuses to disclose its methods for disposing of its mercury, making it impossible for the city to prove one way or another whether Chevron is a source of the bay's mercury poisoning and, consequently, to remediate the pollution.

Chevron also refuses to disclose its utility usage, which affects tens of millions of dollars in annual tax payments. For twenty years, Chevron enjoyed a unique tax arrangement with the city. Chevron alone among Richmond's taxpayers paid a flat rate—usually $1.2 million a month—with an annual cap of $14 million. When City Council member McLaughlin and a few others started to question this unusual arrangement (much to the chagrin of the sitting mayor), Chevron agreed to a slightly revised formula. Richmond's residents pay a 10 percent tax on their utility services. Chevron decided it would do the same and subsequently turned over a check to the city for $390,000 *less* than its usual payment. The city does not know whether the new, reduced payment is accurate, because Chevron still refuses to release energy production or usage information. Mayor McLaughlin is trying to audit Chevron to obtain this information. "The city can't audit our energy usage because of business confidentiality," Chevron refinery spokeswoman Camille Priselac told the local newspaper. "We don't disclose information about our energy production."[100]

Mayor McLaughlin has been disappointed by the lack of support Richmond has received from the rest of the state's elected officials, but she is doggedly optimistic. The people of Richmond put her in office against all odds, so why shouldn't they also succeed in their struggle against Chevron?

McLaughlin's election victory was part of a much broader rejection of business as usual in the 2006 midterm elections. Proving that money does not always win and that the oil companies do not always get their way, candidates across the country at the local and national level who directly expressed opposition to the interests of the oil industry won elections.

THE 2006 PEOPLES' REBELLION

It was a perfect storm: six years of organizing against the Bush administration, four years against the war in Iraq, and at least twenty years spent trying to remove the cloud of doubt about the reality of global warming all came together in one election. The American public was deeply opposed to a war for oil in Iraq. People were angry at the highest profits in oil industry history as gas and home heating prices shot through the roof. They were fed up with an administration that was part and parcel of the oil industry, as scandal after scandal revealed the lengths to which the administration and Congress would go to let its oil industry buddies have their way. The result was a public rebellion that defeated the oil industry in the 2006 midterm elections, voting out oil industry darlings, including Richard Pombo and nine other "Dirty Dozen" members of Congress, and costing the Republicans control of the House and Senate. If Americans could have voted Bush, Cheney, and their entire "oiligarchy" out, they very likely would have.

Among the many groups organizing against the oil industry in 2006 were the League of Conservation Voters, Defenders of Wildlife, and the Sierra Club. These national organizations formed a unique alliance with local groups and activists around the country and succeeded in pinning the infamous ExxonMobil button squarely on the lapels of the industry's favorite candidates. They ran ads that connected the dots between elected officials, their votes, and the oil money they had received. In the ads, "green" candidates said not just what they were against, but also what they were for, speaking up for "a new energy future that brings us new jobs for a new economy with windmills, hydrogen cars, solar power, and sustainable alternatives."

At the same time, the antiwar movement, including groups

such as United for Peace and Justice, Iraq Veterans Against the War, and Code Pink, drove home the connection between the war votes and the oil connections of the same members of Congress. Poll results showed that the war was the single driving issue among Democrats, most of whom clearly identified the war as one for oil. Independent voters, whose votes usually break about 50/50 between Republicans and Democrats, gave 68 percent of their votes to Democrats in 2006. When asked why they rejected the Republicans, their number one answer was because of energy issues broadly and gas prices specifically.[101] "When voters wanted change," Gene Karpinski, president of the League of Conservation Voters, told me, "Big Oil was the single biggest symbol of change that they wanted."[102] The Democrats ran on an alternative energy platform and had the public's backing. But the victory party did not last long.

In their "6 for '06" platform, the Democrats promised to roll back the $14 billion in tax breaks and subsidies given to the oil industry by the Bush administration. They pledged action on climate change and price-gouging, investigations into industry collusion and antitrust practices, and an end to the war in Iraq. The talk was very big. "This is a warning to oil and gas companies," said Representative Rahm Emanuel, Democrat of Illinois and chairman of the House Democratic Caucus, shortly after the Democratic victory. "When you get a Democratic Congress, you are going to get a cop on the beat."[103] The action, unfortunately, has been minimal. The Democrats have been stymied time and again by bills that pass the House but die in the Senate, pass the Senate but die in the House, or even pass both the House and Senate but then die in conference committee. And the war rages on.

There are many explanations for this, but one can certainly be found in the combined lobbying power of the oil industry, which now surpasses that of any other period in the last twenty years. ExxonMobil alone spent twice as much on lobbying in 2006 than in 2005—more than $14.5 million compared with $7 million. ExxonMobil, Chevron, ConocoPhillips, Shell, BP, and

Marathon combined spent $32 million more lobbying the federal government in 2006 than in 2005. Big Oil even started hiring Democrats and Democratic lobbying firms to work for them. The slim majority held by the Democrats in the House and Senate hurts their chances to pass meaningful legislation, as does the threat of a veto from President Bush.

Another explanation of why the Democrats have not achieved greater change is found in the 2008 elections. As I write, the 2008 presidential election is on track to become the most expensive in U.S. history. By some predictions, the eventual nominees will need to raise $500 million apiece to compete—a record for both parties and more than twice the amount raised by Democrats Kerry and Edwards in 2004. The battle for the House and Senate is proving equally groundbreaking. In order to garner these massive sums of money, neither party has been willing to go to extraordinary lengths to see legislation passed opposed by major donors.

The oil industry has maintained its heavy Republican bias thus far in the 2008 electoral season, donating nearly 75 percent of its campaign funds to Republicans, according to the Center for Responsive Politics. Among Democrats for president, however, Senator Hillary Clinton was the oil industry's early and biggest favorite. For months, in fact, she held the third-place seat as the candidate receiving the most oil industry money, behind former mayor Rudolph Giuliani and Governor Mitt Romney. Once it became clear that Senator McCain would be the Republican presidential nominee, however, he pulled ahead of all other 2008 candidates in oil industry contributions. By mid-2008, the oil industry had risen to become one of McCain's largest financial backers, ranking twelve among his top twenty industry supporters.

Senator Obama, meanwhile, renounced money from oil company PACs, while accepting money from executives and other individuals who work for oil companies. In mid-2008, the oil industry did not rank among his top twenty industry contributors, although he had received some $352,000 from the industry. Senator Clinton took in nearly $400,000 from the oil industry by mid-2008, while Senator McCain had taken in more than twice as much, at $1,040,000.

Among all the senators and members of Congress vying for president in 2008, since 1990 Senator McCain has taken the most oil industry money—$1,260,000. Senator Clinton is second with over $561,000 and Senator Obama is third at $417,410, the vast majority of which is due to his 2008 presidential bid.

When ranking each of these candidates' lifetime records on global warming issues, the League of Conservation Voters reported that McCain voted "with the environment" just 27 percent of the time, while Clinton and Obama did so 87 and 86 percent of the time, respectively. In 2007, McCain's percentage was zero. Similarly, Peace Action Education Fund—a project of Peace Action, fifty years old and the nation's largest grassroots peace network—found that in 2007 and 2008, Senator McCain voted with Peace Action none of the time, while Senators Clinton and Obama did so 88 and 100 percent of the time, respectively. Peace groups are, however, quick to criticize both Clinton and Obama for failing to endorse plans to fully and unequivocally end the U.S. occupation of Iraq.

Senators John Edwards and Joseph Biden are in a different oil industry money league, each taking in around $75,000 from the oil industry since 1990. Congressman Dennis Kucinich, meanwhile, has taken in a grand total of $11,200 in the same period. Rounding out the top oil industry recipients for the 2008 presidential race are Bill Richardson ($208,425), Fred Thompson ($162,304), Mike Huckabee ($102,339), and Ron Paul ($99,972).

For now, almost no one is totally clean of oil industry money. As a consequence, despite the American public's demand in the 2006 election for the passage of new legislation, congressional leadership, and action to end the war in Iraq and to meaningfully address climate change, very little has changed. The next two chapters address exactly what Big Oil is hoping to achieve going forward and the costs—from climate chaos to war—associated with allowing business to proceed as usual.

7

Big Oil's Big Plans for the Future, Part I: Environmental Destruction

In the future, you are going to need every molecule of oil that you can get from every source. . . .

—DON PAUL, CHEVRON[1]

You have to kill people, kill wildlife, and kill the last wild places to get what's left of the world's oil.

—RICHARD CHARTER, DEFENDERS OF WILDLIFE[2]

Big Oil would have us believe that it is part of the solution, not the problem. The companies, their commercials declare, are as committed to clean, renewable energy as they are to oil. Do not believe the hype. Oil companies talk big about alternative energy, but their money does not follow their message. Not a single Big Oil company spent more than 4 percent of its total expenditures in 2006 or 2007 on green energy alternatives, and most of the companies spent far less. Instead, the companies are using their massive profits to scour the globe in search of every last available drop of oil—from the tar sands of Canada to the shale regions of the midwestern United States, to deep offshore drilling the world over. Big Oil is using its political muscle to eviscerate existing restrictions on where it can drill and what methods it can use. Big Oil is also using its great financial might to expand its technological capacity to reach record heights and depths in oil extraction. These new methods are even more environmentally harmful than traditional oil production and will, if allowed to continue, drive us even closer to climate catastrophe.

VIVOLEUM

Canada's Gas and Oil Exposition (GO-EXPO) is one of North America's premier industry events. The 2007 GO-EXPO was no exception. A record-breaking twenty-thousand-plus attendees and exhibitors made their way to Calgary in Canada's Alberta Province, not too far across the border from Great Falls, Montana. Two event-filled days in June 2007 included hundreds of exhibitions, workshops, and panels, but one keynote address stole the entire show and captured the world's attention.

ExxonMobil and the U.S. National Petroleum Council (NPC) were scheduled to unveil the results of a new study called "Facing the Hard Truths about Energy: A Comprehensive View to 2030 of Global Oil and Natural Gas." The NPC is an oil industry advisory group to the U.S. Department of Energy. Former ExxonMobil CEO Lee Raymond heads the NPC and is also chair of this study. Chevron CEO David O'Reilly is the study's vice chair.

As the presenters took the stage, three hundred audience members settled into their seats, anxiously awaiting the study results. The NPC representative began by explaining what everyone in the audience already knew: current U.S. and Canadian energy policies—most notably the massive, carbon-intensive exploitation of Alberta's tar sands—are increasing global warming and with it the likelihood of catastrophic global events. He reassured the audience that the oil industry would "keep fuel flowing" by transforming the billions of people who die into oil.

"We need something like whales, but infinitely more abundant," said the NPC representative before describing the technology used to render human flesh into a "new Exxon oil product" called Vivoleum. "Vivoleum works in perfect synergy with the continued expansion of fossil fuel production," noted the speaker. "With more fossil fuels comes a greater chance of disaster, but that means more feedstock for Vivoleum. Fuel will continue to flow for those of us left."

The attendees listened to the lecture with rapt attention. They lit "commemorative candles" supposedly made of Vivoleum obtained from the flesh of an Exxon janitor who died as a result of cleaning up a toxic spill. The audience only reacted when the janitor, in a video tribute, announced that he wished to be transformed into candles after his death.

The gig was up. GO-EXPO had been had.

The "NPC and ExxonMobil representatives" were actually Andy Bichlbaum and Mike Bonanno of the famed Yes Men, a unique theater group that has gained the deep respect of activists and the widespread ire of corporate executives for their ability to slip unnoticed into industry events until their political commentary is made.

As security guards pulled the Yes Men off stage to deliver them into the hands of the Calgary police, Bichlbaum, in character to the last, calmly explained, "We're not talking about killing anyone. We're talking about using them after nature has done the hard work. After all, a hundred and fifty thousand people already die from climate change–related effects every year. That's only going to go up—maybe way, way up. Will it all go to waste? That would be cruel."[3]

BIG OIL = OIL

The real National Petroleum Council report was released a month later, in July 2007. It carries little of the creative zeal of the Yes Men's performance, but, with the exception of Vivoleum, its message does not differ radically from theirs. "Facing the Hard Truths" reflects the views of every major oil company operating in the United States. The working group participants responsible for the report include the CEOs and presidents of

Marathon, ConocoPhillips, Shell, BP America, Halliburton, Hunt Oil, Occidental, Chevron, and ExxonMobil.

Three hard truths dominate the four-hundred-page report. The first is that energy demand is growing. The second is that oil will remain the foremost, indispensable resource for meeting that demand in the immediate and distant future. The third is the oil industry's resounding commitment to leave no stone unturned and no method untried in its pursuit of finding, drilling, and selling every drop of oil left on the planet. The Yes Men's underlying assertion—that given its commitment to increasingly destructive methods to acquire oil, the oil industry might as well stuff our dead bodies directly into the tailpipes of our cars—is well substantiated by the NPC report.

The NPC asserts the need to open every avenue to oil exploitation. To achieve this goal, the report advocates the acceleration of tar sands and oil shale development and the "streamlining of permitting processes"—a nice way of saying "reducing environmental, public health, and safety controls." It also recommends a more explicit integration of oil acquisition and national defense policies, which would be accomplished by "having the Department of Energy share an equal role with the Departments of Defense, State, Treasury, and Commerce on policy issues relating to energy and energy security." Welcome to the United States of Oil.

Big Oil is ready to do whatever is necessary to achieve its goals. In fact, it is on a spending spree. Awash in profits, ExxonMobil, Chevron, ConocoPhillips, Marathon, Shell, and BP are spending big bucks and taking big risks on new technology to take them into uncharted areas of energy production. The spending spree includes expensive media campaigns designed to convince the public that Big Oil's money is being put to good use—namely, that the companies are investing their vast wealth in clean, green, sustainable energy solutions. They are not. Instead, their unprecedented bankrolls, subsidized by our tax dollars, are being used to experiment with expensive, risky, untried, dangerous, and environmentally catastrophic methods of scraping through tar, burrowing under mountains, and barreling into the depths of the ocean to get every last drop of oil left on the planet. In just one example, in 2006 Chevron purchased the most expensive offshore drilling rig in history for $600 million—*twice as much* as it spent on all its green energy investments that year. Big Oil's unwillingness to acknowledge the devastating consequences of this pursuit makes "Vivoleum" seem like an all too reasonable vision of the future.

Just try to get Vivoleum out of your mind when you watch Chevron's next "Human Energy" commercial. The ads in this $15 million campaign include the following line: "Watch as we tap the greatest source of energy in the world—ourselves—this is the power of human energy."[4] The anchor ad is two and a half minutes long and visually stunning. It ought to be: it was filmed in more than thirteen countries by the cinematographer of *Lost in Translation*. The ad first aired during CBS's *60 Minutes,* and additional ads went on to air in eight languages around the globe, including in the Middle East and Kazakhstan.[5] The narrator's sonorous voice conveys both paternal care and scientific authority as he assures us that the people who work at Chevron are "not corporate titans" but rather "part-time poets and coaches." The company not only cares about us, but it is putting its money where its mouth is and investing in clean energy alternatives. The commercials end as the words *oil, geothermal, solar, wind, hydrogen,* and *conservation* appear one at a time for equal duration in between Chevron's three-bar logo. The intent is clear: we are meant to believe that the company is equal parts clean energy and oil.

Chevron is not the only company to engage in "greenwashing." BP changed its name from British Petroleum to Beyond Petroleum in 2000 and has spent millions of dollars assuring us of its green credentials. Shell shot a nine-minute film about a caring, dedicated oil engineer and distributed it on DVD with *National Geographic* magazines.[6] The first thing that greets visitors to ConocoPhillips's Web site is an invitation to read its sustainable development report, energy guide, and information about next-generation biofuels.

The companies would like us to believe that they are, in Chevron's words, "part of the solution" and that we can trust them to do the right thing. This message makes sense to a public that understands that the world is quickly approaching the peak of conventional oil production. It naturally follows that oil companies would lead the way in the development of alternatives because "How else do they plan to stay in business when the oil runs out?" Logical, but wrong. Big Oil plans to stay in business because it does not intend to run out of oil.

The oil companies make token investments in alternatives to appease public opinion, while they push people and their governments to allow them into every last spot on the globe where they can use increasingly destructive methods to draw every last drop of oil out of the earth. Given the chance, they will devastate the earth's last pristine places, destroy local communities, threaten worker safety, increase pollution and global warming, and imperil our future.

CLIMATE CRISIS

The climate crisis . . . is getting a lot worse—much more quickly than predicted. . . . The answer is to end our reliance on carbon-based fuels.
—FORMER VICE PRESIDENT AL GORE, 2008[7]

Our climate is in crisis. Including 2007, seven of the eight warmest years since records began to be kept in 1880 have occurred since 2001, and the ten warmest years have all occurred since 1997.[8] In the United States, the first six months of 2006 were the warmest six-month period ever recorded.[9] As the globe gets warmer, polar ice caps melt, the oceans expand and their levels rise, and floods and storms increase in both intensity and frequency. At the same time, warmer temperatures bring heat waves and droughts, threatening our food supply and spreading disease. While the situation is rapidly worsening, the good news is that we know what the major culprits are: oil, natural gas, coal, and deforestation.

Burning fossil fuels—primarily oil, natural gas, and coal—increases atmospheric concentrations of carbon dioxide (CO_2), the principal greenhouse gas. The more greenhouse gas there is in the earth's atmosphere, the more of the sun's heat is trapped near the earth's surface. The more heat that is trapped, the higher the planet's temperature climbs, and the more our climate is forced into chaos. Forests are the earth's natural mechanism for filtering greenhouse gas emissions from the air. The more forests we cut down, especially older, thicker forests, the less the planet is able to reduce the effects of our emissions.

The United States is by far the single largest per capita contributor to global warming, releasing 30 percent of all global energy-related CO_2 emissions in 2004 (the most recent year for which reliable data is available). The vast majority of the CO_2 emitted by the United States—a full 70 percent   is produced in just two ways: by our cars and trucks, which burn oil, and by our power plants, which burn coal and natural gas. One out of every seven barrels of oil in the world is consumed on America's highways alone. The actual production of oil accounts for another 5 percent of U.S. greenhouse gas emissions.[10]

Just to *stabilize* current greenhouse gas concentrations in the atmosphere, the world must reduce emissions of these gases by 50 to 80 percent by 2050, if not sooner. To accomplish this reduction, the Pew Center on Global Climate Change recently concluded, "Most importantly, the world needs to fundamentally change the way it produces and consumes energy."[11]

The bottom line is clear: burning fossil fuels is the number one activity driving the climate crisis. If we do not make dramatic efforts to reduce these activities, we will hasten the destruction of the earth's capacity to support human life.

ExxonMobil led the charge to deny the mere existence of global warming. Beginning in the late 1990s, Exxon and then

ExxonMobil spent millions of dollars to fund some forty organizations in both the United States and Europe whose purpose was
to undermine the scientific consensus on global climate change
and create the appearance of scientific controversy.[12] The American Petroleum Institute (API), under the guidance of Exxon's Lee
Raymond, joined in the effort. The *New York Times* uncovered
a 1998 API memo outlining a strategy to invest millions to
"maximize the impact of scientific views consistent with ours
with Congress, the media and other key audiences." The document stated: "Victory will be achieved when . . . recognition of
uncertainty [regarding climate change] becomes part of the 'conventional wisdom.' "[13] All of the oil companies have participated
in lobbying to stop the U.S. government and the governments of
the world from taking meaningful action to halt global warming. Their motivations are not mysterious: as the supply of conventional oil is depleted, the available supply of crude oil is
getting dirtier and is being found in more environmentally sensitive areas.

Big Oil knows that it is in trouble. In 2007, while Al Gore
received the Nobel Peace Prize for his work detailing the causes
and consequences of climate change, 67 percent of Americans
polled held a negative view of the oil industry, making it far and
away the most hated industry in the nation. An even higher percentage, 71 percent, said that the effects of global warming had
already begun or would take place within their lifetime.[14] As
public awareness and anger grow, the calls for real policy change
grow as well. What is an oil company executive to do? The oil
industry would like us to believe that the companies' approach
has been "If you can't beat 'em, join 'em"—that they have answered the call for a clean energy future.

They have not.

BIG OIL'S BIG LIES ABOUT ALTERNATIVES

"When you add up all of the various types of emerging energy
technologies, our industry, over the [last] five years, has invested

almost $100 billion—more than two and a half times as much as the federal government and all other U.S. companies combined,"[15] says John Felmy, touting his favorite statistic. As the chief economist of the oil industry's leading trade association, API, Felmy cites this statistic in congressional testimony, speeches, radio interviews, and presentations. He uses it to emphasize to lawmakers and the public that it is both unnecessary and unwarranted to implement new taxes on the oil industry to fund alternative energy. No new taxes are needed because the industry is already using its money to invest in alternatives. "Increasing alternatives is something that the industry supports," Felmy argues. "We're already doing it, we're leading the way."[16]

One hundred billion dollars in investment is an astounding figure that might easily lead one to believe that Big Oil is using its vast resources to pave the way to a clean energy future. It is tempting to imagine that the oil companies are spending tens of billions of dollars on converting from petroleum to biofuels; solar, wind, and tidal power; hybrid and electric cars; fuel cells and hydrogen. The reality is nothing of the sort. Big Oil's big investments in alternatives are, by and large, not related to clean energy at all. Felmy explained to me in an interview that among the oil industry's primary "emerging energy technologies" are investments in "frontier hydrocarbons"—tar sands, oil shale, and gas-to-liquids—methods of oil extraction that are even more environmentally harmful and risky than traditional methods.[17] Felmy also explained that the investments of car companies in hybrid vehicles are included in his dollar count, which of course inflates the figure and leads us to believe that Big Oil rather than Big Auto is making these investments.

Big Oil is investing in a breadth of alternatives, but the actual figure is far less than Felmy's $100 billion would lead us to believe. The oil companies make their money by selling oil and therefore spend their money looking for and producing more oil. To a lesser extent, they make money by selling natural gas and gasoline and therefore spend money on these resources as well.

Almost every major oil company loses money on its alternative energy investments, which is why it is not surprising that relatively speaking they spend almost nothing on these investments.

Given the oil companies' desire to paint themselves as "part of the solution," one might think that it would be easy to find a financial breakdown of exactly how much each company spends on biofuels, solar and wind power, and the like. In fact, the opposite is true. One has to be quite a sleuth to track down their actual expenditures on alternative energy. Their annual tax filings with the U.S. Securities and Exchange Commission (SEC) and annual reports to their shareholders, not their TV commercials, advertisements, or casual visits to their Web sites, provide the only meaningful—albeit incomplete—guide.

The companies' 2006 10K (for U.S. firms) and Form 20-F (for foreign firms) SEC tax filings and annual reports reveal that, even by generous estimates, every oil company investigated here, with the exception of BP and Chevron, spent less than 1 percent of its total capital expenditures on green energy alternatives that year.[18] BP, the company with the highest percentage, still only spent a pitiful 4 percent. Chevron ranked second with 1.8 percent, Shell ranked third with 0.8 percent, followed by Conoco-Phillips with 0.5 percent. Marathon spent next to nothing, and ExxonMobil appeared to spend virtually nothing at all on green energy alternatives.

BP

> Frank Sesno: *So alternatives are still a drop in the bucket.*
> Lord Browne, then CEO of BP: *At the moment, of course they are.*
>
> —CNN INTERVIEW, JUNE 2007[19]

After BP changed its name to Beyond Petroleum in 2000, a group of BP shareholders found that the company had spent more on its new logo than on renewable energy in all of 1998. In response,

CorpWatch, a leading corporate research and watchdog group, offered a more appropriate phrase for the company's rebranding effort: "BP: Beyond Propaganda . . . Beyond Belief."[20]

Public pressure for a transition from fossil fuels to clean energy has been stronger in Europe than in the United States. European governments have responded, and so too has BP—although not nearly to the extent that it would have us believe. BP has pledged more money for alternatives than the other companies and stands out among them for its investments in solar energy. However, the amounts involved are still a pittance relative to its total capital expediture, and hardly qualify the company as being "beyond petroleum."

According to BP's SEC Form 20-F tax filing, in 2006 BP made more than $22 billion in profit and spent an additional $15.5 billion buying back shares of its own stock. It spent another $17 billion on capital expenditures, such as exploration, production, transportation, and marketing. It spent $688 million, roughly 4 percent of its total expenditures, on the company's Gas, Power, and Renewables business division. This division works on "marketing and trading of gas and power; marketing of liquefied natural gas; natural gas liquids; and low-carbon power generation through our Alternative Energy business." BP, like most of the other oil companies, includes renewable energy alternatives in business divisions that have more than one function. As a result, it is often difficult to say exactly what dollar figure went to a particular project, let alone determine exactly how much money was spent on clean energy alternatives. For example, most environmentalists would not consider liquefied natural gas a clean energy alterative, but it is included in BP's figure of $688 million. To keep these numbers simple, however, I am giving BP the entire $688 million in my calculation of its alternative energy investments.

BP became the largest producer of solar energy in the world when it bought the Solarex solar energy corporation for $45 million in 1999.[21] Reuters found that, from 1999 to 2005, BP spent a total of just $500 million on solar energy. It has spent another $300 million on wind energy since 2006.[22]

BP reports in its SEC tax filing that in 2005 the company launched BP Alternative Energy and announced its intention to invest up to $8 billion over the next ten years on "solar, wind, hydrogen, and high-efficiency gas-fired power generation." It also announced a "strategic relationship" with GE to "accelerate the development of hydrogen power technology and the deployment of the concept," as well as plans to invest a measly $500 million over the next ten years to establish the BP Energy Biosciences Institute for researching new transportation fuels. In 2006 U.S. taxpayers generously gave BP $90 million in the form of a federal investment credit for a proposed hydrogen plant in Carson, California.

BP's goals are admirable, and up to $800 million a year is more than any other company has pledged. These goals are simply not significant, however, in comparison with the company's other expenditures. More importantly, in December 2007 the company announced that it was moving into the Canadian tar sands and would be refining the new, dirty crude at its Toledo refinery. BP is expanding its offshore drilling presence, and, as Lord Browne made explicit to CNN, it is just as committed as the other companies to maintaining its nearly singular focus on oil.

Chevron

People who think that peak oil will occur are just looking at conventional oil. You have to think beyond that. Think of all the other hydrocarbon sources, the oil sands in Canada. . . . Think of all the remote areas of the world that have not yet been explored. . . ."
—DAVID O'REILLY, CHEVRON CEO, 2006[23]

Chevron's 2006 annual report reveals that the company took in more than $17 billion in pure profit in 2006. It spent $5 billion buying back its own stock. It also spent another $16.6 billion on capital expenditures. Nearly 80 percent of this amount, some $13 billion, went to exploring for and producing oil and natural gas, including expenditures on Alberta's tar sands, oil shale in Colorado, and offshore drilling the world over. More than $3 billion of this figure was spent on refining oil into finished products and then marketing and transporting those products to the public. Chevron spent another $200 million on its chemical business. It spent $417 million on "all other" expenditures.

It is within this "all other" category that some light is shed on Chevron's "alternative energy" expenditures, although it does not appear in the company's annual report. The supplemental to Chevron's annual report tells us that the "all other" category includes: "the company's interest in Dynegy, mining operations, power generation businesses, worldwide cash management and debt financing activities, corporate administrative functions, insurance operations, real estate activities, alternative fuels, and technology companies." Of these categories, power generation, alternative fuels, and technology companies could include investments in clean energy. To be generous, let's assume that Chevron spent $300 million on clean energy alternatives in 2006. Chevron would therefore have spent, at best, 1.8 percent of its expenditures on green alternatives.

To make sense of such a miniscule investment, we need look no further than the earnings side of Chevron's ledger and remind ourselves that this is a *for-profit* enterprise. Chevron made more than $17 billion selling oil, gas, and refined products in 2006. It lost $516 million on the entire "all other" category.

Chevron's 2006 Corporate Responsibility Report and media materials tout a seemingly larger investment: "From 2002 to 2006, we invested nearly $2 billion in renewable and alternative energy, including energy efficiency services, and expect to invest more than $2.5 billion from 2007 to 2009." There is simply no way to reconcile these figures, which are not broken down anywhere by the company, with its financial reporting, until we learn that

Chevron includes its environmentally destructive and highly polluting development of dirty oil from oil shale as "alternative energy." Chevron's 2006 Corporate Responsibility Report explains: Chevron has undertaken "[s]everal new joint initiatives to develop environmentally responsible and commercially viable technologies and processes to recover crude oil and natural gas from western U.S. oil shale sources, an alternative source of energy."

Chevron has made important investments. According to the company, most of its renewable energy investments are in geothermal energy used for electricity production by utilities. Chevron has four geothermal plants, all located on the Pacific Rim in Indonesia and the Philippines. Chevron has also invested in solar power, including a $12 million solar-powered parking lot in Fresno, California, and a project with the U.S. Postal Service mail processing facility in Oakland, California. Chevron invests in research to determine whether biofuels can "pass a market-commerciality and economics test." It invests in hydrogen fuel technology, including collaboration with General Motors and the state of Florida to build a fleet of hydrogen-fueled buses at the Orlando airport. Chevron recently bought a 22 percent interest in a biodiesel plant in Galveston, Texas.

Chevron's future focus is clear. It is investing in oil wherever it is found, including the Alberta tar sands, Colorado's oil shale, and offshore. Even Chevron's "Human Energy" ads include at least one sentence that honestly describes its future vision: "for today and tomorrow and for the foreseeable future, our lives demand oil."

Shell

Fossil fuels, including coal, currently meet about 80 percent of the world's energy needs—and they are likely to stay the most affordable and accessible source of energy for the coming decades.

—SHELL 2006 SHELL ANNUAL REPORT

Shell's 2006 profits exceeded $25 billion. But, at less than 1 percent, Shell's expenditures on alternatives as a proportion of its overall expenditures put it far behind BP and Chevron. However, Shell has distinguished itself with its investments in wind power. While Shell spent a total of $25 billion on capital expenses in 2006, it spent only about $200 million on a very broadly defined category of "alternatives."

Shell's 2006 annual report states that it has invested over $1 billion in alternative energy over the past five years. This number appears to include investments in several unclean technologies such as "clean coal," gas-to-liquids, oil shale, and tar sands. This number also includes the company's investments in wind, solar, biofuels, and hydrogen. The *San Diego Union-Tribune* found that Shell has the largest wind power business of the oil majors and seventeenth largest in the world, that it has invested $150 million in hydrogen since 1999, and that it is partnering with companies to produce biofuels from waste biomass. The company began investing in solar in 2006, working to develop and produce a "next-generation" thin-film panel. It also announced plans to help create the world's largest hydrogen public transport project, in Rotterdam.

Shell shares, if not surpasses, the other companies' outlays and focus on tar sands, oil shale, and offshore production. As the company states in its annual report, "We are successfully exploring in ever-deeper water, expanding our liquefied natural gas business and developing unconventional sources such as oil sands."

ConocoPhillips

ConocoPhillips favors developing all forms of energy—conventional, renewable and alternative. However, we recognize that . . . fossil fuels must still supply two-thirds of world energy in 2030.

—JOHN LOWE, VICE PRESIDENT,
CONOCOPHILLIPS, 2008[24]

ConocoPhillips certainly talks the alternatives talk, but its related expenditures are virtually nonexistent. Furthermore, what little the company does spend on "alternatives" is largely focused on heavy, dirty oils and environmentally risky endeavors. The company reports in its 10K SEC filing that after spending $15.6 billion in 2006, ConocoPhillips made $15.5 billion in profit. Of its expenditures, 0.5 percent, a measly $80 million, went to its entire Emerging Business segment, which focuses on very broadly defined "alternatives." From 2004 to 2006, the company spent a total of $163 million on this entire segment.

ConocoPhillips explains that it is working on "power generation; carbon-to-liquids; technology solutions, such as sulfur removal technologies; and alternative energy and programs, such as advanced hydrocarbon processes, energy conversion technologies, new petroleum-based products, and renewable fuels." But it then makes clear that the overwhelming focus of this section is not clean energy. In the company's description of its Emerging Business segment, it highlights its focus on tar sands, oil shale, and a plan to release methane trapped in the Arctic—a practice that, if successful, would be highly environmentally destructive and could release enormous quantities of greenhouse gases.

ConocoPhillips, like the rest of Big Oil, is spending billions buying back its stock and a few hundred million, at most, investing in green alternatives. ConocoPhillips announced its intention to buy back $15 billion of its own stock through the end of 2008.

Marathon

In 2006 Marathon spent about $3.5 billion and made more than $5 billion in profit. The company started a $2 billion share repurchase program in January 2006. It does not even pretend to have an alternatives program.

Marathon is unique among the big oil companies, however, for its introduction of renewable fuels to a few of its stations. Marathon claims to be one of the largest blenders of ethanol in the United States. In 2006 Marathon blended approximately 550 million gallons of ethanol and plans to double that amount by 2008. It offers E-10 (90 percent gasoline/10 percent ethanol) and E-85 (85 percent ethanol/15 percent gasoline) at more than forty of its stations and plans to expand that number to nearly sixty. It formed a joint venture to construct and operate "one or more" ethanol plants in the United States. Construction of the first plant in Greenville, Ohio, began in late 2006.

Visitors to Marathon's Web site in 2007 and 2008 are greeted by the smiling young face of Jennifer Bracey, the operations manager for U.S. Production Operations. "I am now responsible for Marathon's operations in the Rockies, the Permian Basin, and the Gulf of Mexico," Bracey tells us. "It is a challenging and interesting role." These are Marathon's operations in oil shale and offshore drilling. The Web site also proudly declares Marathon's 2007 entrance into the Alberta tar sands.

ExxonMobil

[T]he pursuit of alternative fuels must not detract from the development of oil and gas.

—J. S. SIMON, SENIOR VICE PRESIDENT,
EXXONMOBIL, 2008[25]

ExxonMobil spearheaded and financed a movement to deny the existence of global warming. It grudgingly admits that global warming is now an accepted phenomenon, but does not accept responsibility for doing anything about it. Most importantly, ExxonMobil is the most profitable corporation in the history of the world and has no intention of quitting while it is ahead. For all of these reasons and more, ExxonMobil does not invest in alternatives. According to CEO Rex Tillerson, there is nothing in it for them. "What are we going to bring to this area to create value for our shareholders that's differentiating?" asks Tillerson. "Because to just go in and invest like everybody else—well, why would a shareholder want to own ExxonMobil?"[26] In the aptly titled article "Exxon = Oil, G*dammit!" *Fortune* magazine's senior editor Geoff Colvin explains why: "Exxon understands the essence of capitalism: earning a return on capital that exceeds the cost of that capital. At this supremely important job, it is a world champion."

ExxonMobil's 2006 annual report is a testament to its abiding belief in oil and its identification of the key problem in filling the world's energy needs—restrictions placed on where and how oil companies can pursue oil. In 2006 the company reported: "The world is endowed with huge oil resources, which are adequate to meet rising demand through 2030. However, access to these resources . . . [is] essential to develop new supplies. . . . New technology will promote economic development of frontier resources, such as heavy oil and shale oil, to help ensure adequate supplies well past 2030."

The company acknowledges the problem of rising CO_2 emissions but encourages consumers to consider the trade-offs of reducing such emissions: "Rising consumption of oil, gas, and coal means that CO_2 emissions will also increase. . . . Clearly, a variety of options exist to mitigate CO_2 emissions, but they come at a cost, ultimately borne by consumers. Effectively addressing this issue requires understanding the potential scale, cost, and tradeoffs involved."

THIS DETAILED ANALYSIS WAS conducted using the companies' 2006 filings. Their 2007 reports reveal the same spending patterns, with each company continuing to spend less than 4 percent of its total expenditures on green alternatives, and most spending far less. If you are wondering how Big Oil expects to survive in the future if it is not investing in meaningful alternatives, the answer is found, among other locations, in the tar sands of Alberta, the oil shale of the American Midwest, off every coast of the United States, and in the deepest oceans of the world. Estimates of the potential oil in these places run well into trillions of barrels. Unfortunately, the associated methods of extraction come at enormous costs, including greater environmental destruction, harm to coastal communities and public health, risks to the safety and lives of workers, and financial resources that could be put to far better use.

BIG OIL'S BIG SPENDING ON DIRTY, DANGEROUS, AND DEADLY OIL

Canada's Tar Sands: "We Have the Energy!"

The United Nations adopted the international Convention Concerning the Protection of the World Cultural and Natural Heritage in 1972. The treaty encourages the identification, protection, and preservation of cultural and natural heritage around the world "considered to be of outstanding value to humanity." The UN maintains a list of 851 World Heritage Sites, including the Great Wall of China, the Galapagos Islands, the Grand Canyon, and Yellowstone National Park. Canada has thirteen World Heritage Sites, five of which are found in the province of Alberta.

Alberta is a stunning region 600 miles across the U.S.-Canada border from Montana. The landscape is similar to that of the Rocky Mountains of Colorado and Montana. It is home to several native or First Nation communities, including the Mikisew Cree, Athabasca Chipewyan, Dehcho, Akaitcho Dene, and Woodland Cree. It is rich with mountain vistas, lakes, streams, forests, and wildlife. The thick boreal forest and wetlands blanket much of Alberta and are home to bears, wolves, caribou, and lynx. The boreal forest provides a breeding ground for 30 percent of North America's songbirds and 40 percent of our waterfowl.[27] Skiing, fishing, hiking, bird-watching, camping, and tourism rank high among the popular uses of the land.

Drivers making their way through the boreal forest to Fort McNurry near the northern tip of Alberta are greeted with a giant sign announcing, "We have the Energy!" Fort McNurry is home to the northern lights and the Alberta tar sands. Millions of acres of the boreal forest have been transformed into a vast, bar-

ren moonscape. Mammoth, lumbering creatures of steel have replaced the natural wildlife. The machines work twenty-four hours
a day, 365 days a year, ripping vast open pits into the earth, some
as large as three miles wide and 200 feet deep. Among the ma-
chinery is the world's largest dump truck, which stands three
stories high, could conceivably carry about two hundred large
American cars in its trunk (a 400-ton load), and costs $5 million.
"You have fourteen steps going up [to the driver's seat], and at my
house you have fourteen steps to the bedroom," explains driver
Jim Locke. "So it's like going upstairs in my house, sitting on my
bed and driving the house downtown."[28]

The thick, black, tar-filled sand that Locke drives around is a
mixture of 85 percent sand, clay, and silt; 5 percent water; and
10 percent crude bitumen. It is this final 10 percent that has
drawn ExxonMobil, Chevron, ConocoPhillips, Marathon, BP,
Shell, and other oil companies to Alberta's forest. Once the bitumen is separated from the sand and has undergone an intensive
transformation process, it can be sold as conventional oil. Using
available technology, an estimated 175 billion barrels of oil are
believed to be lurking in Alberta's tar. That figure is second only
to Saudi Arabia's 260 billion barrels of conventional oil reserves.
But this is just the beginning. Tar sands–boosters claim that as
much as 1.7 *trillion* barrels of crude will be found, if and when
the right technology becomes available.

Tar Sands and Global Warming
Tar sands oil production generates almost three times more
global warming pollution than does conventional oil production.
Global warming pollution emissions from tar sands production
already totaled 25 megatons in 2003, more than from all the
cars in Maryland that year. As production expands, this figure is
projected to more than *quadruple* to between 108 and 126 megatons by 2015. Tar sands oil production is already the single largest contributor to the increase in global warming pollution in
Canada and is responsible for a regional increase in air pollution

from nitrogen oxides, sulfur dioxide, volatile organic compounds, and particulate matter.[29]

Tar sands production is so polluting because of the massive amounts of energy needed to extract, upgrade, and refine the oil. The enormous equipment is required because it takes 4 tons of earth, as many as 5 barrels of water, and enough natural gas to heat a home for one to five days to create just 1 barrel of oil from the tar sands. Driving the monster trucks, heating the water, and processing the crude bitumen—a particularly heavy, viscous, and dirty oil—produces massive amounts of CO_2.[30] Moreover, in order to get to these sands, millions of acres have been stripped of boreal forest, which has increased the greenhouse effect.[31]

Driving It Home: Choosing the Right Path for Fueling North America's Transportation Future, a critically important report by three leading scientific, legal, and research environmental organizations—the Natural Resources Defense Council (NRDC) and Western Resource Advocates (WRA) of the United States, and the Pembina Institute of Canada—explores tar sands and oil shale production. The report explains that only a small fraction of the bitumen deposits found in the tar sands are close enough to the surface to be mined. More than 80 percent of the established reserves must be extracted by an energy-intensive process of injecting high-pressure steam into the ground to soften the bitumen so it can be pumped to the surface. Tar sands oil production uses enormous amounts of both water and energy—from mining and drilling the tar sands to processing the bitumen that is eventually converted to oil. Natural gas is the current fuel of choice for these tar sands operations, with the industry consuming enough natural gas every day to heat roughly four million American homes.

In order to deliver adequate supplies of natural gas to the region, a vast network of new pipelines has been proposed, including a 758-mile series of pipeline and gas fields through First Nation land and the pristine boreal wilderness of the Mackenzie Valley in the Northwest Territories, one of the last large, intact portions of the forest. Concerns that natural gas may not be able to support the energy-intensive needs of the tar sands oil industry have led to discussions of building nuclear energy facilities to fuel it.

Water Pollution

In addition to global warming, tar sands production creates water pollution. Tar sands mines require extensive human-made wastewater reservoirs. Collectively covering almost 20 square miles, they look like oceans of waste. They are so vast that they can be seen from space. The oil companies dump millions of cubic meters of the sandy, toxic by-product of oil sand processing into these "tailings ponds." The pools have concentrations of highly toxic pollutants that are believed to be leaching into both groundwater and nearby bodies of water, including the Athabasca River.

"The river used to be blue. Now it's brown. Nobody can fish or drink from it. The air is bad. This has all happened so fast," said Elsie Fabian, an elder in a First Nation's community along the Athabasca River. "It's terrible. We're surrounded by the mines."[32] The residents of Fort Chipewyan, a community of about twelve hundred people three hundred kilometers downstream from Fort McMurray, have already been diagnosed with a high number of illnesses, including leukemia, lymphomas, lupus, and other autoimmune diseases.[33]

The oil companies admit that the pools are acutely toxic to aquatic life. To chase off migratory birds, propane cannons go off at random intervals and scarecrows stand guard on floating barrels.

A vast network of First Nation, environmental, indigenous rights, and corporate responsibility groups from across North America has joined forces to halt tar sands production. Their efforts are proving difficult, however, as Big Oil's commitment to the tar sands grows.

Enter Big Oil

While the U.S. oil giants have long dominated Canada's oil industry, the early years of tar sands development were led by the small, limited production capabilities of independent companies. Commercial development of the tar sands began in the late 1960s and continued at a slow pace through the 1970s and 1980s. When the tar sands became more economically desirable, Big Oil entered the picture and began buying up the existing companies and bringing in its own investments.

In consultation with Big Oil, the Canadian government began to provide new tax breaks, lower royalty payments, and other "investment friendly regimes" for entrance into the tar sands. The U.S. government provided its own research, development tax breaks, and other incentives. The oil companies themselves are now wealthy enough to make the massive investments necessary to make tar sands production profitable and to bear the risk if it is not. Their political clout with both the Canadian and U.S. governments has grown accordingly, and the price of oil is now high enough to make the benefits far outweigh the perceived economic costs.

After rebranding the tar sands as "oil sands," ExxonMobil, Chevron, ConocoPhillips, and Shell jumped in and rapidly expanded their investments, such that production of oil from the tar sands doubled in just ten years to approximately 1 million barrels per day in 2005. In 2006 Chevron announced an additional $2 billion investment to expand its oil sands production. In 2007 Marathon entered the tar sands with its purchase of Western Oil Sands, and BP did the same by acquiring a half-share in the Sunrise field in Alberta operated by Husky Energy. In June 2007 Shell announced an eightfold expansion of its Carmon Creek Oil Sands project located near Peace River, Alberta, within the Traditional Territory of the Woodland Cree First Nation.

Plans for an overall fivefold expansion in production across the tar sands have been facilitated in part by streamlined environmental regulations for new projects.[34] U.S. oil companies exert the same lobbying prowess in Canada as they do in the United States, and their goals are the same. The *Driving It Home* report by NRDC, WRA, and the Pembina Institute reveals that the Canadian government's most recent fiscal budget includes plans for a Major Project Management Office to "streamline the review of natural resource projects," "cut in half the average regulatory review period," and develop "legislative and administrative options to further consolidate and streamline regulatory processes."

Coming to a Refinery Near You

The United States imports more oil from Canada than from any other country. Three-fourths of Canada's oil exports go to the United States. And while Canada's domestic demand for oil has stabilized, its exports to the United States continue to climb. Thus, while Canadians get the land, air, and water pollution of tar sands production, the United States gets most of the oil.

Canada's dirty oil is making its way to a refinery near you. Just as the production process for tar sands oil is dirtier than that for conventional oil, so too is the refining process. The crude itself is heavier in sulfur and other toxins that must be "broken off" and released into the air and water through the refining process. Refineries in Colorado, Minnesota, Indiana, Ohio, Wisconsin, and Pennsylvania already process heavy oil from Canada's tar sands. The number of such refineries is set to explode, as ExxonMobil, Chevron, ConocoPhillips, Marathon, BP, and Shell alone plan to retool more than a dozen refineries across the United States to burn the dirtier tar sand oil. Chevron plans to refine its tar sand oil in Richmond.[35]

The United Nations recently identified the Athabasca tar sands region as one of the world's "Top 100 Hotspots"—areas of extreme environmental degradation. However, Canada is not alone in its exposure to extreme forms of oil production. The western United States is vulnerable to a similarly destructive path, as Big Oil sets its sights on the Green River Formation shale region.

Colorado, Utah, and Wyoming's Oil Shale

Bob Randall got stuck working on oil shale. In the fall of 2004, Randall was the new guy at Western Resource Advocates, a law and public policy environmental group in Boulder, Colorado. Randall had just moved from Anchorage, where he had spent seven years as an attorney with the nonprofit law firm Trustees for Alaska, working to protect the Arctic National Wildlife Refuge and Alaska's coastline from oil drills. One month after he started work in Colorado, the Federal Bureau of Land Management announced that it was soliciting public comments on oil shale development in the state. "It was the first that anyone had heard of oil shale in two decades," Randall later told me. "Everyone in the conservation community was shocked. The collective response was, 'Oil shale is back? What the hell?' "[36]

Oil shale, like *oil sands,* is a misnomer, a marketing term. It refers to certain rocks found 2,000 feet below the earth's surface that—when mined, crushed, and heated to temperatures of approximately 900 degrees Fahrenheit—release a small amount of kerogen, a precursor to petroleum. Once the kerogen is released, it must be upgraded by further processing. Only then does this rock become oil—a very heavy, dirty oil—that can be sent off to a refinery to be turned into gasoline or other motor fuels. Just as with tar sand oil, refining oil from shale is dirtier than refining conventional oil.

These kerogen-filled rocks are found in vast quantities in Colorado, Utah, and Wyoming, in what is known as the Green River Formation. Estimates of the potential amount of oil this rock could yield are staggering, ranging from 500 billion to 1.8 trillion barrels of oil. One area of western Colorado alone, the Piceance (pronounced "pee-awnce") Basin, covers 6,000 square miles and estimates of its potential oil run to 500 billion barrels. About 80 percent of the Piceance and over 70 percent of the Green River Formation are in federal lands. Therefore, whatever oil is down there belongs to the American public.

Since 1910 the federal government has been interested in oil shale production as a potential source of reserve supply for the navy. But costs, technological impediments, and environmental harm have always acted as a barrier to production. Commercial development suffered from the same problems, with the added difficulty that it never proved profitable. In the early 1960s, Exxon, Occidental, Shell, Tosco, and Union Oil, among others, began trying their hands at commercial production. At one point Tosco produced 270,000 barrels of oil per day at the Colony Oil Shale mine near Rifle, Colorado, but costs drove Tosco to shut down production in 1972. Exxon bought the Colony project in 1979. After spending more than $1 billion and earning nothing, Exxon announced on May 2, 1982, that it was closing down the project. Shell is the only company that continued its efforts, but for at least the last twenty years Shell has been focused on research, not commercial production.

Colorado's Rocky Mountains

Between Tosco and Exxon, Rifle, Colorado, was an oil boomtown. Rifle is the last town before the road heads north into "shale country." In Rifle, May 2 is known as "Black Tuesday." On that day in 1982, more than two thousand workers lost their jobs when Exxon closed the Colony mine. The company posted armed guards at the gates to stop employees from storming the facility. There was a run on the local bank. The oil boom quickly yielded a massive oil bust, and the closing of the mine was an economic catastrophe.

Twenty-five years later, Rifle has bounced back. Situated in the heart of the Rocky Mountains, Rifle has thrived as a center for outdoor tourism. Like many natives of the area, I grew up skiing, camping, and hiking in Colorado's Rocky Mountains and learned to fish on the Colorado River. The mountains are filled with meadows of wildflowers and colors of all kinds, from the purple state flower to the red earth (which gives Colorado its name: "color red"), shining out from behind green and blue trees, white waterfalls, and snow. Bears, mountain lions, goats, elk, bald eagles, and even buffalo call the state home.

The Colorado River flows through Rifle. The Grand Mesa, Roan Cliffs, and Flat Top Mountains surround the town. The

Grand Mesa is the largest "flat top" mountain in the world, stretching over 70 miles from Rifle to Grand Junction. A short drive north of Rifle on Highway 13 will take you to the trailhead for Rifle Arch, a 60-foot-tall sandstone arch 150 feet across, formed by wind, water, and natural erosion. Outdoor activities such as skiing, camping, hiking, fishing, rock climbing, mountain biking, hunting, whitewater rafting, spelunking (exploring caves), and sightseeing provide one of the largest sources of local revenue.

Just like Fort McNurry, Rifle is quickly becoming better known for the potential energy to be mined from its surroundings than for its natural beauty. Interest in shale is booming once again for the very same reasons that it is booming in the tar sands. Increasing oil company budgets, oil prices, and government handouts are making oil shale more financially attractive than ever. Unlike the tar sands, however, much of the oil shale is found on federal land. Thus, Big Oil depends on the federal government's willingness to open up this national treasure chest to make oil shale a true possibility.

Enter the Bush Administration

Ever since Bob Randall started working on oil shale in 2004, his work has not let up. Rather, it "has only gotten crazier." Driven by heavy industry lobbying—led internally by former interior secretary Norton, undersecretary Griles, and congressman Pombo— oil shale development was put on the fast track by the Bush administration. "There seems to be a real concerted effort on the part of Bush and the Interior Department to get while the getting's good and to hurry up to get these leases out the door before January 2009," Randall told me in an interview.[37]

Exactly two years after Randall started on the job, the federal government handed out six leases to private companies to conduct oil shale research and development (R&D) on federal lands. Five leases in Colorado went to Chevron, Shell, and EGL Resources—a Texas-based independent oil company formed in

1991. The one lease in Utah went to Alabama-based Oil Shale Exploration. ExxonMobil's federal R&D lease application was denied (maybe memories of Colony Oil were too strong in the area). So ExxonMobil bought 11,000 acres of private land and in 2006 began oil shale drilling on six wells in the Dallas–Fort Worth area. Marathon, for its part, also bought private leases, acquiring 200,000 acres in North Dakota and eastern Montana for oil shale development in 2006. According to its annual report, Marathon also holds a private lease in the Piceance Basin.

The federal leases last for ten years, and they were free. Chevron, Shell, and EGL picked the areas with the thickest, richest deposits. They have to pay royalties to the American public only if they find *commercial quantities* of oil, although no one has yet defined the term. Their R&D leases cover just 160 acres of land. However, if the oil companies demonstrate that they can develop commercial quantities of oil on their R&D lease, they will be granted an exclusive right to convert the adjacent 4,960 acres of federal land into a commercial lease under regulations that have not yet been written. Furthermore, the 2005 Energy Policy Act conveniently increased the maximum size of an oil shale lease by ten times the amount of acreage that any one company can hold in a state. Previously, the limit was 5,120; now it is 50,000 acres. Thus, if it all pans out, the companies could become owners of vast tracts of formerly public land all across the West.

Oil Shale and Global Warming

Producing oil from shale takes an enormous amount of energy and causes the emission of higher amounts of global warming pollution than conventional oil development. Notwithstanding the issues associated with refining, there are at least two main problems with oil shale development: the first is getting the shale out of the ground, and the second is getting the oil out of the shale. Both processes are highly destructive environmentally.

Oil shale generally sits 1,000 to 2,000 feet belowground, often with aquifers both above and below. The deposits themselves are usually about 1,000 feet thick. The difficulty lies in getting the shale out of the ground without destroying the mountains above or the aquifers surrounding it. The traditional method ignores these considerations and involves just digging for the shale using the same methods as for coal, open-pit or underground mines. The companies "mine it, haul it, crush it, and cook it," in Randall's words. Holes are dug and the shale is crushed to the size of gravel, then cooked in huge ovens or furnaces called "retorts" at 800 degrees Fahrenheit to convert the kerogen in the shale into liquid petroleum. The spent shale is then disposed of using processes that are highly polluting to groundwater.

The companies are trying to come up with the technology to produce shale oil where it sits in the ground (in situ). These ideas involve snaking pipes in between the aquifers and below the ground, heating the shale where it lies, and then extracting the liquid from the ground with conventional well technology. Each company is trying a different method. All the methods are proprietary, but some information has come out.

Shell has been conducting research into in-situ technologies on private land off and on for the last twenty years and is the furthest along. As described in *Driving It Home*, under Shell's plan, for a full two to three years, electric resister heaters (like ones you find in a toaster oven) would heat the deposit in the ground to the point where the kerogen turns to liquid oil. To keep the liquid from poisoning groundwater, Shell is testing a "freeze wall"—created by refrigerants emitted from wells surrounding the 1,000-foot-wide deposit.[38] Randall explained that freezing the ground around a project to prevent water from flowing through is common in mining, but Shell is proposing to maintain the project for years on end around a heating site, "and that has never been done before," according to Randall. Shell's in-situ production to date—only about 2 barrels per day—has caused a disturbance of virtually 100 percent of the surface area of its site, required substantial amounts of energy, and left behind residual char that could damage the water supply.

Both traditional and in-situ processes are highly polluting and destructive of the environment in a wide variety of ways. Both processes release pollutants into the air that can increase global warming, asthma, and emphysema, cause mercury poisoning, and even lead to premature death. The energy needed to fuel oil shale production is heavily polluting in its own right. The RAND Corporation found that the production of 100,000 barrels of shale oil a day using Shell's in-situ process would require 1,200 megawatts of power. Development of this scale would call for the construction of a power plant as large as any in Colorado history, large enough to serve a city of five hundred thousand people.[39]

Colorado is coal country. If Colorado chose coal as its source of power, the coal-powered plant required for producing 100,000 barrels of shale oil a day would emit 10 million tons of global warming pollution. But oil shale boosters talk of producing 1 million barrels of shale oil a day, which would require construction of ten new power plants that could generate up to 121 million tons of CO_2 per year using coal-powered energy. This would represent a 90 percent increase in the CO_2 emitted by all existing electric utility generating units in 2005 in Colorado, Wyoming, and Utah combined.[40]

Oil Shale and Water Pollution

Shale oil production would both drain existing water sources and pollute those that remain. Like tar sands production, oil shale requires enormous amounts of water. Each barrel of shale oil produced using the traditional mining process requires 2 to 5 barrels of water. The water would come from Colorado's already overworked and depleted rivers. Then there is the possibility that leakage from the in-situ method as well as mine drainage and discharge from the extraction process would cause groundwater contamination. The tailings from such mining operations are often dumped in lakes or streams that have been permitted for waste disposal. Wildlife that lives in or feeds from the lakes and streams also suffers from the effects of pollution.

In addition to potential poisons, salinity is a looming issue, both because water withdrawals increase salinity concentrations and because the salt content of freshly processed shale is significantly higher than that of raw shale. Increases in salinity could destroy fish habitat and cost agricultural, municipal, and industrial users millions of dollars by harming crops and corroding water infrastructure.[41]

Oil Shale and Land Pollution

Surface mining and retorting generate huge quantities of waste. An industry producing just 100,000 barrels of shale oil a day would require disposal of up to 150,000 tons of waste rock each day, or about 55 million tons per year—resulting in large, permanent scars across the landscape. The drilling and support operations of in-situ mining would most likely cause a decade-long displacement of all other land uses in these areas. Significant new infrastructure would accompany any oil shale operation. Surface facilities would be needed to upgrade, store, and transport produced shale oil. Roads, power plants, power distribution systems, pipelines, water storage and supply facilities, construction staging areas, hazardous materials handling facilities, and myriad buildings (residential, commercial, and industrial) would impose additional serious demands on the local landscape.[42]

BIG OIL AND THE Bush administration are pushing to keep oil shale on a fast track. The administration is ready to accept the companies' assessments of the potential environmental impacts of their oil shale leases based on technology that has not yet been developed; it is drafting commercial leases for land that is not yet in use; and it is forcing a speedy timetable that has led a unique alliance of environmentalists, "wise use" land advocates, liberal and conservative elected officials, and others across the region to unite behind one demand: more time. They want the process at a minimum slowed down so that all involved can weigh the pros and cons of shale development before the corporations gain ownership of hundreds of thousands of acres of federal land to exploit as they see fit for years into the future.

Offshore Oil Drilling, Coming to a Shoreline Near You

Eighty-five percent of our coastlines are off-limits to exploration. . . . [W]hat's wrong with our country? Why not open our coast up?
—DAVID O'REILLY, CEO, CHEVRON, 2007[43]

Remember the world's largest truck, driven by Jim Locke to move around the tar sands of Alberta? Take twenty-six of those trucks, stack them one on top of the other, lay the stack on its side, stick an oil derrick in the middle, and ship the whole thing out to sea. That should give you an idea of Chevron's *Discoverer Deep Seas* oil drilling ship, currently at work 190 miles off the coast of New Orleans. It looks like a battleship except that instead of planes and guns it carries an oil derrick and drilling equipment. The *Discoverer* sits in the Gulf of Mexico and sends a diamond-encrusted drill bit down through the bottom of the ship. Engineers attempt to pass the drill through 1 mile of ocean and more than 5 miles of earth in the hope of hitting oil below the ocean floor.

Viewed from the air, the *Discoverer* has been described as "a ghost tanker trying to make off with the Eiffel Tower."[44] It truly is enormous: it is 835 feet long—on end, the height of an 80-story skyscraper—and 125 feet wide. Sitting squat in the middle of its giant deck is a 226-foot-tall oil derrick. It is far from a ghost ship. Two hundred workers call this floating city home. The *Discoverer* comes complete with a movie theater, Internet café, exercise room, and infirmary. The workers rotate on and off the ship, but the *Discoverer* has not been back to shore since it was launched five years ago. Every six months or so, a supply ship pulls up alongside it and pumps a million gallons of diesel on board. The diesel runs six generators, which send 5 megawatts of power to each of six electric thrusters, which keep the ship in position while it drills.[45] Chevron leases the *Discoverer* at a daily rate of $250,000. With the cost of labor and equipment, the price goes up to $500,000 per day.[46] But the *Discoverer* is not alone.

The Cajun Express drilling platform is the *Discoverer*'s $520,000-a-day partner. *Wired Magazine*'s Amanda Griscom offered this vivid description of the Cajun: "Looming like an Erector set version of Hellboy—with cranes for arms, a hydraulic drill for its head, and a 200-foot derrick for a body—the rig appears at once menacing and toy-like."[47] The Cajun Express is a floating platform on top of which very thin-looking bits of steel are pieced together to support an oil derrick. Of course, the pieces only look small when they are viewed against the expanse of the Gulf. Plop the Cajun down in the middle of a city and it would take over several blocks and rival any high-rise.

The Cajun Express is a floating drilling platform. One hundred and fifty workers call it home, and it offers all the amenities of the *Discoverer*. With grueling twelve-hour shifts, however, the workers on both rigs spend most of their free time sleeping, in rooms the size of walk-in closets on cot-sized bunk beds that fold out of the walls.[48] Both rigs are positioned above Chevron's 30-square-mile Tahiti oil field, which sits below 4,000 feet of ocean and more than 22,000 feet of shale and sediment. One of the Gulf's largest deepwater oil discoveries, the field holds 400 to 500 million barrels of oil by Chevron's estimates, although, as of yet, no oil has successfully been pumped from the field.

Believe it or not, the Cajun Express and *Discoverer* are small-fry. Sitting on shore like an expectant father anxiously awaiting his children is the supergiant offshore oil production platform the Tahiti. Just the hull of the Tahiti is a 100,000-ton brown hunk of steel and iron that looks like the gargantuan cork of the world's largest wine bottle. It is 555 feet long—equivalent in height to the Washington Monument. When it is ready (its construction is currently a year behind schedule), the hull will be dragged horizontally out to sea and tipped into place as its bottom fills with saltwater ballasts until it sits vertically. It will be moored to the ocean floor. Placed on top of the hull will be Tahiti's platform, an additional five separate levels with a combined area of about 3 acres, housing three gas turbine generators with enough juice to power thirty thousand homes.[49]

The Tahiti will pump the oil that the Cajun and the *Discoverer* drill out of the ground. That is, if they ever successfully drill any oil. It costs an additional $120 million per well to drill in waters this deep, and there is no guarantee that oil (or natural gas) will be found. Each drill bit (remember, they are encrusted with diamonds) costs $50,000 to $80,000—and a single well can easily chew up a dozen drill bits. The first six exploratory wells that Chevron drilled in the Gulf with the *Discoverer* were dry holes, wells with too little oil to turn a profit. In fact, about 80 percent of all of the exploratory wells drilled in the Gulf are failures. As described by Chevron's Mickey Driver, "It's lots of money, it's lots of equipment and it's a total crapshoot."[50]

Chevron has partnered with Shell and Norway's Statoil on the Tahiti field project. The estimated price tag for developing this field, which has yet to yield any oil, is about $3.6 billion.

Welcome to the new world of offshore drilling, coming to a shoreline near you.

The Big Bang

Some believe that the birth of the modern environmental movement can be pinpointed to 10:45 A.M., Tuesday, January 28, 1969. That was the moment when Union Oil Company of California's (now Chevron) offshore oil rig Platform Alpha suffered a massive underwater blowout. The platform was stationed 5 miles off the coast of Summerland near Santa Barbara, California. Three million gallons of oil spilled directly into the Santa Barbara Channel. Thirty-five miles of shoreline were coated with oil up to 6 inches thick. Upwards of ten thousand birds were killed, marine plant life was suffocated, and large portions of Santa Barbara County smelled like a petroleum refinery.[51]

The Santa Barbara community was ready. Activists had already been campaigning against offshore drilling, and overnight their voices carried significantly greater weight. The environmental community gained both legitimacy and vibrancy. Get Oil Out (GOO) collected 100,000 signatures for a petition to ban new offshore drilling, and California's State Land Commission agreed. Later that year the first Earth Day was held. President Nixon passed the National Environmental Policy Act of 1969, leading the way to the July 1970 establishment of the Environmental Protection Agency.

Federal law gives the states ownership of the land and resources from their coasts to approximately 3 miles offshore. Texas and the Gulf coast of Florida are the exceptions, each having ownership rights to about 9 miles offshore. After the first 3 (or 9) miles offshore, federal jurisdiction kicks in and continues out to 200 nautical miles. The federal area is the Exclusive Economic Zone (EEZ) of the United States. It is the largest EEZ in the world, spanning over 13,000 miles of coastline and almost 1.8 billion acres of land—larger than the combined land area of all fifty states. The Department of the Interior has jurisdiction over this area, known as the Outer Continental Shelf (OCS), and its Mineral Management Service handles federal leasing rights to the minerals found beneath these waters.

In 1981 Congress adopted the OCS Moratorium. The moratorium prevents new leases for oil and gas development off the Atlantic and Pacific coasts as well as in Bristol Bay, Alaska. It must be renewed every year, kicking off an annual confrontation between the oil and gas industry, the environmental community, and voters in coastal states opposed to drilling. For more than twenty-five years, the congressional moratorium has held. In 1990 President George H. W. Bush, hungry for California and Florida's combined 79 electoral votes, sponsored an additional level of presidential protection that deferred new leasing until

2002. Bill Clinton then extended the presidential deferral to 2012.[52]

Drilling continued unabated in the U.S. Gulf of Mexico off the coasts of Texas, Louisiana, Mississippi, Alabama, and west of Florida. It has exploded in the last ten years, with production rising roughly 70 percent. According to data provided by the Mineral Management Service, there are more than 3,850 active offshore oil and gas production facilities in the Gulf. Chevron is the largest overall leaseholder in the Gulf, but all the major oil companies are well represented. BP, for example, announced in its 2007 annual report that it plans to spend $20 billion on deep-sea drilling in the Gulf of Mexico alone. There are hundreds more rigs off the coast of Alaska. The oil leases that were in effect prior to the 1981 moratorium remain in effect today, and thus there are more than twenty oil and gas production facilities in federal waters off California. There was no drilling off the Atlantic Coast prior to 1981, and there remains none today.[53]

There is a lot of oil to be found off America's coastlines, and Big Oil wants in. According to the Department of Energy, there are almost 4.5 billion barrels of proved oil reserves in federal offshore waters. The Department of the Interior estimates that there will be nearly twenty times more—86 billion barrels—once undiscovered fields are uncovered. All of this oil belongs to the American people.

Enter the Bush Administration

> *The Outer Continental Shelf is a vital source of domestic oil and natural gas for America, especially in light of sharply rising energy prices.*
> —DIRK KEMPTHORNE, INTERIOR SECRETARY, 2007[54]

> *Generally speaking, we're for tapping into our oil and gas resources here anywhere we can, because we think they're*

needed. . . . The industry knows, government knows, the
people know there are oil and gas resources off of California.
—MICKEY DRIVER, CHEVRON SPOKESMAN, 2006[55]

Since the Bush administration took office, a radical new course
has been set to expand offshore leasing and open America's
offshore waters to oil and gas drilling. The first step, led in the
Senate by Republican Ted Stevens of Alaska, was the 2003 removal of the congressional moratorium on Bristol Bay, Alaska.
Republican congressman Pombo of California came in next
with a bill to eliminate the entire congressional moratorium in
one fell swoop. Under intense industry lobbying, the bill passed
the Republican-controlled House in 2005, but died in the Senate.

"Pombo's goal from the beginning was to find a way to kill
the moratorium at the behest of Chevron," Richard Charter, cochair of the OCS Coalition, a network of environmental and
community organizations, told me.[56] Charter is one of the original drafters of the moratorium and has spent the last thirty years
working to protect and expand its reach.

In December 2006, the state of Florida, under the direction
of Governor Jeb Bush, made a deal with Congress whereby
President Bush guaranteed that a buffer zone up to approximately 145 miles wide off the Gulf Coast of Florida would be
protected from leasing until at least 2022, in exchange for
immediately opening more than 8 million new acres west of
Florida to new drilling. A few months later, President Bush in-
structed the Interior Department to open an additional 50 million acres to drilling over the next five years. From 2007 to
2012, the Interior Department will sell twelve new leases in the
Gulf of Mexico and eight off the coast of Alaska in vast new
areas of the Beaufort Sea, the Chukchi Sea, and the Cook Inlet.
These areas were not subject to the moratorium, but none had
been tapped before. Starting in 2011, the Interior Department
will also lease out 5.6 million new acres in Bristol Bay along the
Alaska Peninsula.[57] An attempt to open new areas off the coast

of Virginia was successfully halted by the environmental community.

A coalition of Native Alaskans and conservation groups sued the U.S. government to halt the new sales in offshore Alaska. The Beaufort and Chukchi Seas off Alaska are, among other things, prime polar bear habitat. "Short of sending Dick Cheney to Alaska to personally club polar bear cubs to death, the administration could not have come up with a more environmentally destructive plan for endangered marine mammals," argued Brendan Cummings of the Center for Biological Diversity. "Yet the administration did not even analyze, much less attempt to avoid, the impacts of oil development on endangered wildlife."[58]

An additional lease sale proposed in Alaska's Bristol Bay is within critical habitat for the North Pacific right whale, the world's most endangered whale, while two lease sales were proposed for Cook Inlet, home to endangered beluga whales and sea otters. If endangered species "are to survive as the Arctic melts in the face of global warming, we need to protect their critical habitat, not turn it into a polluted industrial zone," added Cummings.

"The cost of drilling will [lie] with the local communities when the effects are seen on a daily life basis affecting our lives and our health," said Rosemary Ahtuangaruk, an Inupiat resident of Nuiqsut and member of the organization Resisting Environmental Destruction on Indigenous Lands (RedOil).[59]

The Ninth Circuit Court of Appeals has tentatively agreed and demanded a halt to production in the area until the case is settled.

OFFSHORE DRILLING IS NOT just an American phenomenon. Big Oil's massive wealth is further subsidized by other national governments and international institutions, including the World Bank and International Monetary Fund. The result is a booming offshore oil business able to plunge into deeper, less hospitable, more environmentally sensitive areas.

One of the hottest new areas for mining oil is off the coast of West Africa. As Big Oil moves in, the U.S. military is concurrently expanding its military presence in the African region, as will be discussed in the next chapter. According to their 2006 10K SEC tax filings, ExxonMobil and Chevron alone currently operate or have plans to begin operating off the shores of Nigeria, Angola, Libya, Australia, Indonesia, the Philippines, Thailand, Vietnam, Cambodia, Ireland, Norway, the Caspian Sea, Russia, Canada, Brazil, Mexico, and elsewhere. ExxonMobil CEO Rex Tillerson has said that by 2010, deepwater drilling will account for over 15 percent of ExxonMobil's global oil production.[60]

Whether in Alaska, the Gulf, or anywhere else in the world, offshore drilling is devastating to wildlife and ecosystems; it produces air, land, and water pollution, including greenhouse gas emissions; it uses vast amounts of energy; and it is alarmingly prone to catastrophic and deadly accidents.

Global Warming

Drilling in water depths greater than 500 feet releases methane, a greenhouse gas at least twenty times more potent than carbon dioxide in its contribution to global warming. Until recently, most offshore drilling in the Gulf of Mexico, for example, took place on simple scaffolds standing on the seafloor in 30 to 200 feet of water. But in the last ten years, the number of rigs drilling in depths of greater than 1,000 feet has catapulted. In 1997 there were seventeen deepwater projects in the Gulf. Today there are at least ninety. The number of ultradeepwater projects in the Gulf, those in more than 5,000 feet of water, has more than doubled in the last two years alone.[61] All of these wells release methane hydrates, icelike structures formed from frozen water and methane, during drilling. The Congressional Research Service reports, "Oil and gas operators have recorded numerous drilling and production problems attributed to the presence of gas hydrates, including uncontrolled gas releases during drilling, collapse of well casings, and gas leakage to the surface."[62] It also reports that methane hydrates easily become unstable, potentially triggering seafloor subsidence and catastrophic landslides.

Air and Water Pollution

At any depth, offshore drilling causes significant air and water pollution. It is estimated that every offshore oil platform generates approximately 214,000 pounds of air pollutants each year, including some 50 tons of nitrogen oxides, 13 tons of carbon monoxide, 6 tons of sulfur dioxide, and 5 tons of volatile organic hydrocarbons. These pollutants are the precursors to smog and acid rain and contribute to global warming.[63]

Offshore drilling also generates huge amounts of polluting waste that is discarded directly into the water. According to the National Academy of Sciences, a single well produces between 1,500 and 2,000 tons of waste material. Debris includes drill cuttings, which is rock ground into pieces by the bit, and drilling mud brought up during the drilling process, which contains toxic metals such as lead, cadmium, and mercury. Other pollutants, such as benzene, arsenic, zinc, and other known carcinogens and radioactive materials, are routinely released in "produced water," which emerges when water is brought up from a well along with the oil or gas.[64]

Damage to Marine Life and Habitat

In testimony before the Senate Committee on Energy and Natural Resources, Sierra Club deputy legislative director Debbie Boger laid out numerous threats to marine life and habitat from offshore drilling.[65] The first step to drilling any offshore well involves doing an inventory of estimated resources. Boger described how every technology employed for this purpose harms marine ecosystems and species. The "seismic survey"—the model used in the Tahiti field—involves ships towing multiple "air gun" arrays with tens of thousands of high-decibel explosive impulses. These air gun arrays fire regular bursts of sound at frequencies in the range of 20 to 150 Hz, which is within the auditory range of many marine species, including whales. Marked changes in behavior in marine species in response to loud underwater noises in the ocean have been well documented. Seismic survey devices and military sonars (which operate at a similar decibel level) have been implicated in numerous whale beaching and stranding incidents, including a mass stranding of sixteen whales in the Bahamas in December 2001.

According to Boger, the auditory organs of fish are particularly vulnerable to loud sounds such as those produced by survey air guns, as fish rely on their ability to hear to find mates, locate prey, avoid predators, and communicate. The sounds have even been known to kill some species outright, including salmon, whose swim bladders have ruptured from exposure to intense sounds.

Both "dart core" and "grab" sampling, additional survey techniques, are extremely destructive to seafloor organisms and fish habitat, discharging silt plumes that are transported on ocean currents and smother nearby life on the seabed.

The onshore infrastructure associated with offshore oil or gas causes significant harm to the coastal zone. For example, the oil and natural gas found in the ocean have to be carried back to land. This is done through miles and miles of pipelines stretching across the ocean floor, through wetlands, and onto the shore. Pipelines crossing coastal wetlands in the Gulf of Mexico are estimated to have destroyed more coastal salt marsh than can be found in the stretch of coastal land running from New Jersey through Maine.[66]

Affected Coastal Communities

Offshore oil and gas development affects commercial fishing, tourism, coastal recreation, and quality of life for those living on shore. Across the country, broad networks of communities that rarely find themselves on the same side of issues have come together to protect their coastlines from drilling. For example, concern for local tourism in North Carolina led the Outer Banks Visitors Bureau to join conservationists in opposition to offshore drilling. Carolyn McCormick, managing director of the Visitors' Bureau, explained, "If there's one spill or one disaster, you could destroy us for a very long time." Similarly, the Hotel-Motel Association of Virginia Beach and the city's mayor have joined in efforts opposing any attempt to lift the moratorium.[67]

Accidents, Spills, and Explosions

Offshore drilling is a Herculean technological and financial feat. All too often, however, technology proves inadequate, appropriate financial investments are not made, and accidents happen. Given the size and scale of these facilities, even a minor incident can have catastrophic impacts. Accidents, spills, leaks, fires, explosions, and blowouts are far too frequent occurrences that have led to the deaths of hundreds of workers.

Many of the platforms operating off the United States and in international waters were built in the 1960s. Many are twenty, thirty, or even forty years old. Even with new facilities, however, deadly and dangerous accidents are frequent. According to the most recent statistics available, compiled by the Department of the Interior, more than seventy incidents on the U.S. Outer Continental Shelf resulted in oil spills between 1980 and 1999. In California alone, at least five major spills occurred on offshore platforms belonging to Exxon and Chevron, among others, from 1991 to 1997. Oil is extremely toxic, and current cleanup methods are incapable of removing more than a small fraction of the oil spilled in marine waters.

The causes of such incidents worldwide include human error, poor equipment, mechanical defects, structural failure, and earthquakes. An increasing problem is extreme weather, particularly hurricanes. As a result of these storms, offshore oil rigs and platforms are tipping, collapsing, exploding, and floating out to sea with increasing frequency. As global warming intensifies, weather conditions will become more extreme and such events will occur with greater frequency—further harming our oceans and threatening the safety of workers.

Union Oil's 1969 Platform Alpha blowout may have been the most influential offshore accident in its effect on U.S. politics, but it hardly ranks among the most serious offshore disasters. Twenty years after Platform Alpha's blowout, 167 people were killed when Occidental's Piper Alpha platform exploded off the Coast of Aberdeen, Scotland, in 1992. A gas leak ignited the first explosion, which set off several others. The fire that eventually burned the entire facility to a crisp could be seen from more than 25 miles away. One hundred sixty-seven men, including two operators of a Fast Rescue Craft, died as a result of the explosions and the fire on board the Piper Alpha. Sixty-two men survived, mostly by jumping into the sea from the high decks of the platform. A number of factors were identified as causes of the incident, including the breakdown of the chain of command and lack of any communication to the platform crew.[68]

Every major oil company has experienced serious accidents on rigs across the United States and around the world. It is estimated that nearly six hundred people have died in them worldwide since 1965.[69]

One hundred twenty-three people died when a Phillips Petroleum platform collapsed in the waters off Norway in 1980. Two years later, Mobil's Ocean Ranger platform sank in storms while drilling 180 miles east of Newfoundland, killing eighty-four workers. Former crew members charged that safety precautions aboard the rig were inadequate and that some crew members were poorly trained.[70] In 1988 one person died when Arco's Ocean Odyssey drilling rig burst into flames in the North Sea. The following year, in Alaska's Cook Inlet, three workers were injured in an explosion and a fire on a Union Oil platform. That same year, another Union Oil platform in the Gulf of Thailand capsized during Typhoon Gay, killing more than ninety men. In 1995 thirteen people were killed on a Mobil oil rig off the coast of Nigeria. The world's largest oil rig, owned by Petrobas, sank in the waters off Brazil in 2001. In 2005 twenty-two people died when a ship collided with the Mumbai High North platform in the Indian Ocean, causing a massive fire that destroyed the entire platform within two hours.[71] As I write, a fire has erupted on Lundin Petroleum's Thistle Alpha facility, a remote North Sea oil platform. Over 170 people have been airlifted to safety.

The Eye of the Storm

*The storm was an eye-opener. . . . How do you brace for
catastrophic events caused by nature? I don't think you can.
Unfortunately, the evil is that we need the oil and gas from
the gulf.*

—CRAIG REYNOLDS, SPECIALTY DIVING,
LOUISIANA, 2006[72]

New Orleans is arguably the first major American city to have been destroyed by global warming. A hallmark of global warming is the increased frequency and intensity of serious weather events, including hurricanes. Before Hurricanes Katrina and Rita touched down on the ground, they pushed through thousands of oil and gas facilities sitting in the Gulf Coast. Fortunately, workers had been evacuated, but the facilities and the ocean water surrounding them were not as lucky. Hurricanes Katrina and Rita destroyed or damaged 167 offshore platforms and more than 450 pipelines and caused nine major oil spills that released at least 7 million gallons of oil and other pollutants into the water.[73]

Reports in the days and months following the storm described platforms snapped off their moorings and simply lost at sea. The Sunday after Katrina hit, one of Chevron's deepwater platforms, ironically named Typhoon, was spotted drifting nearly 80 miles from its original position. It had been operating in 2,100 feet of water about 165 miles southwest of New Orleans when it was severed from its moorings and capsized. One of Diamond Offshore Drilling's rigs was carried 66 miles by the storm and washed up on Dauphin Island. One of Shell's drilling rigs broke free from one of the largest structures in the Gulf of Mexico, Shell's Mars platform. The rig dragged a 12-ton anchor with it. The anchor plowed the sea floor, crushing the twin pipelines that connect the platform to the network of pipes that carry its oil to the coast.

"We were still recovering from Hurricane Ivan when the terrible sisters [Hurricanes Katrina and Rita] came," said Allen J. Verret, president of the Offshore Operators Committee, an industry group. Hurricane Ivan, rated as one of the most severe storms in the Gulf when it struck in 2004, destroyed seven platforms and damaged another twenty-four structures. It created underwater mud slides that uprooted more than a hundred underwater pipelines.[74]

The East Coast, an area where Big Oil would like to go next, is, of course, no stranger to increasingly destructive hurricanes. "We haven't done anything to reduce our vulnerability," said Ted M. Falgout, the director of Port Fourchon, the largest servicing hub for the offshore industry, located about 80 miles south of New Orleans. "I hate to think of the next hurricane season."[75]

Big Oil sees the ocean as the next great oil frontier. Every major company has plans to expand its offshore, deepwater, and ultradeepwater presence in the coming years. Looking out from the tip of the Cajun Express's oil derrick, Chevron's Paul Siegele expressed the views held by the industry, not just for the Gulf of Mexico, but for all of the United States' and the world's waters: "A decade ago, I never even dreamed we'd get here. And a decade from now, this moonscape could be populated with rigs as far as the eye can see."[76]

UNRESTRAINED BY FINANCIAL OR political impediments, Big Oil sees no limits to where the hunt for oil can and should go. Halliburton's John Gibson made this point in 2004 without the usual niceties when he said, "As the CEO of Halliburton Energy Services, the board of directors doesn't sit me down and say 'John, make this a better planet.' They want us to make and create wealth for our shareholders and employees. So the only way we can adopt a sustainability agenda is it must create sustainable wealth for all our shareholders."[77] This is of course also true for Big Oil. To increase profits and the value of its stock, an oil company must have oil. While Big Oil will pursue every avenue to find *new* sources of oil, the companies have not forgotten about the world's remaining existing reserves of conventional oil. Big Oil appears willing to use every tool available to it—up to and including war—to acquire these reserves.

8

Big Oil's Big Plans for the Future, Part II: Wars for Oil

Iraq is the convergence point for two of the greatest threats to America in this new century—al Qaeda and Iran.
—PRESIDENT GEORGE W. BUSH, 2008[1]

I am saddened that it is politically inconvenient to acknowledge what everyone knows: the Iraq war is largely about oil.

—ALAN GREENSPAN, FORMER FEDERAL RESERVE
CHAIRMAN, 2007[2]

Of course it's about oil, we can't really deny that.
—GENERAL JOHN ABIZAID, RETIRED HEAD OF U.S.
CENTRAL COMMAND AND MILITARY OPERATIONS IN
IRAQ, SPEAKING ABOUT THE IRAQ WAR, 2007[3]

Iraq possesses huge reserves of oil and gas—reserves I'd love Chevron to have access to.
—KENNETH T. DERR, CEO OF CHEVRON, 1998[4]

How far will we go to get the world's remaining oil? Who will make this decision? This is the central question guiding this book. This chapter addresses the penultimate threat: war. Big Oil has demonstrated that it has no qualms about driving the world ever further into a climate catastrophe in order to acquire oil. Sadly, the corollary appears equally true: that Big Oil is pushing us into an ever more militarized and war-ravaged future. The reason is largely the same: the world is running out of conventional oil, and so is Big Oil.

Within approximately ten to fifteen years, the major oil companies will have depleted their own reserves unless major changes occur. The Federal Trade Commission estimated in 2004 that ExxonMobil and ConocoPhillips would most likely run out of oil in 2017, Chevron in 2016, and Shell and BP in 2015.[5] If they are going to remain oil companies, as they clearly intend to do, they need greater access to more of the world's oil. Moreover, if Big Oil is going to stay big, it needs to *own* more oil. A significant measure of the value of an oil company's stock is the size of the company's oil reserves. Thus, selling oil is not enough. Big Oil needs to *own* more of the world's oil if it is going to remain on top.

Unfortunately for Big Oil, all of the world's remaining oil is spoken for. Governments own the vast majority of what is left. Even those governments that are U.S. allies are not necessarily inclined to give Big Oil the level and type of access it desires under the terms it prefers. And even when governments accede to the wishes of Big Oil, that does not guarantee a willing and amenable public. Then there are the countries that want nothing to do with Big Oil or the United States. Finally, there is new and growing competition for the oil that is left, from the rising powers of China, Russia, and India, which are increasing both their consumption and their pursuit of oil.

Never has Big Oil had such a bold and willing partner in securing and maintaining access to oil as the George W. Bush administration. Author Kevin Phillips coined the term *petrol-imperialism* to describe the Bush administration's use of the U.S. military, "the key aspect of which is the U.S. military's transformation into a global oil protection force."[6] Under the rubric of the Global War on Terror, the Bush administration has implemented the greatest realignment of U.S. forces since the end of the Cold War. One needs only a map showing Big Oil's overseas operations, the world's remaining oil reserves, and the oil transport routes to track the realignment and predict future deployments of the U.S. military.

The greatest reserves of oil in the world are in the Middle East. Accordingly, since taking office, the Bush administration has opened new U.S. military bases and installations in Iraq, Qatar, Kuwait, Turkey, Afghanistan, and Pakistan and a major U.S. naval base at Diego Garcia in the Indian Ocean.[7] The former French Foreign Legion base, Camp Lemonier, in Djibouti, situated to the north of Somalia and across the Red Sea from Saudi Arabia, became home to U.S. Combined Joint Task Force Horn of Africa in 2003.[8] The United States maintains military installations in Egypt, the UAE, and Oman and has increased its tremendous weapons support to Israel. As former Bush White House speechwriter David Frum wrote in 2003, "the war on terror" was designed to "bring a new stability to the most vicious and violent quadrant of the Earth—and new prosperity to us all, by securing the world's largest pool of oil."[9] U.S. oil companies have operations throughout the Middle East, but certainly not to the extent that they would prefer.

The nearby Caspian region is also home to a wealth of oil and Big Oil companies. Since 2001, new U.S. military facilities have opened in Kyrgyzstan, Uzbekistan, and Tajikistan.[10] The missing link to taking full advantage of Caspian oil has been getting the oil out of the region. The war in Afghanistan, among other goals, was supposed to solve this problem by finally giving U.S. companies their long-sought opportunity to build a pipeline to carry the oil from the Caspian region through Afghanistan and Pakistan and out to the Indian Ocean. The continued strength of the Taliban and overall instability in Afghanistan has thus far stymied such an outcome.

Africa, with almost 10 percent of the world's remaining oil, has become an area of increasing activity for both Big Oil and the U.S. military. Between 2000 and 2007, U.S. imports of oil from Africa increased by 65 percent, from 1.6 to 2.7 million barrels a day, according to the U.S. Department of Energy. These imports, in turn, accounted for a growing percentage of all U.S. oil imports, increasing from 14.5 to 20 percent. According to SEC tax filings, in 2000 ExxonMobil operated in just three African nations—Angola, Equatorial Guinea, and Nigeria—and its production there was negligible relative to the rest of the world. Today ExxonMobil operates in Angola, Cameroon, Chad, Equatorial Guinea, and Nigeria, is set to begin work in Libya, and its African holdings account for nearly 17 percent of the company's global oil reserves. Chevron, ConocoPhillips, Marathon, Shell, and BP are also increasing their presence, with each operating in three or more of the following countries: Algeria, Angola, Cameroon, Chad, the Republic of Congo, the Democratic Republic of Congo, Equatorial Guinea, Egypt, Gabon, Libya, Nigeria, and Tunisia.[11] According to U.S. Energy Secretary Samuel Bodman, U.S. companies hope to expand their operations further, with Madagascar, Benin, Sao Tome and Principe, and Guinea-Bissau among potential future targets.[12]

In recognition of "the emerging strategic importance of Africa," President Bush ordered the creation of the U.S. Africa Command (AFRICOM), in February 2007. Similar to Central Command (CENTCOM) and European Command (EUCOM), AFRICOM centralizes all U.S. military authority for the African region under one command structure. Although AFRICOM is currently headquartered in Germany, the Bush administration intends to "establish a presence" for it on the African continent. There are several options under consideration, including a new naval base and deepwater port on the tiny island of Sao Tome off the coast of Gabon in West Africa. The Pentagon is also considering new bases in Senegal, Ghana, and Mali.[13]

General Charles Wald, deputy commander of U.S. forces in Europe, explained that "a key mission for U.S. forces [in Africa] would be to insure that Nigeria's oilfields, which in the future could account for as much as 25 percent of all U.S. oil imports, are secure."[14] The U.S. government already provides arms and/or direct military services and training to Angola, Algeria, Botswana, Chad, Cote d'Ivoire, the Republic of the Congo, Equatorial Guinea, Eritrea, Ethiopia, Gabon, Kenya, Mali, Mauritania, Niger, Nigeria, Sudan, and Uganda.[15] General James Jones, EUCOM commander, announced that U.S. Navy carrier battle groups would shorten future visits to the Mediterranean and "spend half the time going down the west coast to Africa."[16]

Mexico and Venezuela are among the five largest exporters of oil to the United States, while South and Central America hold about 8.6 percent of the world's remaining oil. Accordingly, the Bush administration has established new military bases in Ecuador, Aruba, Curaçao, and El Salvador, while Puerto Rico has replaced Panama as the U.S. military's hub for the region.[17] U.S. oil companies operate throughout the region, and in spring 2003, seventy U.S. Green Berets reportedly flew into Colombia to secure an Occidental Oil Company pipeline under attack by local "rebels."[18] The U.S. government supplies arms and military aid and training across the region, primarily under the rubric of the war on drugs.

All of these areas are important to Big Oil, but the singular importance of the Middle East cannot be overstated. As then Halliburton CEO Dick Cheney made clear in 1999, "The Middle East, with two-thirds of the world's oil and lowest cost, is still where the prize ultimately lies."[19] In fact, nearly half of all the world's remaining conventional reserves are found in just three countries: Saudi Arabia, Iran, and Iraq. For eighty years, U.S. oil companies and the U.S. government have begged, borrowed, stolen, and destroyed to gain and maintain access to the oil of these three nations.

Saudi Arabia, with more than 260 billion barrels of oil, is the uncontested reigning champion of proved oil reserves in the world. This one country holds 25 percent of the world's remaining oil.

Since their holdings were nationalized in the early 1980s, U.S. oil companies have maintained a constant and generally amicable relationship with the Saudi government, which has signed contracts allowing the U.S. companies to market Saudi oil and to partner with the Saudis on some limited levels of technical assistance. The U.S. government has held a pro-American government in place there by supplying Saudi Arabia with (at a minimum) hundreds of billions of dollars worth of weaponry. U.S. oil companies would certainly like greater access to Saudi oil under more favorable terms but seem satisfied to pursue this goal through negotiations, such as the Bush administration's efforts to create a U.S.–Middle East Free Trade Area, which I discuss in detail in *The Bush Agenda*.

The United States' relations with Saudi Arabia's neighbors, Iraq and Iran, have been far less amiable or stable. Today, as the result of two wars and one occupation, Iraq is poised to proffer up the big prize to U.S. oil companies: control of the oil under the ground. Iran is closed to U.S. oil companies, but the Bush administration and its allies appear to believe that a war may be the best option for changing that situation as well.

Big Oil was seriously weakened by the 1970s oil nationalizations. It has taken some time, but the companies have bounced back. They merged, grew, took control of previously abandoned industry sectors, reclaimed oil reserves, radically increased their profits, and regained their political control. They are ready to roll back the clock and retake the oil that was, not so very long ago, theirs.

I have no smoking gun that uncovers an oil company executive sitting down with George W. Bush and telling him to invade Iraq or Iran so that the oil company can have the nation's oil. The oil companies do not need to hold such meetings. ExxonMobil, Chevron, ConocoPhillips, Marathon, BP, Shell, and the others heavily funded and worked aggressively to elect an administration that had made fully transparent its military ambitions well before taking office. The companies have also played a clear, public role working to ensure that the invasion of Iraq yields them the greatest possible access to and control over Iraq's oil. They have helped define what "winning the war for oil" actually looks like by participating in the Bush administration's attempts to force the Iraqi government to pass a new national oil law. The law would transform Iraq's oil industry from a nationalized model—all but closed to U.S. oil companies—into a privatized model, with at least two-thirds of Iraq's oil open to foreign company control. Big Oil has not hesitated to cash in on the war and has certainly not lobbied to end it.

In a perfect world, I am sure that oil companies would prefer a peaceful route to acquiring their oil, if for no other reason than that wars are risky and there is no telling what their outcomes will be. But peace is not always possible. Nor is oil the sole reason for U.S. military engagement in the Middle East. Israel, Cold War and post–Cold War politics, and regional instability are all powerful motivators. Oil is also about more than oil company profits. Control over the world's oil is an unparalleled source of regional and global hegemony. As Paul Wolfowitz said in 1991, "The combination of the enormous resources of the Persian Gulf, the power that those resources represent—it's power. It's not just that we need gas for our cars, it's that anyone who controls those resources has enormous capability to build up military forces." The danger, Wolfowitz said, could come either from Iran or from a rebuilt Iraq, perhaps by the end of the decade.[20] Threatening leaders are made all the more powerful by their control of oil. The more oil one controls, the more it can be used both to secure alliances and to weaken enemies. With the Bush administration, however, it is particularly difficult to determine where corporate interests begin and political interests end.

BIG OIL IN IRAQ AND IRAN: A BRIEF HISTORY

For eighty-five years, U.S. oil companies and the U.S. government have negotiated an uneasy tango back and forth between Iraq and Iran—the countries with the world's second and third largest oil reserves. Iraq's oil reserves are estimated at 115 billion barrels, about 10 percent of the world's total supply. Energy Intelligence Research, which publishes *Oil Daily* and *Petroleum Intelligence Weekly*, estimates Iraq's reserves at as much as 300 to 400 billion barrels.[21] If that is accurate, Iraq's reserves would be larger than Saudi Arabia's. Iran's reserves are estimated at 130 billion barrels, approximately 12 percent of the world's total supply.

Big Oil in Iraq

From World War I until approximately 1973, British, French, and American oil companies owned and controlled Iraq's oil under the concessionary system. In return for a contract that was to last until the year 2000 giving the companies ownership and control of Iraq's oil, the Iraqi government was to receive royalty payments on the sale of the oil. Following World War I, the Anglo-Persian Oil Company (BP), Shell, Compagnie Française des Petroles (Total), Standard Oil of New Jersey (Exxon), Standard Oil of New York (Mobil), Gulf (Chevron), Standard Oil of Indiana (BP), and the Atlantic Refining Company (BP) took control of Iraq's oil and held it for forty years. In 1958 a popular coup led by General Abdul Karim Qasim overthrew Iraq's British-installed monarchy. Qasim became a national hero when he all but nationalized Iraq's oil, only to be overthrown himself by a CIA-supported coup a few years later.[22] This 1963 coup brought the anticommunist Ba'ath Party to power and stalled the nationalization of Big Oil's Iraqi holdings for another twelve years. In 1973 Iraq fully nationalized its oil and kicked the corporations out.[23]

Spurned by Iraq, U.S. oil companies refocused their efforts on Iran until it too nationalized its oil in 1979. As I describe in *The Bush Agenda*, ousted from Iran, Big Oil, backed by the administrations of Ronald Reagan and George H. W. Bush, returned to Iraq.

Upon taking office in 1981, President Reagan immediately began courting Iraq's new president, Saddam Hussein. The Soviets had invaded Afghanistan two years earlier, threatening U.S. sources of oil across the Middle East. Hussein, having launched an expensive war against Iran in 1980, was eager for American support. Reagan promptly removed Iraq from the list of countries supporting terrorism, which rendered Iraq eligible for a broad range of trade and credits. Reagan then opened full economic and diplomatic relations with Iraq in 1984.

U.S. oil companies, under the rubric of the U.S.-Iraq Business Forum, whose members included representatives of Texaco, Exxon, Mobil, Hunt Oil, and Kissinger Associates, which represented oil company and other corporate clients, lobbied both governments to increase Big Oil's access to Iraq. Hussein did provide U.S. oil companies some renewed access to Iraq's oil, but not nearly as much as they had hoped for. Oil services companies such as Halliburton received infrastructure contracts, and oil companies received contracts to market Iraqi oil. Iraq's oil production was limited, however, due to the war with Iran. With the war's conclusion in 1988, U.S. imports of Iraqi oil skyrocketed—increasing thirteenfold between 1987 and July 1990, from 80,000 to 1.1 million barrels per day.[24]

Upon taking office in 1989, President George H. W. Bush and Secretary of State James A. Baker III immediately went to work to expand U.S. relations with Hussein. Bush was the first U.S. oilman-turned-president, while Baker was the first U.S. oilman-turned-secretary of state. Their efforts on behalf of U.S. business in Iraq were extensive, but ultimately had limited success. U.S. oil companies continued to market Iraqi oil, but Hussein never allowed them to have access to or control over Iraq's oil under the ground. Moreover, Hussein's broader commitment to the U.S. government was weakening on several fronts as his own financial stability worsened and his regional ambitions rose. Hussein's usefulness to the United States was reaching an end.

The First Gulf War

In 1991 the United States launched its first war explicitly for oil. On August 1, 1990, Iraq invaded Kuwait. Days later, President Bush declared, "Our jobs, our way of life, our own freedom and the freedom of friendly countries around the world would all suffer if control of the world's great oil reserves fell into the hands of Saddam Hussein."[25] To this, Secretary Baker added, "The economic lifeline of the industrial world runs from the Gulf and we cannot permit a dictator such as this to sit astride that economic lifeline."[26] The day before he launched the U.S. attack against Iraq, President Bush signed National Security Directive 54. The first line states, "Access to Persian Gulf oil and the security of key friendly states in the area are vital to U.S. national security."[27]

The first Gulf War was over in two months and yielded two immediate victories for the Bush administration and Big Oil. The first was the expulsion of the Iraqi army from Kuwait. The second was a fundamental realignment of U.S. military strength in the Middle East. Instead of just sending weaponry to create and maintain friendly leaders in the region, the United States would for the first time have its own sizable and fixed military presence, stationed directly in the region, to project its own goals. New U.S. bases were established in Bahrain, and existing facilities were expanded in Turkey. Half a million U.S. soldiers had been stationed in Saudi Arabia to fight the war. When the war concluded, most Saudis assumed that the U.S. troops would leave. But five thousand to ten thousand troops remained there for more than a decade, until a new U.S. base was opened in Qatar in 2003.

The overthrow of Hussein failed. The George H. W. Bush administration wanted Hussein out but was not willing to occupy Iraq to achieve that goal. In the words of then defense secretary Dick Cheney in 1991: "Once you've got Baghdad, it's not clear what you do with it. It's not clear what kind of government you would put in place of the one that's currently there. . . . How much credibility is that government going to have if it's set up by the U.S. military when it's there? . . . I think to have American military engaged in a civil war inside Iraq would fit the definition of a quagmire, and we have absolutely no desire to get bogged down in that fashion."[28] To which Paul Wolfowitz, Bush Sr.'s undersecretary for defense policy, added in 1997: "A new regime [in Iraq] would have become the United States' responsibility. Conceivably, this could have led the United States into a more or less permanent occupation of a country that could not govern itself, but where the rules of foreign occupier would be increasingly resented."[29] The thinking of both men would change dramatically by the time they launched the second Gulf War ten years later.

In 1991 the H. W. Bush administration argued that the war itself would create enough instability to unseat Hussein. After the war, the administration returned to more traditional methods: it sent the CIA to foster instability, support Hussein's opponents, and attempt to overthrow his regime from within.[30] To further strangle and isolate Iraq, the Bush administration pushed for and received full economic sanctions against Iraq from the UN Security Council.

The UN initiated the Oil-for-Food program in 1996, through which Hussein was allowed to sell some oil in order to purchase food, medicine, and other humanitarian goods. U.S. companies, including ExxonMobil and Chevron, marketed Iraqi oil under the program. Almost ten years later, it was revealed that Hussein had established a worldwide network of oil companies and countries that secretly helped Iraq generate about $11 billion in illegal income from oil sales under the program. U.S. oil companies were involved in this secret system. Chevron paid $30 million in 2007 to state and federal regulators to settle charges brought by the Securities and Exchange Commission that it had paid illegal kickbacks to the Hussein regime to win marketing contracts.[31]

President Clinton continued U.S. support for the sanctions against Iraq. He continued U.S. financial support to the Iraqi opposition and signed the 1998 Iraq Liberation Act, calling for the removal of Saddam Hussein's regime. He maintained the constant U.S. military presence and activity in the region, including the no-fly zones over northern and southern Iraq. In late 1998, under the pretext that Hussein had not complied fully with UN weapons inspectors, Clinton launched an intensive four-day bombing of Iraq called Operation Desert Fox, followed by increased bombing in the no-fly zones. By the end of 1999, the UN reported 144 civilian deaths as a result of those U.S. raids.[32] Far more deadly, however, were the ongoing economic sanctions. For example, UNICEF reported that from 1991 to 1998, some half a million children under the age of five died in "excess" of the number expected to die without sanctions.

While both devastating and deadly to Iraqis, Clinton's efforts were considered paltry and halfhearted at best by those demanding another full-scale U.S. invasion to oust Hussein and his regime once and for all. In addition to refusing to go the distance to get Big Oil back into Iraq, Clinton also stopped the Iran-Iraq tango and would not facilitate a shift back toward Iran. U.S. companies continued to market Iraq's oil through the Gulf War of 2003. However, oil supplies were severely constrained by the sanctions, while access to Iraq's oil under the soil remained completely elusive.

Big Oil in Iran

The British, later joined by U.S. oil companies, maintained a hold on Iran's oil from the turn of the century until the Iranian revolution of 1979. In 1908 the British were the first to lay claim to Iran's oil, paving the way for the company that would become British Petroleum (BP). BP controlled Iran's oil under the concessionary system until Dr. Mohammad Mossadeq, the democratically elected leader of Iran, nationalized the country's oil in 1951. The nationalization rendered Mossedeq a hero in Iran and throughout the Middle East. Shirin Ebadi, winner of the 2003 Nobel Peace Prize for her lifetime of human rights activism in Iran, eloquently describes the national sentiment toward Mossedeq in her 2007 autobiography, *Iran Awakening*. Ebadi writes of the nationalization, "This bold move, which upset the West's calculations in the oil-rich Middle East, earned Mossadeq the eternal adoration of Iranians, who viewed him as the father figure of Iranian Independence, much as Mahatma Gandhi was revered in India for freeing his nation from the British Empire."[33] A very different image appeared in *Time* magazine, which named Mossadeq 1951's "Man of the Year." The biting article described how Iran's leader had "increased the danger of a general war among nations, impoverished his country, and brought it and some neighboring lands to the very brink of disaster."[34]

The British government tried to choke off the new regime by mounting an embargo, threatening tanker owners with legal action if they transported the "stolen Iranian oil." The British also embargoed goods to Iran, and the Bank of England suspended financial and trade facilities that had been available to Iran. "In short," Daniel Yergin concludes in *The Prize*, the British met the nationalization "with economic warfare."[35] The economic war only strengthened the Iranians' resolve and their support of Mossadeq.

In response, in 1953 the Americans joined the British in engineering a military coup that successfully ousted Mossadeq, reinstalled Mohammad Reza Shah Pahlavi, and put Iran's oil back in corporate hands.[36] As payment for U.S. efforts, the British opened up their Iranian oil holdings to the U.S. Sisters: Standard Oil of New Jersey, Standard Oil of New York, Standard Oil of California, Gulf, and Texaco. Shell and the Compagnie Française des Petroles were also given a piece of the new Iranian consortium.[37]

Over the course of the 1970s, particularly as U.S. oil companies were pushed out of Iraq, every major U.S. oil company eventually gained a portion of Iran's oil. Presidents Nixon, Ford, and Carter made sure that the shah's regime held firm against both domestic opposition and international suitors (namely, the Soviet Union) by facilitating some $12 billion in sales of advanced weaponry to Iran from 1972 to 1978.[38] But to little avail. On October 17, 1978, Ayatollah Ruhollah Khomeini, exiled in Paris, called on Iranians to overthrow the shah and to liberate "the destiny and resources of our country from foreign control."[39] In

1979 a massively popular revolution ousted the shah and named Khomeini as its new leader. It was only a matter of months before Iran's oil was nationalized and the foreign corporations thrown out of the country.

The United States first imposed economic sanctions against Iran in response to the 1979–1981 hostage crisis. While the United States was officially neutral in the Iran-Iraq war, U.S. support clearly flowed more heavily toward Iraq. In 1984, after Iran was implicated in the bombings of the U.S. embassy and a U.S. Marine barracks in Lebanon, Iran was added to the U.S. list of countries that support terrorism.

In a televised address in 1986, President Reagan explained the importance of Iran to the American public: "Iran's geography gives it a critical position from which adversaries could interfere with oil flows from the Arab states that border the Persian Gulf. Apart from geography, Iran's oil deposits are important to the long term health of the world economy."[40]

There was dissension within the Reagan administration, however. Donald Rumsfeld, Reagan's special envoy to the Middle East, promised Iraq that the United States would stop not only its own but also other nations' arms sales to Iran. Yet National Security Advisor Robert McFarlane, CIA Director William Casey, and ultimately Reagan approved secret arms deals to Iran. The deals were short-lived, occurring from 1985 to 1986. After a Beirut magazine uncovered the sales, it was learned that the Reagan administration was overcharging Iran for the weaponry and funneling the extra money to the Nicaraguan Contras.[41] In response, Congress passed the U.S. Arms Export Control Act, prohibiting Iran from receiving U.S. arms. The following year, in 1987, Reagan signed an executive order banning imports of Iranian crude oil to the United States, along with all other Iranian imports.

Cracks emerged in the Iranian government's attitude toward the West in the 1990s, creating new opportunities for U.S. oil companies. These opportunities were quickly shut down by the Clinton administration, however. Like Iraq, Iran emerged from the Iran-Iraq war in 1988 with a fractured economy, enormous financial debt, and a weakened capacity to produce oil. These domestic problems were exacerbated by low global prices for oil and sanctions from the United States. Nonetheless, while the Ayatollah Khomeini was in power and the United States was considered the "Great Satan," there was little opportunity for Big Oil to find its way back into Iran.

In 1989 the Ayatollah Khomeini died and, in response to ongoing popular organizing by Iranians, the political climate changed. Hojjatoleslam Ali Khamenei, who had served as Iran's president, was appointed its new supreme leader, and Hashemi Rafsanjani became president. Khamenei and Rafsanjani were deeply committed to stabilizing Iran's crumbling economy and were willing to work with the West to achieve this goal. Rafsanjani led the effort and turned to the International Monetary Fund (IMF) to facilitate a restructuring of Iran's vast foreign debt, opening Iran to the IMF's economic prescriptions. The IMF advocated, and Rafsanjani sought to implement, fundamental changes to Iran's economy, including limited openings in the oil and natural gas sectors to foreign companies. Support from most of the government was limited, but some changes did occur.

In 1991 Iran began opening certain offshore oil and gas fields to foreign companies, using a buyback system that remains in place today. Iran's oil remains nationalized, and the National Iranian Oil Company exercises full control and ownership of the fields, but it hires foreign companies to develop the fields and pays them "in kind" with a set proportion of the fields' output—either oil or natural gas. The companies have neither ownership rights nor control over decisions about the fields, such as the level of production.

In 1995 Iran signed an oil contract with Conoco, establishing the greatest potential access to Iran for a U.S. oil company since 1979. The $1 billion deal allowed Conoco to develop two large offshore oilfields for the National Iranian Oil Company.[42] It marked a dramatic change for U.S. oil companies and sent shockwaves through Washington. Clinton was advancing a "dual containment" strategy to try to choke off international support for *both* Iran and Iraq. He blamed Iran for funding terrorism, particularly against Israel, for hindering Middle East peace negotiations, and for pursuing nuclear and other weapons of mass destruction. Clinton was trying to convince other countries to join the United States in this strategy and was not at all interested in bending to the will of Big Oil in this instance.

U.S. public outrage against Big Oil grew when it was discovered that, while the U.S. government had imposed a ban on importing Iranian oil, U.S. oil companies had continued to purchase and sell Iranian oil, thereby supporting the Iranian regime. Exxon, Shell-North America, and others began purchasing Iranian oil and selling it abroad as early as 1992.[43] It is unclear whether the U.S. companies had marketing contracts with the Iranian government or purchased the oil from other parties. In either case, it is estimated that for several years U.S. companies purchased some 30 percent of Iran's oil a year, worth about $4 billion, which they then sold outside the United States.[44]

Big Oil hoped that as the door closed to Iraq and opened to Iran, the U.S. government would back its play—just as it had in the past. This time, however, Big Oil was more than disappointed when quite the opposite occurred. The Clinton administration forced Conoco to cancel its contract with Iran. Ten days later, Clinton issued an executive order to ban all U.S. investment in Iran's energy sector. A subsequent Clinton executive order banned all U.S. trade and investment in Iran. Finally, in 1996, under heavy lobbying from the America Israel Public Affairs Committee (AIPAC), Clinton signed the Iran-Libya Sanctions Act, imposing U.S. sanctions on any foreign company that invested in Iran's energy sector.

In 1997 the people of Iran elected a new president, Mohamed Khatami. Where Rafsanjani was considered a centrist, Khatami was a reformer who pushed for greater domestic sociopolitical freedoms. He also continued to advocate for foreign investment in the energy sector—although under the same limited conditions described above. The U.S. sanctions, and the pressure that the United States was applying on other nations to adhere to them, were stifling Iran's economy (as they were intended to do). Khatami announced new oil and gas opportunities for foreign companies. French, Russian, Malaysian, and even Canadian companies began signing limited buyback contracts to develop oil and natural gas fields in spite of the Iran-Libya Sanctions Act. Clinton threatened retaliation but never followed through, as doing so would have entailed imposing U.S. law extraterritorially. Big Oil did not want to be shut out of these deals and immediately went to work lobbying the Clinton administration to cancel the sanctions.

American-Iranian Council and USA*Engage

In 1997 two key organizations were formed to fight back against Clinton's sanctions: the American-Iranian Council (AIC) and USA*Engage. The AIC's board and advisory council includes current and former executives of Chevron, ConocoPhillips, Exxon-Mobil, Halliburton, and others. In fact, Chevron's corporate logo is a permanent fixture on the AIC's Web site. The council facilitates better relations between Iran and the United States, partly through high-level meetings between Iran's government and the CEOs of the nation's largest oil companies.

At a meeting in 2000 organized by the AIC between U.S. oil companies and Iranian government officials, for example, "the companies expressed their concern about sanctions, spoke about their activities against them and asked for some word on what Iran could do," according to council president Hooshang Amirahmadi.[45] ExxonMobil, Chevron, Conoco, and Iran's parliamentary speaker, Mehdi Karroubi, participated in the meeting. Karroubi made an unsuccessful bid for Iran's presidency in 2005 against current president Mahmoud Ahmadinejad and today leads Iran's opposition reformist party, Etemad-e-Melli (the National Trust Party).

USA*Engage was formed by Exxon, Mobil, Conoco, Arco,

Unocal, Chevron, Halliburton, the American Petroleum Institute, and other corporations to lobby against unilateral sanctions. "Conoco had become concerned with the lack of balance in American foreign and trade policy two years ago and championed the formation of the USA*Engage Coalition," Conoco CEO Archie Dunham stated in 1999. He pointed to Iran as Conoco's "most well-known sanctions disappointment."[46]

Mobil ran newspaper advertisements in the United States asking that companies be allowed to negotiate deals with Iran with the understanding that such deals would "remain unconsummated" until sanctions were lifted. Arco just went ahead and held negotiations. Linda Dozier, Arco's spokesperson, told Voice of America radio in 1999 that Arco was having productive conversations with Iran: "We'd characterize our activity in Tehran as an expression of interest subject to lifting of sanctions. We have specified some projects that we would be very interested in, but with the clear understanding that it would be subject to the lifting of the U.S. sanctions."[47]

As CEO of Halliburton, Dick Cheney was one of the most outspoken critics of Clinton's sanctions policies. "We seem to be sanction-happy as a government," Cheney told an oil industry conference in 1996. "The problem is that the good Lord didn't see fit to always put oil and gas resources where there are democratic governments."[48] In 1998 Cheney personally lobbied the Senate, seeking special relief for Halliburton from the Iranian and Libyan sanctions. Two years later, Cheney publicly argued that American companies should be allowed "to do the same thing that most other firms around the world are able to do now, and that is to be active in Iran. We're kept out of there primarily by our own government, which has made a decision that U.S. firms should not be allowed to invest."[49] By the time he was appointed vice president, Cheney was ready to do more than just lobby to gain that access for Halliburton and other U.S. companies.

USA*Engage lobbied against *unilateral* sanctions but did not oppose *multilateral* sanctions, such as those imposed on Iraq.

Unilateral sanctions are imposed by one country against another country, in this case, by the United States against Iran. Multilateral sanctions, on the other hand, are imposed by several countries against another country. In a speech typical of USA*Engage's position, then Chevron CEO and current Halliburton board member Kenneth Derr told a San Francisco audience in 1998, "I think the evidence clearly shows that unilateral trade sanctions just don't work." Derr then said, "Iraq possesses huge reserves of oil and gas—reserves I'd love Chevron to have access to." But he was quick to add, "I fully agree with the sanctions we have imposed on Iraq. Why? Because Iraq's behavior has been especially egregious—so much so that other countries have been willing to join the United States by adding sanctions of their own."[50]

Beyond Derr's feigned humanitarianism, U.S. oil and energy services companies had other reasons to differentiate between the sanctions on Iraq and Iran. If the sanctions against Iraq had been lifted at this time, U.S. oil companies would have been the last to benefit, if they benefited at all. On the other hand, given Iran's deal with Conoco and other close U.S. allies (such as Canadian oil companies), the U.S. oil companies believed that if the U.S. government removed its sanctions against Iran, U.S. oil companies would be in a good position to win contracts—albeit only the limited buyback contracts being offered by the Iranians. Nonetheless, Clinton refused to acquiesce.

Upon George W. Bush's inauguration in January 2001, the AIC hosted a meeting "focused upon the probable impact on US-Iran relations of the new Bush Administration." This meeting was between Dr. Kamal Kharrazi, then Iran's foreign minister and later the appointed head of Iran's Strategic Council on Foreign Relations; Hadi Nejad Hosseinian, then Iran's ambassador to the UN and today Iran's deputy petroleum minister for international affairs; Lee Raymond, then chairman and CEO of ExxonMobil; David O'Reilly, chairman and CEO of Chevron; Archie Dunham, president and CEO of Conoco; and Michael Stinson, senior vice president of Conoco.[51]

Big Oil set out to accomplish its goals in the Middle East by simultaneously lobbying against sanctions, negotiating for access, and putting its money behind the hawks and oil men and women on the Bush team.

The Project for the New American Century

When Big Oil backed Bush, it knew what it was getting: an administration deeply devoted to expanding U.S. military power, invading Iraq, and taking on any other challengers with a big stick. The Bush team had made its goals crystal clear with its participation in the Project for the New American Century (PNAC).

After Bob Dole's resounding loss in the 1996 presidential election, conservatives were keen to circle their wagons and clearly plan and articulate their vision of the future. The key foreign policy platform for both the Republican Party and the upcoming George W. Bush administration was PNAC. Just like USA*Engage and the AIC, PNAC was formed in 1997. Dick Cheney was also a prominent figure in PNAC. Prior to taking the helm of Halliburton in 1995, Cheney had spent his entire career in government. His stint in big business clearly hardened his outlook concerning how far the U.S. military should be willing to go to advance corporate interests.

More than a dozen leading members of George W. Bush's administration were involved in PNAC, including Vice President Cheney, Defense Secretary Donald Rumsfeld, Undersecretary of Defense Paul Wolfowitz, Cheney's chief of staff Scooter Libby, Chair of the Defense Policy Board Richard Perle, U.S. Ambassador to Iraq and then to the United Nations Zalmay Khalilzad, U.S. trade representative and then World Bank president Robert Zoellick, Deputy National Security Advisor Elliott Abrams, Deputy Secretary of State Richard Armitage, U.S. Ambassador to the United Nations John Bolton, Assistant Defense Secretary Peter Rodman, and State Department Counselor Eliot Cohen, among others. Bruce Jackson, who wrote the Republican Party's 2000 foreign policy platform, was a director of PNAC.

The two most well-known and influential documents released by PNAC were a letter to President Clinton calling for military action against Iraq and a report called "Rebuilding America's Defenses: Strategy, Forces and Resources for a New Century." Released in January 1998, the PNAC letter to Clinton called for the removal of Saddam Hussein and his entire regime from power. Arguing that diplomacy had failed, the letter called for military engagement and focused on the threat Hussein posed to "a significant portion of the world's supply of oil." Among the signatories were Rumsfeld, Wolfowitz, Perle, Khalilzad, Zoellick, and Bolton.

PNAC's seminal report was "Rebuilding America's Defenses," released in September 2000. Its arguments were mirrored succinctly in the foreign policy platform of the Republican National Convention of 2000 and formed the basis of the George W. Bush administration's foreign policy. It proposed a $15 billion to $20 billion increase in total defense spending annually— an amount subsequently far surpassed by the administration as it waged its War on Terror. The revamped military should be put to work in Iraq and across the Middle East, the PNAC report argued; "The United States has for decades sought to play a more permanent role in Gulf regional security. While the unresolved conflict with Iraq provides the immediate justification, the need for a substantial American force presence in the Gulf transcends the issue of the regime of Saddam Hussein."

The report established the Axis of Evil by arguing that "adversaries like Iran, Iraq and North Korea are rushing to develop ballistic missiles and nuclear weapons as a deterrent to American intervention in regions they seek to dominate." The report placed Iran next in the shooting order after Iraq: "Over the long-term, Iran may well prove as large a threat to U.S. interests in the Gulf as Iraq has. And even should U.S.-Iranian relations improve, retaining forward-based forces in the region would still be an essential element in U.S. security strategy given the longstanding American interests in the region."

Cheney and the rest of the PNAC team wasted little time putting the platform into action upon taking over the White House in 2000. They brought their Big Oil buddies with them.

BIG OIL IN IRAQ AND IRAN TODAY

From the outset of the new Bush administration, Big Oil played a key role in shaping the path toward its own victory in the Iraq War and immediately cashed in on its success. Big Oil's victory has laid the foundation for a decades-long continuation of the war. As for Iran, instead of the limited goal of simply removing sanctions and hoping for the best, the Bush administration has sought full regime change.

The Cheney Energy Task Force

Just ten days into the first administration of George W. Bush, representatives of the nation's largest oil and energy companies came together for the first of a series of planning meetings with the new administration. Their task was to devise a new energy policy for the United States. The group's official name was the National Energy Policy Development Group, but it is far better known as the Cheney Energy Task Force. While Vice President Cheney fought all the way to the U.S. Supreme Court to keep the content of the meetings and the attendees secret, a few leaks and successful Freedom of Information Act requests have shone light on the proceedings.

Official task force members included former and soon-to-be oil executives and lobbyists who worked for the Bush administration. Among them were task force executive director Andrew Lundquist and Undersecretary of the Interior R. Stephen Griles, who both left the Bush administration to form their own lobbying firm representing the nation's largest oil and energy companies; Interior Secretary Gale Norton, who left the administration to work for Shell; Energy Secretary Spencer Abraham, who joined the board of Occidental Oil Company in 2005 and formed his own corporate lobbying firm specializing in the international energy sector; FEMA director Joe Allbaugh, who left the administration to form New Bridge Strategies, which aids corporate clients in gaining access to postinvasion Iraq; and, of course, Vice President Dick Cheney, former CEO of Halliburton, one of the largest energy services companies in the world.

Attendees of some forty different task force meetings included executives and representatives of every major oil corporation, as well as coal, nuclear, and other energy industries.[52] In 2004 *New Yorker* magazine reporter Jane Mayer revealed a top-secret memo written by a high-level National Security Council (NSC) official directing the NSC staff to cooperate fully with the Energy Task Force as it considered the "melding" of two seemingly unrelated areas of policy: "the review of operational policies towards rogue states," such as Iraq, and "actions regarding the capture of new and existing oil and gas fields." Mark Medish, who served as a senior NSC director during the Clinton administration, told Mayer in response to the memo that "if this little group was discussing geostrategic plans for oil, it puts the issue of war in the context of the captains of the oil industry sitting down with Cheney and laying grand, global plans."[53]

The task force released its final report, "National Energy Policy," in May 2001. It lays out quite succinctly the priorities of the Bush administration and Big Oil, paying particular attention to Middle East oil. The report found that "by any estimation, Middle East oil producers will remain central to the world oil security" and that "the Gulf will be a primary focus of U.S. international energy policy." The report argues that Middle Eastern countries should be urged "to open up areas of their energy sectors to foreign investment." One invasion and a lengthy occupation later, this is exactly what the Bush administration has nearly achieved in Iraq. The report also called for a reevaluation of the U.S. sanctions policies. According to the *Washington Post*, an earlier draft of the report specifically listed Iran, Libya, and Iraq by name.[54]

Of course, quite a lot of the discussions that took place between the Bush administration and Big Oil were left out of the public report—in particular, the meetings' focus on Iraq. Freedom of Information Act requests revealed that, as part of its deliberations, the task force reviewed a series of lists and maps outlining Iraq's entire oil productive capacity.[55] These maps include detailed descriptions of all of Iraq's oil fields, oil pipelines, refineries, and tanker terminals. Two lists entitled "Foreign Suitors for Iraqi Oilfield Contracts" listed more than sixty companies from some thirty countries with contracts in various stages of discussion with Saddam Hussein for oil and gas projects across Iraq. None of these contracts could take effect, however, while the UN Security Council sanctions against Iraq remained in place. Of course, not a single U.S. company was on this list. Hussein was dangling these lucrative contracts before the oil companies in an attempt to entice their governments to cancel the sanctions. Just three countries were holding the largest contracts: China, Russia, and France—all members of the Security Council and all in a position to advocate for the end of sanctions.

It is easy to imagine the lords of the oil industry—both inside and outside the Bush administration—poring over those maps and lists. Running through their minds, if not raised in heated discussion around the table, must have been the reality that if the Hussein regime remained in power and the sanctions were removed, Iraq's oil bonanza would go to all those foreign companies, while the United States would be completely shut out. One can imagine the pangs of frustration they must have felt.

But the frustration must have been short-lived, since we now know that at the same time the Cheney Energy Task Force was meeting, planning for the military invasion of Iraq was also under way. Among those who have revealed the early planning of the war are Paul O'Neill, President Bush's first treasury secretary and an official member of the Cheney Energy Task Force. According to O'Neill, regime change in Iraq was the number one item on the agenda at the very first Bush administration National Security Council meeting on January 30, 2001, and "Already by

February, the talk was mostly about logistics. Not the why [to invade Iraq], but the how and how quickly."[56] The administration's stated focus was regime change: eliminating Saddam Hussein and replacing his government.

The nongovernmental Committee for the Liberation of Iraq (CLI) was the unofficial PR firm for the invasion. Formed in 2002, the CLI was largely an extension of PNAC. Among the many people who overlapped between the two organizations are Robert Kagan and William Kristol, the cofounders and original codirectors of PNAC, and Gary Schmitt, a PNAC executive director. Bruce Jackson left his vice presidency at Lockheed Martin to launch the CLI. The CLI's first president, Randy Scheunemann, is credited with writing the Iraq Liberation Act while working for Senator Trent Lott and later served as codirector of PNAC. Scheunemann is the chief foreign policy adviser to 2008 presidential candidate Senator John McCain. Senator McCain was also a leading member of the Committee for the Liberation of Iraq.[57]

The CLI's high-powered representatives saturated the media with op eds, interviews, and speeches making the case for war. Their arguments are well summarized in the Committee's statement of purpose, which announced that the CLI was formed to replace "the Saddam Hussein regime with a democratic government" because Hussein had "acquired weapons of mass destruction," and because his government "poses a clear and present danger to its neighbors, to the United States, and to free peoples throughout the world."

Prewar Oil Planning

Although the final decision for inviting foreign investment ultimately rests with a representative Iraqi government, I believe in due course the invitation will come.

—PETER J. ROBERTSON, VICE CHAIRMAN,
CHEVRON TEXACO, SEPTEMBER 2003[58]

The strategy implemented to win the war for oil in Iraq by the George W. Bush administration was fundamentally different from that of his father—or from that of any previous U.S. government. Mere arms transfers, CIA-engineered coups, or ploys to create instability would not suffice. Neither would the installation of a new leader. This time the model was more historic, closer to that of colonial Britain. The United States invaded, occupied, and installed an entirely new government, rewrote the nation's legal and political system, and attempted to ensure that, almost *regardless* of who the leader of the country happened to be, U.S. control over and access to the nation's oil could be locked in and guaranteed through international law. The U.S. military, of course, must stay. But according to the PNAC report, this had always been the plan.

Critical changes took place in the ten intervening years between the first George Bush war against Saddam Hussein and the second. The oil companies merged and became far bigger and far wealthier. At the same time, they became far more desperate for oil and perhaps more demanding of the government to meet their needs. After all, they had spent more money to put the Bush-Cheney administration into office than they had spent on any election ever. Many individuals who have spent their lives in "oil families" or worked in the industry for decades have told me that the oil companies' executives themselves changed in the 1990s—succumbing to the influence of their growing size, financial prowess, and desire for more. As one woman whose father was in the industry and whose husband is currently a Big Oil executive candidly told me, those in the industry seemed to have "lost their moral compass."

There are other important differences between the Bush administrations. When he became president, George W. had spent more time working as an oil executive than he had working for government. Likewise, prior to her appointment as national security advisor, Condoleezza Rice had spent more time on Chevron's board of directors—eventually serving as the head of its

Policy Committee—than in government service. Cheney had spent the previous six years heading one of the largest oil services companies in the world, and his personal commitment to extreme methods for obtaining corporate access had grown. Bush, Rice, and Cheney brought with them an administration filled to the brim with oil men and women.

The fall of the Soviet Union had also served to harden the view by neoconservatives that the United States could and should exercise imperial powers around the world. These neoconservative thinkers had roles of greater prominence in the George W. Bush administration than they had in his father's. Those who served in both Bush administrations learned through experience that getting their way in the Middle East was more difficult than they had originally imagined. Then the September 11 terrorist attacks opened the door to a far greater military response than what had been available to the U.S. government following Hussein's invasion of Kuwait. And while Iranian buyback and Iraqi marketing contracts are better than nothing, to many within both the oil industry and the Bush administration, the nationalizations of the past thirty years are a mere historical aberration whose time should now finally come to an end.

Big Oil Takes the Lead

We know where the best [Iraqi] reserves are [and] we covet the opportunity to get those some day.
—ARCHIE DUNHAM, CEO, CONOCOPHILLIPS, 2003[59]

Big Oil was brought in at the earliest stages to advise the Bush administration and to run and oversee Iraq's postwar oil industry. We will most likely never know exactly when the postwar planning between Big Oil and the Bush administration began. It seems logical to assume, however, that it began at least as early as the Cheney Energy Task Force in 2001. Press reports date discussions for postwar planning between the two groups to late 2002 and early 2003. Philip Carroll, former CEO of Shell Oil's U.S. division, was one of the first U.S. oil industry advisers in Iraq. He was brought in to help develop "contingency plans for Iraq's oil sector in the event of war."[60] Carroll told BBC reporter Greg Palast that he was tapped for the position six months before the invasion.[61] The *Wall Street Journal* reported that representatives from Exxon-Mobil, Chevron, ConocoPhillips, and Halliburton, among others, met with Cheney's staff in January 2003 to discuss plans for Iraq's postwar industry.[62] While there is a level of mystery about when Big Oil's role began, however, there is no question about the level of authority Big Oil acquired after the invasion.

Representatives of U.S. oil companies ran Iraq's oil ministry immediately following the invasion and held high-level oversight roles thereafter. Executives of ConocoPhillips, ExxonMobil, Chevron, Shell, and BP each took a turn guiding Iraq's oil industry. Philip Carroll of Shell and Gary Vogler, a former ExxonMobil executive, were the first on the ground. They arrived in April 2003, just one month after the invasion. Officially, the two were the ranking U.S. advisers to the Iraqi Oil Ministry. Unofficially, the two ran the ministry. Hussein's oil minister, Amir Mohammed Rashid, was on the Bush administration's "Most Wanted" list and had fled his post. "The ministry once again has a strong man at its helm," reported Germany's *Spiegel* magazine upon Vogler's arrival at the Iraqi Oil Ministry. "This was quite evident in the first order he presented to the undersecretary: Until further notice, all employees of the ministry are to be forbidden from independently making any operational or staffing decisions."[63] The *New York Times* ran a similar report of Vogler's meeting under the headline "U.S. Tells Iraq Oil Ministers Not to Act Without Its O.K."[64]

With Hussein ousted and the U.S. oil industry firmly in charge, Bush went to the United Nations in April and asked that the sanctions against Iraq be dropped. The Security Council not only agreed, but also gave the U.S. government decision-making authority over how Iraq's oil funds would be used. Chevron received one of the first postinvasion contracts to market Iraqi oil.

The U.S. occupation government, the Coalition Provisional Authority, named Thamir Ghadhban as the interim head of the Oil Ministry in May. Philip Carroll, the former Shell executive, was simultaneously appointed chair of a new advisory committee formed to oversee the entire ministry. Ghadhban was a returned Iraqi exile and an advocate of the privatization of Iraq's oil industry.[65] He advised that the process would need to be slow and would involve the rewriting of Iraq's existing oil laws by a new Iraqi government.

Robert McKee took over for Carroll in October. McKee retired from his position as executive vice president of ConocoPhillips just days after the invasion of Iraq to become chairman of Enventure, a joint venture between Halliburton and Shell. The *Houston Chronicle* referred to McKee as the "Bush administration's energy czar in Iraq" and stated that his appointment had drawn fire from congressional Democrats "because of his ties to the prime contractor in the Iraqi oil fields, Houston-based Halliburton Co."[66] ChevronTexaco vice president Norm Szydlowski also took a position as a liaison between the Coalition Provisional Authority and the Iraqi Oil Ministry in October. Terry Adams and Bob Morgan of BP and Mike Stinson of ConocoPhillips would also serve terms as advisers.

Big Oil's Big Plans: The International Tax and Investment Center

Of course, Big Oil wanted to do more than advise. It wanted in. Big Oil's ultimate goal was laid out in "Petroleum and Iraq's Future: Fiscal Options and Challenges" by the International Tax and Investment Centre (ITIC). The ITIC, with some eighty-five corporate sponsors, advocates for corporate-friendly tax and investment policies abroad. Chevron was an original sponsor of the ITIC and, like BP, has held a seat on the ITIC's Executive Committee for the last ten years. The current board of directors includes representatives of Chevron, ConocoPhillips, Exxon-Mobil, BP, Shell, and Halliburton.

The ITIC began its Iraq project in the summer of 2003. Six oil companies participated in and funded the project: Chevron, ExxonMobil, BP, Shell, Total, and Spain's Eni SpA.[67] Each of these companies is today poised to sign big oil contracts in post-Hussein Iraq. The ITIC's report, "Petroleum in Iraq's Future," released in the fall of 2004, made the case for opening Iraq's oil industry to foreign oil companies to a degree not seen since the original concessionary system of the post–World War I period. The report recommended that while the Iraqi government should retain the literal ownership of Iraq's oil, the rest of the industry should be all but fully privatized. It recommended the use of Production Sharing Agreements (PSAs), which are the industry's favorite contract model because they give oil companies the right to explore for and produce oil under the ground. PSAs have contract lives ten times longer than the most commonly used models: twenty to thirty years compared with two to three. PSAs give the foreign company a far greater level of control, ownership, and profit.

Consider PSAs as the politically correct version of the old concessionary system. As industry consultant Daniel Johnston writes in a standard textbook on petroleum fiscal systems: "At first [PSAs] and concessionary systems appear to be quite different. They have major symbolic and philosophical differences, but these serve more of a political function than anything else. The terminology is certainly distinct, but these systems are really not that different from a financial point of view."[68] Similarly, Professor Thomas Wälde, an expert in oil law and policy at the University of Dundee, describes "a convenient marriage between the politically useful symbolism" of the PSA and "the material equivalence" of this contract model with concession regimes. "The government can be seen to be running the show and the company can run it behind the camouflage of legal title symbolizing the assertion of national sovereignty."[69]

None of the top oil producers in the Middle East use PSAs. In fact, PSAs are only used for 12 percent of the world's oil. Iraq's neighbors—Iran, Kuwait, and Saudi Arabia—maintain nationalized oil systems and have outlawed foreign control over oil development. They all hire international oil companies as contractors to provide specific services as needed, for a limited duration, and without giving the foreign company any direct interest in the oil produced.[70]

Oil industry expert Greg Muttitt of the London-based research and advocacy organization Platform writes that in strategy planning meetings in late 2004 and early 2005, the ITIC's directors and sponsors argued that the ITIC's goal should be "to go beyond Iraq itself and regain oil companies' access to the region's other oil rich countries. . . . Specifially, they mentioned the oil-rich states of Iran and Libya."[71]

The ITIC report was delivered personally to Iraq's finance minister, Abdel Abdul Mahdi, by Britain's ambassador to Iraq, Edward Chaplin, in 2004. ITIC president Dan Witt then presented the report to officials of the Iraqi Ministries of Finance, Oil, and Planning at a meeting in Beirut in 2005.[72]

The report was right in line with the plans of the Bush administration, or possibly vice versa. All were working toward the same goal: a new law to open Iraq's oil industry to foreign oil companies under the most corporate-friendly terms possible.

Bush Administration Prewar Planning
State Department Oil and Energy Working Group
The Bush administration was mapping out its postinvasion plans for Iraq's oil in late 2002. One forum was the U.S. State Department's Future of Iraq Project's Oil and Energy Working Group, composed of administration officials, expatriate Iraqis, and others. Meeting four times between December 2002 and April 2003, the members of the working group agreed that Iraq "should be opened to international oil companies as quickly as possible after the war."[73] Differences appear to have emerged in the working

group as well as within the Bush administration over just how far Iraq should be "opened."

There are varying degrees of privatization. At one end of the spectrum, private companies would own all of Iraq's oil—a situation that does not even exist in the United States, where oil found in public land, whether on- or offshore, belongs to the public. Such a wholesale transformation of Iraq's most vital industry was considered but ultimately abandoned. Some of the loudest opponents appear to have been oil company executives themselves, who knew that such a move would surely have been met with mass opposition from the Iraqi public. The model ultimately agreed upon was the same model advocated by the ITIC: the Production Sharing Agreement (PSA).

A key member of the working group, Ibrahim Bahr al-Uloum, a U.S.-educated Iraqi oil engineer, was then named Iraqi oil minister by the U.S. occupation government in September 2003. He promptly went to work implementing the working group's proposal, supporting privatization through PSAs.

BearingPoint, Inc.

The blueprint for the Bush administration's economic overhaul of the Iraqi economy was ready at least a month prior to the invasion. The 107-page, three-year contract between the Bush administration and BearingPoint, Inc. of McLean, Virginia, provided the company with $250 million in return for "technical assistance" to the U.S. Agency for International Development (USAID).[74] BearingPoint's lawyers and economists, who provide consulting services to businesses and governments, wrote the framework to restructure Iraq from a state-controlled economy to one that guarantees "free markets, free trade and private property." The contract, entitled "Economic Recovery, Reform and Sustained Growth in Iraq," specifically states the need for "private-sector involvement in strategic sectors, including privatization, asset sales, concessions, leases and management contracts, *especially those in the oil and supporting industries*" (emphasis added).

While USAID and BearingPoint signed the company's contract on July 24, 2003, BearingPoint's plan was ready and in Bush administration hands at least five months earlier. Bearing-Point's Draft Statement of Work, "Stimulating Economic Recovery, Reform and Sustained Growth in Iraq," was completed on February 21, 2003—one month before the invasion—and does not differ substantially from the final contract.

BearingPoint was asked to prepare a second, more specific report on Iraq's oil industry in December 2003. The report, "Options for Developing a Long-Term Sustainable Iraqi Oil Industry," overwhelmingly supports the introduction of foreign oil company participation in the Iraqi oil sector. It finds that for both national oil companies "as well as a majority of other oil producing countries around the globe, using some form of PSAs with a competitive rate of return has proved the most successful way to attract IOC [International Oil Company] investment to expand oil productive capacity significantly and quickly."[75] Amy Jaffe, the senior adviser for the report, who works for former secretary of state James A. Baker III's Institute for Public Policy, describes the report as being "guided by a handful of oil industry consultants and executives."[76] In late 2004, BearingPoint's contract was extended for an additional three years, through at least 2007.

TURNING ON THE SPIGOT

Restoration and protection of Iraq's oil industry was an immediate focus of the war. When U.S. soldiers invaded Iraq, priority was given to the protection of the Oil Ministry, oil facilities, and oil infrastructure. Big Oil's presence was felt on the ground during the initial assault on Baghdad when soldiers set up bases nicknamed "Camp Shell" and "Camp Exxon."[77] Halliburton received a series of contracts, including for oil facilities restoration, that have yielded the firm more than $20 billion in Iraq War earnings to date. In addition to U.S. soldiers, Operation Task Force Shield employed approximately fourteen thousand private security guards, deployed along Iraq's oil pipelines in 175 critical installations, including 120 mobile patrols, to provide continual protection against sabotage.[78]

Oil production, which was halted during the invasion, resumed shortly after the occupation and reached prewar levels of 2.5 million barrels per day in March 2004. With a few significant bumps, production has held remarkably steady at between approximately 2 and 2.5 million barrels a day ever since. As explained earlier, Chevron received one of the first contracts to market Iraq's oil. It has since signed subsequent longer-term deals, as have ExxonMobil, Marathon, Shell and BP, among others.[79] The companies have been shipping large quantities of their Iraqi oil into the United States ever since. In August 2005, for example, Energy Intelligence Research reported that more than 50 percent of all Iraq's oil exports went to the United States that month.[80]

The Iraq Oil Law

The next step was to introduce a new law to transform Iraq's oil sector from a nationalized to a privatized model. During the period of formal occupation, L. Paul Bremer, the head of the U.S. occupation government—the Coalition Provisional Authority— implemented BearingPoint's broader economic plan through a series of laws that sought to open virtually all of Iraq's economy to foreign companies. Oil production was, however, explicitly excluded from Bremer's laws. There were those who wanted Bremer to open Iraq's entire oil sector to private investment at this time. More rational minds prevailed. The Hague Conventions bar occupying governments from doing exactly what the Bush administration has done in Iraq: fundamentally altering the laws of the occupied country. Oil contracts signed by Big Oil based on a law implemented by Bremer and the U.S. occupation government could easily be challenged under international law. Moreover, privatization of the oil industry by the occupation government within weeks of the invasion would clearly raise red flags of a war for oil. The safer approach was to have an elected Iraqi government pass its own oil law—albeit one drafted by Big Oil and the Bush administration.

The U.S. occupation of Iraq formally concluded in June 2004 when power was handed over to the interim Iraqi government. Iraq's interim prime minister, Iyad Allawi, was widely viewed as "the Americans' choice," in the words of Lakhdar Brahimi, UN special envoy to Iraq.[81] Having left Iraq for London at the age of twenty-five in 1971, by 1979 Allawi had organized a leading anti-Hussein network that became the Iraqi National Accord in 1990 and later became a direct financial beneficiary of the CIA. Allawi worked with the CIA on a failed coup attempt against Hussein in 1996.[82] He returned to Iraq after the 2003 invasion.

Just two months after taking office, Allawi proposed a new oil law that would bring "an end to the centrally planned and state-dominated Iraqi economy." Allawi recommended that the Iraqi government "disengage from running the oil sector, including management of the planned Iraq National Oil Company (INOC), and that the INOC be partly privatized in the future." He further recommended that the Iraqi field services industry "should be exclusively based in the private sector, that domestic wholesale and retail marketing of petroleum products should be gradually transferred to the private sector, and that major refinery expansions or grassroots refineries should be built by the local and foreign private sectors." Most important, Allawi's guidelines turned all undeveloped oil and gas fields over to private international oil companies.[83]

Just seventeen of Iraq's eighty known oil fields have been developed. According to a 2003 Energy Intelligence Research (EIR) report boldly titled "Iraqi Oil and Gas: A Bonanza-in-Waiting," only modest development work has been carried out in recent years anywhere in Iraq, and no significant exploration has been done in the last twenty years. The twenty-two largest known fields are evenly distributed between the north and the south of Iraq. Other fields are located in central Iraq, and the EIR reports that East Baghdad could be a giant field once it has been fully appraised. The largest known fields are Kirkuk in the north and Rumaila in the south, but there is potential for vast amounts of oil across virtually all of Iraq, including the western desert. EIR estimates that while Iraq's proved oil reserves are second only to Saudi Arabia's, "its 200 billion-plus barrels of probable reserves could put it in competition for the top spot." The development of untapped fields could therefore yield billions of gallons of oil and trillions of dollars in revenue.[84]

The plans for Iraq's new oil law were made public at a December 2004 press conference in Washington, D.C., hosted by the State Department. Iraqi finance minister Abdel Abdul Mahdi joined U.S. undersecretary of state Alan Larson in announcing Iraq's plans for a new national oil law that would open the oil sector to private foreign investment. Mahdi commented, "I think this is very promising to the American investors and to American enterprise, certainly to oil companies."[85] A few weeks later, Mahdi was appointed one of Iraq's deputy presidents.

In January 2005, a national parliamentary election was held in Iraq. The election has been challenged as illegitimate for many reasons, including the inability of voters to vote in a free and secure environment and without fear or intimidation, the inability of candidates to have access to voters for campaigning, and the lack of a freely chosen and independent election commission. However, it has generally been felt in Iraq that the parliament— particularly after the later inclusion of Sunni representatives— ultimately emerged as a generally consistent and fair representation of the Iraqi public.

The process of naming the cabinet, however, has been fraught with far more controversy. Three months of politicking, heavily influenced by the Bush administration, followed the parliamentary elections, during which the parliament appointed the president and two vice presidents, who then named the prime minister, Ibrahim al-Jaafari. Al-Jaafari was later replaced by Nouri al-Maliki. From the outset, a clear rift emerged, which has grown more pronounced with time, between the cabinet and the parliament, with the former, as a group not popularly elected, generally finding security in the continued presence of the foreign occupation and thus more willing to follow the agenda of the Bush administration, while the latter sees its fate more clearly tied to the Iraqi public—nearly 80 percent of whom say they oppose the presence of coalition forces in Iraq—and is therefore far less willing to support the Bush agenda.[86]

Ever since the new government took office, the Bush administration and U.S. oil companies have been pushing the Iraqis to pass the Iraq Oil Law. Dan Witt of the ITIC has stated matter-of-factly that the ITIC helped draft the law.[87] The law gives the Iraq National Oil Company control of only currently producing oil fields. All other fields, including all new discoveries, are to be opened to private companies using PSAs. Private companies would therefore have control of 64 percent of Iraq's known reserves. If another 100 billion barrels are found, as is widely predicted, foreign companies could control 81 percent of Iraq's oil—or 87 percent, if 200 billion are found, as the Oil Ministry has predicted.[88]

Under the terms of the Iraq Oil Law, as currently drafted, foreign companies would not have to invest their earnings in the Iraqi economy, partner with Iraqi companies, hire Iraqi workers, or share new technologies. None of the oil produced from Iraq's fields would need to stay in Iraq; it could all be exported. The companies could ride out Iraq's current instability by signing contracts while the Iraqi government is at its weakest, and then wait at least two years before setting foot in the country. The companies would also have control over production decisions on their fields—potentially jeopardizing Iraq's membership in OPEC. Without control over how much oil is produced from its fields, Iraq could not adhere to OPEC production quotas. Any disputes arising from the contracts would be handled in international rather than Iraqi courts. The law would grant the companies contracts of up to thirty-five years.[89]

The Iraq Study Group Report

The highly anticipated report of the bipartisan Iraq Study Group was released in December 2006. With James A. Baker III as cochair and Amy Jaffe as a lead author, it should have surprised no one that page one of the report laid out Iraq's importance to the Middle East region, the United States, and the world with this reminder: "It has the world's second-largest known oil reserves."[90] The report specifically (and publicly) called on the Bush administration to "assist Iraqi leaders to reorganize the national oil industry as a commercial enterprise" and to "encourage investment in Iraq's oil sector by the international community and by international energy companies." Much of the Iraq Study Group report was ignored, such as its recommendation to increase negotiations with Iran and Syria, but its recommendations for Iraq's oil were, of course, in lockstep with the Bush administration's existing agenda.

Within a few days of the Iraq Study Group report's release, President Bush made his first public demand of the Iraqi government to pass the oil law. Shortly thereafter, as reported by the *New York Times,* Bush's highest officials in Iraq made the same public demand: "Gen. George W. Casey Jr., the senior American commander here, and Zalmay Khalilzad, the American ambassador, have urged Iraqi politicians to put the oil law at the top of their agendas, saying it must be passed before the year's end."[91] The al-Maliki government in Iraq responded, announcing that it would work to complete the oil law by the end of 2006. All were unsuccessful.

The Surge and the Benchmarks

In January 2007, in a nationally televised and highly anticipated speech, President Bush announced the surge of twenty thousand additional American troops to Iraq. Bush stated that the surge would be successful where other U.S. efforts had failed in Iraq, because the Iraqi government would be held to a set of specific benchmarks. Those benchmarks were laid out in a White House fact sheet released the same day, which stated that the Iraqi government had committed to several economic and political measures, including to "enact [a] hydrocarbons law to promote investment, national unity, and reconciliation"—that is, the Iraq Oil Law. The president said that the surge would provide the Iraqis with the "political space" that they needed to achieve the benchmarks. The Congress later adopted the president's benchmarks and added its own pressure in advocating for their achievement.

The pressure worked. In February 2007, the Iraq Oil Law passed what seemed to be the most important hurdle, Iraq's cabinet. The cabinet signed off on the law and sent it to the parliament. Only passage in the parliament would put the national oil law into force. At the same time, the Kurdistan Regional Government passed its own oil law—following the Bush–ITIC model to a tee— and began signing PSAs with international oil companies, including longtime Bush supporter Hunt Oil of Texas. The central Iraqi government, however, immediately challenged the legality of this regional Kurdish law as a usurpation of its authority. Thus far, the major oil companies have all stayed away from Kurdistan, waiting for the conflict to be resolved. The conflict is an old one, but the current issues surrounding the oil law can be largely summarized with just two words: independence and Kirkuk. The Kurds want independence from Iraq and they hope that the Bush administration (and the U.S. military) will help them achieve it. They also want to retain authority over Kirkuk, not only for cultural reasons, but also because it sits atop one of the world's largest oil fields. The fate of Kirkuk has been a stumbling block to passage of the national oil law as both the Kurds and the central Iraqi government hope to lay claim to it. So too has been the Iraqi parliament, which has thus far been unwilling even to consider the law.

The Opposition

The Iraqi parliament has thus far refused to take up the Iraq Oil Law because of immense popular opposition, both in Iraq and abroad. A global education and resistance campaign spread from Iraq to Europe to the United States. Iraqis opposed to the law teamed up with activists in the countries that were perpetrating the war and where the oil corporations reside. Iraq's oil workers' unions, women's organizations, academics, and parliamentarians joined forces to raise awareness of and opposition to the law. Iraq's trade unionists went on strike, marched, rallied, and peacefully protested time and again against the law. Iraq's five trade union federations released a statement rejecting "the handing of control over oil to foreign companies, which would undermine the sovereignty of the state and the dignity of the Iraqi people."[92] Usama al-Nujeyfi, a member of Iraq's parliamentary energy committee, quit in protest over the oil law, saying that it would cede too much control to global companies and "ruin the country's future." He vowed to work to defeat the draft in parliament.

Six Nobel Peace Prize laureates from around the world signed their own statement in opposition to the Iraq Oil Law, writing that "it is immoral and illegal to use war and invasion as mechanisms for robbing a people of their vital natural resources."[93]

Labor, peace, women's, faith-based, student, and other activist groups in Europe and the United States educated themselves, their elected officials, and the public. Members of the British Parliament and the U.S. Congress joined the opposition, as did 2008 presidential candidate and congressman Dennis Kucinich. Iraqi spokespeople came to the United States, and American and British activists went to Iraq. They wrote analyses, set up Web sites, and held marches, rallies, and protests. Activists in London protested at the headquarters of BP. In California, on the fourth anniversary of the war, protestors blockaded Chevron's world headquarters by locking themselves to oil barrels spray-painted with the words "Stop the Iraq Oil Theft Law."

Big Oil Digs In

American officials are girding for an open-ended
commitment to protect the country's oil industry.
                    —CHIP CUMMINS, *Wall Street Journal*, 2007[94]

The national Iraq Oil Law remains the big prize in Iraq. If it becomes law, Big Oil will have the access it most desires to Iraq's oil. While it awaits the law's passage, Big Oil has begun negotiations with Iraq's oil minister to sign contracts for the seventeen currently producing oil fields under Iraq's existing oil laws. This means that the rest of Iraq's oil fields would still be open for a future law using PSAs. The contracts now under consideration involve the more common service arrangement found in Saudi Arabia and Iran whereby the state still owns the oil and the national oil company hires the foreign company to perform work on its behalf.

Big Oil has held regular meetings with Iraq's government and oil ministry in and outside of Iraq since the invasion. For example, Chevron and ExxonMobil were among the corporate sponsors of the Iraq Procurement 2004—Meet the Buyers conference at which Iraqi ministers met with U.S. and other corporations in Amman, Jordan, to "further their business relations with the rest of the world."

Chevron has been flying Iraqi oil engineers to the United States free of charge for four-week training courses since early 2004. ExxonMobil signed a memorandum of understanding with the Oil Ministry in late 2004, laying the groundwork to provide technical assistance and conduct joint studies. In January 2005, BP signed a contract to study the Rumaila oil field near Basra, and the Royal Dutch/Shell Group signed an agreement to study the Kirkuk field. Shell is also helping to write a master plan for Iraq's natural gas sector for free.[95] The purpose of all these free services and memorandums has been to keep their foot in the door and be the first companies in line when the real deals began.

The real deals began to solidify in late 2007. Iraq's oil minister, Hussain al-Shahristani, who has done just about everything possible to try to get the oil law passed, announced that he was in negotiations with the major oil companies for currently producing fields all across Iraq. Ben Lando, energy editor for United

Press International, was at the conference in Dubai where many of the negotiations took place and wrote about the fields of interest to Big Oil. "Shell, which produced a technical study of Kirkuk in 2005, wants a deal for the field. BP wants one for Rumaila, which it studied last year. Shell and BHP Billiton are angling for the Missan field in the south. ConocoPhillips is talking with the ministry about the West Qurna oil field. . . . ExxonMobil is interested in the southern Zubair field. . . . Chevron and Total have teamed up in a bid for the Majnoon field."[96] If these companies—ExxonMobil, Chevron, Total, Shell, and BP—sound familiar, it is because they are the very same companies that owned and controlled Iraq's oil following the First World War (with Chevron's purchase of Gulf in 1984).

ExxonMobil vice president Daniel Nelson, speaking in Houston in February 2008, said: "My guess is every international oil company in the world, knowing Iraq is blessed with terrific god-given natural resources, is interested in Iraq. I'm not giving any competitive secrets away there." While noting that security is crucial, Nelson added, "more important is you have confidence you have a system of laws and a system of fiscal stability that's going to be together for not only the 6, 7, 8, 9 years that it takes from the time you start up working in a venture to the time you have significant production and through that 30-year period you really need to get the returns back." That "30-year period" just happens to be the length of time that contracts would be granted under the Iraq Oil Law.[97]

If and when U.S. oil companies get to work in Iraq, under whatever terms, the companies will require protection. What better protective force is there than the U.S. military? A confidential intelligence report on the Iraq Oil Law prepared for U.S. officials was leaked to ABC News. The report concluded that if "major foreign oil companies" were going to go to work in Iraq, they would need to be "heavily underwritten by the U.S. government."[98] The Bush administration has openly discussed a U.S. military commitment along the lines of our "Korea policy"—a presence that could last for as long as fifty years to separate the warring factions between regions of Iraq.

On January 3, 2008, at a town hall styled campaign appearance in Derry, New Hampshire, Senator John McCain was asked specifically about the potential for U.S. troops to be in Iraq for another fifty years, to which McCain answered, "Maybe 100. We've been in South Korea, we've been in Japan for 60 years. We've been in South Korea for 50 years or so. That'd be fine with me as long as Americans are not being injured or harmed or wounded or killed. Then it's fine with me. I would hope it would be fine with you if we maintain a presence in a very volatile part of the world where Al Qaeda is training, recruiting, equipping, and motivating people every single day."[99]

Meanwhile, none of the leading Democratic candidates for president—including Barack Obama—were willing to commit to withdrawing all U.S. troops from Iraq by 2012, what would be the end of their first term in office.

The Bush administration is building the largest U.S. embassy in the world in Iraq, as well as permanent military bases (although it does not use the word *permanent*). For example, the U.S. Navy is building a command-and-control facility atop one of Iraq's offshore oil terminals. The terminal is conveniently located just a stone's throw away from the Iranian border and the headquarters of the Iranian Revolutionary Guards Corps. From the facility, U.S. and "coalition officers will monitor ship traffic and coordinate the movement of coalition warships circling the oil terminals," demonstrating "a more lasting military mission in the oil-rich north Persian Gulf," reports Chip Cummins in the *Wall Street Journal*. Cummins also reported that the U.S. embassy in Baghdad had formed a new special task force of American officials to coordinate U.S. policy regarding "Iraqi energy-related issues, including security of oil infrastructure." Congress recently committed nearly $300 million just for energy-infrastructure protection in Iraq.[100]

The implication of the base atop the oil terminal is clear. The

United States is digging in its heels in Iraq and has its eyes on Iran. The oil and the U.S. oil companies will be protected, and their access may yet expand into Iran in the very near future.

IRAN: THE NEXT WAR?

My message to the Iranian people is, "You can do better than this current government. You don't have to be isolated. You don't have to be in a position where you can't realize your full economic potential."

—PRESIDENT GEORGE W. BUSH, 2007[101]

We hope Iraq will be the first domino and that Libya and Iran will follow. We don't like being kept out of markets, because it gives our competitors an unfair advantage.

—JOHN GIBSON, CEO, HALLIBURTON ENERGY SERVICE GROUP, 2003[102]

Since taking office the Bush administration has been girding for war to replace the Iranian regime. Bush has slowly built up the U.S. military presence surrounding Iran. Since 2000, the U.S. military has installed new bases and personnel in Iraq, on Iran's western border; in Afghanistan, on Iran's eastern border; in Turkey, to the west; and in Qatar, across the Persian Gulf to the south. Existing U.S. military facilities sit in virtually every country on Iran's borders. U.S. Navy carrier battle groups patrol the Persian Gulf and the Arabian Sea. American naval tactical aircraft, operating from these carriers, have been flying simulated nuclear weapons delivery missions—rapid ascending maneuvers known as "over the shoulder" bombing—since 2005, within range of Iranian coastal radar.[103] In January 2007 Bush explained in a televised "Address to the Nation" that he had deployed Patriot Air Defense Systems to the region "to reassure our friends and allies."[104]

Bush further emphasized the importance of the navy to U.S.

efforts in the Middle East when he appointed a naval aviator, Admiral William Fallon, as the new head of U.S. Central Command in the Middle East in January 2007. In response, the *New York Times* reported, "Admiral Fallon's appointment comes amid a series of indications that the Bush administration is increasingly focused on putting pressure on Iran and, perhaps, veering toward open confrontation."[105]

Unfortunately for Bush, Admiral Fallon would ultimately prove a liability for the administration's objectives in Iran. As the administration rhetoric against Iran—including the threat of military engagement—intensified, press reports of internal conflict between Fallon and others in the administration grew. In September, Fallon appeared on Al Jazeera television in his dress whites and warned that talk of bombing Iran is not helpful,"This constant drumbeat of conflict is what strikes me—which is not helpful and not useful," he said. "I expect that there will be no war and that is what we ought to be working for. . . . It is not a good idea to be in a state of war. We ought to try and to do our utmost to create different conditions."[106] The following April, Fallon was the subject of an *Esquire* article entitled "The Man Between War and Peace," which described Fallon as a lone voice in the Bush administration against taking military action against Iran and which warned, "President Bush is not accustomed to a subordinate who speaks his mind as freely as Fallon does, and the president may have had enough."[107] One week later, under headlines stating "Admiral William Fallon Quits Over Iran Policy," Fallon retired his post.

The administration has taken a different approach to regime change in Iran from that in Iraq. An all-out invasion and occupation of Iran may well have been the original plan, but with the U.S. military strained beyond its limits in ongoing ground wars in Iraq and Afganistan, and U.S. public opinion firmly against— at a minimum—the former, such a plan for Iran was ultimately out of the question. Instead, Bush created a hybrid of older, proved models with a more aggressive nuclear twist. The administration has sought to build antigovernment groups in Iran that would be situated and ready to overthrow the Iranian regime, a tried and true tactic. At the same time, the administration planned for the U.S. Navy to launch an aerial bombardment of key facilities in Iran. In April 2006, Pulitzer Prize–winning journalist Seymour Hersh revealed these plans after speaking with leading military and policy makers both within and outside of the administration. Their willingness to speak, Hersh explained, was their belief that going public would head off an administration hell-bent on war.[108]

Hersh revealed that air force planning groups had drawn up lists of targets, and teams of undercover American combat troops had gone into Iran to collect targeting data and to establish contact with "anti-government ethnic-minority groups," with the ultimate goal of regime change. Among the targets for the aerial bombardment are Iran's nuclear facilities. Nuclear weapons are among those being considered for use by the U.S. military—a truly terrifying scenario.[109]

A former defense official who still deals with sensitive issues for the Bush administration told Hersh that the military planning was premised on a belief that "a sustained bombing campaign in Iran will humiliate the religious leadership and lead the public to rise up and overthrow the government." He added, "I was shocked when I heard it, and asked myself, 'What are they smoking?'"

The real issue for the Bush administration is "who is going to control the Middle East and its oil in the next ten years," a high-ranking diplomat told Hersh. A senior Pentagon adviser on the War on Terror expressed a similar view: "This White House believes that the only way to solve the problem is to change the power structure in Iran, and that means war."

Rather than end sanctions, the administration has sought both to expand the scope of the sanctions and to make them multilateral, like those against Iraq in the 1990s, which Big Oil supported. Expanding the sanctions serves not only to isolate

Iran further, but, if the sanctions are expanded far enough, to stop Iran from signing oil and gas deals with companies from other countries. For as the Bush administration has been planning for war, Iran has been signing oil and natural gas contracts with China, Russia, Pakistan, and India.

Secretary Rice went to the UN in 2006 to say that the UN Security Council's delay in approving further economic sanctions on Iran was "leaving the administration with little choice but unilateral action." The administration followed Rice's statement by intensifying its rhetoric. It designated the Iranian Revolutionary Guard, the largest branch of Iran's military, as a terrorist organization. It has made the case that Iran is providing arms and other support to Shiite militias in Iraq and to Taliban militants in Afghanistan. And, of course, the administration argues that Iran is pursuing weapons of mass destruction, including nuclear weapons. "This time, however, I think the empirical evidence is clear that the negotiations have failed," argued former UN ambassador John Bolton on Fox News in May 2007. "They have not slowed the Iranians down, they have not dissuaded them from their ultimate strategic objective, and that's why I think moving toward significantly greater pressure up to and including regime change and the use of force has to be the way to go."[110]

Thus far, the administration's efforts to expand the sanctions have largely failed and were dealt a particularly rough blow when the 2007 U.S. National Intelligence Estimate (NIE) for Iran, reflecting the consensus view of all sixteen U.S. intelligence agencies, found that Iran had halted development of a nuclear bomb four years earlier and was less determined to develop nuclear weapons than U.S. intelligence agencies had earlier claimed. In January 2008, on his first trip to the Middle East as president, Bush met with Israeli prime minister Ehud Olmert. According to Michael Hirsch of *Newsweek,* "the President all but disowned the [NIE] Document." Hirsch quoted a senior administration official who accompanied Bush on the trip as saying of Bush, "He told the Israelis that he can't control what the intelligence community says, but that [the NIE's] conclusions don't reflect his own views."[111]

The existing UN sanctions against Iran still have a powerful effect, and the fear of an invasion is ever-present among Iran's leaders. "Under sanctions, Iran cannot develop its hydrocarbon potential," an Iranian oil ministry adviser explained, "and this inability to deliver its supply of much-needed energy to the world could lead the stronger consuming states to invade it in order to develop its huge reserves."[112]

The oil companies, for their part, have never been shy about their desire to gain greater access to Iran's oil. And the Bush administration has not been shy about the lengths to which it is willing to go to secure that oil. But to date their plans have not worked out. Neither the American public nor the global public has any stomach for another front in the War on Terror. The U.S. military is stretched far too thin: it is suffering from critical recruitment shortfalls and from internal dissension against the war. If Big Oil and the Bush administration thought that the war in Iraq would turn their goals for the rest of the region into a cakewalk, they were wrong. At first the threat of war forced many nations to acquiesce to the Bush administration's demands, but the fear has since largely turned to anger. The war in Iraq has created far more enemies than allies and has also solidified support for those leaders, such as Iran's Ahmadinejad, who are willing to stand up to the agendas of Bush and Big Oil.

"The threat of regime change by military force," writes Iran's Shirin Ebadi, "while reserved as an option by some in the Western world, endangers nearly all of the efforts democracy-minded Iranians have made in these recent years. . . . It makes Iranians overlook their resentment of the regime and move behind their unpopular leaders out of defensive nationalism. I can think of no scenario more alarming, no internal shift more dangerous than that engendered by the West imagining that it can bring democracy to Iran through either military might or the fomentation of violent rebellion."[113]

When viewed through such a lens, the future looks bleak. In addition to the demands of Big Oil, there is the competition from other global powers, particularly China. China has been increasingly making arms deals with other nations—including Iran, Sudan, Libya, and Syria—in exchange for oil. Simultaneously, the rhetoric among hawks in the United States against China has grown. The U.S. military has emerged as an oil-protective force that has drawn shockingly little response from Congress or any other of our elected officials. Hopefully, the Bush regime will prove to be the apex of how far a U.S. presidency will go in the service of Big Oil.

There is hope. In April 2008, opposition to the Iraq war reached a new high, with 63 percent of Americans saying that the United States had made a mistake in sending troops to Iraq. It is the highest "mistake" percentage Gallup has ever measured for an active war involving the United States—surpassing the 61 percent who said the Vietnam War was a mistake in May 1971.[114]

Americans are not only talking about their opposition, they are taking action. It is a resistance movement against war and Big Oil very much in the spirit of the populist struggles more than a hundred years ago.

RESISTANCE

On the fourth anniversary of the U.S. invasion of Iraq, a dozen people chained themselves to oil barrels and blockaded the main entrance of Chevron's world headquarters in San Ramon, California. They were clothed all in red, and pinned to their chests were black-and-white patches that read "No Blood for Chevron." Before sunrise, and before police and security guards had time to react, the protestors had set up the empty barrels on Chevron Way, the road leading into Chevron's corporate campus. They sat down on the ground and locked each hand into a barrel, creating a human-barrel chain. Behind them, others quickly unfurled giant banners that read "End Chevron's Crimes from Richmond to Iraq" and "End Oil Wars."

"I've had enough," said one protestor. "I've had enough of corporations determining who lives and dies. . . . It's time for democracy to come back and for the people to decide the important issues." A young woman explained, "I couldn't stand one more day of silently supporting this oil war." "I'm here to protest Chevron's seventeen billion dollars in profits from war and global climate chaos," said protestor Scott Parkin.

As the sun came up, members of the Ronald Reagan Home for the Criminally Insane theater group arrived, posing as Condoleezza Rice, Dick Cheney, and George W. Bush. The song "Money Makes the World Go Round" boomed from a portable sound system as the three impersonators danced and laughed, cash flowing from their pockets, unable to conceal their glee at the vast wealth their war was bringing to Chevron. Giant 20-foot-tall puppets representing Chevron CEO David O'Reilly and other chief executives joined in the celebration. The mood grew more somber as a mock funeral dirge announced the approach of a procession for "the world's last cube of ice," which was carried in a coffin by pallbearers dressed in black. The group watched as the ice melted in the hands of the "priest" conducting the service.

Hundreds of others came out to join the protest over the course of the day. They rallied, chanted, held signs, and waved as passing cars honked their horns in support. They handed out literature to both passersby and Chevron employees, who by and large took the protest in stride and willingly received the proffered materials. The handouts discussed, among other topics, the Iraq Oil Law and Chevron's role in the war.

The protest was the lead story on every local television news program that night. Reporters interviewed protestors as they sat chained to the barrels. Local and national newspapers covered the event, and the video documenting the protest remains a favorite on YouTube.

The day concluded with a symbolic tug of war between "Chevron's representatives, Bush, Cheney, and Rice" and "the people" over the future of the planet.

The people won.

IN THE NEXT CHAPTER, I propose new policies, ideas for activism, and a way forward to end the tyranny of Big Oil.

9

Taking On Big Oil

We also have to reexamine whether having only a handful of giant oil companies can coexist with the needs of the American consumer and a rational energy policy in this country—I do not believe it does. And so I'll be offering an amendment . . . that will require a complete examination as to whether or not we should break up the big oil companies. Enough is enough.

—SENATOR CHARLES SCHUMER, APRIL 25, 2006[1]

A new spirit of populism is alive and well in the United States. Just a few months before Senator Barack Obama declared that he would end both the tyranny of oil and the war in Iraq, as he delivered his historic victory speech at the 2007 Iowa Caucus, hundreds of people took action at the nation's Capitol in Washington, D.C. On October 22, 2007, students, veterans of the Iraq War, religious leaders, peace activists, and environmentalists protested against Big Oil, war, and global warming. Chanting "No War, No Warming!" one group sat down before an entrance to the Cannon House Office Building. Carrying a banner calling for "Separation of Oil and State," they blocked the doors leading to the offices of members of Congress.

As the blockaders took up the chant "ExxonMobil, BP, Shell: Take your war and go to hell!" U.S. servicemembers who had served in Iraq and were members of Iraq Veterans Against the War circled the building. Dressed in their full desert camouflage and pretending to carry machine guns at the ready, the soldiers walked in formation as if they were protecting an oil company executive. Just as they had done in Iraq, the soldiers then prepared to guard an oil derrick. This 25-foot derrick was, however, being erected in the middle of Pennsylvania Avenue.

Simultaneously a group of high school and college students sat in the middle of the intersection of Independence and New Jersey Avenues. Legs and arms entwined, they blocked traffic in both directions. Members of Congress and their staffs tried to get to work while the students shouted "No blood for oil!" At which point the "polar bear contingent" arrived. Dressed in furry white costumes from head to toe, the bears chanted their opposition to global warming and danced near the various blockades until Capitol Hill Police put them in handcuffs. Arrested as well were the Iraq war veterans, the students, and some sixty others, ranging in age from fourteen to seventy two.

Colonel Ann Wright, who retired from the U.S. Army Reserves to protest the invasion of Iraq, said of the day's events, "Millions of Americans—the vast majority of us—want immediate action on the twin global threats of the Iraq War and global warming. We are demonstrating today because as the violence, chaos, and death in Iraq continue and we hit another year of increasing climate disasters, our government is failing, once again, to respond to the will of the people."[2]

"The link between war and warming is oil," said Steve Kretzmann of Oil Change International. "The oil industry gave $10 million in campaign contributions to this Congress. Perhaps this explains Congress's inability to address these issues. We're here today to demand a separation of oil and state."[3]

THE UNITED STATES IS an "oiligarchy"—a nation in which a small cadre of oil interests governs the most pressing decisions of our time. Consequently, oil and gasoline prices are skyrocketing, feeding the already overstuffed pockets of Big Oil at the expense of investments in meaningful and sustainable clean energy alternatives. But this is just the most obvious tip of a much larger iceberg. As oil becomes harder to find, more competitive to acquire, more expensive to produce, and more polluting to refine, we will be further pressed to decide just how far we are willing to go to get the last drops. Will our climate crisis be expanded? Will communities be destroyed? Will more wars be fought?

As long as the nation's largest oil companies continue to use their unparalleled access to both money and political power to pursue their goals, we will continue to follow the more destructive path. Only by restoring democracy and bringing the oil companies into check will we have a chance to choose a more peaceful, sustainable, and secure future.

Today Big Oil is the most profitable industry in the United States and in the world. The largest oil companies operating in the United States took in $133 billion in profits in 2007, making ExxonMobil, BP, Shell, Chevron, ConocoPhillips, Valero, and Marathon together the fiftieth largest economy in the world. Their combined profits were larger than the individual gross domestic products of New Zealand, Egypt, Kuwait, Peru, Morocco, and Bulgaria, among 129 additional countries. Each company is also dramatically increasing its profits. For example, between 2003 and 2007, Chevron's profits increased by an astounding 158 percent, ConocoPhillips's by 153 percent, and ExxonMobil's by 89 percent. And their profits just keep growing.

The oil industry reached its current behemoth proportions through megamergers that in most cases should not have been permitted. These megamergers have led not only to market consolidation on a massive scale but to skyrocketing prices. Over the stern objections of members of Congress, state officials, consumer advocates, and antitrust experts, the FTC permitted the mergers of BP, Amoco, and then Arco; Exxon and Mobil; Chevron, Texaco, and then Unocal; Conoco and Phillips; Shell and

Pennzoil; and numerous joint ventures between these companies, among other mergers. The FTC permitted the mergers in the face of its own econometric analysis, which should have made these mergers unthinkable—or at least called for placing significantly greater conditions on the mergers than the token gestures ultimately required by the FTC.

The FTC's primary determinant for whether a merger should be challenged is the level of concentration that exists in the market or can be predicted to occur if the merger takes place. The FTC prefers unconcentrated markets because, all things being equal, the more concentrated a market, the more likely it is that a company or a group of companies working within it will be able to exert undue control over market price. Under the FTC's guidelines, if a market is "moderately" concentrated, a proposed merger should be critically scrutinized and the FTC should be highly skeptical of allowing it to take place. If a market is "highly" concentrated, the FTC should investigate the market for antitrust violations, and will often flatly reject a proposed merger.

The FTC reported in 2004 that concentration levels in the U.S. oil and gasoline industry increased everywhere in the United States from 1985 to 2003 such that virtually every region is now overconcentrated in both refining and marketing. This means that the few refiners and sellers that exist are able to exert control over price. Using the FTC's measurements, the American Antitrust Institute calculated that, between 1996 and 2006, refinery concentration increased by 95 percent on the East Coast, by 56 percent in the Midwest, and by 104 percent in the Gulf Coast.[4] In California, the FTC allowed the refining market to become an oligopoly, with the top four refiners owning nearly 80 percent of the market. Six refiners also owned 85 percent of the retail outlets, selling 90 percent of the gasoline in the state.[5] This is the primary explanation for why gasoline prices in California are often the highest in the nation.

The oil industry keeps its records very close to its chest. Thus, no government agency or any other public organization has regular access to data on retail gas stations or the prices they charge. The FTC is left to measure the effect of concentration on gasoline marketing using wholesale price data.

If you live in Iowa, South Carolina, Arkansas, or Mississippi, you can breathe a slight sigh of relief because these are the only four states in the nation that are unconcentrated in wholesale gas prices. Everyone else lives in a concentrated market. From 1994 to 2004, concentration in wholesale gas prices on the East Coast increased by 32 percent, in the Midwest by 48 percent, in the Gulf Coast by 45 percent, in the Rockies by 10 percent, and in the West Coast, Alaska, and Hawaii by 19 percent.[6] The U.S. government's General Accounting Office concluded in 2004 that "Mergers and increased market concentration generally led to higher wholesale gasoline prices in the U.S."[7] "Mergers influenced some, but not all, of the [concentration] changes in these states," agreed the FTC.

The permission to merge in the face of existing concentration gave Big Oil the keys to the kingdom. As a result, we have been paying higher gasoline prices that have contributed to the highest oil company profits in history.

The mergers also facilitated Big Oil's reacquisition of sizable portions of the world's oil following nationalizations of their holdings during the 1970s and 1980s. By buying up smaller companies and then merging with each other, Big Oil has recaptured about 13 percent of the world's oil market. ExxonMobil, Chevron, ConocoPhillips, Marathon, Shell, and BP hold approximately 40 billion barrels of oil reserves among them. Were these companies one country, it would be tied for ninth place among the nations with the largest oil reserves in the world.

Big Oil has used its political influence to persuade the federal government to abdicate its regulatory authority over the crude oil futures market, which is today the primary determinant of the price of a barrel of oil. Energy traders working for Big Oil companies on the regulated NYMEX have been found guilty of or have been charged with intentionally manipulating energy markets. We know nothing of what these traders are up to on the unregulated exchanges. The actions of energy traders on the futures market have contributed to the second-highest run-up in oil prices in world history. The skyrocketing price of crude oil drives Big Oil's profits and is the primary determinant of the companies' recent record-setting profits.

Big Oil has turned this megawealth into mega–political influence. ExxonMobil, BP, Shell, Chevron, ConocoPhillips, Valero, Marathon, and other major oil companies use their money to create a labyrinth of financial control that weaves through state houses across the nation, into the courts, and up through the U.S. Capitol and the White House. It blocks virtually all other players and seeps through all of the nation's policy-making. With the help of front groups, trade associations, creative media, and the revolving door, more often than not we are not even aware of Big Oil's actions against the public good.

The cost of "business as usual" has been borne out most destructively on our environment, on communities caught in the cross fire, and on workers at oil facilities, while it weakens the entire national security posture of the United States government and its military. Oil from the tar sands of Canada, the shale regions of Colorado, and in the world's waters is extracted at enormous financial and environmental costs. The pursuit of these methods of oil extraction imperils the globe's very ability to sustain life. Communities unlucky enough to reside near decrepit refineries are forced to suffer health risks, environmental pollution, and political manipulation. Those living where oil is produced face mass human rights abuses, the rule of corrupt governments, and death. Nations unwilling to turn over their oil face invasion and war.

The United States has already invaded Iraq to acquire its oil. Our military is laying down its roots for the long term, while U.S. oil companies contemplate thirty-five-year contracts for control over Iraqi oil. Iran appears next on the horizon. The U.S. military has become an international security force for Big Oil, with bases and deployments following the world's oil supply and transportation routes. People from Ecuador to Indonesia and from Angola to Oman confront the constant visible presence of the U.S. military, and the threat of force looms over their daily lives.

As I write, none of the leading candidates for president in 2008 have spoken to this massive realignment of the U.S. military, nor have they addressed our current *petrol-imperialism*. As the chance of war grows daily, it becomes all the more clear that our actions do not take place in a vacuum. China, for example, pursues oil in the same manner that the U.S. government has for decades: by supplying arms in return for oil. We see the grim effects of this policy in areas like Sudan. New alliances that threaten global stability are quickly emerging as oil and war become twin threats looming over the globe.

The costs associated with the wars in Iraq and Afghanistan are many. Well over a hundred thousand Iraqi civilians are estimated to have died as a result of the invasion of Iraq, while some 4 million have been displaced from their homes.[8] Civilian casualties from Afghanistan are far more difficult to come by, but conservative estimates add to some 5,000 deaths.[9] As of this writing, there have been 4,373 confirmed deaths among coalition soldiers in Iraq, including 4,064 Americans, 2 Australians, 176 Britons, 13 Bulgarians, 1 Czech, 7 Danes, 2 Dutch, 2 Estonians, 1 Georgian, 1 Hungarian, 33 Italians, 1 Kazakh, 1 Korean, 3 Latvians, 23 Poles, 3 Romanians, 5 Salvadorans, 4 Slovaks, 11 Spaniards, 2 Thai, and 18 Ukrainians.[10] One hundred twenty-seven journalists have been killed in the war. Approximately 29,829 U.S. soldiers have been physically injured in Iraq while tens of thousands suffer deep psychological trauma. More than 1.6 million U.S. soldiers have been deployed to Iraq and Afghanistan. In Afghanistan, 889 coalition soldiers—including 556 Americans—have died, while the Pentagon reports at least 2,257 U.S. personnel have been wounded in action.[11] The U.S. government has appropriated some $800 billion to fund both wars. Economists Joseph Stiglitz and Linda Bilmes have estimated, however, that when costs such as future military operating expenditures, health care and other needs of veterans and their families, interest on the war debt, and costs on the broader economy are taken into account, the war in Iraq alone will ultimately cost U.S. taxpayers more than $3 trillion.[12]

Yet the larger costs may ultimately lie in future petrol-imperialism conflicts. Dr. Steven Kull, director of the Program on International Policy Attitudes at the University of Maryland, stated in testimony before the U.S. Congress, "In the world as a whole, negative views of the United States have increased sharply in recent years. A key factor contributing to these feelings is that the United States is perceived as unconstrained in its use of military force. . . ." He went on to say that the institute's research "does show that anti-American feelings do make it easier for al Qaeda to operate and to grow in the Muslim world. In this context it is not surprising that three out of four respondents favor the goal of getting the U.S. to withdraw its military forces troops [sic] from all Islamic countries. . . . Though al Qaeda and America are both seen as largely illegitimate, America is seen as the greater threat. It is as if Muslims are living in a neighborhood where there are two warlords operating. They do not like either one, but one is much more powerful."[13]

Similarly, in 2004 the Defense Science Board, a federal advisory committee appointed by the U.S. Defense Department to report to then defense secretary Paul Wolfowitz, conducted a study of Muslim attitudes toward the United States. It found that the War on Terror and, in particular, the invasions of Iraq and Afghanistan had increased antipathy toward the United States and support for radical Islamists:

American direct intervention in the Muslim world has
paradoxically elevated the stature of, and support for,
radical Islamists, while diminishing support for the
United States to single digits in some Arab societies. . . .
In the eyes of Muslims, the American occupation of

Afghanistan and Iraq has not led to democracy there, but only [to] more chaos and suffering. U.S. actions appear to be motivated by ulterior motives, and deliberately controlled in order to best serve America national interests at the expense of truly Muslim self-determination. . . . Muslims see American rhetoric about freedom and democracy as hypocritical and American actions as deeply threatening.[14]

These are sobering findings that should convince the most cynical reader that the United States is on an unsustainable course. We are digging ourselves into a hole from which we may soon be unable to get out.

THE BREAKUP OF BIG OIL

How are we to change course? The first step must be to unlock the hold that Big Oil has on our government's decision-making. We cannot engage in a truly democratic process for determining the best path forward for the United States with the 800-pound gorilla of Big Oil in the room and the public all but shut out.

One hundred years ago, activists, journalists, politicians, and others looked at an analogous set of problems and chose as their solution the breakup of the largest corporation in the world, the Standard Oil Company. They introduced a new set of powerful antitrust laws specifically designed to counter the unchecked power of corporations over the U.S. government.

Anthony Sampson's description of Standard Oil could easily be written of Big Oil today: "It was almost untouchable by the state governments which seemed small beside it, or the federal government in Washington, whose regulatory powers were minimal. By bribes and bargains it established 'friends' in each legislature and teams of lawyers were ready to defend its positions. Its income was greater than that of most states."[15] This description of the intent of the Clayton Antitrust Act from a congressional report written in 1914 could also have been written today: "The concentration of wealth, money, and property in the United States under the control and in the hands of a few individuals or great corporations has grown to such an enormous extent that unless checked it will ultimately threaten the perpetuity of our institutions."[16] And finally, President Woodrow Wilson's words while campaigning for the presidency in 1912 may be even more relevant today: "The trusts are our masters now, but I for one do not care to live in a country called free even under kind masters. I prefer to live under no masters at all. . . . The government has never within my recollection had its suggestions accepted by the trusts. On the contrary, the suggestions of the trusts have been accepted by the government."[17]

The nation's antitrust laws were written to ensure that corporations did not grow so large that they could overrule the power of the government. I have sought to demonstrate that today our nation is once again ruled by a handful of corporate oil interests— and the stakes are arguably far higher. Any formula designed to lessen the control of Big Oil over our government and the world's most vital natural resource must therefore consider the breakup of the nation's largest oil corporations, the spawn of Standard Oil: ExxonMobil, Chevron, ConocoPhillips, Marathon, Valero, Shell-U.S., and BP America.

We know that this can be done because we did it once before. The breakup of Standard Oil provides inspiration, tools, and guidance for the "do's and don'ts" of breaking up Big Oil today. The most significant failures of the 1911 breakup of Standard Oil were allowing the company to design its own dissolution, and the failure of the government to enforce the breakup through regulatory action. Moreover, the people largely left the fight against Standard Oil to the government after the breakup was achieved. Vigilance was not maintained. Any breakup or even attempt at a breakup today should be carried out simultaneously with a host of other proposals and actions required of both the government and the people. We should reduce not only Big Oil's size, but also our reliance on its product. These efforts would weaken Big Oil's hold on our government and thereby make the government more willing to regulate the postbreakup companies.

I am not alone in making this proposal. The quote that introduces this chapter was made by New York's senior senator, Democrat Charles Schumer, in response to a speech by President Bush on energy policy. Elected to the Senate in 1998, Schumer sits on four key Senate committees: Finance; Banking, Housing, and Urban Affairs; Judiciary; and Rules. The head of the Senate Democrats' 2006 reelection committee, Schumer is credited more than any other senator with regaining Democratic control of the Senate in that election. He is generally progressive on economic issues and has been outspoken on oil company price-gouging, collusion, and market manipulation. However, few anticipated that when Schumer took to the Senate floor in April 2006 he would call for an investigation into the breakup of the nation's largest oil companies.

Schumer first responded directly to President Bush's energy speech: "The president today just spoke about high gas prices. And to listen to the president, you'd think that it's the local gas station that's the problem. We all know it's the big oil companies who are causing these massive price increases that go way beyond what supply and demand would merit. There were five words missing from the president's speech today: 'Get tough on Big Oil.' The president refuses to do that." The senator renewed his message one month later at a press conference in Albany, calling for a study by the General Accounting Office (GAO) into the feasibility of breaking up the biggest oil companies. According to *The Albany Business Review*, Schumer said that the country needed the "trust-busting spirit of former New York governor Theodore Roosevelt" and that "the entrenched oil giants form an ultra-powerful lobby in Washington that is preventing the country from getting serious about developing alternative energy sources to relieve the United States' over-dependence on Middle East oil."[18] Hearings into the industry followed, and the GAO is at work on its investigation as I write.

State attorneys general and consumer advocacy groups have been at the forefront in seeking action against the nation's oil companies. Richard Blumenthal, the attorney general of Connecticut, told a congressional hearing in mid-2007, "Consumers need and deserve swift Congressional action to halt oil company mergers, [and] break up oil companies who misuse market power to engage in predatory practices against competitors. . . ."[19] There have been several other calls for moratoriums on new mergers as well as new legislation introduced to better facilitate antitrust action. Wenonah Hauter of Public Citizen proclaimed before a congressional committee that we must "stop oil company merger mania. While mergers give greater power to individual companies, industry consolidation makes the industry itself more influential as power becomes concentrated in the hands of the very few."[20]

Lawsuits have also been filed all across the United States citing antitrust violations by the industry. Unfortunately, the "antitrust revolution" of the Reagan era appears, at least for now, to have been won in the nation's courtrooms. Reagan's judicial appointees follow the most conservative approach to antitrust and in case after case have thrown out any attempt to take action against corporate consolidation, collusion, or conspiracy. Antitrust experts have therefore suggested to me that antitrust action against the oil companies would best be brought before courts in a more liberal judicial environment, such as that in California.

One key obstacle to action has been the enormous black hole of information that surrounds the oil industry. I have attempted to fill much of that void here, but time and again I have heard from government regulators, lawyers, investigative journalists, and consumer advocates that they do not have adequate access to, or are unable to afford, vital information about the industry. Both the FTC and the GAO present their critical studies of the effects of mergers in the U.S. petroleum industry with a caveat concerning the inadequacy of the information available to them. Critically, no government agency or any other public organization has regular access to data on retail gas stations or the prices they charge. Oil companies are not required to provide this information to the public. This information can be had, but the price is steep. Employees of private firms literally sit in front of gas stations all across the country recording price changes, data that these firms collect and sell for a fee. Thus this data and a good deal of other critical industry data is only available from private companies for a fee or not at all. This leads to inadequate and infrequent investigations. For example, I was told by an author of the GAO's 2004 study on oil industry mergers that the agency has been unable to update the report because it cannot afford to do so.

The oil industry has also perfected the art of obfuscating its financial investments and expenditures. Transparency International, a London-based anticorruption research organization, evaluated forty-two leading oil and gas companies operating in twenty-one different countries around the world. It found that only a handful of companies sufficiently report on their payments to governments where they operate, particularly for resource extraction rights. ExxonMobil rated as one of the least transparent companies in the world.[21] Similarly, as discussed in chapter 7, determining the exact amount of money that Big Oil spends on renewable energy alternatives is extremely difficult. The same problem emerged in determining the full extent to which the companies participate in the crude oil futures market. The FTC reports its own difficulty in tracking oil company finances: "Energy firms' capital structures have become more complicated over the years. These arrangements sometimes allow firms to screen many details of these units' operations under the umbrella of equity method accounting, in which reporting obligations are limited. . . ."[22] The lack of information hinders all kinds of lawsuits, from small business complaints to federal antitrust suits.

On occasion information does get out. Government regulators do come up with the funds to acquire data and conduct investigations. Legal proceedings do force companies to reveal information they would prefer not to reveal. Investigative journalists do get behind company doors, and interviewees do talk. This book brings as much of this information as possible to you.

The industry does not like talking to the public directly. That is what the American Petroleum Institute and the Chamber of Commerce are for. But this, too, makes getting information directly about and from individual companies extremely difficult. I tried, for example, to interview several representatives of the oil companies for this book and was unsuccessful in every attempt. I thought my best hope had emerged when API's John Felmy provided me with the names of the chief economists at ExxonMobil, ConocoPhillips, and Chevron. I assumed that Felmy's name would open doors. I was wrong.

When I made my first call to ConocoPhillips's chief economist, Marianne Kah, Felmy's name may have made it possible for me to get ten words out that I would otherwise have been unable to say. But once I told Kah that I was writing a book on the oil industry and wondered if I could ask her a few questions, she stayed on the phone only long enough to assure me that she was not permitted to speak unless first cleared by ConocoPhillips's communications department. I tried to convince her otherwise, but to no avail. She seemed quite relieved when I finally relented and said good-bye.

Michael Tanner of ConocoPhillips's communications department then told me in so many words that few people actually end up interviewing the company's staff. He explained that in order to interview Kah, I would first have to sign a contract with ConocoPhillips indicating that the company would be able to review the entire book prior to publication before determining whether to allow the interview material to be used. After getting the green light from my publisher to at least review the contract, I sent back an e-mail to Tanner indicating my interest in the interview. I never heard back.

Chevron's senior economist, Edgard Habib, meanwhile, returned one of my phone calls and asked that I send an interview request by e-mail. After sending the e-mail, I never heard back.

The best sources of information have been lawsuits and congressional hearings and investigations. Congress has in fact put enormous effort into digging deeply into the industry, and many members have put forward serious legislation to enact reform. This leads me to believe that the most effective way to break up the companies and to implement any sort of meaningful reform today would be through congressional action in combination with other organizing efforts discussed below.

As discussed earlier, in the 1970s numerous bills were introduced with great support in both congressional chambers to break up the nation's largest oil companies. A list of the companies under consideration in one 1975 bill looks like an oil merger "to-do list" for the years that followed: Exxon (ExxonMobil), Texaco (Chevron), Mobil (ExxonMobil), Standard Oil of California (Chevron), Gulf (Chevron), Standard Oil of Indiana (BP), Shell, Atlantic Richfield (BP), Continental (ConocoPhillips), Occidental, Phillips (ConocoPhillips), Union (Chevron), Sun, Ashland (Marathon), Cities Service (Occidental), Amerada Hess, Getty (Chevron), and Marathon. Rather than being broken up, these eighteen companies merged into seven megacompanies, today's ExxonMobil, Chevron, BP, ConocoPhillips, Marathon, Occidental, and Hess.

A *New York Times* reporter argued in 1976 that the success or failure of Big Oil's "massive public-relations drive could determine whether the industry is broken up by the United States Congress and restructured along somewhat more economically modest and politically manageable lines."[23] Big Oil's PR worked and none of the bills passed. Most of the bills followed a model of "vertical divestiture," by which the companies would only be permitted to operate in one area—production, refining, or transportation/marketing—and would be required to sell off other parts of the company. Big Oil called it "dismemberment." The FTC sought a similar plan to break the eight oil companies into separate production, pipeline, refining, and marketing operations.

Although I am not a lawyer and do not have enough information to know the best method for such a breakup, I do know that it is high time for another call to action. Congressional investigations are only meaningful if they are supported by popular appeal. In most cases, congressional action has been spurred by public outrage over prices, which has led to bills that primarily focus on issues of price-gouging. Were the public to expand its critique to not only the market power but also the political power of the industry, the movement toward breaking up Big Oil would be far more powerful.

Breaking up the companies is a key place to start, but, if the past has taught us anything, we know that it cannot be achieved in isolation. If Congress is the source of both the problem and the solution, new proposals for reducing Big Oil's hold on our nation must be pursued in tandem with new calls for a breakup. These proposals should present tools for getting Big Oil's money out of politics; cutting off its subsidies and taxing its operations; constraining and regulating Big Oil's activities; investing in public transportation and sustainable alternative energy; reducing our consumption of oil; and demanding that our military get out of the oil-protection business altogether.

Separation of Oil and State: Electoral and Campaign Reform

Elected officials at all levels of government should demonstrate that they are not and will not be beholden to Big Oil. A fundamental demand of all people running for and holding elected office should be that they are committed to a "separation of oil and state": a commitment to renounce money from the oil industry and support sustainable clean energy alternatives. Such a commitment could provide an element of demonstrable proof that election promises can turn into real policy change once the electioneering is over. At the same time, voters can pledge only to vote and campaign for the least "oily" candidates.

Separation of Oil and State (SOS) is a campaign launched by the Washington, D.C.–based Oil Change International and endorsed by another twenty organizations, including Greenpeace

USA, Rainforest Action Network, the Sierra Club Student Coalition, and the Center for American Progress. Oil Change International works to remove the legal and political impediments to shifting our economy away from oil. SOS is modeled after the successful campaigns of the 1990s that led many politicians to reject campaign contributions from the tobacco industry. Through public education and protest, politicians came to view any association with the tobacco industry as a toxic relationship better to be avoided altogether. As a consequence of these campaigns, the power of the tobacco industry has been significantly reduced. Meaningful legislation has been passed at the local, state, and national levels regulating the industry, eliminating subsidies, and even eliminating tobacco altogether from restaurants, neighborhoods, and cities. Such an outcome was believed impossible in the heyday of the tobacco industry's political power. If it could happen to tobacco, it can also happen to oil—another product for which the nation has developed a deadly addiction.

A vital corollary to the SOS campaign is the need for real campaign finance reform that removes the stain of corporate money from our elections. The first meaningful campaign finance laws in the United States were put in place by the same political momentum that reined in corporate power over government with the nation's antitrust laws. I recommend Public Citizen's "Clean Up Washington" Web site, which provides legislative proposals for both campaign finance reform and for curtailing the power of lobbyists.

While spending on campaigns is clearly manipulating our political decision-making, elections only occur every few years. The expenditures on lobbying made by Big Oil and other corporations are significantly greater and far out of proportion to those of groups advocating for the rights of workers, consumers, public health, and the environment. These expenditures must be constrained. In this regard, Senator Barack Obama's declaration early in his campaign for president that he would renounce money from federal lobbyists was an important development. By mid-2008, Senator Hillary Clinton had received more money from lobbyists than any other presidential candidate of any party, taking in over $850,000 from this group as of May 2008—almost eight times as much as Obama had received (he does take money from state lobbyists) and over $200,000 more than Republican presidential candidate Senator John McCain, according to the Center for Responsible Politics.

Senator McCain's money from lobbyists may have trailed behind that of Senator Clinton, but that has not stopped lobbyists from fund-raising for him or from exercising significant influence over his campaign. In May 2008, McCain listed seventy lobbyists as "bundlers"—fund-raisers whose success at raising money is large enough to be directly monitored and reported upon by the candidates. Clinton listed twenty two lobbyists and Obama listed fourteen (Obama's bundlers had previously been registered as, but are no longer, lobbyists).[24] Moreover, *McClatchy News Service* reported in April 2008 that more than two dozen lobbyists were working in the McCain campaign.[25] Among them were McCain's campaign manager, Rick Davis; his chief fund-raiser, Thomas Loeffler; and senior adviser Charles Black Jr. Amid a great deal of public pressure, the McCain campaign ultimately issued an edict requiring all senior staff to resign or drop their lobbying and outside political connections. Loeffler left the campaign, while Davis and Black stayed on. Meanwhile, the Republican National Committee's primary McCain spokesperson, with the "catchy" title "McCain for President Victory '08 Chair," is Carly Fiorina, the former CEO of Hewlett Packard Corporation.

In the past, Senator McCain has been a national leader for campaign finance reform, while Senator Obama is standing out in attempts at ethics reform and trying to close the revolving door between government and private practice.

Today, the nation's rules and laws governing conflict of interest and the revolving door are at best porous and at worst nonexistent. Aggressive proposals are necessary to ensure that the public interest is served.

Ending Big Oil's Free Ride

Big Oil maintains its wealth and size through billions of dollars of local, state, federal, and international tax breaks, subsidies, royalty relief, and loopholes. We should no longer consider it a priority of the U.S. government at any level to subsidize the activities of Big Oil. Our national wallet is too small and the costs associated with Big Oil's wealth are too large. Big Oil is also more than capable of financing its own affairs. Eliminating Big Oil's free ride will help to create a more level playing field for the development of alternatives to oil and free up money for direct investments in public transportation.

In order to eliminate Big Oil's free ride, the industry must be adequately taxed. State measures such as California's Proposition 87 to impose excise taxes on oil production should be supported and implemented across the country. A windfall profits tax should also be imposed. Such a measure would bring an additional tax to bear on Big Oil's current tax liability whenever the price of oil tops a certain predetermined marker. There is tremendous support for such legislation all across the nation. "Once again, ExxonMobil has reaped the largest windfall in U.S. history at the expense of hard-working families," Wisconsin governor Jim Doyle said in a 2006 statement. "I hope that this news will finally convince the U.S. Congress to take action and force the oil companies to give consumers a refund."[26]

In this book I have only touched the surface of the many ways in which Big Oil uses existing legislative loopholes to skirt meaningful tax payments. Big Oil spends big bucks on loophole strategies—from offshore tax havens such as the Cayman and Jersey Islands, to elaborate joint venture, subsidiary, and partnership corporate structures—to avoid paying its fair share of taxes. Organizations including the Center for Tax Justice and Institute on Taxation and Economic Policy in the U.S. and the London-based Tax Justice Network are working to expose and shut down such schemes and to hold Big Oil to account.

Transparency must be the guiding principle applied to every

aspect of the oil industry. New laws to require greater divulgence of financial records, pricing, and other data are needed to ensure that the public can adequately monitor and regulate the industry. Lack of transparency is a problem that permeates the industry. Similar to the lack of reporting requirements for gas stations and gasoline pricing are the inadequate reporting requirements for refineries. For example, refineries do not have to report outages or planned outages. All too often, state oversight boards only learn of refinery outages from the press and therefore have little capacity to determine if refiners are shutting down to reduce supply or for valid reasons such as necessary repairs. Reporting issues associated with the health and safety of workers are another pressing problem that dictates whether government regulators can pinpoint a refinery operating at risk to its employees.

Consumer advocacy groups, such as Consumer Watchdog and Public Citizen, provide excellent oversight and advocacy services that bring a greater level of transparency to the inner workings of the industry.

Regulation

It is time, once and for all, to abandon Ronald Reagan's obsession with deregulation. The federal government has abdicated far too much of its regulatory authority in every arena of Big Oil's activities. Environmental, worker, human rights, public health, consumer, and other advocacy groups have been newly formed, and existing ones have dedicated their limited energy and severely constrained financial resources, to fill this regulatory void. But of course, nongovernmental organizations cannot enforce laws. When they uncover wrongdoing by companies, they cannot force compliance, but must rather turn to the courts or appeal to the government for redress. It is time to empower our government to enforce our laws written for our companies. Not only must existing laws be enforced, but new laws to constrain Big Oil's activities must be passed.

Chevron's Richmond Refinery is representative of a far greater problem affecting refineries across the nation and the world.

Refineries routinely abuse local communities through land, air, and water pollution, unsafe operations, old and aging infrastructure, and corruption of local politics. There is no earthly reason why the most profitable corporations in the history of the world cannot afford to invest their money in the world's most state-of-the-art refineries. Instead of spending $1 million a day drilling for oil in the Tahiti field off the coast of Florida, why shouldn't Chevron spend $1 million a day improving the Richmond Refinery?

It is within this context that we must turn a very skeptical eye toward the "cap and trade" proposals gaining currency with, among others, ConocoPhillips, BP, and Shell, as well as both Senators McCain and Obama. Under this system, the government decides how many tons of a given pollutant can be emitted state- or nationwide and passes out credits to the emitters. Polluters then trade the credits. Energy traders will then step in to facilitate and seek to make a profit off the trades.

There are several problems with such a system, the most pressing is that it does not work. The European Union implemented a cap and trade system in 2005, but, thanks in good part to intense industry lobbying, the initial cap was set so high that the polluters fell under it without making any reductions at all. The Europeans are trying to fix the system, but the politicization inherent in the allocation process makes this very difficult. One can only imagine the type of industry influence that could be expected under a U.S. system. Larry Lohman, an expert on the European experiment and editor of *Carbon Trading: A Critical Conversation on Climate Change, Privatization and Power*, said, "The experience from Europe's [Emissions Trading Scheme] has been a well-documented disaster. Emissions actually increased, the worst polluters were given the largest windfall profits on record, energy costs for consumers increased, and the use of global 'offsets' funded oppressive projects the world over. The U.S. should really learn from Europe's mistakes, not copy them."[27]

The editors of the *Los Angeles Times* have also warned about the potential for increased costs: "Say there's a very hot summer week in California. Utilities would have to shovel more coal to produce more juice, causing their emissions to rise sharply. To offset the carbon, they would have to buy more credits, and the heavy demand would cause credit prices to skyrocket. The utilities would then pass those costs on to their customers, meaning that power bills might vary sharply from one month to the next."[28] Energy traders could also step in to drive up price, just as they have done with oil and gasoline futures.

Companies are also allowed offsets, which has created a very distorted system in which tree planting in one area, for example, allows the companies to increase pollution in another area. Fear that both the trading and the offsets will consolidate pollution even further among those already disproportionately impacted today, including low-income people of color, has led a broad coalition of environmental justice and human rights groups to join forces such as "EJ Matters" in opposition to cap and trade systems.[29] The answer, they say, is not to allow polluters to choose the places where it is most convenient for them to pollute, but rather to regulate pollution everywhere.

Rather than allow companies to trade in pollution, local, state, and national governments around the world need support in their efforts to better enforce and expand control over polluters, particularly as companies seek to retool refineries to burn dirtier crude. The same is true for pipelines, gasoline stations, ships, trucks, trains, and, of course, production and exploration facilities as well. Only when facilities have proved that they are using the safest, most technologically superior equipment and maintaining the highest standards of worker safety and public health should companies be allowed to expand existing refineries, refit them to burn dirtier crude, or build new refineries. Local groups such as West County Toxics Coalition and Communities for a Better Environment in Richmond as well as national groups such as the Refinery Reform Campaign need support in their efforts.

Transparency is as great a problem in international exploration, production, and refining as it is in every other oil sector. Oil companies do not have to report where they operate abroad, much less how they operate. Any reporting or oversight is also left to local and international organizations with limited resources. Generally, it is only when the worst abuses are revealed—such as the mass human rights abuses in Indonesia and Nigeria and the environmental and health abuses in Ecuador—that an appropriate spotlight shines on the activities of oil companies operating abroad. There are many proposals for international corporate accountability and international law to require best practices of corporations when they operate outside of their home country that have been put forward by organizations including Human Rights Watch and Amnesty International. However, Big Oil has enjoyed a virtual free pass in its operations around the globe. Meanwhile, exploration and production is expanding in areas such as Angola, Nigeria, Sudan, and in other countries whose governments are notorious for permitting brutal corporate repression against local populations. The need for international coordination in oversight and the enforcement of strict rules on the companies is greater today than ever.

International financial institutions such as the World Bank are a part of this problem. As described by the End Oil Aid Campaign, since 1992, the World Bank alone has provided more than $5 billion in subsidies to the oil industry, including the world's largest oil corporations, while devoting only 5 percent of its energy budget to clean, renewable energy sources. In Chad, for example, the World Bank provided critical financial assistance to a project led by ExxonMobil that has only exacerbated conflict and poverty. As oil started flowing, Chad's authoritarian president increased military spending and ripped up an agreement with the World Bank that was supposed to ensure that oil revenues were used to fight poverty. At first the World Bank objected, but it backed down as soon as the president threatened to cut off the oil if his terms were not accepted.[30] An international campaign led by groups including the Bank Information Center, Jubilee USA Network, Friends of the Earth, and Oil Change

International is demanding an end to this "Oil Aid." Similarly, organizations such as Rainforest Action Network are working to expose and confront private banks that finance the oil industry.

We could also declare certain areas simply off the table for oil development, such as offshore coastal areas or the shale regions of the midwestern United States. Canadians could choose to reject further exploration of the tar sands. The National Outer Continental Shelf Coalition has organized not only to maintain the existing moratoriums on offshore drilling, but to expand offshore preserves that deny drilling access for all time in specific areas. Similar coalitions exist around the world in areas that already have moratoriums or are seeking to impose them. Environmental organizations such as Earthjustice, Sierra Club, and Defenders of Wildlife have all taken the lead in protecting our offshore areas.

We need an informed national debate and discussion about where we believe our companies should and should not go in search of oil. At a minimum we can decide whether we will allow companies to hunt for oil on public land. Clearly it is pure folly, however, to continue to give them free leases to hunt for oil on public land in the shale regions and royalty relief for offshore drilling. Many organizations—such as Western Resource Advocates, Polaris Institute, Natural Resources Defense Council, and the Pembina Institute—have unified their efforts to protect the Midwest from shale production and Alberta from tar sand production.

Oil Futures Markets

Calls for greater transparency and regulation are also crucial for the crude oil, gasoline, and other energy futures markets. It is high time to heed the calls from government regulators, industry experts, and consumer advocates to introduce U.S. government regulation and oversight to the Intercontinental Exchange (ICE), increase regulation and enforcement of the NYMEX, and once and for all close the Enron Loophole. Legislation has been introduced in Congress to achieve each of these ends, and the Energy Market Oversight Coalition—com-

posed of groups including the Municipal Electric Utilities of
Wisconsin, the Virginia Petroleum Convenience and Grocery
Association, Fuel Merchants Association of New Jersey, and
Public Citizen—has formed to close the Enron Loophole. They
have even launched a Web site by the same name, www.closeloop-
hole.org. In June 2008, Senator Obama added his voice to those
calling for the close of the loophole and for increased regulation
of oil futures markets.[31]

We should also consider if it makes sense to continue treating
oil as if it were just like any other good traded on the market. Energy traders, even when following the letter of the law, can act to
push oil prices ever higher without any public discussion. How
high oil prices should rise, how to prepare the world's economies
for rising prices, and how to invest the profits are all of critical interest to the public good. They should not remain exclusively in the
realm of private actors seeking only to maximize personal profits.

Prices
Were we to calculate the external costs associated with the exploration, production, transportation, refining, selling, and disposing of oil and oil products, the prices we pay for oil, gasoline,
home-heating fuel, and the like would be far higher than the
prices we are paying today. A common misconception is that the
price of oil and gasoline is too high, when the real problem is
that our alternatives are too minimal. In addition, Big Oil is cap-
turing the profits of rising prices and using its wealth to maintain
a stranglehold over our public decision-making processes. Therefore, taxes should be levied to capture a greater share of the price
of oil and gasoline, while government resources should be shifted
from support of the oil industry to support of meaningful renewable, sustainable, and clean energy alternatives.

Public transit in all forms, all across the country, is the most vital alternative. We have all the ideas and available technology that
we need to create clean, efficient, financially affordable public transit in every corner of the United States and across the world. What

is missing is the financial commitment to put these systems in place. In the 1920s and 1950s, the U.S. government successfully implemented a massive construction effort to build the national highway system. The new roads fueled the nation's obsession with cars, created the suburbs, and sapped money and energy from public transit. Nations around the world are today planning to mimic this effort. Before they do so, wouldn't it be better to offer a different model on the scale and with the same level of commitment as the national highway effort, for a massive investment in clean, affordable, and accessible public transit across the United States?

A corollary to a renewed commitment to public transit is the many plans across the nation and the world for "green cities," which are designed to shorten the distances people must travel for goods and services, increase pedestrian access, and the like.

Ronald Reagan literally took the solar panels off the White House. It is time to put them back on. The United States was able to dramatically reduce energy consumption in the 1970s and early 1980s, until Reagan simply changed the policy course. We can get back on track if we significantly increase fuel efficiency requirements for cars. We must also make enforceable commitments to increase support for and use of solar and wind energy. We must require and subsidize the increased production of electric and hybrid cars, increase meaningful rebates for their purchase, and invest in the infrastructure necessary to support their broad usage. Those who continue to produce and purchase Hummers and other gas-guzzlers must be taxed for their decision to do so.

Consumption

What better way is there to reduce the power of Big Oil than to make its product obsolete? We hold in our power the ability to dramatically reduce the wealth and influence of Big Oil by simply refusing to use its products. Reducing our consumption of oil and gasoline is paramount to strengthening our own democratic voice. In the United States the first order of business is reducing how much we drive. Next would be using resources other than fossil fuels in our vehicles. However, the bottom line must still entail reducing consumption. For example, ethanol is a good idea, but only in moderation. Trying to replace gasoline with ethanol is leading to the clearing of rain forests and the coversion of vast tracts of land from agricultural production for human consumption to biofuel production. Similarly, a global shift away from industrial agriculture which uses energy-intensive crop production for export and toward small-scale, sustainable production of crops for local consumption would address food security issues and reduce consumption of oil and gas. We can help countries like China and India leapfrog the oil stage of development altogether both by leading by example and by providing support (financial and otherwise) for alternative energy solutions. We can also lead by example by committing our nation to meaningful international climate change agreements, including and exceeding the Kyoto Protocol.

Among the countless dedicated groups and people working to break our addiction to oil is Energy Action, a coalition of almost fifty youth groups organized on campuses and in communities across the United States.

Public Control

Many proposals have been made to increase public control over the U.S. oil industry. State-owned refineries have been proposed all across the country. California's assistant attorney general for antitrust, Tom Greene, told me that he supports a strategic reserve of oil held by the state of California.[32] A national oil company to produce the oil on federal land has been proposed. Nationalizing the nation's largest oil companies—taking ownership from the private sector and putting it into the federal government's hands—has also been proposed. Most countries in the world place ownership and control of oil in the hands of the public. Doing so in the United States would simply put us in line with the majority of the people on the planet. All such ideas should be debated and discussed.

Ending Wars for Oil

The previous chapter begins with a quote from former Federal Reserve chairman, deep Washington insider, and longtime ultraconservative Alan Greenspan, drawn from his 2007 memoir, *The Age of Turbulence: Adventures in a New World*. It appears near the end of the 500-plus-page book as the closing to chapter 24, "The Long-Term Energy Squeeze." While Greenspan later backtracked somewhat from his statement that "everyone knows that the Iraq war is largely about oil," it is clear that he wrote those words with sincerity and conviction. Greenspan argues in his book that, as the world is running out of conventional oil, the world and the United States in particular appear ready to go to whatever lengths necessary to acquire what is left. The places that still have oil are "politically volatile regions" where we have already gone to war in the past. According to Greenspan, "U.S. national security will eventually require that we see petroleum as an energy source of choice, not necessity"—though we are not at that point today. Rather, we are at a point where our national foreign policy posture is governed by oil and will be for the near future. Within this context Greenspan finds it quite rational that President Bush would go to war in Iraq for oil, but he calls this an unstable path to follow that puts "industrial economics and hence the global economy" at risk.

Greenspan's words reflect the tenor of the discussions on oil and war that take place routinely—although generally outside of public view—among foreign policy experts for whom it is a given that the United States has engaged in numerous armed conflicts, CIA operations, and wars for oil, and will continue to do so. It is also a given that oil corporations participate in and benefit from these arrangements.

I have described as clearly as possible the relationship between Big Oil and the war in Iraq, as well as a possible war against Iran. As our military spreads out across the globe as an oil-protective force, we, the public, must declare our unwillingness to fight for either oil or oil companies. Our troops should not remain in Iraq, as neither the Iraqis nor the Americans want them there. Our military should not be used as a security force for Big Oil. Those who argue that we need the oil must ask if they are really willing to accept the daily continuation of war against other countries to acquire and maintain it. Nor is there any sort of guarantee that oil securely in the hands of ExxonMobil, Chevron, or Conoco-Phillips in any way ensures increased access to oil for Amercan consumers, lower oil prices, or lower prices for gasoline at the pump. Wars fought for natural resources are not only morally reprehensible, but they are also illegal under international law. Furthermore, they are dangerous, not only harming those directly in their paths, but also precipitating blowback in the form of widespread anger, hatred, and even violence toward the aggressors. Fortunately, groups both small and large organizing for peace abound. They include United for Peace and Justice, Iraq Veterans Against the War, the Institute for Policy Studies, Code Pink, Peace Action, a newly reborn Students for a Democratic Society, and many, many more. By identifying the role of oil and oil corporations in the war in Iraq, the drive for war against Iran, and the military buildup across the world, we can put one more stake into the war machine and help shut it down.

WE NOW FIND OURSELVES in a critical moment of opportunity. We have information that can empower our action. We have organizations, community groups, elected officials, journalists, academics, unions, and people around the world who are inspired to bring change. To disentangle ourselves from the natural resource that has guided global economics, politics, and consumption for a hundred and fifty years is a profound endeavor. To break the lock of the largest corporations on the planet is equally challenging. We must think radically, challenge ourselves in new ways, and believe in our own capacity to stop wars, protect our climate, communities, and workers, and build a more secure, sustainable, and peaceful future.

Acknowledgments

This book would not have been possible without the superb and meticulous research talents and extreme dedication of Sam Edmondson, whose commitment to finding the truth when surrounded by misdirection and lies is utterly invaluable; the dogged research prowess of Megan Kelek Stevenson; the many people who gave freely of their time and knowledge in extensive personal interviews, including Leila Salazar, Michael Pertschuk, Mayor Gayle McLaughlin, Dr. Henry Clark, Terry Tamminen, Diana Moss, Gene Karpinski, Yusef Robb, Bob Randall, Jim Miller, Timothy Muris, John Felmy, Bob Pitofsky, Dan Berkovitz of the Senate Permanent Subcommittee on Investigations, Ilyse Hogue of MoveOn.org, Seth Bloom of the Senate Judiciary Committee's Subcommittee on Antitrust, Michael Spiegel, Herman Schwartz, Michael Greenberger, Assistant Attorney General Tom Greene, Richard Charter, and Michael Tecklenburg of Congresswoman Nancy Pelosi's office; Meredith Dearborn's legal research; Tyson Slocum, director of Public Citizen's Energy Program, whose research, testimony, and one-on-one conversations were invaluable to me, particularly for chapters 4 and 5; Judy Dugan, research director of Consumer Watchdog, who provided both research information and editorial assistance; the expertise and writing of Greg Muttitt, codirector of Platform; the tireless efforts of EarthRights International; the invaluable information and support provided by my colleagues at Oil Change International—Steve Kretzmann, Trina Zahller, Nadine Bloch, Samantha Miller, Kenny Bruno, and Andy Rowell—and at the Institute for Policy Studies—Emira Woods, Erik Leaver, John Cavanagh, Sara Anderson; and particularly Phyllis Bennis, whose tireless commitment to both knowledge and justice is awe-inspiring and utterly invaluable; Diana Finch for being an editor, a researcher, a motivator, a friend, and a great agent; the absolutely fabulous and supportive team at HarperCollins—Cal Morgan, Brittany Hamblin, Sarah Burningham, Michael Barrs; and Anna Bliss for her incredible editing.

Among the many books and authors of particular importance to this book are Dilip Hiro and every book he has ever written, Anthony Sampson's *The Seven Sisters*, Sonia Shah's *Crude: the Story of Oil*, Linda McQuaig's *It's the Crude, Dude*, and Kevin Phillips's *American Theocracy*.

I am indebted to the incredible efforts of activists all across the world, including but far from limited to Medea Benjamin and everyone with Code Pink, Colonel Ann Wright (Ret.), David and Rebecca Solnit, all the members and allies of Iraq Veterans Against the War, Leslie Cagan and the entire team with United for Peace and Justice, the incredible inspiration provided to me by everyone associated with the Nobel Women's Initiative, Bay Rising Affinity Group, and Direct Action to Stop the War; all of my friends at Global Exchange and Rainforest Action Network; my entire family, all of whom pitched in and helped in one way or another; and Nan Neak and all of my friends at Church Street Café, who gave me a home away from home at which to write.

And finally, a special word of tribute to Ida Tarbell, whose actions and words inspired this book.

Notes

Chapter 1: Big Oil's Last Stand

1. Sheila McNulty, "Big Oil Drills for Vote of Approval," *Financial Times,* July 25, 2007.
2. See John Edwards: "Edwards Delivers Major Speech on Lifting Up America's Middle Class," Ames, Iowa, December, 16, 2007; "Remarks as Prepared for Delivery: 'To Build One America, End the Game,'" Hanover, New Hampshire, August 23, 2007; "Address by Senator John Edwards on Restoring Our Democracy," Keene, New Hampshire, October 13, 2007; http://www.johnedwards.com.
3. Eric Pooley, "John Edwards Fires Up His Populism," *Time,* July 19, 2007.
4. William Jennings Bryan, *The First Battle: A Story of the Campaign of 1896* (Hammond, IN: W. B. Conkey, 1898), 294.
5. Daniel Yergin, *The Prize: The Epic Quest for Oil, Money, and Power* (New York: Simon & Schuster, 1991), 46, 51, 53, 95.
6. Jonathan B. Baker, "A Preface to Post-Chicago Antitrust," Social Science Research Network, June 2001; http://papers.ssrn.com.
7. Richard Blumenthal, Connecticut attorney general, Testimony before the Antitrust Task Force of the House Committee on the Judiciary, May 16, 2007.
8. Schwartz, Nelson, "The Biggest Company in America Is Also a Big Target," *Fortune,* April 13, 2006.
9. J. S. Simon, senior vice president, ExxonMobil, "Testimony before U.S. House Committee on Energy Independence and Global Warming," April 3, 2008.
10. Paul R. Lally, Andrew W. Hodge, and Robert J. Corea, "Returns for Domestic Nonfinancial Business," U.S. Bureau of Economic Analysis, May 2008.
11. Marianne Lavelle, "Exxon's Profits: Measuring a Record Windfall," *U.S. News & World Report,* February 1, 2008.

12. Rachel Bronson, *Thicker Than Oil: America's Uneasy Partnership with Saudi Arabia* (Oxford: Oxford University Press, 2006), 19.

13. Amanda Griscom, "Pumped Up: Chevron Drills Down 30,000 Feet to Tap Oil-Rich Gulf of Mexico," *Wired Magazine*, August 21, 2007.

14. Louise Durham, "Saudi Arabia's Ghawar Field," American Association of Petroleum Geologists, January 2005. http://www.aapg.org/explorer/2005/01jan/ghawar.cfm.

15. Richard Heinberg, *The Party's Over: Oil, War and the Fate of Industrial Societies* (Gabriola Island, BC: New Society Publishers, 2003), 95.

16. Sonia Shah, *Crude: The Story of Oil* (New York: Seven Stories Press, 2006), 133.

17. "Worldwide Look at Reserves and Production," *Oil & Gas Journal* 104, no. 47 (2006): 24–25.

18. Ian Rutledge, *Addicted to Oil: America's Relentless Drive for Energy Security* (New York: I. B. Tauris, 2006), 102.

19. "NOAA: 2007 a Top Ten Warm Year for U.S. and Globe," National Oceanic and Atmospheric Administration, December 13, 2007, http://www.noaanews.noaa.gov.

20. "Climate Change 101; Understanding and Responding to Global Climate Change," Pew Center on Global Climate Change and Pew Center on the States, October 2006.

21. Ibid.

22. U.S. Census Bureau, U.S. Department of Energy, Energy Information Administration, "World Oil Balance Chart 2003–2007," http://www.eia.doe.gov.

23. U.S. Department of Energy, Energy Information Administration, "Top World Oil Consumers, 2006 Table," http://www.eia.doe.gov.

24. Shah, *Crude: The Story of Oil*, 133.

25. Dilip Hiro, *Blood of the Earth: The Battle for the World's Vanishing Oil Resources* (New York: Nation Books, 2007), 56.

Chapter 2: The Birth and Breakup of Standard Oil

1. Grover Cleveland, Fourth Annual State of the Union Address, December 3, 1888.

2. Jules Abels, *The Rockefeller Billions* (New York: Macmillan, 1965), 1.

3. Gallup Polls, "Big Business," February 28–March 1, 2006, and "Business and Industry Sector Ratings," August 13–16, 2007, http://www.Gallup.com.

4. Henry Demarest Lloyd, *Wealth Against Commonwealth* (1894; repr., Englewood Cliffs, NJ: Prentice-Hall, 1963), 151.

5. Ida M. Tarbell, *The History of the Standard Oil Company, Briefer Version*, ed. David M. Chalmers (New York: Dover Publications, 1966), xxiii.

6. Ibid., 155.

7. Howard Zinn, *A People's History of the United States: 1492–Present* (New York: HarperCollins, 2003), 339.

8.   Daniel Yergin, *The Prize: The Epic Quest for Oil, Money, and Power* (New York: Simon & Schuster, 1991), 105.

9.   Ibid., 36.

10.   Ohio History Central, Social Darwinism, http://www.ohiohistory-central.org/entry.php?rec=1528.

11.   Ida Tarbell, *All in a Day's Work: An Autobiography* (1939; repr., Champagne: University of Illinois Press, 2003), 82.

12.   David Olive, *The Quotable Tycoon* (Naperville, IL: Sourcebooks, 2004), 115.

13.   Tarbell, *All in a Day's Work*, 8.

14.   Tarbell, *History of the Standard Oil Company*, 21.

15   Ron Chernow, *Titan: The Life of John D. Rockefeller, Sr.* (New York: Vintage Books, 1998), 6.

16.   Ibid., 17.

17.   Yergin, *The Prize*, 30–36.

18.   Anthony Sampson, *The Seven Sisters: The Great Oil Companies and the World They Made* (New York: Coronet Books, 1975), 43.

19.   Tarbell, *History of the Standard Oil Company*, 33.

20.   Lloyd, *Wealth Against Commonwealth*, 20.

21.   Tarbell, *History of the Standard Oil Company*, 37.

22.   Tarbell, *All in a Day's Work*, 24.

23.   Ibid., 84.

24.   Tarbell, *History of the Standard Oil Company*, 41.

25.   Yergin, *The Prize*, 95.

26.   Ibid., 42.

27.   Tarbill, *History of the Standard Oil Company*, 93.

28.   Ibid., 163.

29.   "The Rockefellers," PBS, *The American Experience*, http://www.pbs .org/wgbh/amex/rockefellers/timeline/index.html.

30.   Yergin, *The Prize*, 45.

31.   Allan Nevins and Henry Steel Commager, *A Pocket History of the United States*, 9th rev. ed. (New York: Pocket Books, 1992), 270.

32.   Ibid.

33.   Linda McQuaig, *It's the Crude, Dude: Greed, Gas, War, and the American Way* (New York: St. Martin's Press, 2006), 209.

34.   Kevin Phillips, *Wealth and Democracy: A Political History of the American Rich* (New York: Broadway Books, 2002), 23.

35.   Nevins and Commager, *Pocket History of the United States*, 348.

36.   Lloyd, *Wealth Against Commonwealth*, 71.

37.   Ibid., 132.

38.   Tarbell, *History of the Standard Oil Company*, 144.

39.   Sampson, *Seven Sisters*, 43.

40.   Yergin, *The Prize*, 104.

41.   Chernow, *Titan*, 548.

42.   Lloyd, *Wealth Against Commonwealth*, 13.

43.   Ibid., 131.

44.   Tarbell, *History of the Standard Oil Company*, 146.

45. Zinn, *People's History the United States*, 286.
46. William Letwin, *Law and Economic Policy in America: The Evolution of the Sherman Antitrust Act* (Chicago: University of Chicago Press, 1965), 85.
47. Ibid., 85–87.
48. Zinn, *People's History of the United States*, 286.
49. Ibid., 288.
50. Roger E. Meiners, Al H. Ringleb, and Frances L. Edwards, *The Legal Environment of Business,* 4th ed. (St. Paul, MN: West Publishing, 1991), 423.
51. Charles Mueller, "The Latest Antimonoply 'Swindle,'" December 23, 1997, http://legalminds.lp.findlaw.com/list/antitrust/msg00774.html.
52. Chernow, *Titan*, 298.
53. Thomas J. DiLorenzo, "The Ghost of John D. Rockefeller," *The Freeman*, June 1998.
54. George F. Hoar, *Autobiography of Seventy Years*, vol. 1 (New York: Charles Scribner's Sons, 1903), http://www.gutenberg.org/files/19548/19548.txt.
55. http://www.amc.gov/public_studies_fr28902/remedies_pdf/AAI_Remedies.pdf.
56. Jonathan B. Baker, "A Preface to Post-Chicago Antitrust," Social Science Research Network, April 29, 2002, http://papers.ssrn.com.
57. William Jennings Bryan, *The First Battle: A Story of the Campaign of 1896* (Hammond, IN: W. B. Conkey, 1898), 523.
58. Bill Meyers, "Money and Politics," *Justice Rising,* Spring 2005.
59. Chernow, *Titan,* 388.
60. William Jennings Bryan, "The Trust Question" (speech at Lincoln, Nebraska, July 21, 1908).
61. Zinn, *People's History of the United States*, 306.
62. Ibid., 299.
63. Ibid., 301.
64. Tarbell, *All in a Day's Work*, 195.
65. Zinn, *People's History of the United States*, 313.
66. George Hoar, "The Lust for Empire," Record, 55 Congress, 3 Session, 493–503.
67. Zinn, *People's History of the United States*, 310.
68. Yergin, *The Prize*, 98, 100.
69. Ibid., 105.
70. Letwin, *Law and Economic Policy in America*, 199.
71. Chernow, *Titan*, 434.
72. Yergin, *The Prize*, 108.
73. James S. Hogg, Texas State Library & Archives Commission, http://www.tsl.state.tx.us/governors/rising/hogg-p01.html.
74. James S. Hogg, Texas State Historical Association, TSHA Online, http://www.TSHAonline.org/hardbook/online/articles/HH/fhol7.html.
75. Robert C. Cotner, "Hogg, James Stephen," Handbook of Texas

Online, Texas State Historical Association Online, http://www.tsha online.org.

76. Yergin, *The Prize*, 89.

77. Kenny Bruno and Jim Valette. "Cheney and Halliburton: Go Where the Oil Is," *Multinational Monitor,* May 2001, http://www.thirdworld traveler.com/Oil_watch/Cheney_Halliburton.html.

78. Tarbell, *All in a Day's Work*, 244–45.

79. Meiners, Ringleb, and Edwards, *Legal Environment of Business,* 431.

80. Yergin, *The Prize*, 109.

81. Chernow, *Titan,* 525.

Chapter 3: Big Oil Bounces Back

1. Anthony Sampson, *The Seven Sisters: The Great Oil Companies and the World They Made* (New York: Coronet Books, 1975), 103.

2. John D. Rockefeller IV and Olympia Snowe, "The 'Obfuscation Agenda': The Letter to ExxonMobil," *Wall Street Journal,* December 6, 2006.

3. Phone interview with the author, August 11, 2007.

4. Ron Chernow, *Titan: The Life of John D. Rockefeller, Sr.* (New York: Vintage Books, 1998), 557.

5. Daniel Yergin, *The Prize: The Epic Quest for Oil, Money and Power* (New York: Simon & Schuster, 1992), 110.

6. Chernow, *Titan,* 557.

7. Kevin Phillips, *Wealth and Democracy: A Political History of the American Rich* (New York: Broadway Books, 2002), 50.

8. Myrna Santiago, "Rejecting Progress in Paradise: Huastecs, the Envi- ronment, and the Oil Industry in Veracruz, Mexico, 1900–1935," *Environmental History,* April 1998.

9. Ibid. See also Toyin Falola and Ann Genova, *The Politics of the Global Oil Industry: An Introduction* (Westport, CT: Praeger, 2005), 125.

10. Santiago, "Rejecting Progress in Paradise."

11. Ibid.

12. Russ Banham, *Conoco: 125 Years of Energy* (Old Saybrook, CT: Greenwich Publishing Group, 2000), 22.

13. Ibid., 22, 34.

14. Garrick Bailey, "Review of the Underground Reservation," *American Indian Quarterly* 10, no. 3 (1986): 251–52.

15. "Osage Indian Murders FBI Files," http://www.paperlessarchives.com/osage.html.

16. Michael Wallis, *The Real Wild West: The 1010 Ranch and the Creation of the American West* (New York: St. Martin's Press, 1999), 330.

17. Ibid., 330.

18. Banham, *Conoco,* 29.

19. Arco—Chronological History, http://www.arco-ampm.com/history .htm.

20. Yergin, *The Prize*, 82.

21. Ibid., 91–92.

22. Ibid., 90.

23. Ibid., 93.

24. Sampson, *Seven Sisters*, 209.

25. Linda McQuaig, *It's the Crude, Dude: Greed, Gas, War, and the American Way* (New York: St. Martin's Press, 2006), 215.

26. Woodrow Wilson, *The New Freedom* (New York and Garden City: Doubleday, Page, 1913) (Project Gutenberg EBook 14811).

27. William Letwin, *Law and Economic Policy in America: The Evolution of the Sherman Antitrust Act* (Chicago: University of Chicago Press, 1965), 275.

28. Roger E. Meiners, Al H. Ringleb, and Frances L. Edwards, *The Legal Environment of Business*, 4th ed. (St. Paul, MN: West Publishing, 1991), 424.

29. "Annual Report of the Federal Trade Commission for the Fiscal Year Ended June 30, 1922" (Washington, DC: Government Printing Office, 1922), 48.

30. "Annual Report of the Federal Trade Commission for the Fiscal Year Ended June 30, 1917" (Washington, DC: Government Printing Office, 1917), 32.

31. Jonathan W. Cuneo, director, American Antitrust Institute, Testimony before the U.S. Senate Committee on Energy and Natural Resources, January 28, 1999.

32. Sampson, *Seven Sisters*, 72.

33. U.S. State Department, "The 1928 Red Line Agreement," http://www.state.gov/r/pa/ho/time/id/88104.htm.

34. Sampson, *Seven Sisters*, 88.

35. Dilip Hiro, *Blood of the Earth: The Battle for the World's Vanishing Oil Resources* (New York: Nation Books, 2007), 26.

36. Ian Rutledge, *Addicted to Oil: America's Relentless Drive for Energy Security* (New York: I. B. Tauris, 2005), 40.

37. Louise Overacker, "Campaign Funds in the Presidential Election of 1936," *American Political Science Review* 31, no. 3 (1937): 473–98.

38. Sampson, *Seven Sisters*, 110–12.

39. Ibid., 121.

40. Rachel Bronson, *Thicker Than Oil: America's Uneasy Partnership with Saudi Arabia* (New York: Oxford University Press, 2006), 116.

41. Sampson, *Seven Sisters*, 137.

42. Ibid., 139.

43. Ibid., 139.

44. Ibid., 137–43.

45. Shirin Ebadi, *Iran Awakening: One Woman's Journey to Reclaim Her Life and Country* (New York: Random House, 2007), 5.

46. Bronson, *Thicker Than Oil*, 124.

47. Hiro, *Blood of the Earth*, 54.

48. Sampson, *Seven Sisters*, 198.

49. Philip Dougherty, "Esso to Be Exxon," *New York Times*, May 10, 1972.

50. Complaint for Equitable Relief Damages, in the *United States District Court for the District of Columbia, John Doe I, et al. vs. ExxonMobil Corporate, et al.*, filed June 11, 2001.

51. Ibid.

52. John Aglionby, "U.S. Court Orders Exxon to Answer Aceh Suit," *Financial Times,* January 18, 2007.

53. Ibid.

54. Ibid.

55. Neela Banerjee, "Lawsuit Says Exxon Aided Rights Abuses," *New York Times,* June 21, 2001.

56. See Ike Okonta and Oronto Douglas, *Where Vultures Feast: Shell, Human Rights and Oil* (London: Verso, 2003).

57. Ibid., 131.

58. Ibid., 135.

59. Ibid., 134–35.

60. "The Price of Oil: Corporate Responsibility and Human Rights Violations in Nigeria's Oil Producing Communities," *Human Rights Watch,* January 1999.

61 Earth Rights International, "Bowoto v. Chevron Texaco," September 2, 2008.

62. Ibid.

63. Rick Jurgens, "Chevron Scrutinized for Role in Nigeria," *Contra Costa Times,* May 18, 2003.

64. Rick Herz and Marco Simons, "Bowoto v. ChevronTexaco Case Overview," EarthRights International, October 22, 2007.

65. McQuaig, *It's the Crude, Dude,* 242; Frank Church, "The Impotence of Oil Companies," *Foreign Policy,* Summer 1977, 27–51.

66. Sampson, *Seven Sisters,* 178.

67. Yergin, *The Prize,* 596.

68. Michael C. Jensen, "Attacks on Oil Industry Grow Fiercer," *New York Times,* February 3, 1973.

69. Bronson, *Thicker than Oil,* 124.

70. Kevin Philips, *American Theocracy: The Peril and Politics of Radical Religion, Oil, and Borrowed Money in the 21st Century* (New York: Penguin, 2006), 40.

71. Sampson, *Seven Sisters,* 289, 309.

72. Yergin, *The Prize,* 718.

73. William Robbins, "Oil Profits Up 46% on 6% Volume Rise," *New York Times,* January 22, 1973.

74. Phone interview with the author, July 10, 2007.

75. Ralph Nader, "Breaking the Energy Monopolies," February 24, 1974, http://www.nader.org/template.php?/archives/898-Breaking-the-Energy-Monopolies.html.

76. "Assailing the Giants," *Time,* November 3, 1975.

77. Sampson, *Seven Sisters,* 285.

78. Robert Sherrill, "Breaking Up Big Oil," *New York Times,* October 3, 1976.

79. Irvin Molotsky, "It Sometimes Seems Like the Federal Tirade Commission," *New York Times,* June 3, 1984.

80. Carole Shifrin, "FTC Asks for Authority to Stop Conglomerates," *Washington Post,* July 28, 1978.

81. Edward Cowan, "Attorneys Quit F.T.C. Oil Case," *New York Times,* June 26, 1978.

82. Interview at the San Francisco office of Michael Spiegel with the author, June 11, 2007.

83. Rhys Jerkins, *Transnational Corporations and Uneven Development* (London: Routledge, 1988), 53.

84. Hiro, *Blood of the Earth,* 45.

85. Winston Williams, "Big Oil Starts Thinking Smaller," *New York Times,* March 17, 1985.

86. Yergin, *The Prize,* 685; Joel Jacobson, "Government and the Oil Industry: The Myth and the Reality," *New York Times,* January 11, 1981.

87. Hobart Rowen, "A Tidal Wave of Big Oil Takeovers," *Washington Post,* March 15, 1984.

88. Steven Greenhouse, "An Unsettling Shift in Big Oil," *New York Times,* March 11, 1984.

89. Marc Allen Eisner, *Antitrust and the Triumph of Economics: Institutions, Expertise, and Policy Change* (Chapel Hill: University of North Carolina Press, 1991), 214.

90. Irvin Molotsky, "At the FTC, the Trade in Mud Is Brisk," *New York Times,* August 29, 1984.

91. Phone interview with the author, July 6, 2007.

92. Daniel Yergin and Joseph Stanislaw, *Commanding Heights: The Battle for the World Economy* (New York: Simon & Schuster, 1998), 342.

93. Eisner, *Antitrust and the Triumph of Economics,* 212.

94. Phone interview with the author, August 1, 2007.

95. Eisner, *Antitrust and the Triumph of Economics,* 215.

96. Leonard Silk, "Economic Scene; A Free Lunch? Yes, Indeed," *New York Times,* October 30, 1981.

97. Eisner, *Antitrust and the Triumph of Economics,* 214.

98. John Yemma, "Weighing the Impact of Recent Company Mergers on US Economy," *Christian Science Monitor,* May 1, 1984.

99. Phone interview with the author, July 6, 2007.

100. Thomas J. Lueck, "Oil Industry's Push to Merge," *New York Times,* February 9, 1984.

101. Winston Williams, "Frenzy and Style in the Merger Boom," *New York Times,* January 15, 1984.

102. Steven Greenhouse, "An Unsettling Shift in Big Oil," *New York Times,* March 11, 1984.

103. William Hall, "Marshalling Reserves to Plug an Oil Drain," *Financial Times,* January 10, 1984.

104. Stephen Koepp, "History's Biggest Takeover?" *Time,* January 16, 1984.

105. Ibid.

106. Michael Isikoff and Mark Potts, "Texaco Acquires Getty in Largest Corporate Merger," *Washington Post,* February 14, 1984.

107. William Hall, "Way Clear for Chevron to Justify Gulf Deal," *Financial Times,* June 19, 1985.

108. Robert D. Hershey Jr., "Congress Studies the Urge to Merge," *New York Times,* March 18, 1984.

109. "Senator Johnston's Prescription for Merger Fever: An Interview," *Washington Post,* March 11, 1984.

110. Ibid.

111. Susan Fraker, "Brawl in the Family at Superior Oil," *Fortune,* May 30, 1983.

112. Ibid.

113. Nathaniel Nash, "Now Mobil Enters the Merger Game," *New York Times,* March 18, 1984.

114. Fraker, "Brawl in the Family at Superior Oil."

115. Ibid.

116. Edwin Chen, "It All Began with a 'Friendly' Lawsuit," *Los Angeles Times,* March 12, 1989.

117. Phone interview with the author, August 11, 2007.

118. Federal Trade Commission, Bureau of Economics, "The Petroleum Industry: Mergers, Structural Change, and Antitrust Enforcement," August 2004, 38.

119. Timothy J. Muris, et al., Counsel for ExxonMobil Corporation, "ExxonMobil Corporation's Request for Review of Denial of Petition to Limit Civil Investigative Demand." United States of America Before Federal Trade Commission, Received by Federal Trade Commission Secretary, January 18, 2006, File No. 051-0243.

120. John Micklethwait and Adrian Wooldridge, *The Right Nation: Conservative Power in America* (New York: Penguin, 2004), 71.

121. Robert E. Litan and Carl Shapiro, "Antitrust Policy During the Clinton Administration," July 2001, Paper for "American Economy Policy in the 1990s," Harvard University, June 27–30, 2001.

122. Ibid.

123. Jonathan B. Baker and Carl Shapiro, "Reinvigorating Horizontal Merger Enforcement," Paper prepared for the Conference on Conservative Economic Influence on U.S. Antitrust Policy, Georgetown University Law School, April 10, 2007.

124. James Love, Center for Study of Responsive Law, "Antitrust Considerations and the Petroleum Industry," Statement before the House Committee on the Judiciary, March 29, 2000.

125. Richard Blumenthal, Connecticut attorney general, Testimony before the Antitrust Task Force of the House Committee on the Judiciary, May 16, 2007.

126. Jeffrey Garten, "Mega-Mergers, Mega-Influence," *New York Times,* October 26, 1999.

127. Albert A. Foer, president, American Antitrust Institute, letter to the Honorable Robert Pitofsky, chairman, Federal Trade Commission, April 2, 1999.

128. Andrew Ross Sorkin and Neela Banerjee, "Chevron Agrees to Buy Texaco for Stock Valued at $36 Billion," *New York Times,* October 16, 2000.

129. Neela Banerjee, "An Oil Merger That Assumes that Bigger Is Not Just Better, It's Necessary," *New York Times,* October 16, 2000.

130. Nancy Brooks and James Peltz, "Critics Line Up Against Chevron-Texaco Merger," *Los Angeles Times,* October 17, 2000.

131. Neela Banerjee and Andrew Sorkin, "Phillips and Conoco to form U.S. Gasoline Giant," *New York Times,* November 19, 2001.

132. Dennis K. Berman, "The Game: Handicapping Deal Hype and Hubris," *Wall Street Journal,* January 16, 2007.

Chapter 4: Driving the Price of Crude

1. Steve Hargreaves, "Investors: Don't Blame Us for High Oil Prices," CNNMoney.com, February 12, 2008.

2. Alla McMullen, "Gas, Oil Prices to Double by 2012, CIBC Economist Predicts," *Financial Post,* April 24, 2008.

3. "Oil Drops as Iraq Supply Fears Ebb," Associated Press, March 28, 2008.

4. Adam Davidson, "Is the Weak Dollar to Blame for High Oil Prices?" National Public Radio, *All Things Considered,* April 29, 2008.

5. C. Fred Bergsten, "A Call for an 'Asian Plaza,'" *International Economy,* Spring 2008.

6. Kathleen Pender, "Experts Disagree on Why Oil Prices Go Up," *San Francisco Chronicle,* August 28, 2005.

7. Bhusan Bahree and Ann Davis, "Oil Settles Above $70 a Barrel, Despite Inventories at 8-Year High," *Wall Street Journal,* April 18, 2006.

8. Carl Levin, chairman, Permanent Subcommittee on Investigations, Statement before a Joint Hearing with the Subcommittee on Energy on Speculation in the Crude Oil Market, December 11, 2007.

9. "The Role of Market Speculation in Rising Oil and Gas Prices: A Need to Put the Cop Back on the Beat," Staff Report, Permanent Subcommittee on Investigations, U.S. Senate, June 27, 2006.

10. Fadel Gheit, senior energy analyst, Oppenheimer & Company, Statement before a Joint Hearing with the Subcommittee on Energy on Speculation in the Crude Oil Market, December 11, 2007.

11. Katherine Reynolds Lewis, "Tricks of the Trade," *Star-Ledger,* May 7, 2006.

12. Roberta Romano, "The Political Dynamics of Derivative Securities Regulation," *Yale Journal* on *Regulation* 14, no. 2 (1997): 292.

13. "How the Exchange Works," NYMEX.com.

14. Lewis, "Tricks of the Trade."

15. Ann Davis, "Where Has All the Oil Gone?" *Wall Street Journal,* October 6, 2007.

16. Thomas Lippman and Mark Potts, "Oil Traders: Turning on a Dime," *Washington Post,* January 11, 1991.

17. Report of the Senate Committee on Agriculture, Nutrition, and For-

estry, to accompany S. 2019, Futures Trading Act of 1982, S. Rept. 97-384, 97th Cong., 2nd Sess. 11 (1982).

18. Dan Morgan, *Merchants of Grain* (New York: Viking Press, 1979), 57.

19. "Two Potato Futures Traders Suspended and Fined in Default," *New York Times*, March 9, 1978.

20. H. J. Maidenberg, "The Peeling of the Potato Speculators," *New York Times*, May 30, 1976.

21. Michel Marks, "Crude Oil Futures: A Form of Pricing that Went to the Soul of the Industry," NYMEX, News [no date listed] http://www .nymex.com/energy_in_news.aspx?id=eincrudeprice.

22. Daniel Yergin, *The Prize: The Epic Quest for Oil, Money, and Power* (New York: Simon & Schuster, 1991), 725.

23. Ibid.

24. Adrian Binks, "Clash Between Titans Nears," *Financial Times*, March 2, 1984.

25. Stuart Diamond, "Setting Crude Prices in the Pits," *New York Times*, December 9, 1984.

26. Binks, "Clash Between Titans Nears."

27. Jeff Fleming and Barbara Ostdiek, "The Impact of Energy Derivatives on the Crude Oil Market," *Energy Economics* 21, no. 2 (1999).

28. Yergin, *The Prize*, 725.

29. "Commodity Boom Puts Temptation in Traders' Way," *Financial Times*, September 19, 2006.

30. Representatives of BP North America, Koch Industries, Coastal Corporation, Mobil, Conoco, Phibro Energy, Enron, Phillips, and J. Aron, letter to Ms. Jean A. Webb, secretary, Commodity Futures Trading Commission, re: "Application for Exemptive Relief in Connection with Contracts for the Purchase and Sale of Physical Commodities," November 16, 1992. Pdf copy of letter provided to the author by the CFTC.

31. David Ivanovich, "Wyatt Enters Pleas in Oil Trial," *Houston Chronicle*, October 2, 2007.

32. Tyson Slocum, "Gasoline Prices, Oil Company Profits, and the American Consumer," Testimony before the U.S. House Committee on Energy and Commerce, Subcommittee on Oversight and Investigations, May 22, 2007.

33. Pdf copies of the letters were provided to the author upon request by the CFTC.

34. "U.S. Strategic Petroleum Reserve: Recent Policy Has Increased Costs to Consumers but Not Overall U.S. Energy Security," Report prepared by the Minority Staff of the Permanent Subcommittee on Investigations of the Committee on Governmental Affairs, U.S. Senate, March 5, 2003.

35. Slocum, "Gasoline Prices, Oil Company Profits."

36. "Budget Office 'Czar' Named," *Los Angeles Times*, October 9, 1985.

37. Center for Responsive Politics online database, http://www.opensecrets .org.

38. Robert Manor, "Gramms Regulated Enron, Benefited from Ties," *Chicago Tribune*, January 18, 2002.

39. Slocum, "Gasoline Prices, Oil Company Profits."

40. Transcript of testimony before the Hearing on Reauthorization of the Commodity Futures Trading Commission, Agriculture Committee, Subcommittee on Risk Management, Research, and Specialty Crops, U.S. House of Representatives, May 20, 1999.

41. Slocum, "Gasoline Prices, Oil Company Profits."

42. "Excessive Speculation in the Natural Gas Market," Staff Report, Permanent Subcommittee on Investigations, U.S. Senate, June 25 and July 9, 2007, 119.

43. Bethany McLean and Peter Elkind, *The Smartest Guys in the Room: The Amazing Rise and Scandalous Fall of Enron* (New York: Penguin, 2003), 275.

44. McLean and Elkind, *Smartest Guys in the Room*, 283.

45. Robert McCollough, Testimony before the Senate Democratic Policy Committee, "Lessons from Enron: An Oversight Hearing on Gas Prices and Energy Trading," May 8, 2006.

46. Michael Greenberger, Testimony before the Senate Democratic Policy Committee, "Lessons from Enron: An Oversight Hearing on Gas Prices and Energy Trading," May 8, 2006.

47. McLean and Elkind, *Smartest Guys in the Room*, 272.

48. Greenberger, "Lessons from Enron."

49. Charles Lewis, *The Buying of the President 2004: Who's Really Bankrolling Bush and His Democratic Challengers—and What They Expect in Return* (New York: HarperCollins, 2004), 11.

50. Senator Byron Dorgan, Opening remarks before the Senate Democratic Policy Committee, "Lessons from Enron: An Oversight Hearing on Gas Prices and Energy Trading," May 8, 2006.

51. David Lazarus, "Vocal Citizens Berate PUC," *San Francisco Chronicle*, April 4, 2001.

52. Dana Hull, "First of 'Outrageous' Power Bills Hits Bay Area," *San Jose Mercury News*, January 24, 2001.

53. Lazarus, "Vocal Citizens Berate PUC."

54. Charles Krauthammer, "Gas and Fog," *Washington Post*, February 16, 2001.

55. Bill Day and Elizabeth Allen, "It's Riches to Rags for Enron's Retirees," *San Antonio Express-News*, December 23, 2001.

56. Phone interview the author, October 30, 2007.

57. Terry Pristin, "Houston Tries to Banish Enron's Ghosts," *New York Times*, March 3, 2004.

58. Alexei Barrionuevo, "Energy Trading, Post-Enron," *New York Times*, January 15, 2006.

59. Saijel Kishan, "Commodity Traders Drive Hiring Amid Credit Shakeout," Bloomberg.com, October 17, 2007.

60. Ann Davis, "The New Rushmore: Commodities," *Wall Street Journal*, October 30, 2007.

61. Jed Horowitz, "Moving the Market—Tracking the Numbers," *Wall Street Journal,* June 3, 2004.

62. Michael R. Sesit, Jo Wrighton, and Peter A. McKay, "Global Banks Rush to Profit from Oil Boom," *Wall Street Journal,* August 26, 2004.

63. Author's analysis of NYMEX data provided at www.NYMEX.com.

64. "Role of Market Speculation," 17.

65. Author's analysis of ICE data provided at www.TheIce.com.

66. Slocum, "Gasoline Prices, Oil Company Profits."

67. "Role of Market Speculation," 40.

68. "Ice Reports October Volume and OTC Commission," ICE press release, Atlanta, November 2, 2007.

69. Lewis, "Tricks of the Trade."

70. "Oil: A Bubble, Not a Spike?" *BusinessWeek online,* April 27, 2005.

71. Bahree and Davis, "Oil Settles Above $70 a Barrel."

72. "Behind Runaway Prices: Supply Issues Are Real, but Hype Sets Bar," *Natural Gas Week,* September 5, 2005.

73. Davis, "Where Has All the Oil Gone?"

74. "Role of Market Speculation," 2.

75. Allan Chernoff, "Rush of Investors to Oil Costly for All," *CNN Money Magazine,* March 4, 2008.

76. Statement of Fadel Gheit, senior energy analyst, Oppenheimer & Company, Statement before a Joint Hearing with the Subcommittee on Energy on Speculation in the Crude Oil Market, December 11, 2007.

77. Peter C. Fusaro, "Energy Trading and Risk Management 2.0," Global Change Associates, UtiliPoint Issue Alert, June 11, 2007.

78. Levin, "Statement before a Joint Hearing."

79. U.S. Commodity Futures Trading Commission, "The Economic Purpose of Futures Markets and How They Work," http://www.cftc.gov/educationcenter/economicpurpose.html.

80. Slocum, "Gasoline Prices, Oil Company Profits."

81. Ann Davis and Russell Gold, "Marathon Pays Up in 'Platts Window' Case," *Globe and Mail,* August 2, 2007.

82. U.S. Commodity Futures Trading Commission, "Former BP Trader Paul Kelly Agrees to Pay $400,000 Civil Penalty," Release: 5402–07, October 25, 2007.

83. U.S. Commodity Futures Trading Commission, "BP Agrees to Pay a Total of $303 Million in Sanctions," Release: 5405–07, October 25, 2007.

84. Peter C. Fusaro and Gary M. Vasey, "Hedge Funds Change Energy Trading," International Research Center for Energy and Economic Development Occasional Papers No. 39, August 20, 2005.

85. Thomas R. Dye, *Who's Running America? The Bush Restoration,* 7th ed. (Englewood Cliffs, NJ: Prentice Hall, 2002), 144.

86. Ann Davis, "Morgan Stanley Trades Energy in Barrels," *Wall Street Journal,* March 3, 2005.

87. Davis, "The New Rushmore."

88. Jad Mouawad and Heather Timmons, "Trading Frenzy Adding to Rise in Price of Oil," *New York Times,* April 29, 2006.

89.   Kishan, "Commodity Traders Drive Hiring."
90.   Ann Davis, "Trader Hits Jackpot in Oil," *Wall Street Journal*, February 28, 2008.
91.   Kishan, "Commodity Traders Drive Hiring."
92.   Slocum, "Gasoline Prices, Oil Company Profits."
93.   Jeanine Prezioso, "Lehman Deal Reflects Interest in Physical Energy Markets," *Dow Jones MarketWatch*, May 9, 2007.
94.   Davis, "Morgan Stanley Trades Energy in Barrels."
95.   Ibid.
96.   Davis, "Morgan Stanley Trades Energy in Barrels."
97.   Fusaro, "Energy Trading and Risk Management 2.0."
98.   Peter C. Fusaro and Dr. Gary M. Vasey, "Today's Energy and Environmental Hedge Funds," *Commodities Now*, September 29, 2005, 1–3; and Peter C. Fusaro, "Green Hedge Funds: The New Commodity Play," *Commodities Now*, March, 2005.
99.   Fusaro, "Energy Trading and Risk Management 2.0."
100. Rich Blake, A. D. Barber, and Robert LaFranco, "Trader Monthly 100: Top Hedge Fund Traders," *Trader Monthly Magazine*; April/May, 2006.
101. "Brian Hunter: From Hero to Zero in Two Years," "Wall Street's Biggest Losers," MSN.money.com, September 20, 2006; Jenny Anderson, "The Private Lives of Hedge Funds," *New York Times*, December 29, 2006.
102. Carl Levin, chairman, Permanent Subcommittee an Investigations, Opening statement at the Permanent Subcommittee an Investigations Hearing on Amaranth Speculation in Natural Gas Prices, July 10, 2007.
103. Clifford Krauss, "Volatility of the Markets Carries on in 2008," *New York Times*, January 3, 2008.
104. Heather Thomas, "India's Solution for Oil Prices: Ban Speculation by Banning Trading," *New York Times*, November 8, 2007.

Chapter 5: Paying the Price

1.   "Gas Prices: How Are They Really Set?" Hearings before the Permanent Subcommittee on Investigations of the Committee on Governmental Affairs, U.S. Senate, April 30 and May 2, 2002, 624.
2.   Senator Arlen Specter, "Bipartisan Legislation Seeking to Foster Competition and Reduce Oil and Gas Prices Receives Committee Approval," press release, April 27, 2006.
3.   Testimony of Tom Greene, senior assistant attorney general for Antitrust, California Department of Justice, Hearing before the Permanent Subcommittee of Investigations Committee on Government Affairs, U.S. Senate, "Gas Prices: How Are They Really Set?" May 2, 2002.
4.   Richard Blumenthal, Connecticut attorney general, Testimony before the Antitrust Task Force of the House Committee on the Judiciary, May 16, 2007.

5. "Gas Prices" and author's analysis of industry data.
6. Blumenthal, Testimony before the Antitrust Task Force of the House Committee on the Judiciary.
7. "Gas Prices," 428.
8. U.S. Department of Energy, Energy Information Administration, Refinery Tables.
9. Federal Trade Commission, Bureau of Economics, "The Petroleum Industry: Mergers, Structural Change, and Antitrust Enforcement," August 2004, 227.
10. M. Jodi Rell, governor, State of Connecticut, "Governors Across Nation Join Governor Rell to Fight Rising Gas Prices," press release, May 21, 2007.
11. "Gas Prices," 624.
12. Tim Hamilton, "The 'Katrina Syndrome': Low Supplies—High Profits in 2007," Foundation for Taxpayer and Consumer Rights, July 23, 2007.
13. Diana Moss, "Competition in U.S. Petroleum Refining and Marketing: Part I—Industry Trends," American Antitrust Institute, January 2007, 5.
14. U.S. Department of Energy, Energy Information Administration data, "Company Level Imports," http://www.eia.doe.gov.
15. U.S. Department of Energy, Energy Information Administration, "U.S. Crude Oil Stocks," http://www.eia.doe.gov.
16. U.S. Department of Energy, Energy Information Administration, "Finished Motor Gasoline," http://www.eia.doe.gov.
17. "Antitrust Class Action against Oil Companies May Proceed," *Class Action Law Monitor,* May 15, 2007.
18. "Gasoline Cost Suit Green-Lighted," *Los Angeles Times,* March 29, 2007.
19. Rhys Jenkins, *Transnational Corporations and Uneven Development* (London: Routledge, 1988), 53.
20. "Gas Prices," 335.
21. Ibid., 558.
22. Senator Ron Wyden, "Campaign of Inaction: The Federal Trade Commission's Refusal to Protect Consumers from Consolidation, Cutbacks and Manipulation in America's Oil and Gasoline Markets," June 15, 2004, 4.
23. Senator Ron Wyden, "The Oil Industry, Gas Supply and Refinery Capacity: More Than Meets the Eye," June 14, 2001.
24. "Gas Prices," 43, 553.
25. Wyden, "The Oil Industry, Gas Supply and Refinery Capacity."
26. Energy Information Administration, *Performance Profiles of the Major Energy Producers,* 2005, 6; Tyson Slocum, "Oil Mergers, Manipulations and Mirages: How Eroding Legal Protections and Lax Regulatory Oversight Harm Consumers," *Public Citizen,* April 2007.
27. Robert Pirog, "Petroleum Refining: Economic Performance and Challenges for the Future," Congressional Research Service Report for Congress, March 23, 2007.

28.   Slocum, "Oil Mergers, Manipulations and Mirages."
29.   D. J. Peterson and Serej Mahnovski, *New Forces at Work in Refining: Industry Views of Critical Business and Operations Trends* (Santa Monica, CA: RAND Corporation, 2003).
30.   U.S. Department of Energy, Energy Information Administration, Annual Energy Review, 2002.
31.   "Are Refiners Boosting the Pain at the Pump?" *Business Week*, March 19, 2004.
32.   "Gas Prices," 378–79; U.S. Department of Energy, Energy Information Administration data.
33.   General Accounting Office, "Energy Markets: Effects of Mergers and Market Concentration in the U.S. Petroleum Industry," Report to the Ranking Minority Member, Permanent Subcommittee on Investigations, Committee on Governmental Affairs, U.S. Senate, May 2004, 1.
34.   Hamilton, "The 'Katrina Syndrome."
35.   Federal Trade Commission "Petroleum Industry," 8.
36.   Wyden, "Campaign of Inaction," 9.
37.   General Accounting Office, "Energy Markets," 11.
38.   National Petroleum Council, "Observations of Petroleum Product Supply," December 2004.
39.   "Oil Refineries Targeted for Global Warming Emissions Cuts," Earthjustice, press release, August 28, 2007.
40.   Terry Tamminen, *Lives Per Gallon: The True Cost of Our Oil Addiction* (Washington, DC: Island Press, 2006), 14, 36.
41.   California Environmental Protection Agency, Department of Toxic Substances Control, "Draft Non-RCRA Hazardous Waste Facility Post-Closure Permit," December 2002.
42.   "Unfathomable: EPA Decides Oil Refinery Air Pollution Is Clean Enough to Ignore," Natural Resources Defense Council, press release, August 23, 2007.
43.   Elizabeth Douglass, "Concern Grows on Refinery Safety," *Los Angeles Times*, March 23, 2007.
44.   *Investigation Report, Refinery Explosion at Fire (15 killed, 180 Injured)*, U.S. Chemical Safety at Hazard Investigation Board, Report No. 2005-04-1-TX, March 2007.
45.   Ibid.
46.   Ibid.
47.   Lise Olsen, "Murky Stats Mask Plant Deaths," *Houston Chronicle*, May 16, 2005.
48.   Ibid.
49.   David Barstow, "U.S. Rarely Seeks Charges for Deaths in Workplace," *New York Times*, December 22, 2003.
50.   Ibid.
51.   "A Dangerous Business," PBS, *Frontline*, January 9, 2003.
52.   Julia May, *Refinery Flaring in the Neighborhood* (Oakland and Huntington Park, CA: Communities for a Better Environment, Spring 2004).

53. National Petroleum Council, "Observations of Petroleum Product Supply."

54. Chevron USA, Richmond, CA, Refinery Locator, Refinery Reform Campaign, http://www.refineryreform.org.

55. U.S. Environmental Protection Agency, "Sector Facility Indexing Project: Facility Level Statistics," Chevron USA Inc., Richmond Refinery, April 2004.

56. Scott Sherman, "Environmental Justice Case Study: West County Toxics Coalition and the Chevron Refinery, Richmond, California," University of Michigan, 1996.

57. "Chevron Continues to Probe into March Refinery Fire," Chevron press release, September 16, 1999.

58. "Chevron's Big Bang," Counterpunch.org, 1999.

59. Chevron USA, Richmond, CA, Refinery Locator.

60. Benjamin A. Goldman and Laura J. Fittons "Toxic Wastes and Race Revisited" (Washington, DC: Center for Policy Alternatives, 1994).

61   Interview with the author, September 17, 2007.

62. Gayle McLaughlin, "Richmond Must Insist that Chevron Do Better," *Contra Costa Times,* August 11, 2007.

63. Chevron Richard Refinery, Draft Hazardous Waste Facility Post-Closure Permit, California Department of Toxic Substances Control, Fact Sheet, December 2002. http://www.dtsc.ca.gov.

64. Craig Flournoy, "Refinery Accidents, Anxiety Increase, Minorities 'Ticking Time Bombs,' " *Dallas Morning News,* October 1, 2000.

65. Contra Costa Health Services, "A Framework for Contra Costa County," http://www.cchealth.org/groups/chronic_disease/framework .php.

66. Martha Matsuoka, ed., "Building Healthy Communities from the Ground Up: Environmental Justice in California," (Oakland, CA: Asian Pacific Environmental Network et al., 2003).

67. Liz Tascio, "Chevron to Settle Violations at Refinery with $330,000," *Contra Costa Times,* January 14, 2004.

68. Jane Kay, "Chevron Plant Hit with Fine," *San Francisco Chronicle,* March 27, 2001.

69. Red Cavaney, American Petroleum Institute, Testimony before the Gasoline: Supply, Price, and Specifications Hearing of the House Committee on Energy and Commerce, May 11, 2006.

70. Dinesh Ramde, "Gas Station Shuts Down Pump for 24 Hours to Protest Oil Prices," Associated Press, May 25, 2007.

71. Federal Trade Commission, "Petroleum Industry," 214; U.S. Federal Highway Administration data.

72. "Gas Prices," 628.

73. General Accounting Office, "Energy Markets."

74. "Gas Prices," 629.

75. Ibid., 630.

76. Ibid., 634.

77. Elizabeth Douglass and Gary Cohn, "What's Driving Gas Prices?

Refiners Maintain a Firm but Legal Grip on Supplies," *Los Angeles Times,* June 18, 2005.

78. Patrick D. Meadowcroft, Testimony before the Senate Democratic Policy Committee, "An Oversight Hearing on Record High Gasoline Prices and Windfall Oil Company Profits," September 19, 2005.

79. "Gas Prices," 384.

80. Ramde, "Gas Station Shuts Down Pump."

81. "Stations Boycott Their Own Gas Over Prices," CBS/Associated Press, May 24, 2007.

82. U.S. Department of Energy, Energy Information Administration, "The U.S. Petroleum Refining and Gasoline Marketing Industry," updated August 19, 2004.

83. Federal Trade Commission, "Petroleum Industry," 227.

84. C. W. Nevius, "Dealer Prices Gas over $4 in Protest," *San Francisco Chronicle,* May 10, 2007.

85. John Roberts, "Playing Politics with Gas Prices," CNN, April 25, 2006.

86. Meadowcroft, Testimony.

87. General Accounting Office, "Energy Markets," 4.

88. *United States v. Container Corp. of America,* 393 U.S. 333 (1969) and *In re Coordinated Pretrial Proceedings in Petroleum Products Antitrust Litigation v. Standard Oil Co.,* 906 F.2d 432 (9th Cir. Cal. 1990).

89. Sonya Hoo and Robert D. Ebel, "An International Perspective on Gasoline Taxes," Urban Institute, September 26, 2005.

90. John Greenwald, "Why Not a Gas Tax?" *Time,* February 15, 1993.

91. "Gallons Guzzled," *Business Week,* June 16, 2008.

92. "Almost 85 Million More Trips Taken Than in the First Quarter of 2007," American Public Transit Association, June 2, 2008.

93. "Import of Rising Fuel Costs on Transit Services," American Public Transportation Association, May 2008.

Chapter 6: Lobbyists, Lawyers, and Elections

1. Phone interview with the author, May 19, 2007.

2. Robert G. Allen, *Multiple Streams of Income: How to Generate a Lifetime of Unlimited Wealth!* (Hoboken, NJ: John Wiley, 2000), 11.

3. Phone interview with the author, May 23, 2007.

4. Phone interview with the author, July 2, 2007.

5. John Pomfret, "California Battle Over Big Oil May Be Costliest in U.S. History," *Washington Post,* October 20, 2006.

6. Phone interview with the author, May 23, 2007.

7. David Baker, "Economists Weigh Prop. 87," *San Francisco Chronicle,* October 15, 2006.

8. Charles Lewis, *The Buying of the President 2004: Who's Really Bankrolling Bush and His Democratic Challengers—and What They Expect in Return* (New York: HarperCollins, 2004), 86.

9.   *Times* Editorial, " 'Nuts' to Gulf Drilling," *St. Petersburg Times,* June 21, 2006.

10. Lewis, *Buying of the President,* 83.

11. Daniel J. Weiss and Anne Wingate, "Big Oil's Favorite Representatives," Center for American Progress Action Fund, August 22, 2007.

12. "Follow the Oil Money," Oil Change International, http://www.Price ofOil.org.

13. Center for Responsive Politics, http://www.opensecrets.org

14. Lewis, *Buying of the President,* 116–117.

15. Ibid., 116

16. Interview with the author, May 14, 2007.

17. Scot J. Paltrow, "Bon Appetit: On Overseas Trips, Congress's Rules Are Often Ignored," *Wall Street Journal,* October 27, 2006.

18. Tom Chorneau, "Big Oil Lobbyists Stall Bills in Legislature That Industry Opposes," *San Francisco Chronicle,* July 14, 2006.

19. Richard Karp, Speaker Bio for World Bank Conference, "Business, NGOs and Development—Strategic Engagement to Meet the Millennium Development Goals," April 11, 2006.

20. Antonia Felix, *Condi: The Condoleezza Rice Story* (New York: Simon and Schuster, 2004), 192.

21. Willie Soon and Sallie Baliunas, *Lessons and Limits of Climate History: Was the 20th Century Climate Unusual?* (Washington, DC: George C. Marshall Institute, 2003).

22. Chris Mooney, "Earth Last," *American Prospect,* April 13, 2004.

23. Lauren Morello, "Environment and Energy Daily—House Probe Turns to Role of Cheney's Office," Government Accountability Project, March 20, 2007.

24. Phone interview with the author, June 27, 2007.

25. Dana Milbank, "Bush Energy Order Wording Mirrors Oil Lobby's Proposal," *Washington Post,* March 28, 2002.

26. Matt Stoller, "U.S. Chamber of Commerce: The Right Wing's Right Hand in D.C.," AlterNet.org, December 14, 2006.

27. Ibid.

28. Tom Donohue, "Undeniable Energy Facts," Uschamber.com weekly, May 22, 2007.

29. Peter H. Stone, "Donohue's Pro-Oil Pitch," *National Journal,* January 6, 2007.

30. Kevin Philips, *American Theocracy: The Peril and Politics of Radical Religion, Oil, and Borrowed Money in the 21st Century* (New York: Penguin Group, 2006), 71.

31. See, for example, Christian S. White, Designated Agency Ethics Official, "Post-Employment Ethics Restrictions," Memorandum, U.S. Federal Trade Commission, Washington, DC, September 16, 2002, http://www.ftc.gov/ogc/postempmem.htm and "Statement of Chairman Deborah Platt Majoras Concerning Petition Seeking My Recusal from Review of Proposed Acquisition of Hellman & Friedman Capital

Partners V, LP (DoubleClick Inc.) by Google, Inc.," December 14, 2007, http://www.ftc.gov/opa/2007/12/google.shtm.

32. Robert Vosper, "Under Pressure: Chevron's GC Takes on Some of the Toughest Legal Challenges in Corporate America," *Inside Counsel*, June 2006.

33. "*Doe v. Unocal,*" http://www.earthrights.org/legal/unocal/, Earth-rights International; "The Questions Over Aiding and Abetting: Alien Tort Statute: An Oil Company's Fight with the Human Rights Lobby Tests and 18th Century Law," *Financial Times*, August 2, 2004.

34. "Oil Giant Chevron Urged to Cut Ties with Burmese Military Junta," *Democracy Now!* WBAI Radio, October 12, 2007; "The Human Cost of Energy: Chevron's Continuing Role in Financing Oppression and Profiting from Human Rights Abuses in Military-Ruled Burma (Myan-mar)," EarthRights International, April 2008.

35. "Exxon Oil Spill, Part 1," Hearing before the Committee on Commerce, Science, and Transportation, United States Senate, April 6, 1989, 8.

36. "Exxon Oil Spill, Part 2," Hearings before the National Ocean Policy Study and Subcommittee on Merchant Marine of the Committee on Commerce, Science, and Transportation, United States Senate, 1989, 260.

37. Steve Lohr, "Tanker in Big Spill Typifies Freewheeling Industry," *New York Times*, July 3, 1989.

38. Nina Totenberg, "Supreme Court Weighs Exxon Valdez Damages," *National Public Radio, Morning Edition,* June 27, 2008.

39. Davis Wright Tremaine LLP, plaintiffs' attorneys, "Exxon Valdez Oil Spill Disaster Fact Sheet," downloaded June 28, 2008, http://www.dwt .com/news.htm.

40. Statement of Michelle O'Leary, Cordova District Fishermen United, "Exxon Oil Spill, Part 2," Hearings before the National Ocean Policy Study and Subcommittee on Merchant Marine of the Committee on Commerce, Science, and Transportation, United States Senate, 1989, 233.

41. Statement of Dennis Kelso, commissioner, Department of Environmental Conservation, State of Alaska, "Exxon Oil Spill, Part 2," Hearings before the National Ocean Policy Study and Subcommittee on Merchant Marine of the Committee on Commerce, Science, and Transportation, United States Senate, 1989, 151–52.

42. "Exxon Oil Spill," parts 1 and 2.

43. Barnaby J. Feder, "Exxon Valdez's Sea of Litigation," *New York Times,* November 19, 1989.

44. Davis Wright Tremaine LLP, plaintiffs' attorneys, "Exxon Valdez Oil Spill Disaster Timeline and History of the Litigation," downloaded June 28, 2008, http://www.dwt.com/news.htm; Lynda V. Mapes, "Supreme Court Drastically Cuts Payouts for Plaintiffs in Exxon Valdez Oil Spill," *Seattle Times*, June 26, 2008.

45. Office of the Clerk, U.S. Court of Appeals for the Ninth Circuit, Summary of *Baker v. Exxon,* prepared by court staff, November 7, 2001.

46. Mapes, "Supreme Court Drastically Cuts Payouts for Plaintiffs in Exxon Valdez Oil Spill."

47. Tom Kizzia and Megan Holland, "Plaintiffs React to Exxon Decision," *Anchorage Daily News,* June 25, 2008.

48. O'Melveny & Myers, "Class Actions," at http://web.omm.com/class actions/, June 27, 2008.

49. Richard Parker, O'Melveny & Myers bio, http://web.omm.com/richard parker/.

50. Timothy Muris, O'Melveny & Myers bio, http://www.omm.com/law-yers/detail.aspx?attorney=6334; Timothy J. Muris, et al., Counsel for ExxonMobil Corporation, "ExxonMobil Corporations' Request for Review of Denial of Petition to Limit Civil Investigative Demand," in the Matter of ExxonMobil Corporation, United States of America Before Federal Trade Commission, File No. 051-0243, December 19, 2005.

51. Christine Wilson, O'Melveny & Myers bio, http://web.omm.com/christinewilson/ and "Christine Wilson Named Executive Assistant to FTC Chairman," Federal Trade Commission, September 6, 2001, http://www.ftc.gov/opa/2001/09/wilson.shtm.

52. Bilal Sayyed, O'Melveny & Myers bio, http://web.omm.com/Bilal Sayyed/.

53. Statement of Bilal Sayyed Pursuant to Sections 2.7(D)(2) and 3.22 (F) of the Code of Federal Regulations," in the Matter of ExxonMobil Corporation, File No. 051-0243, in Timothy J. Muris et al., Counsel for Exxon-Mobil Corporation, "ExxonMobil Corporations' Request for Review of Denial of Petition to Limit Civil Investigative Demand," United States of America Before Federal Trade Commission, December 19, 2005.

54. "FTC Says It Is Investigating Gas Price Gouging," MSNBC News Services, September 22, 2005.

55. Brad Foss, "FTC Finds Some Gas Price Gouging After Katrina," Associated Press, May 22, 2006.

56. *Theresa Aguilar et al. vs. Atlantic Richfield Company et al.,* in the Supreme Court of California, S086738, Filed June 14, 2001; Stephen Labaton, "Bush Nominee to Lead FTC Is Questioned Intensely About Gasoline Prices," *New York Times,* June 3, 2004.

57. Noel J. Francisco, Jones Day bio, http://www.jonesday.com/njfrancisco/.

58. Lawsuit for alleged damages filed before the president of the Superior Court of Nueva Loja in Lago Agrio, Province of Sucumbios, on May 7, 2003, by forty-eight inhabitants of the Orellana and the Sucumbio Province.

59. Results of several studies, including Anna-Karin Hurtig and Miguel San Sebastian, "Geographical Differences in Cancer Incidence in the Amazon Basin of Ecuador in Relation to Residence Near Oil Fields," *International Journal of Epidemiology* 31 (2002): 1021–1027.

60. Carlyn Kolker, "Jungle Warfare," *Litigation 2006: A Supplement to the American Lawyer & Corporate Counsel,* 2006.

61. Vosper, "Under Pressure."

62. Statement of Senator Patrick Leahy, Ranking Member, Senate Judiciary Committee Confirmation Hearing on the Nominations of Daniel J. Bryant to be Assistant Attorney General for the Office of Legislative Affairs and Charles A. James to be Assistant Attorney General for Antitrust, May 2, 2001.

63. "A Chat with the Justice Dept.'s Charles James," *BusinessWeek,* Legal Affairs/Online Extra, August 13, 2001.

64. Statement of Commissioner Mozelle W. Thompson, "Concerning the Abandoned Memorandum of Agreement Between the Federal Trade Commission and the Antitrust Division of the United States Department of Justice Concerning Clearance Procedures for Investigations," January 2002, www.FTC.gov.

65. Texas Review of Law & Politics, Sean Royall Steering Committee bio, http://www.trolp.org/main_pgs/steering_committee/sroyall.htm.

66. Sean Royall Gibson, Dunn & Crutcher bio, http://www.gibsondunn.com/Lawyers/sroyall.

67. Vosper, "Under Pressure."

68. Jones Day Web site, professional biographies and client listing, http://www.jonesday.com/kmfenton/, http://www.jonesday.com/jsims/, http://www.jonesday.com/experience/experience_detail.aspx?exID=S8837.

69. *Anderson v. Chevron Corp.,* 190 F.R.D.S, D.D.C., 1999, November 5, 1999.

70. Cecile Kohrs Lindell, "Sources: FTC Antitrust Chief to Join Linklaters," The Deal, Law.com, March 4, 2008.

71. Tom Smith, Jones Day bio, http://www.jonesday.com/tdsmith/, and Robert Jones, Jones Day bio, http://www.jonesday.com/rcjones/.

72. Michael S. McFalls, Jones Day bio, http://www.jonesday.com/msmcfalls/.

73. Interview with the author, August 11, 2007.

74. Lisa Lambert, "At the Crossroads of Environmental and Human Rights Standards: Aguinda v. Texaco, Inc.," *Journal of Transnational Law & Policy* 10, no. 1 (Fall 2000): 10–32.

75. "Experts Say Health Studies Promoted by Lawyers and Activists Are Flawed, Biased, and Inconclusive," Quito, Ecuador, ChevronTexaco, February 2, 2005, Texaco in Ecuador, http://www.texaco.com/sitelets/ecuador/en/releases/2005-02-02.aspx.

76. "Letter from Fifty Scientists to Texaco and Its Consultants," *International Journal of Occupation Health,* 11, no. 2 (April/June 2005), http://www.chevrontoxico.com/article.php?id=61.

77. Interview with the author, May 14, 2007.

78. Andrew Revkin, "Bush Aide Softened Greenhouse Gas Links to Global Warming," *New York Times,* June 8, 2005.

79. "Cooney Moves to Exxon," *The Oil Daily,* June 16, 2005.

80. Dan Van Natta Jr. with Neela Banerjee, "Bush Policies Have Been Good to Energy Industry," *New York Times*, April 21, 2002.

81. Robert F. Kennedy Jr., "Texas Chainsaw Management," *Vanity Fair,* May 2007.

82.   Karl Vick, "In Colorado, Drilling Some Holes in the Republican Base," *Washington Post,* September 16, 2007.
83.   Steve McMillan, "Norton Will Join Regal Dutch Shell," *Denver Post,* December 27, 2006.
84.   Jeffrey St. Clair, "Meet Steven Griles: Big Oil's Inside Man," Counterpunch.org, June 28, 2003.
85.   Center for Responsive Politics online database, http://www.opensecrets.org.
86.   Ken Silverstein, "Meet the Revolvers," *Harper's Magazine,* March 28, 2007.
87.   St. Clair, "Meet Steven Griles."
88.   John Heilprin, "Ex-Deputy Pleads Guilty in Abramoff Case," Associated Press, March 23, 2007; John Heilprin, "Lobbyist, Fed Lawyer Share Vacation Home," Associated Press, February 14, 2007.
89.   Heilprin, "Ex-Deputy Pleads Guilty."
90.   "Italia Federica Sentenced for Evading Taxes and Obstructing Senate Investigation into Abramoff Computer Scandal," Department of Justice, December 14, 2007.
91.   "The UnGreening of America," *Mother Jones,* September 2003.
92.   Edmund Andrews, "Blowing the Whistle on Big Oil," *New York Times,* December 3, 2006.
93.   Ibid.
94.   Ibid.
95.   John Warnock, "Selling the Family Silver: Oil and Gas Royalties, Corporate Profits, and the Disregarded Public," Parkland Institute and Canadian Centre for Policy Alternatives, Saskatchewan, Canada, November 2006.
96.   Robert S. McIntyre and T. D. Coo Nguyen, "Corporate Income Taxes in the Bush Years," a joint project of Citizens for Tax Justice and the Institute on Taxation and Economic Policy, September 2004.
97.   U.S. Congressional Budget Office, "Historical Effective Federal Tax Rates: 1979 to 2005," http://www.cbo.gov/ftpdocs/88xx/doc8885/EffectiveTaxRates.shtml.
98.   Interview with the author, home of Gayle McLaughlin, Richmond, CA, September 17, 2007.
99.   E-mail exchange between author and Gayle McLaughlin, Richmond mayor, December 2, 2007.
100. John Geluardi, "Utility Tax Recalculation Costs City," *Contra Costa Times,* September 8, 2006.
101. Greenberg Quinlan Rosner, "A New Energy Future: The Role of Energy in the 2006 Election," Research for LCV, November 17, 2006.
102. Interview with author, May 14, 2007.
103. Edmund Andrews, "Democrats Plan Oil Royalties Inquiry," *New York Times,* December 9, 2006.

Chapter 7: Big Oil's Big Plans for the Future, Part I: Environmential Destruction

1. Cora Daniels, "Fast Talk: Chevron's Underground Researcher," *Fast Company*, October 2007.
2. Phone interview with the author, December 6, 2007.
3. "Exxon Proposes Burning Humanity for Fuel If Climate Calamity Hits," Yes Men, press release, June 14, 2007, http://www.TheYesMen.org.
4. Joan Voight, "POV: Chevron Teaches Big Brands What Not to Do," *Ad Week*, October 15, 2007.
5. David Baker, "Chevron Campaign Tries to Balance Need for Oil with Global Warming," *San Francisco Chronicle*, September 28, 2007.
6. Ibid.
7. Al Gore, "A Generational Challenge to Repower America," Washington, D.C., July 18, 2008.
8. "NOAA: 2007 a Top Ten Warm Year for U.S. and Globe," National Oceanic and Atmospheric Administration, December 13, 2007, http://www.noaanews.noaa.gov.
9. "Climate Change 101: Understanding and Responding to Global Climate Change," Pew Center on Global Climate Change and Pew Center on the States, October 2006.
10. Ibid.
11. Ibid.
12. Chris Mooney, "Some Like it Hot," *Mother Jones*, May/June 2005.
13. Andrew Buncombe and Stephen Castle, "EU: Exxon Spends Millions to Cast Doubt on Warming," *Independent* (UK), December 7, 2006.
14. Gallup polls, http://www.gallup.com/poll/12748/Business-Industry-Sector-Ratings.aspx; http://www.gallup.com/poll/1615/Environment.aspx.
15. John Felmy, Statement to the House Judiciary Committee Antitrust Task Force Hearing on "Prices at the Pump: Market Failure at the Oil Industry," May 16, 2007.
16. Energy Tomorrow radio interview with John Felmy, June 19, 2007.
17. Phone interview with the author, June 27, 2007.
18. Research conducted by author and Sam Edmondson based exclusively on information provided by the companies in their annual reports, 10-K SEC tax filings, Corporate Responsibility Reports, and on their Web sites.
19. Frank Sesno, CNN Special Correspondent, "We Were Warned: Out of Gas," *CNN: Special Investigations Unit*, CNN, June 2, 2007.
20. Kenny Bruno, "BP: Beyond Petroleum or Beyond Preposterous?" CorpWatch, December 14, 2000.
21. Ibid.
22. "Factbox: Oil Major's Investments in Renewable Energy," Reuters, April 13, 2007.
23. Edward Iwata, "Chevron CEO Doesn't See Oil Crisis Looming," *USA Today*, June 13, 2006.
24. John Lowe, vice president, ConocoPhillips, Testimony before U.S.

House Committee on Energy Independence and Global Warming, April 2008.

25.   J. S. Simon, senior vice president, ExxonMobil, Testimony before U.S. House Committee on Energy Independence and Global Warming, April 2008. ,

26.   Geoff Colvin, "Exxon = Oil, G*dammit!" *Fortune,* April 23, 2007.

27.   Ann Bordetsky et al., "Driving It Home: Choosing the Right Path for Fueling North America's Transportation Future," a joint report by Natural Resources Defense Council, Western Resource Advocates, and Pembina Institute, 2007.

28.   Bob Simon, "The Oil Sands of Alberta," CBS, *60 Minutes,* January 22, 2006.

29.   Bordetsky et al., "Driving It Home."

30.   Doug Struck, "Canada Pays Environmentally for U.S. Oil Thirst," *Washington Post,* May 31, 2006.

31.   Katherine Bourzac, "Dirty Oil," *Technology Review,* December 2005.

32.   Struck, "Canada Pays Environmentally for U.S. Oil Thirst."

33.   Bordetsky et al., "Driving It Home."

34.   Ibid.

35.   Bordetsky et al., "Driving It Home"; author's analysis of 2006 corporate annual reports.

36.   Phone interview with the author, June 12, 2007.

37.   Ibid.

38.   Bordetsky et al., "Driving It Home."

39.   Ibid.

40.   Ibid.

41.   Ibid.

42.   Ibid.

43.   Geoff Colvin, "Chevron's CEO: The Price of Oil," *Fortune,* November 28, 2007.

44.   Bryant Urstadt, "The Oil Frontier," *Technology Review,* July 1, 2006.

45.   Ibid.

46.   Joe Carroll, "Rig Shortage Slows Chevron Bid to Tap Offshore Fields," Reuters, December 6, 2006.

47.   Amanda Griscom, "Pumped Up: Chevron Drills Down 30,000 Feet to Tap Oil-Rich Gulf of Mexico," *Wired Magazine,* August 21, 2007.

48.   Ibid.

49.   Kristen Hays, "Gulf of Mexico's Tahiti Is an Island of Steel," *Alexander's Gas and Oil Connections* 12, no. 7 (April 11, 2007).

50.   Carroll, "Rig Shortage Slows Chevron Bid."

51.   Daniel Haier, "'69 Oil Spill Leaves Mark on SB Environmentalism," *Daily Nexus,* January 28, 2005; K. C. Clarke and Jeffrey J. Hemphill, "The Santa Barbara Oil Spill, A Retrospective," *Yearbook of the Association of Pacific Coast Geographers,* ed. Darrick Danta, vol. 64 (Honolulu: University of Hawaii Press, 2002), 157–62.

52.   Sierra Club, "The Threat of Offshore Drilling: America's Coasts in Peril," May 24, 2006. http://www.sierraclub.org/wildlands/coasts/.

53.   U.S. Department of the Interior, Mineral Management Service, Off-shore Minerals Management, http://www.mms.gov/offshore.

54.   Edmund L. Andrews, "Administration Proposes Expanded Energy Drilling Off Coasts," *New York Times*, May 1, 2007.

55.   David Baker, "Underwater Resources," *San Francisco Chronicle*, August 3, 2006.

56.   Phone interview with the author, December 6, 2007.

57.   *Strategic Plan 2007–2012*, U.S. Department of the Interior, Minerals Management Service, Offshore Minerals Management, October 2007.

58.   Center for Biological Diversity, "Bush-Cheney Offshore Oil Plan Will Destroy Polar Bear and Whale Habitat," press release, July 2, 2007.

59.   Center for Biological Diversity, "Shell Oil Can't Drill This Year in Beaufort Sea, Court Rules," press release, August 15, 2007.

60.   Rex Tillerson, "The State of the Energy Industry: Strengths, Realities and Solutions" (opening address to CERA [Cambridge Energy Research Associates] Week 2007, Houston, Texas, February 13, 2007).

61.   U.S. Department of the Interior, Mineral, Management Service, Gulf of Mexico Region, http://www.goms.mms.gov.

62.   James Mielke, "RS20050: Methane Hydrates: Energy Prospects or Natural Hazard?" CRS Report for Congress, February 14, 2000.

63.   Sierra Club, "Threat of Offshore Drilling."

64.   Ibid.

65.   Debbie Boger, deputy legislative director, Sierra Club, Testimony before the Senate Committee on Energy and Natural Resources, April 19, 2005.

66.   Ibid.

67.   Ibid.

68.   Oil Rig Disasters, Deadliest Accidents, Piper Alpha, http://www.oilrigdisasters.co.uk/.

69.   Accidents Do Happen! . . . http://oilrigwork.netfirms.com/Accidents.htm.

70.   "Wreck of the Ocean Ranger," *Time*, March 1, 1982.

71.   Oil Rig Disasters, Deadliest Accidents, http://www.oilrigdisasters.co.uk/.

72.   Jad Mouawad, "Fixing Up Offshore U.S. Oil Rigs," *International Herald Tribune*, March 1, 2006.

73.   The Sierra Club, "Threat of Offshore Drilling."

74.   Jad Mouawad, "Divers Work the Gulf Floor to Undo What Hurricanes Did," *New York Times*, March 1, 2006.

75.   Ibid.

76.   Griscom, "Pumped Up."

77.   John Gibson, "Sustainability: An Unexpected Source of Profit," *Leading Edge* 23, no. 2 (February 2004): 169–70.

Chapter 8: Big Oil's Big Plans for the Future, Part II: Wars for Oil

1.   President George W. Bush, "President Bush Discusses Iraq," http://www.whitehouse.gov/news/releases/2008/04/20080410-2.html.

2. Alan Greenspan, *The Age of Turbulence: Adventures in a New World* (New York: Penguin, 2007), 463.

3. Gerry Shih and Susana Montes, "Roundtable Debates Energy Issues," *Standard Daily,* October 15, 2007.

4. Kenneth T. Derr, "Engagement—A Better Alternative" (speech to the Commonwealth Club of California, San Francisco, November 5, 1998).

5. Federal Trade Commission Bureau of Economics, "The Petroleum Industry: Mergers, Structural Change, and Antitrust Enforcement," FTC Staff Study, August 2004, 68.

6. Kevin Philips, *American Theocracy: The Peril and Politics of Radical Religion, Oil, and Borrowed Money in the 21st Century* (New York: Penguin, 2006), 78.

7. The Editors, "U.S. Military Bases and Empire," *Monthly Review* 53, no. 10 (March 2002).

8. "Combined Joint Task Force Horn of Africa," http://www.globalsecurity .org/militery/agency/dod/cjtf-hoa.htm.

9. Philips, *American Theocracy,* 83.

10. The Editors, "U.S. Military Bases and Empire."

11. All corporate data drawn from 2007 SEC tax filings.

12. Energy Secretary Samuel Bodman, Keynote address for Corporate Council on Africa Oil and Gas Forum, December 1, 2006.

13. Philips, *American Theocracy,* 85.

14. Ibid., 85.

15. Michael Klare and Daniel Volman, "America, China and the Scramble for Africa's Oil," *Review of African Political Economy* 22, no. 108 (June 2006): 297–309.

16. Philips, *American Theocracy,* 85.

17. Editors, "U.S. Military Bases and Empire."

18. Matthew Yeomans, *Oil: A Concise Guide to the Most Important Product on Earth* (New York: New Press, 2004), 137.

19. Dick Cheney, Speech at the Institute of Petroleum Autumn Lunch, 1999, http://www.energybulletin.net/559.html.

20. James Mann, *Rise of the Vulcans: The History of Bush's War Cabinet* (New York: Penguin, 2004), 199.

21. "Iraqi Oil and Gas: A Bonanza-in-Waiting," Energy Intelligence Research, Special Report Update, Spring 2003.

22. Con Coughlin, *Saddam: His Rise and Fall* (New York: Harper Perennial, 2002), 37–38.

23. Much of this discussion on the history of U.S. economic relations with Iraq is drawn from the author's *The Bush Agenda: Invading the World, One Economy at a Time* (New York: HarperCollins, 2006).

24. Alan Friedman, *Spider's Web: The Secret History of How the White House Illegally Armed Iraq* (New York: Bantam Books, 1993), 163.

25. R. W. Apple Jr., "Bush Invokes U.S. Values," *New York Times,* August 16, 1990.

26. Friedman, *Spider's Web,* 173.

27. Robert Bryce, *Cronies: Oil, the Bushes and the Rise of Texas* (New York: Perseus Publishing, 2004), 161–62.

28. Christian Parenti, *The Freedom: Shadows and Hallucinations in Occupied Iraq* (New York: New Press, 2004), 15.

29. Mann, *Rise of the Vulcans,* 190.

30. Among many sources, see Coughlin, *Saddam.*

31. "Chevron Pays Fine in Oil-For-Food Case," Associated Press, November 14, 2007.

32. Phyllis Bennis, *Before and After: U.S. Foreign Policy and the September 11th Crisis* (New York: Olive Branch Press, 2003), 72.

33. Shirin Ebadi, *Iran Awakening: One Woman's Journey to Reclaim Her Life and Country* (New York: Random House, 2007), 4.

34. "1951 Man of the Year: Mohammed Mossadegh," *Time,* January 7, 1952.

35. Daniel Yergin, *The Prize: The Epic Quest for Oil, Money, and Power* (New York: Simon & Schuster, 1991), 462.

36. See, among other sources, Stephen Kinzer, *All the Shah's Men: An American Coup and the Roots of Middle East Terror* (New York: Wiley, 2008).

37. Dilip Hiro, *The Iranian Labyrinth* (New York: Nation Books, 2005), 196.

38. Mann, *Rise of the Vulcans,* 84.

39. Hiro, *The Iranian Labyrinth,* 126.

40. Ibid., xxxvii.

41. Mann, *Rise of the Vulcans,* 154.

42. "White House and a Senator Criticize Conoco Oil Deal with Iran," *New York Times,* March 8, 1995.

43. Youssef M. Ibrahim, "OPEC Dealing with Threat of an Oil Glut Linked to Iraq," *New York Times,* June 6, 1996.

44. Elaine Sciolino, "Iran's Difficulties Lead Some in U.S. to Doubt Threat," *New York Times,* July 5, 1994; Thomas L. Friedman, "Foreign Affairs; Wednesday News Quiz," *New York Times,* March 29, 1995.

45. "ExxonMobil at Anti-Iran Sanctions Meeting," *Forbes,* September 1, 2000.

46. Archie Dunham, "The Impact of Sanctions on American Interests in the Middle East," *Middle East Insight,* May/June 1999.

47. Nejla Sammakia, "Oil Sanctions," Voice of America Radio, Report Number 5-43151, April 16, 1999.

48. "Cheney Pushed for More Trade with Iran," Associated Press, October 9, 2004.

49. James Risen, "Cheney's Path: From Gulf War to Mideast Oil; In Business, He Benefited from His Pentagon Days," *International Herald Tribune,* July 28, 2000.

50. Kenneth T. Derr, "Engagement—A Better Alternative" (speech to the Commonwealth Club of California, San Francisco, November 5, 1998).

51. American-Iranian Council Web site, list of past events, http://www.american-iranian.org/events/.

52. Dana Milbank and Justin Blum, "Document Says Oil Chiefs Met with Cheney Task Force," *Washington Post,* November 16, 2005; Michael Abramowitz and Steven Mufson, "Papers Detail Industry's Role in Cheney's Energy Report," *Washington Post,* July 18, 2007.

53. Jane Mayer, "Contract Sport: What Did the Vice-President Do for Halliburton?" *New Yorker,* February 16, 2004.

54. Peter Behr and Alan Sipress, "Cheney Panel Seeks Review of Sanctions," *Washington Post,* April 19, 2001.

55. Lawsuit filed by Judicial Watch, tables available at http://www.judicial watch.org/iraqi-oil-maps.shtml.

56. Ron Suskind, *The Price of Loyalty: George W. Bush, the White House, and the Education of Paul O'Neill* (New York: Simon & Schuster, 2004), 96.

57. Matt Bai, "The McCain Doctrines," *New York Times Magazine*, May 18, 2008.

58. "Economic and Energy Development in the Middle East; A Time for Optimism," Peter J. Robertson, vice chairman, ChevronTexaco, Statement at the Middle East Petroleum and Gas Conference, Dubai, United Arab Emirates, September 8, 2003, http://www.chevron.com/news/speeches/Release/?id=2003-09-08.probertson.

59. Carola Hoyos, "Big Players Anticipate Iraq's Return to Fold," *Financial Times,* February 20, 2003.

60. Greg Palast, "OPEC on the March," *Harper's Magazine,* April 2005.

61. E mails with the author, December 17, 2007.

62. Thaddeus Herrick, "U.S. Oil Wants to Work in Iraq—Firms Discuss How to Raise Nation's Output After a Possible War," *Wall Street Journal,* January 16, 2003.

63. Bernhard Zand, "Iraq: An End to Saudi Dominance," *Spiegel,* May 4, 2003.

64. Sabrina Tavernise, "U.S. Tells Iraq Oil Ministers Not to Act Without Its O.K.," *New York Times,* April 30, 2003.

65. James Glanz, "Derelict Plants Are Crippling Iraq's Petroleum Industry," *New York Times,* March 3, 2005.

66. David Ivanovich, "Houston Exec Gets Top Iraq Energy Post," *Houston Chronicle,* September 23, 2003.

67. Greg Muttitt, "Hijacking Iraq's Oil Reserves: Economic Hit Men at Work," in *A Game as Old as Empire: The Secret World of Economic Hit Men and the Web of Global Corruption*, ed. Steven Hiatt (San Francisco: Berrett Koehler, 2007), 144.

68. Greg Muttitt, "Crude Designs: The Rip-Off of Iraq's Oil Wealth," Global Policy Forum, November 2005.

69. Ibid.

70. Ibid.

71. Muttitt, "Hijacking Iraq's Oil Reserves," 144.

72. Ibid.

73. Muttitt, "Crude Designs."

74. Award/Contract, BearingPoint, Inc. and USAID/Iraq, "Technical

Assistance for Economic Recovery, Reform, and Sustained Growth in Iraq," July 18, 2003; Darwin G. Johnson, senior vice president, BearingPoint, Inc., Anne Quinlan, Contracting Officer, USAID.

75. BearingPoint report to USAID (U.S. Agency for International Development), "Options for Developing a Long-Term Sustainable Iraqi Oil Industry," December 19, 2003.

76. Palast, "OPEC on the March."

77. Paul Farhi, "The Soothing Sound of Fighting Words," *Washington Post,* March 26, 2003.

78. Gal Luft, "Iraq's Oil Sector One Year after Liberation," Saban Center for Middle East Policy at the Brookings Institution, June 17, 2004.

79. Verne Kopytoff, "Iraqi Oil Reaches California," *San Francisco Chronicle,* October 15, 2003.

80. "Iraq Plans Kirkuk Tender for Ambitious August Export Program," *International Oil Daily* (Energy Intelligence Group, Inc.), August 19, 2005.

81. Briefing by Lakhdar Brahimi, Special Advisor to the Secretary General for Iraq, Baghdad, unofficial transcript, *UN News Service,* June 2, 2004.

82. Rajiv Chandrasekaran, "Former Exile Is Selected as Interim Iraqi Leader," *Washington Post*, May 28, 2004.

83. "Iraqi Plan for Radical Oil Reform Runs into Controversy," *Iraq Oil Daily*, September 30, 2004.

84. "Iraq Oil and Gas: A Bonanza-in-Waiting," Energy Information Research.

85. Transcript, National Press Club Afternoon News Conference with Alan Larson, undersecretary of state, and Abil Abd Al-Mahdi, Iraqi minister of finance, Washington, D.C., December 22, 2004.

86. Iraq Index, Saban Center for Middle East Policy at the Brookings Institution, poll of Iraqis taken in September 2007.

87. Daniel Witt, interviewed on *Marc Steiner Show,* WYPR, 88.1 FM, Baltimore, Maryland, May 14, 2007.

88. Muttitt, "Crude Designs."

89. Draft Oil and Gas Law Prepared by the Committee on February 15, 2007, Council of Ministers Oil and Energy Committee, Republic of Iraq, Draft Iraq Oil and Gas Law, No. of 2007, February 15, 2007.

90. James A. Baker III and Lee Hamilton, cochairs, *The Iraq Study Group Report*, December 6, 2006.

91. Edward Wong, "Iraqis Near Deal on Distribution of Oil Revenues," *New York Times,* December 2006.

92. "Statement on the Draft Oil and Gas Law," Executive Bureau, General Federation of Iraqi Workers, July 10, 2007.

93. "In Opposition to the Iraq Oil Law," Betty Williams, Mairead Corrigan Maguire, Rigoberta Menchu Tum, Prof. Jody Williams, Dr. Shirin Ebadi, and Prof. Wangari Maathai, May 2007.

94. Chip Cummins, "U.S. Digs In to Guard Iraq Oil Exports," *Wall Street Journal*, November 12, 2007.

95. Antonia Juhasz, *The Bush Agenda: Invading the World, One Economy at a Time* (New York: HarperCollins, 2006), 256–57.

96. Ben Lando, "Big Oil to Sign Iraq Deal Soon," United Press International, December 6, 2007.

97. Ben Lando, "Exxon, Shell: Iraq Oil Law Needed for Deal," United Press International, February 13, 2008.

98. Brian Ross, "Secret Report: No Iraq Oil Deal by September," The Blotter, ABC News, http://blogs.abcnews.com/theblotter/2007/07/secret report-n.html.

99. Mark Silva, "DNC: McCain 100-Year War Ad Stays," *Baltimoresun.com, The Swamp*, April 28, 2008.

100. Cummins, "U.S. Digs In to Guard Iraq Oil Exports."

101. President George W. Bush, "President Bush Discusses American Competitiveness Initiative During Press Conference," Transcript of Press Conference, White House Office of the Press Secretary, August 9, 2007.

102. "Halliburton Execs Want More Work in Iraq," *Oil Daily,* May 8, 2003.

103. Seymour M. Hersh, "The Iran Plans: Would President Bush Go to War to Stop Tehran from Getting The Bomb?" *New Yorker,* April 8, 2006.

104. George W. Bush, "President's Address to the Nation," Office of the White House Press Secretary, January 10, 2007.

105. John Kifner, "Gunboat Diplomacy: The Watch on the Gulf," *New York Times,* January 14, 2007.

106. Tim Reid, "Admiral Fallon Quits Over Iran Policy," *The Times of London,* March 12, 2008.

107. Thomas P. M. Barnett, "The Man Between War and Peace," *Esquire,* April 23, 2008.

108. Hersh, "The Iran Plans."

109. Ibid.

110. John Bolton, Fox News, May 16, 2007.

111. Michael Hirsch, "Bothersome Intel on Iran," *Newsweek,* January 12, 2008.

112. Valerie Marcel, *The Oil Titans: National Oil Companies in the Middle East* (Washington, DC: Brookings Institution Press, 2006), 150.

113. Ebadi, *Iran Awakening,* 244.

114. Jeffrey M. Jones, "Opposition to Iraq War Reaches New High," *Gallup .com,* April 24, 2008.

Chapter 9: Taking On Big Oil

1. Senator Chuck Schumer, "Schumer: There Were Five Words Missing from the President's Energy Speech Today—'Get Tough on Big Oil,'" Press Release, April 25, 2006.

2. "'No War, No Warming' Actions Held on Capitol Hill," Global Exchange Press Room, October 22, 2007.

3. Ibid.

4. Diana Moss, "Competition in U.S. Petroleum Refining and Marketing: Part I—Industry Trends, American Antitrust Institute, January 2007, 16.

5.   Richard Blumenthal, Connecticut attorney general, Testimony before the Antitrust Task Force of the House Committee on the Judiciary, May 16, 2007.

6.   Moss, "Competition in U.S. Petroleum," 22

7.   General Accounting Office, "Energy Markets: Effects of Mergers and Market Concentration in the U.S. Petroleum Industry," Report to the Ranking Minority Member, Permanent Subcommittee on Investigations, Committee on Investigations, Committee on Governmental Affairs, U.S. Senate, May 2004, 6.

8.   Just Foreign Policy, http://www.justforeignpolicy.org/iraq/iraqdeaths.html; Emma Batha, "Iraq Refugee Crisis Hits 'Epic Proportions,'" *Reuters AlertNet*, April 12, 2007.

9.   Compiled by the author from several sources, including the United Nations, Human Rights Watch, and Afghanistan Conflict Monitor.

10.   Iraq Index, Saban Center for Middle East Policy at the Brookings Institution, April 23, 2008.

11.   "U.S. and Coalition Casualties," CNN.com/world, http://www.cnn.com/SPECIAL/2004/oef.casualties/.

12.   Joseph E. Stiglitz and Linda J. Bilmes, *The Three Trillion Dollar War* (New York: W. W. Norton & Company, Inc., 2008).

13.   Dr. Steven Kull, "Negative Attitudes Toward the United States in the Muslim World: Do They Matter?" Testimony before House Committee on Foreign Affairs, Subcommittee on International Organizations, Human Rights, and Oversight, May 17, 2007.

14.   "Report of the Defense Science Board Task Force on Strategic Communication," Department of Defense, Office of the Undersecretary of Defense for Acquisition, Technology, and Logistics, September 2004.

15.   Anthony Sampson, *The Seven Sisters: The Great Oil Companies and the World They Made* (New York: Coronet Books, 1975), 43.

16.   Linda McQuaig, *It's the Crude Dude: Greed, Gas, War, and the American Way* (New York: St. Martin's Press, 2006), 215.

17.   Woodrow Wilson, *The New Freedom* (New York and Garden City: Doubleday, Page, 1913) (Project Gutenberg EBook 14811).

18.   Joel Stashenko, "Schumer Seeks GAO Study on Breaking Up Oil Companies," *Business Review* (Albany), May 8, 2006.

19.   Richard Blumenthal, Connecticut attorney general, Testimony before the Antitrust Task Force of the House Committee on the Judiciary, May 16, 2007.

20.   Wenonah Hauter, director, Public Citizen's Critical Mass Energy and Environment Program on Solutions to Competitive Problems in the Oil Industry, Testimony before the House Committee on the Judiciary, June 28, 2000.

21.   "Promoting Revenue Transparency: 2008 Report on Revenue Transparency of Oil and Gas Companies," Transparency International, 2008.

22.   Federal Trade Commission, Bureau of Economics, "The Petroleum Industry: Mergers, Structural Change, and Antitrust Enforcement," August 2004, 95.

23. Robert Sherrill, "Breaking Up Big Oil," *New York Times,* October 3, 1976.

24. Public Citizen, "White House for Sale," http://www.whitehouseforsale .org.

25. David Goldstein, "Presidential Candidates Are No Stranger to Lobbyists," *McClatchy Newspapers,* April 24, 2008.

26. Joe Benton, "High Gas Prices Wearing Thin: Record Oil Company Prices Putting Pressure on Congress," February 6, 2006; http://www .consumeraffairs.com.

27. "Broad Environmental Justice Coalition Releases Declaration Against Carbon Trading and Offset Use to Address Global Warming in California," Los Angeles, Sacramento, San Diego, Fresno, Bay Area, California, February 19, 2008, http://www.ejmatters.org

28. "Time to Tax Carbon," The Editors. *Los Angeles Times, May 28,* 2007.

29. *EJ* Matters, http://www.ejmatters.org.

30. "Where Oil Flows, Debt Grows," *Financial Times* advertisement, www .endoilaid.org.

31. "Obama Vows to Close 'Enron Loophole' for Oil Speculators," *U.S. News & World Report* Political Bulletin, June 23, 2008.

32. Interview with author at the office of Tom Greene in Sacramento, CA, May 15, 2007.

Index